AUTHENTIC
Veneto Friuli

TOURING CLUB
OF ITALY

Touring Club Italiano
President and Chairman: *Roberto Ruozi*
General Manager: *Guido Venturini*

Touring Editore
Managing Director: *Alfieri Lorenzon*
Editorial Director: *Michele D'Innella*

International Department
Fabio Pittella
fabio.pittella@touringclub.it

Senior Editor: *Paola Pandiani*
Editor: *Monica Maraschi*
Writer and Researcher: *Vittoria Majocchi*
with Banca Dati Turistica for Practical info
Translation: *Timothy Dass, Jennifer Robson,*
Studio Queens
Maps: *Touring Club Italiano*
Design and layout: *Studio Gatelli, Milano*
Cover photo: *Gondolas moored*
on the Gran Canal (G. Carfagna)

Advertising Manager: *Claudio Bettinelli*
Local Advertising: *Progetto*
www.progettosrl.it - info@progettosrl.it

Typesetting and Color Separations:
Emmegi Multimedia, Milano
Printing and Binding: *CPM, Casarile*

Distribution
USA/CAN – *Publishers Group West*
UK/Ireland – *Portfolio Books*

Touring Club Italiano, corso Italia 10, 20122 Milano
www.touringclub.it
© 2006 Touring Editore, Milan

Code K8R
ISBN-13: 978 – 88365 – 3770 – 9
ISBN-10: 88 – 365 – 3770 – 7

Printed in April 2006

SUMMARY

Long Tradition, Great Prestige

For over 110 years, the Touring Club of Italy (TCI) has offered travelers the most detailed and comprehensive source of travel information available on Italy.
The Touring Club of Italy was founded in 1894 with the aim of developing the social and cultural values of tourism and promoting the conservation and enjoyment of the country's national heritage, landscape and environment.

Advantages of Membership

Today, TCI offers a wide rage of travel services to assist and support members with the highest level of convenience and quality. Now you can discover the unique charms of Italy with a distinct insider's advantage.

Enjoy exclusive money saving offers with a TCI membership. Use your membership card for discounts in thousands of restaurants, hotels, spas, campgrounds, museums, shops and markets.

These Hotel Chains offer preferred rates and discounts to TCI members!

JOIN THE TOURING CLUB OF ITALY

How to Join

It's quick and easy to join.
Apply for your membership online at
www.touringclub.it
Your membership card will arrive within
three weeks and is valid for discounts
across Italy for the entire year.
Get your card before you go and start
saving as soon as you arrive.
Euro 25 annual membership fee
includes priority mail postage for
membership card and materials.
Just one use of the card will more than
cover the cost of membership.

Benefits

- Exclusive car rental rates with Hertz
- Discounts at select Esso gas stations
- 20% discount on TCI guidebooks
and maps purchased in TCI bookstores
or directly online at
www.touringclub.com
- Preferred rates and discounts available
at thousands of locations in Italy: Hotels -
B&B's - Villa Rentals - Campgrounds -TCI
Resorts - Spas - Restaurants - Wineries -
Museums - Cinemas - Theaters - Music
Festivals - Shops - Craft Markets - Ferries -
Cruises - Theme Parks - Botanical Gardens

ITALY: INSTRUCTIONS FOR USE

Italy is known throughout the world for the quantity and quality of its art treasures and for its natural beauty, but it is also famous for its inimitable lifestyle and fabulous cuisine and wines. Although it is a relatively small country, Italy boasts an extremely varied culture and multifarious traditions and customs. The information and suggestions in this brief section will help foreign tourists not only to understand certain aspects of Italian life, but also to solve the everyday difficulties and the problems of a practical nature that inevitably crop up during any trip. This practical information is included in brief descriptions of various topics: public transport and how to purchase tickets; suggestions on how to drive in this country; the different types of rooms and accommodation in hotels; hints on how to use mobile phones and communication in general. This is followed by useful advice on how to meet your everyday needs and on shopping, as well as information concerning the cultural differences in the various regions. Lastly, there is a section describing the vast range of restaurants, bars, wine bars and pizza parlors.

TRANSPORTATION

From the airport to the city

Public transportation in major cities is easily accessible and simple to use. Both Malpensa Airport in Milan and Fiumicino Airport in Rome have trains and buses linking them to the city centers. At Malpensa, you can take a bus to the main train station or a train to Cadorna train station and subway stop.

Subways, buses, and trams

Access to the subways, buses, and trams requires a ticket (tickets are not sold on board but can be purchased at most newsstands and tobacco shops). The ticket is good for one ride and sometimes has a time limit (in the case of buses and trams). When you board a bus or tram, you are required to stamp your previously-acquired ticket in the time-stamping machine. Occasionally, a conductor will board the bus or tram and check everyone's ticket. If you haven't got one, or if it has not been time-stamped, you will have to pay a steep fine.

Trains

The Ferrovie dello Stato (Italian Railways) is among the best and most modern railway systems in Europe. Timetables and routes can be consulted and reservations can be made online at www.trenitalia.com. Many travel agents can also dispense tickets and help you plan your journey. Hard-copy schedules can be purchased at all newsstands and most bookstores.

Detail of a palazzo in the historic center of Belluno

Automated ticket machines, which include easy-to-use instructions in English, are available in nearly all stations. They can be used to check schedules, makes reservations, and purchase tickets. There are different types of train, according to the requirements:

Eurostar Italia Trains **ES★** : Fast connections between Italy's most important cities. The ticket includes seat booking charge;

Intercity /C and **Espresso E** Trains: Local connections among Italy's towns and cities. Sometimes /C and E trains require seat booking. You can book your seat up to 3 hours before the train departure. The seat booking charge is of 3 euro.

Interregionale Trains iR move beyond regional boundaries. Among the combined local-transport services, the iR Trains are the fastest ones with the fewest number of stops. No seat booking available.

Diretto D and **Regionale R** Trains can circulate both within the regions and their bordering regions. No seat booking available.

DO NOT FORGET: You can only board trains in Italy with a valid ticket, which must be time-stamped before boarding; there are numerous time-stamping machines in every station. You cannot buy or stamp tickets on board.

If you don't have a ticket - or did not stamp before boarding - you will be liable to pay the full ticket price plus a 25 euro fine. If you produce a ticket that is not valid for the train or service you're using (i.e. one issued for a different train category at a different price, etc.) you will be asked to pay the difference with respect to the full ticket price, plus an 8 euro surcharge.

Taxis

Taxis are a convenient but expensive way to travel in Italian cities. There are taxi stands scattered throughout major cities. You cannot hail taxis on the street in Italy, but you can reserve taxis, in advance or immediately, by phone: consult the yellow pages for the number or ask your hotel reception desk or maitre d'hotel to call for you.

Taxi drivers have the right to charge you a supplementary fee for every piece of luggage they transport, as well as evening surcharges.

Driving

Especially when staying in the countryside, driving is a safe and convenient way to travel through Italy and its major cities. And while it is best avoided for obvious reasons, driving in the cities is not as difficult as it may seem or may have been reported to be. It is important to be aware of street signs and speed limits, and many cities have zones where only limited traffic is allowed in order to accommodate pedestrians. Although an international driver's license is not required in Italy, it is advisable. ACI and similar associations provide this service to members.

The fuel distribution network is reasonably distributed all over the territory. All service stations have unleaded gasoline ("benzina verde") and diesel fuel ("gasolio"). Opening time is 7am to 12:30 and 15 to 19:30; on motorways the service is 24 hours a day.

Type of roads in Italy: The *Autostrada* (for example A14) is the main highway system in Italy and is similar to the Interstate highway system in the US and the motorway system in the UK. Shown on our Touring Club Italiano 1:200,000 road maps as black. The Autostrada are toll highways; you pay to use them. The *Strada Statale* (for example SS54) is a fast moving road that may have one or more lanes in each direction. Shown on our Touring Club Italiano 1:200,000 road maps as red. *Strada Provinciale* (for example SP358) can be narrow, slow and winding roads. They are usually one lane in each direction. Shown on our Touring Club Italiano 1:200,000 road maps as yellow. *Strada Comunale* (for example SC652) is a local road connecting the main town with its sorrounding. Note: In our guide you will sometime find an address of a place in the countryside listed, for example, as "SS54 Km 25". This means that the you have to drive along the Strada Statale 54 until you reach the 25-km road sign. Speed limits: 130 kmph on the

Autostrada, 110 kmph on main highways, 90 kmph outside of towns, 50 kmph in towns.

The town streets are patrolled by the Polizia Municipale while the roads outside cities and the Autostrada are patrolled by the Carabinieri or the Polizia Stradale. They may set up road blocks where they may ask you to stop by holding out a small red sign.

Do not forget:

- Wear your seat belt at all times;
- Do not use the cellular phone while driving;
- Have your headlights on at all times when driving outside of cities;
- The drunk driving laws are strict - do not drink and drive;
- In case of an accident you are not allowed to get out of your car unless you are wearing a special, high-visibility, reflective jacket.

ACCOMMODATION

Hotels

In Italy it is common practice for the reception desk to register your passport, and only registered guests are allowed to use the rooms. This is mere routine, done for security reasons, and there is no need for concern.

All hotels use the official star classification system, from 5-star luxury hotel to 1 star accommodation.

Room rates are based on whether they are for single ("camera singola") or double ("camera doppia") occupancy. In every room you will find a list of the hotel rates (generally on the back of the door). While 4- and 5-star hotels have double beds, most hotels have only single beds. Should you want a double bed, you have to ask for a "letto matrimoniale". All hotels have rooms with bathrooms; only 1-star establishments usually have only shared bathrooms.

Most hotel rates include breakfast ("prima colazione"), but you can request to do without it, thus reducing the rate. Breakfast is generally served in a communal room and comprises a buffet with pastries, bread with butter and jam, cold cereals, fruit, yoghurt, coffee, and fruit juice. Some hotels regularly frequented by foreign tourists will also serve other items such as eggs for their American and British guests.

The hotels for families and in tourist localities also offer "mezza pensione", or half board, in which breakfast and dinner are included in the price.

It's always a good idea to check when a hotel's annual closing period is, especially if you are planning a holiday by the sea.

Farm stays

Located only in the countryside, and generally on a farm, "agriturismo" – a network of farm holiday establishments – is part of a growing trend in Italy to honor local gastronomic and wine traditions, as well as countryside traditions. These farms offer meals prepared with ingredients cultivated exclusively on site: garden-grown vegetables, homemade cheese and local recipes. Many of these places also provide lodging, one of the best ways to experience the "genuine" Italian lifestyle.

Bed & Breakfast

This form of accommodation provides bed and breakfast in a private house, and in the last few years has become much more widespread in Italy. There are over 5,000 b&bs, classified in 3 categories, and situated both in historic town centers, as well as in the outskirts and the countryside. Rooms for guests are always well-furnished, but not all of them have en suite bathrooms.

It is well-recommended to check the closing of the open-all-year accommodation services and restaurants, because they could have a short break during the year (usually no longer than a fortnight).

COMMUNICATIONS

Nearly everyone in Italy owns a cellular phone. Although public phones are still available, they seem to be ever fewer and farther between. If you wish to use public phones, you will find them in subway stops, bars, along the street, and phone centers generally located in the city center. Phone cards and pre-paid phone cards can be purchased at most newsstands and tobacco shops, and can also be acquired at automated tellers. For European travelers, activating personal cellular coverage is relatively simple, as it is in most cases for American and Australian travelers as well. Contact your mobile service provider for details. Cellular phones can also be rented in Italy from TIM, the Italian national phone company. For information, visit its website at www.tim.it. When traveling by car through the countryside, a cellular phone can really come in handy.

Note that when dialing in Italy, you must always dial the prefix (e.g., 02 for Milan, 06 for Rome) even when making a local call. For cellular phones, however, the initial zero is always dropped.

Freephone numbers always start with "800". For calls abroad from Italy, it's a good idea to buy a special pre-paid international phone card, which is used with a PIN code.

Internet access

Cyber cafés have sprung up all over Italy and today you can find one on nearly every city block. The Italian national phone company, TIM, has also begun providing internet access at many of its public phone centers.

EATING AND DRINKING

The bar

The Italian "bar" is a multi-faceted, all-purpose establishment for drinking, eating and socializing, where you can order an espresso, have breakfast, and enjoy a quick sandwich for lunch or even a hot meal. You can often buy various items here (sometimes even stamps, cigarettes, phone cards, etc.). Bear in mind that table service ("servizio a tavola") includes a surcharge. At most bars, if you choose to sit, a waiter will take your order. Every bar should have a list of prices posted behind or near the counter; if the bar offers table service, the price list should also include the extra fee for this.

Lunch at bars will include, but is not limited to, "panini," sandwiches with crusty bread, usually with cured meats such as "prosciutto" (salt-cured ham), "prosciutto cotto" (cooked ham), and cheeses such as mozzarella topped with tomato and basil. Then there are "tramezzini" (finger sandwiches) with tuna, cheese, or vegetables, etc. Often the "panini" and other savory sandwiches (like stuffed flatbread or "focaccia") are heated before being served. Naturally, the menu at bars varies according to the region: in Bologna you will find "piadine" (flatbread similar to pita) with Swiss chard; in Palermo there are "arancini" (fried rice balls stuffed with ground meat); in Genoa you will find that even the most unassuming bar serves some of the best "focaccia" in all Italy. Some bars also include a "tavola calda". If you see this sign in a bar window, it means that hot dishes like pasta and even entrées are served.

A brief comment on coffee and cappuccino: Italians never serve coffee with savory dishes or sandwiches, and they seldom drink cappuccino outside of breakfast (although they are happy to serve it at any time).

While English- and Irish-type pubs are frequented by beer lovers and young people in Italy, there are also American bars where long drinks and American cocktails are served.

Breakfast at the bar

Breakfast in Italy generally consists of some type of pastry, most commonly a "brioche" – a croissant either filled with cream or jam, or plain – and a cappuccino or espresso. Although most bars do not offer American coffee, you can ask for a "caffè lungo" or "caffè americano", both of which resemble the American coffee preferred by the British and Americans. Most bars have a juicer to make a "spremuta", freshly squeezed orange or grapefruit juice.

Lunch and Dinner

As with all daily rituals in Italy, food is prepared and meals are served according to local customs (e.g., in the North they prefer rice and butter, in South and Central Italy they favor pasta and olive oil).

Wine is generally served at mealtime, and while finer restaurants have excellent wine lists (some including vintage wines), ordering the house table wine generally brings good results (a house Chianti to accompany your Florentine steak in Tuscany, a sparkling

Prosecco paired with your creamed stockfish and polenta in Venice, a dry white wine with pasta dressed with sardines and wild fennel fronds in Sicily). Mineral water is also commonly served at meals and can be "gassata" (sparkling) or "naturale" (still).

The most sublime culinary experience in Italy is achieved by matching the local foods with the appropriate local wines: wisdom dictates that a friendly waiter will be flattered by your request for his recommendation on what to eat and drink. Whether at an "osteria" (a tavern), a "trattoria" (a home-style restaurant), or a "ristorante" (a proper restaurant), the service of lunch and dinner generally consists of – but is not limited to – the following: "antipasti" or appetizers; "primo piatto" or first course, i.e., pasta, rice, or soup; "secondo piatto" or main course, i.e., meat or seafood; "contorno" or side-dish, served with the main course, i.e., vegetables or salad; "formaggi", "frutta", and "dolci", i.e., cheeses, fruit, and dessert; caffè or espresso coffee, perhaps spiked with a shot of grappa.

The pizzeria

The pizzeria is in general one of the most economical, democratic, and satisfying culinary experiences in Italy. Everyone eats at the pizzeria: young people, families, couples, locals and tourists alike. Generally, each person orders her/his own pizza, and while the styles of crust and toppings will vary from region to region (some of the best pizzas are served in Naples and Rome), the acid test of any pizzeria is the Margherita, topped simply with cheese and tomato sauce. Beer, sparkling or still water, and Coca Cola are the beverages commonly served with pizza. Some restaurants include a pizza menu, but most establishments do not serve pizza at lunchtime.

The wine bar (enoteca)

More than one English-speaking tourist in Italy has wondered why the wine bar is called an enoteca in other countries and the English term is used in Italy: the answer lies somewhere in the mutual fondness that Italians and English speakers have for one another. Wine bars have become popular in recent years in the major cities (especially in Rome, where you can find some of the best). The wine bar is a great place to sample different local wines and eat a light, tapas-style dinner.

CULTURAL DIVERSITY

Whenever you travel, not only are you a guest of your host country, but you are also a representative of your home country. As a general rule, courtesy, consideration, and respect are always appreciated by guests and their hosts alike. Italians are famous for their hospitality and experience will verify this felicitous stereotype: perhaps nowhere else in Europe are tourists and visitors received more warmly. Italy is a relatively "new" country. Its borders, as we know them today, were established only in 1861 when it became a monarchy under the House of Savoy. After WWII, Italy became a Republic and now it is one of the member states of the European Union. One of the most fascinating aspects of Italian culture is that, even as a unified country, local tradition still prevails over a universally Italian national identity. Some jokingly say that the only time that Venetians, Milanese, Florentines, Neapolitans, and Sicilians feel like Italians is when the national football team plays in international competitions. From their highly localized dialects to the foods they eat, from their religious celebration to their politics, Italians proudly maintain their local heritage. This is one of the reasons why the Piedmontese continue to prefer their beloved Barolo wine and their white truffles, the Umbrians their rich Sagrantino wine and black truffles, the Milanese their risotto and panettone, the Venetians their stockfish and polenta, the Bolognese their lasagne and pumpkin ravioli, the Florentines their bread soups and steaks cooked rare, the Abruzzese their excellent fish broth and seafood, the Neapolitans their mozzarella, basil, pizza, and pasta. As a result of its rich cultural diversity, the country's population also varies greatly in its customs from region to region, city to city, town to town. As you visit different cities and regions throughout Italy, you will see how the local personality and character of the Italians change as rapidly as the landscape does. Having lived for millennia with their great diversity and rich, highly heterogeneous culture, the Italians have taught us many things, foremost among them the age-old expression, "When in Rome, do as the Romans do."

NATIONAL HOLIDAYS

New Year's Day (1st January), Epiphany (6th January), Easter Monday (day after Easter Sunday), Liberation Day (25th April), Labour Day (1st May), Italian Republic Day (2nd June), Assumption (15th August), All Saints' Day (1st November), Immaculate Conception (8th December), Christmas Day and Boxing Day (25th-26th December).
In addition to these holidays, each city also has a holiday to celebrate its patron saint's feast day, usually with lively, local celebrations. Shops and services in large cities close on national holidays and for the week of the 15th of August.

EVERYDAY NEEDS

State tobacco shops and pharmacies
Tobacco is available in Italy only at state licensed tobacco shops. These vendors ("tabaccheria"), often incorporated in a bar, also sell stamps.
Since 11 January 2005 smoking is forbidden in all so-called public places - unless a separately ventilated space is constructed - meaning over 90% of the country's restaurants and bars.
Medicines can be purchased only in pharmacies ("farmacia") in Italy. Pharmacists are very knowledgeable about common ailments and can generally prescribe a treatment for you on the spot. Opening time is 8:30-12:30 and 15:30-19:30 but in any case there is always a pharmacy open 24 hours and during holidays.

Shopping
Every locality in Italy offers tourists characteristic shops, markets with good bargains, and even boutiques featuring leading Italian fashion designers. Opening hours vary from region to region and from season to season. In general, shops are open from 9 to 13 and from 15/16 to 19/20, but in large cities they usually have no lunchtime break.

Tax Free
Non-EU citizens can obtain a reimbursement for IVA (goods and services tax) paid on purchases over €155, for goods which are exported within 90 days, in shops which display the relevant sign. IVA is always automatically included in the price of any purchase, and ranges from 20% to 4% depending on the item. The shop issues a reimbursement voucher to present when you leave the country (at a frontier or airport). For purchases in shops affiliated to 'Tax Free Shopping', IVA may be reimbursed directly at international airports.

Banks and post offices
Italian banks are open Monday to Friday, from 8:30 to 13:30 and then from 15 to 16. However, the afternoon business hours may vary.
Post offices are open from Monday to Saturday, from 8:30 to 13:30 (12:30 on Saturday). In the larger towns there are also some offices open in the afternoon.

Currency
Effective 1 January 2002, the currency used in many European Union countries is the euro. Coins are in denominations of 1, 2, 5, 10, 20 and 50 cents and 1 and 2 euros; banknotes are in denominations of 5, 10, 20, 50, 100, 200 and 500 euros, each with a different color.

Credit cards
All the main credit cards are generally accepted, but some smaller enterprises (arts and crafts shops, small hotels, bed & breakfasts, or farm stays) do not provide this service. Foreign tourists can obtain cash using credit cards at automatic teller machines.

Time
All Italy is in the same time zone, which is six hours ahead of Eastern Standard Time in the USA. Daylight saving time is used from March to October, when watches and clocks are set an hour ahead of standard time.

Passports and vaccinations
Citizens of EU countries can enter Italy without frontier checks. Citizens of Australia, Canada, New Zealand, and the United States can enter Italy with a valid passport and need not have a visa for a stay of less than 90 days.
No vaccinations are necessary.

Payment and tipping
When you sit down at a restaurant you are generally charged a "coperto" or cover charge ranging from 1.5 to 3 euros, for service and the bread. Tipping is not customary in Italy. Beware of unscrupulous restaurateurs who add a space on their clients' credit card receipt for a tip, while it has already been included in the cover charge.

USEFUL ADDRESSES

Foreign Embassies in Italy

Australia
Via A. Bosio, 5 - 00161 Rome
Tel. +39 06 852721
Fax +39 06 85272300
www.italy.embassy.gov.au.
info-rome@dfat.gov.au

Canada
Via G.B. de Rossi, 27 - 00161 Rome
Tel. +39 06 445981
Fax +39 06 445983760
www.canada.it
rome@dfait-maeci.gc.ca

Great Britain
Via XX Settembre, 80/a - 00187
Rome
Tel. +39 06 42200001
Fax +39 06 42202334
www.britian.it
consularenquiries@rome.
mail.fco.gov.uk

Ireland
Piazza di Campitelli, 3 - 00186
Rome
Tel. +39 06 6979121
Fax +39 06 6792354
irish.embassy@esteri.it

New Zealand
Via Zara, 28 - 00198 Rome
Tel. +39 06 4417171
Fax +39 06 4402984
nzemb.rom@flashnet.it

South Africa
Via Tanaro, 14 - 00198 Rome
Tel. +39 06 852541
Fax +39 06 85254300
www.sudafrica.it
sae@flashnet.it

United States of America
Via Vittorio Veneto, 121 - 00187
Rome
Tel. +39 06 46741
Fax +39 06 4882672
www.usis.it

Foreign Consulates in Italy

Australia
2 Via Borgogna
20122 Milan
Tel. +39 02 77704217
Fax +39 02 77704242

Canada
Via Vittor Pisani, 19
20124 Milan
Tel. +39 02 67581
Fax +39 02 67583900
milan@international.gc.ca

Great Britain
via S. Paolo 7
20121 Milan
Tel. +39 02 723001
Fax +39 02 86465081
ConsularMilan@fco.gov.uk

Lungarno Corsini 2
50123 Florence
Tel. +39 055 284133
Consular.Florence@fco.gov.uk

Via dei Mille 40
80121 Naples
Tel. +39 081 4238911

Fax +39 081 422434
Info.Naples@fco.gov.uk

Ireland
Piazza San Pietro in Gessate 2 -
20122 Milan
Tel. +39 02 55187569/02 55187641
Fax +39 02 55187570

New Zealand
Via Guido d'Arezzo 6,
20145 Milan
Tel. +39 02 48012544
Fax +39 02 48012577

South Africa
Vicolo San Giovanni Sul Muro 4
20121 Milan
Tel. +39 02 8858581
Fax +39 02 72011063
saconsulate@iol.it

United States of America
Via Principe Amedeo, 2/10
20121 Milan
Tel. +39 02 290351
Fax +39 02 29001165

Lungarno Vespucci, 38
50123 Florence
Tel. +39 055 266951
Fax +39 055 284088

Piazza della Repubblica
80122 Naples
Tel. +39 081 5838111
Fax +39 081 7611869

Italian Embassies and Consulates Around the World

Australia
12, Grey Street - Deakin, A.C.T.
2600 - Canberra
Tel. 02 62733333, 62733398,
62733198
Fax 02 62734223
www.ambitalia.org.au
embassy@ambitalia.org.au
Consulates at: Brisbane, Glynde,
Melbourne, Perth , Sydney

Canada
275, Slater Street, 21st floor -
Ottawa (Ontario) K1P 5H9
Tel. (613) 232 2401/2/3
Fax (613) 233 1484 234 8424
www.italyincanada.com
ambital@italyincanada.com
Consulates at: Edmonton,
Montreal, Toronto, Vancouver,

Great Britain
14, Three Kings Yard, London
W1K 4EH
Tel. 020 73122200
Fax 020 73122230
www.embitaly.org.uk
ambasciata.londra@esteri.it
Consulates at: London, Bedford,
Edinburgh, Manchester

Ireland
63/65, Northumberland Road -
Dublin 4
Tel. 01 6601744
Fax 01 6682759
www.italianembassy.ie
info@italianembassy.ie

New Zealand
34-38 Grant Road, Thorndon,

(PO Box 463, Wellington)
Tel. 04 473 5339
Fax 04 472 7255
www.italy-embassy.org.nz
ambwell@xtra.co.nz

South Africa
796 George Avenue, 0083 Arcadia
Tel. 012 4305541/2/3
Fax 012 4305547
www.ambital.org.za
ambital@iafrica.com
Consulates at: Johannesburg,
Capetown, Durban

United States of America
3000 Whitehaven Street, NW
Washington DC 20008
Tel. (202) 612-4400
Fax (202) 518-2154
www.italyemb.org
stampa@itwash.org
Consulates at: Boston, MA -
Chicago, IL - Detroit, MI - Houston,
TX - Los Angeles, CA - Miami, FL -
Newark, NJ - New York, NY -
Philadelphia, PA - San Francisco, CA

ENIT (Italian State Tourist Board)

Australia
Level 4, 46 Market Street
NSW 2000 Sidney
PO Box Q802 - QVB NSW 1230
Tel. 00612 92 621666
Fax 00612 92 621677
italia@italiantourism.com.au

Canada
175 Bloor Street E. Suite 907 –
South Tower
M4W3R8 Toronto (Ontario)
Tel. (416) 925 4882
Fax (416) 925 4799
www.italiantourism.com
enit.canada@on.aibn.com

Great Britain
1, Princes Street
W1B 2AY London
Tel. 020 7408 1254
Tel. 800 00482542 FREE from
United Kingdom and Ireland
italy@italiantouristboard.co.uk

United States of America
500, North Michigan Avenue
Suite 2240
60611 Chicago 1, Illinois
Tel. (312) 644 0996 / 644 0990
Fax (312) 644 3019
www.italiantourism.com
enitch@italiantourism.com

12400, Wilshire Blvd. – Suite 550
CA 90025 Los Angeles
Tel. (310) 820 1898 - 820 9807
Fax (310) 820 6357
www.italiantourism.com
enitla@italiantourism.com

630, Fifth Avenue – Suite 1565
NY – 10111 New York
Tel. (212) 245 4822 – 245 5618
Fax (212) 586 9249
www.italiantourism.com
enitny@italiantourism.com

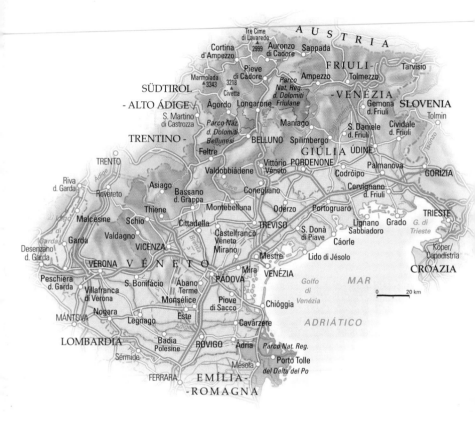

The Veneto, home to Petrarch, Palladio, Tiepolo and St Anthony, is a land of tremendous contrasts: Venice itself, the Adriatic coast, the lagoon, the Veneto Plain, Lake Garda, the Dolomites. Exposed to Roman, Frankish, Byzantine and Austrian influences, its artistic and historical heritage are remarkable. Behind the modern veneer, the Veneto will impress, intrigue and delight.
Friuli Venezia Giulia, in the far north-east corner of Italy, is quite unique. Romans, Lombards and Byzantines left their mark.

Heritage

For over 500 years it was part of the Austro-Hungarian Empire. It now shares borders with Austria and Slovenia. The result: a rich multi-ethnic tapestry, Italian, yet with fascinating Central and Eastern European traits for the visitor to explore.

Highlights

- The historical sights of Venice
- The Teatro Olimpico in Vicenza and the Roman Arena in Verona
- Trieste, its castle of San Giusto, the quays
- Udine, its squares, churches and palazzi

Bold, stars and italics are used in the text to emphasize the importance of places and works of art:

bold type ** → not to be missed
bold type * → very important
bold type → important
italic type → interesting

Inside

Though the old part of the town is obviously Venetian, nothing remains from the medieval or Roman periods. Defensive walls were built around the Roman stronghold of *Belunum* during the medieval period. Venetian rule began in 1404. 400 years of peace ended with Napoleon's arrival in 1806. However, the town became a provincial capital of his Italic Kingdom. The earthquake of 1873 halted neither the rise in population nor the urban development of the 19th century when the vast Piazza dei Martiri became the new focus of the town, outside the old walls. During the two world wars, in 1917-18, it was occupied by the Austrians and, in 1943, invaded by the Nazis. It is the birthplace of Bartolomeo Alberto Cappellari, pope from 1831-46 with the name of Gregory XVI, and writer Dino Buzzati.

Detail of the facade of the Duomo

Piazza dei Martiri ❶

The lively town center was built in 1500 north of the walls. Laid out as a garden, the square is dedicated to martyrs murdered by the Nazis in 1944.
The *church of S. Rocco*, built in the 16th century and restored in the 19th century, overlooks the square.
It contains a painting of St Francis in Ecstasy (1727). Nearby, in Piazza Vittorio Emanuele is the *Teatro Comunale* (1835) and *Palazzo Doglioni* (16th century), with an elegant loggia.

S. Stefano ❷

The church in the eponymous square dates from 1468. On the right side of the church is a 15th-century doorway. Inside, in the left aisle, are paintings by Cesare Vecellio. On the right of the presbytery, the *cappella Cesa* is decorated with frescoes from the second half of the 15th century. On the altar is a 15th-century polychrome wooden sculpture. Next-door is a 15th-century *cloister*.

Piazza del Mercato ❸

The square with the *fontana di S. Lucano* (1410) in the center is built on the site of the old Roman forum. The porticoed buildings around the edge date from the Renaissance. They include *Monte di Pietà*, decorated with crests and inscriptions, founded in 1501.

Via Mezzaterra ❹

The town's main street is lined with Venetian-style palaces. Nearby is the **church of S. Pietro** (14th century), rebuilt in 1750, with a plain facade. Inside are fine paintings by Andrea Schiavone and Sebastiano Ricci (above the high altar) and two carved wooden altar-pieces. The adjacent *Seminario Gregoriano* (Gregorian Seminary) has two cloisters, the oldest of which dates from the 15th and 16th centuries.

Piazza del Duomo ❺

A lively, monumental square overlooked by the Cathedral, the Baptistery, Palazzo dei Rettori and the clock-tower. The **Duomo*** was rebuilt in the early 16th century; the unfinished facade has two Gothic one-light windows and the fine

BELLUNO
IN OTHER COLORS...

ITINERARIES: page 118, 122
FOOD: page 140, 145, 152, 167
SHOPPING: page 177, 181, 183
EVENTS: page 186, 189
WELLNESS: page 195
PRACTICAL INFO: page 205

Baroque bell tower beside it is by Filippo Juvarra (1743). The elegant Renaissance *interior* has fine altar-pieces by Andrea Schiavone (1st altar on the right) and Palma il Giovane (4th on the right). In the *crypt*, above the altar formed by a 14th-century tomb with reliefs, is a 15th-century polyptych. Opposite the cathedral is the **Battistero** (1520), converted in the 19th century, with a fine font. On the north side of the square is **Palazzo dei Rettori*** (now the Police Headquarters), with a portico, two-light windows and beautiful loggias, begun in 1491. On the right is the *Torre dell'Orologio* (1549) and *Palazzo dei Vescovi-conti* (1190), now the municipal auditorium, now completely re-built;

The clock on the tower of Palazzo dei Rettori

the *clock-tower* is the only original part left.

Museo Civico ⑥

The museum in Palazzo dei Giuristi (1664) was created in 1876. In addition to Paleolithic and Roman finds, it has a **Pinacoteca**, with a fine collection of Venetian art from the 14th to 19th centuries, with works by Sebastiano Ricci (*Hercules at the Crossroads*, *Fall of Phaeton*). There are also works by Palma il Giovane and Domenico Tintoretto.

Porta Doiona ⑦

Porta Doiona was the main entrance to the old town. Although the outside of the gate dates from 1553, the inside facade, built with large sandstone blocks, dates from 1268.

Belluno 1 : 11 000 (1 cm = 110 m) 0 100 200 m

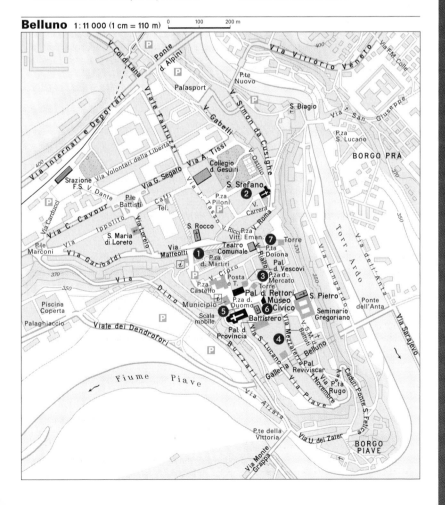

ÀGORDO [30 km]

Associated with the fate of Belluno since the 10th century, for many years it was a mining town. Now a popular holiday resort, it has several craft traditions (the town is famous for eye-glasses) and mining (it sent iron from its mines to the sword-makers of Belluno and the mint of the Venice). Here the **Collezioni Ottiche e Occhiali - Raccolta Rathschüler-Luxottica** comprise the collections of Leonardo Del Vecchio, who manufactured eye-glasses on an industrial scale, and the Genoese optician Fritz Rathschüler. More than 1,200 exhibits are on display, including eye-glasses, telescopes and binoculars, microscopes, optical instruments, the Luxottica company's key products, and ex votos, prints, engravings and paintings. The **Museo della Storia Mineraria** has more than 3,000 exhibits about mining from all over the world (from 190 sites abroad and 290 in Italy), with a splendid collection of rocks and fossils.

ÀLLEGHE [50 km]

A holiday resort in summer and winter, Àlleghe stands on a promontory jutting out into the lake of the same name (1,500 m long and 18 m deep), formed in 1771 by a landslide. Monte Civetta (3,220 m) towers above the town.

COMÈLICO [50 km]

Most of its traditional houses are built of wood. The green meadows, woods and mountain ridges form a particularly peaceful landscape, very different to that of the nearby Dolomites. This corner of the Cadore, where the dialect is similar to Ladino, is a crossed by the Pàdola (north-west) and Piave (north-east) rivers. The villages in the area are holiday resorts and winter sports centers.

CORTINA D'AMPEZZO [70 km]

The international fame of this "pearl of the Dolomites" is well justified. Not only is the scenery around the town wonderful but its quality as a tourist destination is unrivalled. It is called the "capital" of the Dolomites because the mountains nearby offer considerable potential in terms of hiking and rock-climbing – with more than 300 km of footpaths, 56 huts and

ORANGE FLAG
THE QUALITY LABEL FOR TOURISM AND ENVIRONMENT IN ITALY'S INLAND AREAS

The ORANGE FLAG is a label of quality for the development of tourism in Italy's inland areas. Municipalities with less than 15,000 inhabitants may be awarded it if selected criteria are achieved and maintained: cultural heritage, respect for the environment, hospitality, information and services, and quality local production. The ORANGE FLAG program is run by the Touring Club of Italy. The World Tourism Organisation has chosen the ORANGE FLAG PROGRAM as a success in the sphere of environmental tourism. For more information: www.touringclub.it/bandierearancioni

Eight towns have been awarded the Orange Flag in the Veneto, whereas none has been awarded in the region of Friuli-Venezia Giulia. Arquà Petrarca and Montagnana (Padova), Àsolo (Treviso), Maròstica (Vicenza), Mel (Belluno) and Soave (Verona) are described in the following pages; the last two are described below.

MALCÉSINE (VERONA)

The medieval town of Malcésine lies on a strip of land between Lake Garda and Monte Baldo. With its castle perched on a rock high above the lake, this small fishing-town, its houses linked by arches and porticoes, has a charming atmosphere. Next to the picturesque harbor stands the Renaissance-style Palazzo dei Capitani del Lago. Isolated on its hill above the town, the castle houses a Natural History Museum, with rooms devoted to various topics.

PORTOBUFFOLÈ (TREVISO)

The town was built on the bend of a river, although the riverbed has been dry since the Livenza was diverted in 1911. In the past it was regarded as a small island on dry land, and an important strategic and commercial center. It is approached by two stone bridges. It has a small castle built around Piazza Maggiore. Other notable buildings on the square include the Loggia Comunale and the Duomo (cathedral), an unusual example of a converted synagogue. Nearby is the house of Gaia da Camino, a noblewoman whose exceptional beauty was described by Dante in the "Divina Commedia". The 13th-century building has elegant two-light windows and a portico. It houses a Cycling Museum.

a magnificent network of ski runs – and it also offers every comfort in terms of modern hotel facilities. Corso Italia, the town's main street, is now a pedestrian precinct. The **Municipio** houses the *Museo della Grande Guerra*, with a collection of c. 10,000 exhibits relating to WWI, including books, photos, uniforms and memorabilia. Just beyond it is the *church of Ss. Filippo e Giacomo* (18th century). Behind the parish church stands the **Casa delle Regole** (1827). It houses a *Modern Art Collection* with many works by leading Italian artists (Carrà, De Chirico, Morandi); the *Museo Etnografico "Regole d'Ampezzo"* with objects representing local craft activities (wrought iron, musical instruments) and work tools; and the *Museo Paleontologico "Rinaldo Zardini"* with a collection of fossils found in the Dolomites. In 1956, the **Stadio Olimpico del Ghiaccio** (Olympic Ice-Rink) was built for the Winter Olympics. Opposite, the bronze plaque is to the French geologist who first described Dolomite rock in the late 18th century.

the piazza. It is overlooked by the *church of S. Rocco* (1599), preceded by a large fountain (1520), *Palazzo della Ragione* (the *town hall*) with a fine portico (inside is a little wooden theater dating from 1802), *Palazzo Gazzi*, with a fine portico and *Palazzo Guarnieri*. The **Museo Civico**, opened in 1928, occupies part of *Palazzo Villabruna* (16th century) and has an archeological section, an art gallery with Venetian works from the 16th to 18th centuries, and a historical section with exhibits from the Risorgimento, (memorabilia, weapons, documents and photos). It has a fine collection of local antique furniture. The 15th-century **chiesa di Ognissanti** (church of All

Feltre: the old town center with the castle keep

FELTRE [35 km]

This small attractive hill-town was once the seat of a bishop, in 1404, Feltre agreed to supply Venice with iron, copper and silver from its mines, and timber. Venetian money paid for its reconstruction in the 16th and 17th centuries, earning its historic center the title of *urbs pincta* ("painted town") because of the many frescoed facades. The main street of the old town is **Via Mezzaterra**, accessed through *Porta Imperiale* (late 15th century). Here, the *church of S. Giacomo Maggiore* has a marble Renaissance doorway. Nearby, the **Galleria d'Arte Moderna "Carlo Rizzarda"** is housed in *Palazzo Cumano*, left to the town by Carlo Rizzarda (1883-1931), with his priceless wrought-iron collection. The gallery also has paintings, sculptures and ceramics by leading 19th- and 20th-century Italian artists (Casorati, Fattori, Signorini and Carrà). Built on several levels, **Piazza Maggiore** is decorated with monuments to illustrious citizens of the town (Panfilo Castaldi). The square keep of the castle dominates

Saints) has a bell tower from the 9th and 10th centuries. Inside, above the 2nd altar on the left, is an altar-piece by Jacopo Tintoretto (Madonna Enthroned with St Victor and St Nicholas of Bari). The present **Cattedrale**, dedicated to St Peter, is very old but was re-built in the 16th century. There is still a 15th-century apse and a bell tower (1392), with a fine 15th-century tomb with a relief at its base. Behind the cathedral is the *Battistero*, formerly the Oratorio di S. Lorenzo, with a 15th-century apse and a font (1399). The facade overlooks the ruins of the paleo-Christian baptistery.

LONGARONE [18 km]

There is still dramatic evidence of the disaster which struck here on the night of October 9, 1963 when the town (473 m, population 4,202) was swept away by a huge mass of water from the *Vajont Dam*. Although the concrete reconstruction of the town is open to debate, it helps to convey the impact

A fairy-tale landscape: the Dolomites of Cadore at dawn

of the catastrophe. Initiated by a landslide on Monte Toc which hurtled into the artificial lake below, the mass of displaced water killed 1,909 people, virtually destroying the town. The *parish church* (1966-76), by Giovanni Michelucci stands next to the memorial to the victims of the disaster. Now mainly an industrial town, Longarone is the main trade-fair center of the Belluno area.

The **Mostra Fotografica Permanente del Vajont - "Vajont per non dimenticare"** tells the story of Longarone and the Vajont Dam disaster through photos and excerpts of film.

The **Museo del Vajont** illustrates the culture of the local mountain community before the Vajont Dam disaster.

MEL [16 km]

This town, which has been awarded the TCI's "Bandiera Arancione" (Orange Flag), stands on the site of an early Venetian settlement. It has an attractive center with palaces and churches containing many works of art.

The **Museo Civico Archeologico** in Palazzo delle Contesse, opened in 1996, contains grave-goods from a nearby necropolis and items from private collections.

MISURINA [82 km]

The classic view of Misurina is of the large, old-fashioned hotel which overlooks the lake. This is a popular holiday and ski resort. A road leads around the edge of the **Lago di Misurina***, the largest natural lake in the Cadore region (1 km long and 300 m wide). The mountains to the north of the lake include the **Tre Cime di Lavaredo***. The scenic drive around their perimeter takes about 2 hours.

PIEVE DI CADORE [40 km]

The historical capital of the Cadore region overlooks the artificial lake created by the dam across the River Piave. The elegant decoration of the buildings belies the wealth of the local merchants, who felled local timber and sold it to Venice. The Renaissance *Palazzo della Magnifica Comunità di Cadore* houses the Museo **Archeologico della Magnifica Comunità di Cadore**, with archeological finds from the proto-historic and Roman periods.

The **Casa natale di Tiziano Vecellio** (Titian's birthplace) (1488/90-1576), is a typical 15th-century house. It contains prints and reproductions of Titian's works, as well as antique furniture and household objects. In the *parish church of S. Maria Nascente* (rebuilt 1761) is a **Madonna and Child*** by Titian. The **Museo dell'Occhiale** was opened in 1990. It contains one of the most complete collections of its kind, with more than 3,000 pairs of eye-glasses dating from the medieval period to the present, including eyewear from the East.

SELVA DI CADORE [58 km]

Set amid meadows and woods, the town is dominated by Monte Pelmo (3,168 m) and Marmolada. A mining town until the 18th century, it has recently become a tourist attraction. The *church of S. Lorenzo* dates from the 15th and 16th centuries.

The **Museo Civico della Val Fiorentina "Vittorino Cazzetta"**, inaugurated in 1982, has an archeological section with the original skeleton and grave-goods of *Mondeval Man* from a 6th-century BC burial discovered nearby in 1987, and stone and pottery finds dating from the late 4th millennium BC to the early 3rd millennium BC; a historical section and a geo-paleontological section.

PADOVA

This active provincial capital with its medieval layout and artistic wealth has become a focus for tourism. The presence of a university here since 1222 made Padua one of Europe's great cultural centers. Padua's strong Roman Catholic tradition is rooted in the preaching of the Fransciscan monk Anthony (1195-1231), who spent the last years of his life here and was proclaimed saint shortly after his death.

The presence of Giotto, Donatello and Mantegna qualifies Padua as capital of Italian art in the 14th and 15th centuries. According to Virgil, the city was founded by Antenor of Troy. Local archeological finds point to civilization dating from the 11th to 10th centuries BC. It came under full Roman rule in the 2nd century AD, and became one of the Empire's richest cities. The earliest permanent markets date from the 12th century, roughly where Piazza delle Erbe and Piazza della Frutta are today. In 1318, the da Carrara family came to the fore, providing the town with a solid set of walls, but were overwhelmed by the Visconti of Milan (1388-90). In 1406 they were ousted by the Venetians who ruled Padua until it was invaded by Napoleon in 1797. The city became part of the Kingdom of Italy in 1866.

Palazzo della Ragione ➊

The palazzo separates *Piazza delle Frutta* from **Piazza delle Erbe**, closed on the east side by 15th-century **Palazzo Comunale** and site of a colourful daily market. The palazzo was built on a rectangular plan in 1218-19 as a lawcourt. Enlarged in 1306-09 by adding external loggias and a ship's keel roof, a fire in 1420 destroyed Giotto's frescoes. Subsequently restored, the frescoes cover more than 200 m of walls and are divided into 12 sections. The huge wooden *horse* (1446) is a copy of Donatello's equestrian statue of Gattemelata.

(1532), with Italy's earliest clock (1344). Beyond, the *Corte Capitaniato* is surrounded by 16th-century buildings and the **Liviano** (1939), the seat of the

Palazzo della Ragione on Piazza delle Erbe

Piazza dei Signori ➋

Named after the da Carrara family, the square is overlooked by the 17th-century *church of S. Clemente* and the elegant marble **Loggia del Consiglio*** (1496-1553), with a ground-floor portico and a broad staircase; at the far end is *Palazzo del Capitanio* (1605), whose facade incorporates the **Arco dell'Orologio**

University Arts Faculty; in the atrium, frescoes by Massimo Campigli and a statue of Livy by Arturo Martini (1942). A **monumental staircase*** leads up to the first floor to the vast *Sala dei Giganti*, decorated in the 16th century with frescoes of kings and heroes (in one corner is a 14th-century portrait of Petrarch). The Liviano houses the **Museo di Scienze Archeologiche e d'Arte**, with a fine collection of ceramics, votive and domestic objects from pre-history to late Antiquity, and a plaster-cast museum Greek and Roman sculpture.

PADOVA
IN OTHER COLORS...

▪ **ITINERARIES:** page 130
▪ **FOOD:** page 141, 145, 152, 158, 168
▪ **SHOPPING:** page 178, 181, 183
▪ **EVENTS:** page 186, 189
▪ **WELLNESS:** page 194, 196, 197
▪ **PRACTICAL INFO:** page 212

Battistero ➌

The 12th-century Baptistery is built on a square plan with a broad dome. The interior is covered with exceptional frescoes* (1374-76), the masterpiece of Giusto de' Menabuoi. He also painted the polyptych at the altar: a prime example of Italian 14th-century painting. The font in the center dates from 1260.

Duomo ④

Founded in the Early Middle Ages, re-built in the 9th and 10th centuries and again before 1124, its present appearance reflects the reconstruction begun in 1551, to a design by Michelangelo. The warm brick facade is unfinished. The interior is bare and majestic, dominated by mighty pilasters. In the walls of the transept: monumental tombs of the 14th to 16th centuries. In the *Sagrestia dei Canonici*: 14th-century panels and fine paintings.

One of Giotto's frescoes in the Scrovegni Chapel

Museo Diocesano di Arte Sacra ⑤

Housed in the prestigious **Palazzo Vescovile** (Bishop's Palace), the museum (visitors should book) contains precious examples of painting, sculpture, gold- and silver-ware, codices, incunabulae and vestments from the diocese of Padua. Highlights include a 9th-century ink-well, an 11th-century panel depicting *Christ making the sign of benediction*, the 12th-century cover of a book of the the Gospels, a cycle of paintings depicting the *Stories of St Sebastian* (1367), panels by Giorgio Schiavone and paintings by G.B. Tiepolo (*S. Francesco di Paola*). The *cappella di S. Maria degli Angeli* (1495), with frescoes, is now part of the museum.

Piazza Insurrezione ⑥

Piazza Insurrezione lies in the heart of the modern city. Nearby, the 18th-century **church of S. Lucia** has a harmonious interior decorated with statues and fine paintings, and, high up, monochrome paintings, with works by G.B. Tiepolo (**St Luke***). Not far away, in Via Marsilio da Padova is the 13th-century *Casa di Ezzelino*.

I Carmini ⑦

The complex of the Church of the Carmelites, a.k.a. *S. Maria del Carmine*, documented as early as 1212, was re-built in the late 15th century. For centuries, it was the fulcrum of the town north of the city walls. Badly damaged by bombs in WWII, the sacristy and the nearby **Scuola del Carmine***, built in the 14th century, completed in 1494 and decorated with 16th-century frescoes, survived. The school was re-built in the early 16th century.

Nuovi Musei di Palazzo Zuckermann ⑧

This new museum complex, inaugurated in June 2004, comprises the *Museum of Art and Applied and Decorative Arts* and the *Museo Bottacin*. The first contains more than 2,000 objects from the collections of the Civic Museum of Medieval and Modern Art: glass, inlay work, ceramics, silver, ivories, jewelry, fabrics and furniture used in Padua from the Middle Ages until the late 19th century. The second museum has an exhibition of coins and medals, paintings, furniture, sculptures, Chinese ceramics, antique weapons and other items collected by Nicola Bottacin, a merchant who donated his art and coin collection to the city in the mid-19th century.

Museo di Mineralogia ⑨

The museum contains various collections (systematics, mineral deposits, genetics, and the "G. Gasser" regional collection) and is the most important mineralogical collection in the Veneto. There are also smaller collections of gemstones, geological phenomena, crystals, meteorites, and fluorescent minerals. It also has displays of equipment and instruments used in the 19th and 20th centuries for analyzing and studying minerals, models of crystalline structures and early illustrated books on mineralogy.

Cappella degli Scrovegni ⑩

The Scrovegni Chapel, named after the man who commissioned it, stands in the Giardino Pubblico dell'Arena, named after the 1st-century *Roman amphitheater* which once stood on this site. The *little church*, also called S. Maria dell'Annunciata, was consecrated in 1305. *Inside* are the **famous frescoes by Giotto****, executed with the aid of his assistants and completed by 1305. They constitute one of the finest examples of

Padova: the Scrovegni Chapel

(Episodes of Joachim and Ann)
1 Joachim is driven from the Temple
2 Joachim retreats to live among the shepherds
3 The Angel tells Ann that she will have a child
4 The Angel tells Joachim that his prayers will be granted
5 Joachin's dream
6 Joachim meets Ann at the golden gate of Jerusalem

(Episodes from the Life of Mary)
7 Birth of Mary
8 The presentation of Mary at the Temple
9 The handing over of the rods to St Simeon
10 The prayer for the flowering of the rods
11 Marriage of Mary and Joseph
12 The wedding procession
13 God the Father instructs the Archangel Gabriel to tell Mary the news
14 The Annunciation

(Episodes from the Life and Death of Christ)
15 The visitation
16 The Birth of Jesus

17 The Adoration of the Magi
18 The Presentation of Jesus at the Temple
19 The Flight into Egypt
20 The Slaughter of the Innocents
21 Christ among the Doctors of the Temple
22 The Baptism of Christ
23 The Wedding at Cana
24 The Raising of Lazarus
25 Christ's Entry into Jerusalem
26 The Expulsion of the Merchants from the Temple
27 Judas betrays Jesus
28 The Last Supper
29 Christ washes the feet of his Disciples
30 The Kiss of Judas
31 Jesus appears before Caiphas
32 Jesus is mocked and made to wear a Crown of Thorns
33 The Road to Calvary
34 The Crucifixion
35 The Deposition
36 The Resurrection
37 The Ascension
38 Pentecost

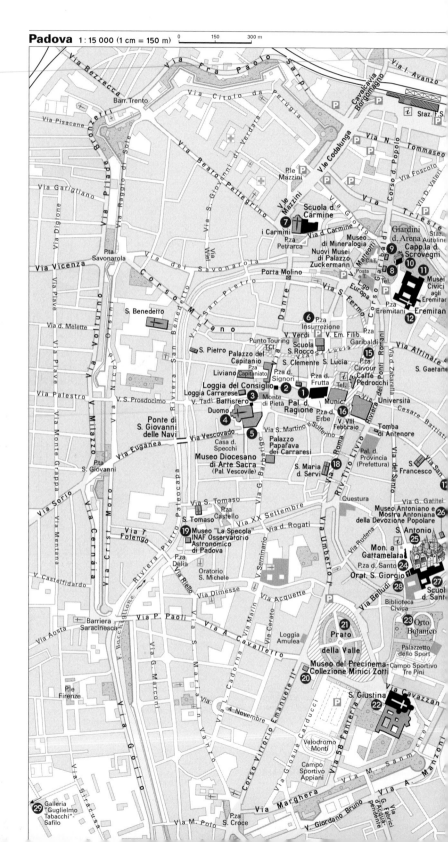

Padova

1 : 15 000 (1 cm = 150 m)

0   150   300 m

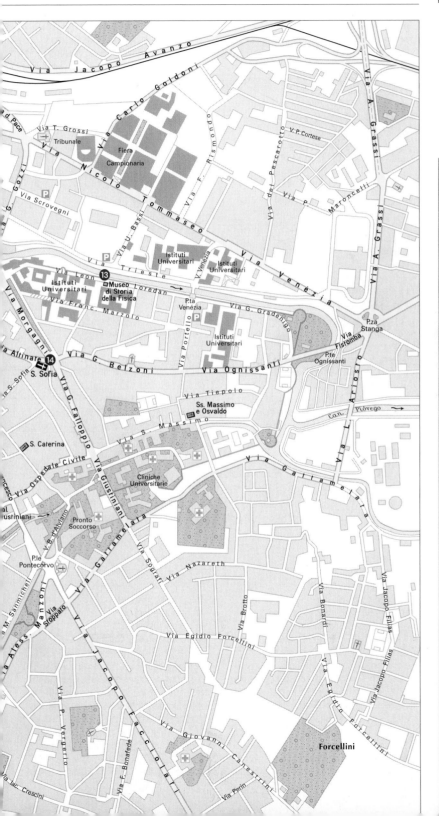

Italian painting. On the wall above the entrance is the Last Judgement. On the side-walls (below) are the 7 vices and 7 virtues, and above are 38 panels depicting the Life of Christ and the Life of Mary. The frescoes reflect the special characteristics of Giotto's art: monumental composition, simplicity of representation and great use of melodrama. In the presbytery, the statues above the altar are a **Madonna and two Angels*** by Giovanni Pisano.

Eremitani ⑪

The church of the Eremitani, dedicated to St Philip and St James, was built between 1276 and 1306. Half-destroyed by bombs in 1944, it has been lovingly restored. Inside, the single nave has a wooden ceiling. On the walls of the nave are tombs and sculptures from the 14th and 16th centuries: the *tomb of Jacopo da Carrara*, with an inscription by Petrarch, and the *tomb of Ubertino da Carrara* (both 14th-century). At the far end, on the right is the **Cappella Ovetari***. The chapel's famous frescoes by Andrea Mantegna and other artists were destroyed by the bombs. Some of Mantegna's works have survived: the **Assumption*** (behind the altar), two scenes of the *Martyrdom of St Christopher* (on the right) and the *Martyrdom of St James* (on the left, partly destroyed).

Musei Civici agli Eremitani ⑫

Housed in the restored cloisters of the monastery of the Eremitani monks, the **Museo Archeologico** has pre-Roman, Roman, Egyptian, Etruscan and paleo-Christian exhibits. Highlights include the 88 items, including some finely decorated candle-sticks, from the *tomb of the embossed Vases* (700 BC) and various Roman remains: a *head of Augustus* (1st century AD), a *bust of Silenus* (2nd century BC), and an aedicular tomb. The **Pinacoteca** has a splendid range of paintings from the Venetian School (14th to 20th centuries) and important works by Giotto (*Christ on the Cross*, from the Scrovegni Chapel), Tintoretto (*Dinner at the house of Simon*) and Veronese (*Martyrdom of St Primus and St Felicianus*). The **Emo Capodilista Collection** has a nucleus of 543 paintings by Venetian and Flemish

artists. Highlights include paintings by Giorgione (*Leda and the Swan*), Titian (*Mythological Scenes*) and Giovanni Bellini (*Portrait of a Young Senator*).

Museo di Storia della Fisica ⑬

The museum contains a collection of scientific apparatus dating from the 16th to 20th centuries. The exhibits include 16th-century astronomical instruments, some extremely rare microscopes from the 17th and 18th centuries and a fine collection of instruments used in the study of physics in the 18th and 19th centuries.

S. Sofia ⑭

The oldest church in Padua, S. Sofia was possibly founded in the 9th century. It was altered and rebuilt several times. It has an interesting facade (11th to 14th centuries) and a beautiful **apse*** with three overlapping tiers of blind arcading. The somber interior has a nave and two side-aisles and an ambulatory around the far end of the presbytery.

Piazza Cavour ⑮

Piazza Cavour is the liveliest square in the city. In a small square nearby is **Caffè Pedrocchi**, an elegant neo-classical building dating from 1831. It was once known as the "café with no doors", because it stayed open all night. It was a popular meeting-place for intellectuals, writers and politicians and the focus of the life of the city.

Via VIII Febbraio ⑯

On the left of Via VIII Febbraio is the University and on the right, Palazzo del Municipio. The **University**, known as *Palazzo del Bo'* (from "bue" - ox -, the name of an inn which once stood on the spot) is one of the oldest in Europe (1222) and has many cultural traditions. Frequented by students from all over Europe (Galileo Galilei taught here), it is regarded as the cradle of modern medicine. *Palazzo del Municipio* (16th century) has a very fine **courtyard*** with a portico and loggias. From here, steps lead up to the upper floor, where the most interesting rooms are located: the **anatomy theater***, the first of its kind (1594), the *Sala dei Quaranta* (with Galileo's wooden "cattedra") and the *Aula Magna* (Great Hall), which is decorated with numerous coats of arms.

Via S. Francesco ⑰

In Piazzale Antenore, which is crossed by this street, is the **Tomb of Antenor**, a spired aedicule (1283). It stands above the tomb traditionally regarded as that of Antenor, the mythical founder of Padua. In fact, it is the tomb of a warrior of the 2nd or 4th century. Further on is the 15th-century **church of S. Francesco**, which has a porticoed entrance. Gothic in style, it has a nave and two side-aisles. The *Ascension* above the doorway is attributed to Paolo Veronese.

Via Roma ⑱

One of Padua's busiest streets, Via Roma is overlooked by the side of the *church of S. Maria dei Servi* (1372-92), with its 16th-century doorway. Inside are some fine frescoes (the *Pietà* in the right aisle) and Renaissance sculptures.

Museo "La Specola" INAF Osservatorio Astronomico di Padova ⑲

In the late 18th century, the University of Padua converted the *Great Tower* of the old castle into an astronomical observatory. "La Specola" was divided into two parts. The lower observatory, called the *Sala della Meridiana* (Room of the Sun-dial), was used for making observations at midday using the sun-dial incorporated in its floor and for observing stars at the celestial meridian. The octagonal *upper observatory* has large windows which enabled students of astronomy to observe the stars in every direction. The museum also has an exhibition room (*Sala Colonna*) with astronomical instruments from the 18th and 19th centuries.

Museo del Precinema - Collezione Minici Zotti ⑳

The museum focuses on the pre-cinema age and the "magic lantern", an optical instrument invented in 1650 for projecting images painted on glass onto a screen. There are numerous magic lanterns, hand-painted panes of glass used in magic-lantern shows, a photography and stereoscopy section and optical games. Almost all the exhibits are original, except the ones which have been reproduced to give visitors a "hand's on" experience.

Prato della Valle ㉑

One of Europe's largest squares, Prato della Valle was laid out in 1775-76. In the center of the square is an island planted with trees, *Isola Memmia*, surrounded by a pool and 78 statues.

Padua: the square of Prato della Valle

S. Giustina ㉒

In a corner of Prato della Valle, the grand 16th-century **church of S. Giustina** has a bare facade and eight domes. Its vast *interior* has a nave and two side-aisles separated by pilasters. The right transept leads into the **sacello di S. Prosdocimo*** (church of St Prosdocimus), the remains of a primitive church of the 5th and 6th centuries, which still has part of the old marble iconostasis (6th century) on one side. In the **old choir*** (1462), formerly the apse of the previous church, are wooden *choir-stalls* with fine inlay work (1477). In the adjoining rooms is a 15th-century terracotta statue (*Madonna and Child*), and the lunette and architrave from the Romanesque doorway of the earlier church (c. 1080), with fine sculptures. In the apse is the **choir***, made of walnut, carved and inlaid in 1566, and the **Martyrdom of St Giustina***, a large altar-piece by Paolo Veronese (c. 1575). In the 2nd chapel on the left, the painting (*St Gregory the Great frees Rome from the Plague*) is by Sebastiano Ricci

Orto Botanico ㉓

Created in 1545 for acclimatizing and studying plant species of potential pharmacological value, this is the oldest university botanical garden in the world. The layout of the garden is original: a circular walled garden with four sectors containing numerous, mainly perennial, botanical species. Outside the walls are the glass-houses and the arboretum. The collection of carnivorous and acquatic plants is particularly interesting. Since 1997, it has been a UNESCO World Heritage Site.

Piazza del Santo and Monumento al Gattamelata ㉔

Heart of the so-called "Cittadella antoniana", Piazza del Santo is a vast square decorated with a bronze equestrian statue, the **monument to Gattamelata***, a mercenary soldier of the Republic of Venice (c. 1370-1443). This masterpiece of the Italian Renaissance is by Donatello (1453), who also designed and created the pedestal. Site of the Basilica del Santo, the Oratorio di S. Giorgio and the Scuola di S. Antonio, part of the historic square is lined with porticoed houses and shops selling souvenirs and religious mementoes.

S. Antonio ㉕

St Anthony's Basilica, or, simply, **Il Santo**, is one of Italy's most famous sanctuaries. It was built between 1232 and the mid-14th century to enshrine the tomb of St Anthony of Padua (who was born in Lisbon in 1195 and died in Padua in 1231). The *exterior* has eight domes arranged in the form of a cross. *Inside*, in the *right transept* is the 14th-century **chapel of S. Felice***, decorated with

Padova: Santa Giustina

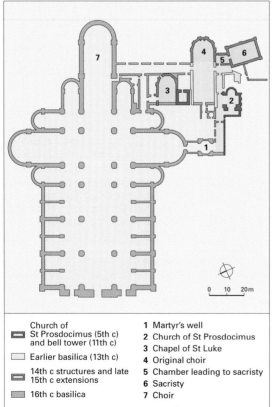

0   10   20m

	Church of St Prosdocimus (5th c) and bell tower (11th c)	**1** Martyr's well
	Earlier basilica (13th c)	**2** Church of St Prosdocimus
	14th c structures and late 15th c extensions	**3** Chapel of St Luke
	16th c basilica	**4** Original choir
		5 Chamber leading to sacristy
		6 Sacristy
		7 Choir

The church of S. Giustina from Prato della Valle

frescoes (*Legend of St James, Crucifixion*) by Altichiero (1374-78). In the *presbytery*, the high altar is decorated with fine **bronzes by Donatello**** (1443-50) and his assistants. On the left of the altar is a bronze *candle-stick* (1515). The *ambulatory* leads around behind the presbytery, with chapels leading off its outer edge. The fifth chapel, the Chapel of the Reliquaries, contains a fine **treasury***, with some unusual reliquaries: little incense-burners in the shape of ships (15th century) and the wooden boxes which once contained the bones of the Saint. At the end of the ambulatory, the Chapel of the Black Madonna lies next to the Chapel of the Blessed Luca Belludi (1382), which is decorated with **frescoes*** by Giusto de' Menabuoi. In the *left transept*, the **cappella dell'Arca del Santo*** (Chapel of the Tomb of St Anthony) was begun in 1500. On the walls are nine reliefs depicting the Life of the Saint, executed by 16th century sculptors including Jacopo Sansovino (*St Anthony revives a drowned woman*, 1563). In the middle of the chapel is an exquisite altar dating from 1593, behind which lies the tomb of St Anthony. The right aisle leads to the **cloisters** (13th to 15th centuries). The first, the *Cloister of the Chapter*

or of the Magnolia, is the oldest part of the monastery (1240). It leads to the Consiglio della Presidenza dell'Arca, where there is a fresco of **St Anthony and St Bernard in Prayer** by Andrea Mantegna.

Museo Antoniano and Mostra Antoniana della Devozione Popolare ㉖

Founded in 1895, the Museum of St Anthony's Basilica was re-opened to the public on the occasion of its centenary having had its collection re-organized to highlight two main themes: first, testimonials of popular veneration for St Anthony over the centuries (ex-votos and various donations) and the many art-works created for the basilica and the Scuola which, for various reasons, were removed from their original setting. The gold- and silver-ware section is particularly interesting, with some valuable 18th-century altar-pieces and numerous fabrics.

Scuola del Santo ㉗

The School of St Anthony was begun in 1427 and the height was raised in 1504-1505. An 18th century staircase leads up to the council chamber, which has some very fine early 16th-century **frescoes*** (the most important works from that period in Padua), depicting the miracles of the saint. Starting at the bottom on the right, the 1st, 12th and 13th scene are by Titian.

S. Giorgio ㉘

This 14th-century oratory stands to the right of the basilica, next to the *Mausoleum of Rolando da Piazzola*. The interior of the oratory is entirely covered with **frescoes*** (stories from the lives of St Catherine and St George) by Altichiero (1379-84). The cycle, organized in horizontal tiers similar to Giotto's frescoes in the Scrovegni Chapel, is one of the most interesting examples of Italian 14th-century painting.

St Anthony's Basilica, Padua

St Anthony's Basilica, or rather, the Basilica "del Santo" – of the saint – as the locals call it, is shown here in the three ways, namely an axonometric section, a plan (seen from above) and a view of the facade. In the plan, you can clearly see the Latin-cross shape of the church, with its eight domes (the last dome over the Chapel of the Treasury which was added in the 18th century beyond the apse is not shown) and the layout of the cloisters. The view of the facade shows and simplifies the shape of the roof, showing the domes over the transepts at the sides and the first central dome, with a with the truncated-cone shape of the central dome behind it (the third dome above the nave). The truncated cone has an octagonal bell tower on each side. A small spired bell tower is shown at the apex of the architrave. The axonometric cross-section gives an idea of how the space is organized inside the church, together with the height of the nave and side-aisles and the depth of the presbytery.

KEY

1 Monument to Gattemelata
2 School of St Anthony
3 Oratory of St George
4 Cloister of the Chapter (or of the Magnolia)
5 Cloister of the Novitiate (or of the Sacristy)
6 Cloister of the General (or of the Library)
7 Cloister of Blessed Luca Belludi (or of the Infirmary)
8 Minarets
9 Domes
10 Dome of the Angel
11 Bell towers
12 Chapel of St Anthony
13 Chapel of St Felix
14 Nave
15 Matroneum
16 Chapel of the Tomb of St Anthony
17 Presbytery
18 High altar
19 Choir
20 Dome over the choir
21 Ambulatory
22 Entrance to the Chapel of the Black Madonna and Blessed Luca Belludi (St Anthony's companion)
23 Chapels
24 Chapel of the Reliquaries or of the Treasury

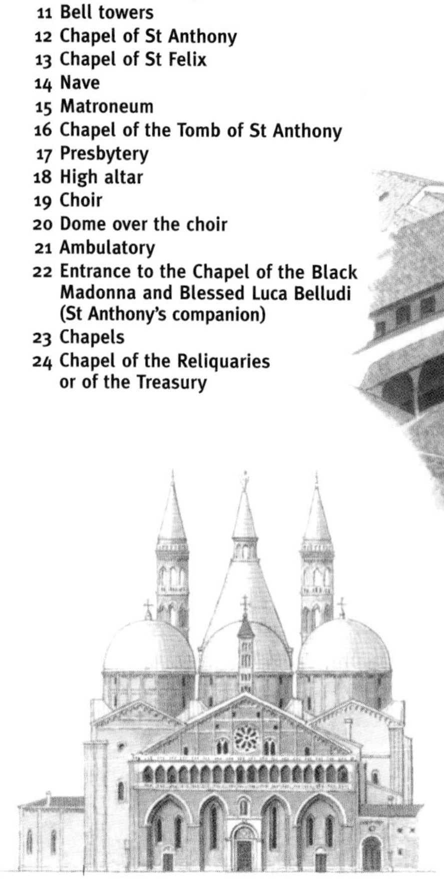

View of the Facade

Plan of the Basilica complex
The eight-domed Basilica
is on the right

Galleria "Guglielmo Tabacchi" – Safilo ㉙

This museum of eyewear and optical equipment is arranged on three floors. The imaginative interior has been created through the juxtaposition of different thicknesses of glass and metal. The first room has optical equipment from the 16th to 20th centuries: eye-glasses, eye-glass cases, telescopes, binoculars and other optical accessories. Another focuses on the history of the Safilo company and traces the history of the Italian eyewear industry, from its simple Cadore origins to its modern international scale. The exhibition is enhanced by photographs, documents and advertisements. There is also a section devoted to eye-glasses worn by famous personalities and goggles worn by top ski champions. Upstairs, there is a display of protective equipment worn during WWII, a more scientific section with instruments and charts used for testing eye-sight, and an artistic section with early paintings and prints of eye-glasses from the 17th to 20th centuries.

DAY TRIPS

ÀBANO TERME [12 km]

This famous *spa town*, with its eclectic 20th-century buildings with floral decoration lies below the Euganean Hills. The hotels exploit springs of thermal water which surfaces at a temperature of between 70°C and 80°C (158°F and 176 °F). The water is not, as was once thought, heated volcanically. It flows down from the mountains of the Piccole Dolomiti, penetrates deep underground, is then mineralized, heated and pushed up to the surface again by the pressure of local cold water. *Mud* is made for mud therapy, by adding special heat-loving algae.
Viale delle Terme is a long avenue of trees lined with hotels and shops, connecting the old part of the town to the new. Beyond Piazza della Repubblica is the neo-classical facade of *Hotel dell'Orologio* (1825). Opposite it is the *Albergo Trieste e Vittoria*, another interesting example of elegant spa accommodation.
The 12th century **Duomo**, dedicated to St Lawrence, has been altered several times. It now has a modern

"neo-Romanesque" facade (dating from 1967) and a 14th-century bell tower.
Via Pietro d'Àbano leads to **Montirone**, a small hill where one of the hottest thermal springs is located, famous even in Roman times. Near a Corinthian-style *colonnade* (early 20th century) stands a Doric *column* erected in 1825 to mark the visit of Emperor Francis I. The **Pinacoteca Civica al Montirone** has about 50 paintings and drawings from the 15th to 20th centuries, with important works from the Venetian and Lombard Schools and other works, including some contemporary works of art. Via Montirone continues 2 km to Monteortone, to the **Santuario della Vergine***. It was built in the 15th century in the place where, according to tradition, a miraculous image of the Virgin was found. Its simple facade has a Baroque doorway. Inside, the presbytery is decorated with marble low reliefs and *frescoes* dating from 1495. The chapel left of the presbytery has a *Crucifixion and Saints* by Palma il Giovane.

ABBAZIA DI PRAGLIA [12 km]

The **abbey**** is an important monumental complex founded in the

Praglia Abbey

12th century and almost completely rebuilt in the 15th and 16th centuries. Steps lead up to the *chiesa dell'Assunta* (1490-1560). Its Romanesque bell tower is the only part of the original church still standing. Inside are paintings dating from the 16th century. Above the altar is a 14th-century *wooden crucifix*. To the right of the church is the entrance to the **monastery**, which was also rebuilt in the 15th century around a *hanging cloister* dating from the late 15th-century. This is accessed by an 18th-century staircase leading up from the *garden cloister*. The *large refectory* contains Baroque wooden choirstalls and a fresco of the *Crucifixion* (1499-1500). There is an *old library*, reserved for scholars, a *chapter house* and a *double cloister* (closed to the public) with a portico and loggia (1461).

ARQUÀ PETRARCA [32 km]

This town has been awarded the "Bandiera Arancione" (Orange Flag) of the TCI. Petrarch was born in Arezzo on July 20, 1304. He spent the last years of his life here and died aged 70 (in July 1374) in view of the Euganean Hills. The **Casa di Petrarca** is a little house between an olive grove and a vineyard in this remote medieval village. It has retained many of its 14th-century features but the little loggia with two arches was added in 1546. Inside the house are mementoes associated with the poet. Some of the frescoes on the walls are original; others, which were added later, depict themes associated with Petrarch's works.

The **Oratorio della Trinità** is a simple building from the 12th to 14th centuries, not far from Petrarch's house. Next to it, the remains of the *Loggia dei Vicari* are decorated with the coats of arms of the town's rulers. When Humanism was at its height, the memory of this celebrated poet attracted cultured nobles who built residences and villas here.

CITTADELLA [38 km]

The walls around the town, built with stones from the River Brenta, form an irregular oval. Within the walls, the porticoed houses form a grid of streets parallel to the roads from Padua to Bassano and from Vicenza to Treviso, which cross in the town center. It was founded by Padua in 1220-1221 on the site of an earlier town. The sturdy, elegant **walls** are c. 12 m high and 1,461 m long, with 12 large towers and 16 smaller ones built at regular intervals: the essence of a medieval fortified town. Four gates, many with their original towers, of which *Porta Bassano* is the most interesting, lead out at the town's cardinal points.

In the **parish church of Ss. Prosdocimo e Donato**, built in the 13th century and altered later, are paintings from the 16th to 18th centuries, including a *Flagellation* by Palma il Giovane. The parish church houses the *Museo del Duomo*. Near Porta Treviso is **Palazzo Pretorio**, the residence of Pandolfo Malatesta. The **Museo Archeologico Torre di Malta** is housed in the *Torre di Malta*, a fortified structure incorporated in the walls in 1251 and once used as a prison. It contains archeological finds dating from the Bronze Age to the Middle Ages, discovered during excavations in the vicinity.

Arquà Petrarca: medieval houses

ESTE [33 km]

The town, founded by the Veneti between the 9th and 8th centuries BC, was a kind of river port, and led a quiet life until it was conquered by the Romans six centuries later. In about the year 1000 it became the stronghold of the Este family. The Este built the first fortified town, rebuilt in about 1340 and extended after 1405 when members of the Venetian nobility chose to holiday here. Today, the **Castello**, rebuilt in 1339-40, consists of a rectangle of merloned walls with 12 large and small towers, part of which is built on the hill around the keep. The area inside the walls is now a public park. In the lower part of the town, the Venetian Mocenigo family built a palace, which was destroyed by a fire in the late 18th century. Since 1887, the only surviving wing has housed the **Museo Nazionale Atestino**. The museum contains archeological finds which illustrate the culture of the Veneti. Highlights of the collection include the famous *Situla Benvenuti* (a vase in the shape of an upturned truncated cone), and a masterpiece of bronze plate made by skilled craftsmen in the 7th century BC. There are also many prehistoric finds of European importance found locally, fine collections from the Roman town of Ateste and interesting examples of local pottery up to the present day. The last room contains a fine *Madonna and Child* (1504) by Cima da Conegliano.

The **Duomo** was rebuilt after the 1688 earthquake which destroyed the paleo-Christian church on this site.

The imposing oval interior has various sculptures and paintings, including one in the apse (**St Tecla frees Este from the Plague of 1630***) by G.B. Tiepolo (1759). The **church of S. Maria delle Consolazioni** dates from the early 16th century. At the end of the left aisle is the *cappella della Vergine*, with a magnificent Roman floor mosaic found nearby during excavations. The large *cloister* next to the church has 15th-century capitals.

The 11th-century **church of S. Martino** has a 13th century bell tower which has been leaning since 1618. The 18th-century **church of S. Maria delle Grazie** was built over a previous 15th-century church. It has a bare brick facade, richly-decorated altars and a 15th-century panel of the Madonna and Child, venerated for its miraculous properties.

MONSÉLICE [24 km]

Monsélice has an exceptionally beautiful setting. The lower part of the town is medieval but it extends up to the Rocca (fort) at the top of the hill. Its fine period buildings are set in lush green landscape. This small cone of rock in the plain, south-west of the Euganean Hills, was called *Mons Silicis* (hill of flint) in Roman times. On the east side of the hill is a trachyte quarry which twice supplied the stone to pave St Mark's Square in Venice. **Piazza Mazzini**, the town's main square, is overlooked by the 13th-century **Torre dell'Orologio**, the height of which was raised in the 16th century. In an area at the bottom of the road leading up to the castle is a building with a loggia,

The public garden below the towers and walls of the Castle of Este

Monte di Pietà (16th century), now the *municipal library*, and a Gothic palace. **Via al Santuario**, a charming cobbled street, leads to the top of the hill passing some of the town's finest monuments. There are beautiful views on the way up. The **Castello** is an interesting complex begun in the 11th century. (The *castelletto* and *Palazzo di Ezzelino* were added in the 13th century and *Palazzo dei Marcello* in the 15th and 16th centuries.) The castle contains a collection of weapons, Renaissance furniture and tapestries. There is a **monumental fireplace*** in one of the rooms, in the shape of a tower. A little further on is *Villa Nani-Mocenigo*, which dates from the 16th century. The walls around the villa are decorated with curious 18th-century statues of dwarfs, and its grounds are landscaped with elegant flights of steps and terraces. The **Duomo vecchio** (1256) is dedicated to S. Giustina. A 14th-century porch enhances its simple facade. Beside the apse is a bell tower dating from the 13th century. The single-nave interior has a few frescoes and some 15th-century altar panels. Behind the Duomo vecchio, the *Piazzale della Rotonda* leads to the **Santuario delle Sette Chiese**. The sanctuary comprises six chapels which are aligned among the cypress trees, designed by Vincenzo Scamozzi, with paintings (1605) by Palma il Giovane, and the little *church of S. Giorgio*, built on an octagonal plan. At the end of the avenue is **Villa Duodo**, also designed by Scamozzi (1593). It was enlarged in the 18th century, when the monumental staircase to the Italianate garden was built. At the top of the hill (152 m) are the ruins of the **Rocca**, built by Frederick II. The *keep* within its rectangular walls is all that survives of the castle. Situated on the slopes of the hill, the old *church of S. Tommaso* contains some fine 13th-century frescoes. The **Museo delle Macchine Termiche "Orazio e Giulia Centanin"** (Steam-engine Museum) was a fruit and vegetable market in the 1950s. Carefully restored so as to maintain its original appearance, it now houses a fascinating collection of steam-engines donated by Professor Orazio Centanin to the Province of Padova in 1980. It includes late 19th-century farm machines (steam tractors, steam-engines, steam generators) which played an important role in the modernization of farming methods and land reclamation.

MONTAGNANA [50 km]

One of the best preserved fortified towns anywhere, it has been awarded the TCI's "Bandiera Arancione" (Orange Flag). The 2 km of brick walls built to defend the town sometimes makes visitors feel that they have stepped back into the Middle Ages. But the town is not only medieval: many features date from later periods. The structure of the town still respects the 700-year-old layout, yet in this small area, there are more than a dozen buildings of historical or artistic importance. A Roman town was built on the site of a Bronze Age settlement. It later came under the rule of the Este family, and then, from 1405, under the rule of Venice. The **walls*** were built in 1360-62 over earlier fortifications. The 24 towers are about 18 m high and face inwards towards the town. The main gates in the rectangular walls are the **Rocca degli Alberi**** or Porta Legnago and the **Castello di S. Zeno**** or Porta Padova, built in 1242 and now the *Museo Municipale*. It has sections on archeology, musical and medieval ceramics. The **Duomo***, begun in 1431 and finished in 1502, has a triumphal arch over the doorway dating from about 1530, by Sansovino. Inside, the many artworks, include a *Madonna Enthroned* (1507, on the right wall), and a **Transfiguration*** by Veronese (1555) over the high altar. The *church of S. Francesco* dates from the 14th century and the apse and bell tower were added a century later. The interior has a single nave and the *Madonna and Child* in the apse is by Palma the Younger.

TEÒLO [21 km]

This beautiful holiday location was supposedly the home of the Roman writer, Livy. In the center is the 16th-century *palazzetto* (now the municipal library), with a loggia and a clock tower (its mechanism dates from 1543). In the higher part of the town, the *parish church of S. Giustina*, begun in the 13th century and rebuilt in the 18th century, has a bell tower dating from the 15th century.

Capital of the Polésine, the town is first mentioned in the 9th-century. In 1194 the Este family of Ferrara came to power until 1482, when it submitted to Venice, which left its mark on the town's buildings for the next 300 years. It benefited from the construction of the Padua-Rovigo railway in 1866. In the 19th century, the walls were destroyed and the ramparts and moat transformed into public parks. In the 1950s and 1960s Rovigo finally developed from being a traditional market town to an industrial center.

Duomo ❶

The Cathedral, dedicated to St Stephen, founded a long time ago, was rebuilt in the late 17th century; its facade is unfinished and the dome was added in the 18th century. It contains sculptures and paintings (at the altar, *Resurrection* by Palma il Giovane). Near the cathedral, **Torre Donà** (one of the tallest medieval buildings in Italy) and a *truncated tower*, both of which are leaning, are all that remains of the castle founded in 920.

"Flagellation" by Palma il Vecchio at the Accademia dei Concordi

Piazza Vittorio Emanuele II ❷

This irregularly shaped square in the heart of the town is decorated by a column of Istrian stone (1519) with the Lion of St Mark (1881). **Palazzo del Municipio** (16th century), with a portico, a loggia and a niche with a statue of the Madonna and Child (1590) overlooks the square. Next to it is the 18th-century *clock tower*. The columns and pilasters of the portico and part of the courtyard of *Palazzo Roverella*, built in the 14th century. are original. To the left of the Town Hall, in Via Laurenti, is the stern facade of *Palazzo Roncale* (1555).

Accademia dei Concordi ❸

Conceived in 1580 as an association for lovers of music and literature, in the 18th century, the Accademia dei Concordi created a special farming section to find a scientic solution to the hydraulic problems of the Polésine. In this format, between 1833 and 1901, it received bequests of art collections from many local landowners, particularly works of the Venetian School from the 14th to18th centuries. They now form the **Pinacoteca dei Concordi***. Highlights include: *Coronation of the Virgin* by Nicolò di Pietro, **Madonna and Child*** and **Christ carrying the Cross*** by Giovanni Bellini, *Flagellation* by Palma il vecchio, *Venus at her Mirror* by Jan Gossaert, *Death of Cleopatra* by Sebastiano Mazzoni, and a set of portraits by G.B. Piazzetta, G.B. Tiepolo and Alessandro Longhi. The third floor houses the **Pinacoteca del Seminario** (Seminary Art Gallery), the most important works of Count Silvestri's collection which, in 1876, was bequeathed and divided randomly between the Academy and the Bishop's Seminary. Now the collection is under one roof, especially the 18th-century paintings. They include: *Flagellation* by Palma the Younger, **The Three Advocates*** by Sebastiano Bombelli, *The Tribute Money* by Bernardo Strozzi, **Venus and Psyche*** by Luca Giordano, *St John the Baptist* by

ROVIGO
IN OTHER COLORS...

- ITINERARIES: page 124, 128, 131
- FOOD: page 146, 168
- SHOPPING: page 181, 183
- EVENTS: page 186
- PRACTICAL INFO: page 215

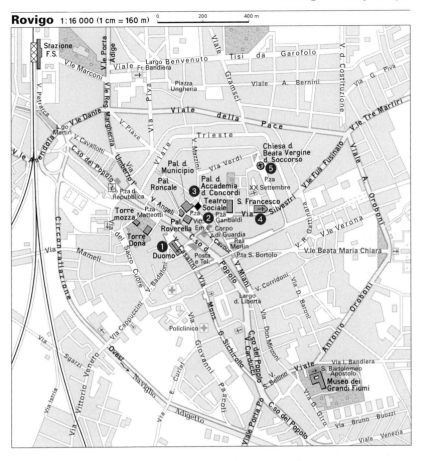

Rovigo 1:16 000 (1 cm = 160 m)

G.B. Piazzetta and **The Little Peasant***
by Pietro Longhi.
The collection also has an *archeological
section*, with Egyptian artifacts, a room
with four large tapestries by the workshop
of Rubens and a large **library** with 382
incunabulae and almost 200,000 books.

S. Francesco ❹

Built between 1300 and 1430 (see
original features on right of church),
St Francis was modernized in the 19th
century; the bell tower dates from 1520;
inside, various works from the 16th
century and a few sculptures.

Beata Vergine del Soccorso ❺

A.k.a. "*La Rotonda*", the church is built on
a central octagonal plan (1594-1613) with a
portico around the base; the imposing bell
tower beside it is by Baldassarre Longhena
(1655-73). Inside, the wooden altar dates
from 1607 and there are some 17th-century
paintings of the Venetian School.

DAY TRIPS

ADRIA [22 km]

The town gave its name to the Adriatic
Sea when it was an important port. By
the 6th century BC, it was a cross-roads
for trading and intercourse between
different cultures, until the silting up
of the coastline eventually rendered the
port impracticable. The quays, once
about 10 km from the sea, probably
followed the line of the modern Canal
Bianco. Today, Adria is the second-largest
town in the Polésine after Rovigo, with an
economy orientated towards the
hinterland. In Piazza Garibaldi stands the
Cattedrale nuova dedicated to St Peter
and St Paul, built in the early 19th
century next to a free-standing bell tower
(1688). It contains paintings of the
Venetian School and, on the 3rd pilaster
on the left, a Byzantine 6th-century *low
relief*. The left aisle leads into the

Cattedrale vecchia (Old Cathedral), where the early octagonal font and remains of the crypt belong to the original church, with Byzantine frescoes which possibly date from the 8th century. Corso Vittorio Emanuele II crosses the Canal Bianco, and continues past the facade of **S. Nicolò da Tolentino**, rebuilt in the 17th century, and the 1931 War Memorial, where there is a 15th-century terracotta statue of the Madonna. The street ends beyond the park near **S. Maria Assunta della Tomba**, a very old church rebuilt and altered several times up to the 18th century. Inside: an octagonal 8th-century baptismal font and a 15th-century fresco in the 1st altar on the left. The finds in the remarkable **Museo Archeologico Nazionale***, inaugurated in 1961, are based on a collection made by the local Bocchi family since the 18th century. The Town Council acquired it in 1904 and has incorporated finds from local excavations. In chronological order, on the first floor: vases with black figures on a red background (6th century BC), an amphora depicting scenes of the myths of Hercules (some of the earliest imports from Greece) and cups of Attic origin with red figures on a black background (1st century BC). The inside of one **cup** is decorated with a **dancing Maenad***. A necropolis on the Canal Bianco has produced some Etruscan and Roman gold artifacts, as well as *glass vases* from the Roman period. Note the **burial*** of a Venetian or Celtic warrior (3rd century BC), known as a chariot burial because it included some horse skeletons and iron and bronze trimmings of a chariot. In the courtyard, other Roman material includes a **milestone*** (131 BC) with one of the oldest Latin inscriptions found in the north of Italy.

DELTA DEL PO

The northern Delta. Following the bank of the Canal Bianco, the SS 443 leads from Adria to **Lorèo**, a historic river port on the eponymous canal. Further back from the water, the *parish church of the Assumption* (1675) is by

A little egret in the Botanical Garden at Porto Caleri

Baldassarre Longhena, who also designed the high altar; at the 1st altar on the left, *Death of Joseph* by G.B. Piazzetta. Since 1963, the coast at nearby **Rosolina** has been developed as a tourist resort, especially Rosolina Mare. Not far from here, great efforts are being made at the *Botanical Garden* on the tip of the peninsula at Porto Caleri to promote local conservation work. The road which leads to the resort area passes the Via delle Valli on the right and emerges after several wiggles on the bank of the **Po di Levante**. From here it is only c. 5 km to *Isola Albarella*, the most exclusive part of Rosolina. The most important town in the northern delta is **Porto Viro**. The provincial highway following the left bank of the river reveals how recently the land has been reclaimed, passing farmland (wheat, maize, silage and sugar beet) below the level of the river. At *Ca' Venier*, with its eponymous rambling palazzo, a ferry crosses over to **Porto Tolle**. Further on still, *Ca' Zuliani* and *Pila* are situated where the *valle* landscape gives way to that of the *Bocche di Po* (Po Estuary), now protected, underlining the importance of this wetland habitat. *The southern Delta.* **Taglio di Po** is named after the cut of Porto Viro, started in 1600. Further east, beyond the Strada Romea, the old pumping station of Ca' Vendramin (1903, now derelict) lies just before **Ca' Tiepolo**, seat of the scattered municipality of Porto Tolle, which includes most of the delta area. This is the *Isola della Donzella* and most of it is reclaimed land. At *Ca' Dolfin*, having crossed the Po delle Tolle to *Isola di Polésine*, there is a thermo-electric power plant. At **Scardovari**, the local economy is based on fishing. From here, you can drive around the peninsula at the mouth of the Po delle Tolle, passing the mussel farms of Sacca degli Scardovari. After the mouth of *Po di Gnocca* and the bridge of boats at **Santa Giulia**, lies **Goro Gorino Veneto**, on the Po di Goro. The trees of the Mésola Estate on the opposite bank are in the region of Emilia-Romagna.

TREVISO

Treviso began as a medieval town. During 5th to 11th centuries, the town grew in importance as a river port, on an island between two branches of the River Cagnàn. Its most glorious period began in the 13th century: its first statutes date from 1207 and, in 1210, a new town hall was built, Palazzo dei Trecento, for the 300 members of the Grand Council. In 1219, the walls were extended. Treviso, loyal to Venice from 1339 until 1381, joined the Venetian Republic in 1389. Under Venice, the town began to decline, isolated from the surrounding area behind its fortifications. Not until the agricultural revolution of the 18th century, with the building of patrician residences north of the town, did Treviso begin to venture beyond its walls.

Old Treviso reflected in the Canale dei Buranelli

In the 19th century, under Austrian rule (1813-66), the opening of a railway line between Treviso and Venice shifted the town center south towards the station, and at the turn of the century, a public park was created between it and Porta San Tomaso, enhancing the town's quaint charm.

Duomo ❶

Originally medieval, the cathedral apse was rebuilt in the 15th and 16th centuries, the rest in the 18th century. The pronaos dates from 1836. The *interior*, with a nave and two side-aisles supported by large pilasters, and seven domes has some fine works of art. On the 1st pilaster on the right: (in a niche) a statue of John the Baptist (1565?); on the 2nd pilaster on the right, a marble low relief of the Visitation. The far end of the right aisle lead to the 16th-century **chapel of the Annunciation** (1518-23). In the vestibule: some medieval sculptures (12th and 14th centuries), *Adoration of the Shepherds* by Paris Bordon and *Madonna and Child Enthroned with Saints* known as the "Madonna del Fiore" (in the center,1487). Above the altar: **Annunciation*** by Titian (1520); on the walls, early 16th-century frescoes. In the *presbytery* (1488) and the *chapel of the Holy Sacrament* (on the left, 1513), various Renaissance **sculptures**. The fine **crypt*** (11th and 12th centuries), with a nave and two side-aisles, is supported by 68 slender columns with re-used capitals (possibly 8th century).

Battistero ❷

Left of the Duomo, the Romanesque Baptistery (11th to 12th centuries) has a 14th-century low relief on the architrave, Roman friezes by the door and, inside, in the apses, parts of frescoes from the 12th to 14th centuries. Behind is the massive unfinished *bell tower* (11th to 12th centuries).

Via Calmaggiore ❸

The lively main street of the old town is lined by porticoes and houses dating from the 15th and 16th centuries.

S. Lucia and S. Vito ❹

In Piazza San Vito, the two adjoining churches of St Lucy and St Vitus are medieval. The most interesting is **St Lucy,** with a nave and two side-aisles, dedicated to the patron saint of eyesight in 1389. Inside are frescoes by Tommaso da Modena and sculptures of busts of saints around the balustrade

TREVISO
IN OTHER COLORS...
- **ITINERARIES:** page 132
- **FOOD:** page 141, 146, 152, 159, 168
- **SHOPPING:** page 178, 181, 183
- **EVENTS:** page 186, 189
- **PRACTICAL INFO:** page 217

dating from the 14th and 15th centuries. The church of **St Vitus**, built in the 11th and 12th centuries and rebuilt in 1561 (a portico with high arches was added), has some paintings (at the high altar, an *altar-piece* by Marco Vecellio; a 12th- to 13th-century fresco in the right apse) and sculptures.

Piazza del Monte di Pietà ❺

Behind Piazza dei Signori, in Piazza del Monte di Pietà, *Palazzo del Monte di Pietà* is an early building incorporating the **Cappella dei Rettori***, a small 16th-century building with an apse. The interior is richly decorated with paintings, a fine ceiling and 17th-century gilded-leather panels on the walls.

Piazza dei Signori ❻

The civic buildings on three sides of this square in the town center give it a strongly medieval flavor (many have been rebuilt). On the east side of the square, **Palazzo dei Trecento*** (Palace of the Three Hundred) is from about 1210 (rebuilt 1946-52), with a portico and three-light windows (the side facing Piazza Indipendenza has an early

13th-century outside staircase; on the ground floor, a monumental 16th-century loggia). Next door is *Palazzo del Podestà* (now the police headquarters), rebuilt in the late 19th century, with the bell tower known as "il Campanon" above and, on the west side, old *Palazzo Pretorio*, with a 17th-century rusticated facade facing Via Calmaggiore, and a 19th-century facade facing the piazza. Nearby is **Loggia dei Cavalieri**, dating from the 12th and 13th centuries, under whose arches (1276-77) the medieval aristocracy of the town gathered.

Museo Diocesano di Arte Sacra ❼

Since 1988, the sacred art collection of the Diocese of Treviso has occupied the Canoniche Vecchie. It has Roman archeological finds, paintings and furnishings of the Venetian School and other art-works (12th to 14th centuries). There are Romanesque marble reliefs from the Duomo, medieval detached frescoes from the Bishop's Palace, silver-ware and a wooden crucifix.

S. Nicolò ❽

The brick-built church of St Nicholas dates from the 13th and 14th centuries, with very high one-light windows at the sides and in the three slender apses. The *interior* has a nave and two side-aisles, transepts and five chapels. On the huge round pilasters supporting the ship's keel roof: *frescoes* by Tommaso da Modena (2nd pilaster on the left) and his workshop (14th century); many paintings adorn the inner wall of the west facade and the walls of the aisles. Right aisle: 2nd altar, triptych of the *Resurrection*, with statues; large fresco of *St Cristopher* (1410); a fine *organ*, with painted organ-doors. In the chapel right of the presbytery: 14th-century frescoes (contemporary with those in the sacristy); at the altar: *Incredulity of Thomas*. In the *presbytery*: in the apse, **Sacra Conversazione**, an altar-piece by Gerolamo Savoldo, completed 1521; on the left wall, an early 16th-century **monument to Senator Agostino Onigo***, by Giovanni Buora (sculpture) and Lorenzo Lotto (painting). In the 2nd chapel left of the altar: Madonna Enthroned with St Peter and St Paul (late 15th-century).

Treviso: Piazza dei Signori

Seminario vescovile ⑨

Next to the church of St Nicholas, the Bishop's Seminary contains the **Chapterhouse of the Dominicans*** (13th and 14th centuries), decorated with splendid frescoes (*important Dominicans*) by Tommaso da Modena (1352), and three small **museums**: the *Ethnographical Museum of the Indios of Venezuela*, with tribal artifacts from the Amazon jungle of Venezuela; the *Museum of Pre-Colombian Archeology and Paleontology of South America*; and the *"Giuseppe Scarpa" Zoological Museum*, a collection of Italian vertebrates and exotic reptiles.

Tommaso's frescoes in the Chapterhouse of the Dominicans

S. Maria Maggiore ⑩

The church, also known as the *Santuario della Madonna Granda*, stands in the eponymous square, with a harmonious facade and a curved top. Though rebuilt and altered several times to permit the building of the town walls (1511), it began in the 8th and 9th centuries as the shrine of a capital thought to have miraculous properties. Inside, the apse and the chapel dedicated to the Madonna have Renaissance lines. The sacristy leads into the *cloister*, with one original side dating from 1474.

S. Caterina dei Servi di Maria ⑪

The church of St Catherine, dating from the 14th century, was deconsecrated in the 18th century; devastated by bombs in 1944 and restored, it is used for art exhibitions. The *Chapel of the Innocents* has an early 15th-century fresco cycle. Inside the *church*: fresco fragments and detached frescoes; the latter include a cycle depicting the **Stories of the Life of St Ursula** by Tommaso da Modena, removed in 1883 from a chapel of the deconsecrated church of S. Margherita. The **Stories of the Life of St Eligio*** and the **Madonna and Saints*** on the right are attributed to Pisanello. The church of St Catherine is to become the main seat of the **Musei Civici** of Treviso. The considerable land, the underground hall beneath the cloister, the long corridor on the first floor of the former convent and the workshops are being converted into a modern, dynamic museum of early art and archeology, with facilities for education, research and experimentation in contemporary art and venues for cultural and social events.

Pescheria ⑫

The **Pescheria*** is a tiny island in the middle of the River Cagnàn, occupied by the fish market. It is a fascinating place because of the network of channels and narrow streets which converge on it. The present fish market dates from 1851.

Porta S. Tomaso ⑬

Porta S. Tomaso is the most monumental of the three gates in the Venetian walls. Built in 1518, the outer facade is decorated with trophies of arms and coats-of-arms with the Lion of St Mark.

S. Francesco ⑭

The Gothic church of St Francis, from 1230, was rebuilt in 1928. It has a ship's keel ceiling and five apses (the side-chapels were added between the 14th and 16th centuries). On the walls, various frescoes from the 13th to 15th centuries. On the 4th pilaster on the right: the tombstone of Francesca, daughter of Petrarch (died 1384). In the left transept: the *tomb of Pietro*, son of Dante Alighieri (died 1364).

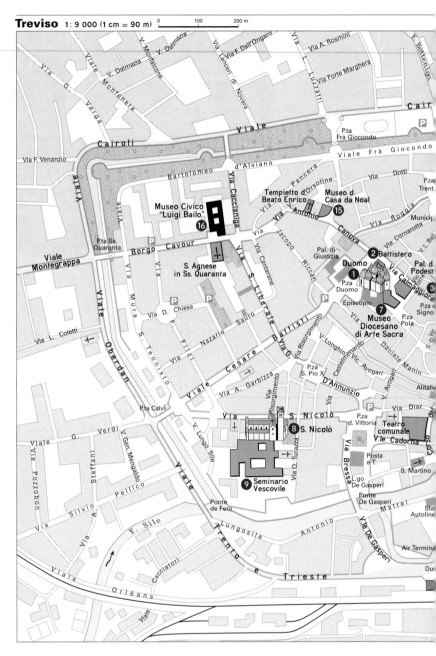

Treviso 1 : 9 000 (1 cm = 90 m)

Museo della Casa da Noal ⑮

This museum, located in the Casa da Noal, a late-Gothic building in the Venetian style, is part of the Museo Civico and focuses on the minor arts and crafts of the Treviso area. Exhibits include majolicas, terracotta ware, weapons, wrought-iron, insignia and other products. There is also a section on the iconography of the town.

Museo Civico "Luigi Bailo" ⑯

Opened in 1879, the museum occupies the buildings of a former 16th-century monastery, extended in the same style in the early 20th century. It has a large archeological collection, with swords from the late Bronze Age, funerary finds from paleo-Venetian settlements, and early Christian and medieval sculpture. The *art gallery*, formed by

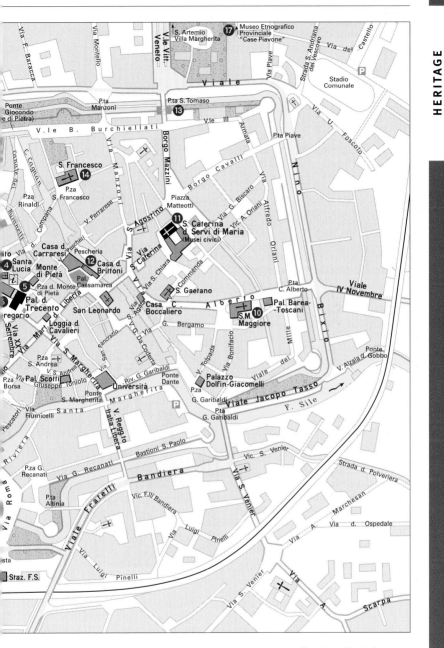

the donations of Margherita Grimaldi Prati (1851) and Emilio Sernagiotto (1888), includes paintings from the 12th to 20th centuries, by Giovanni Bellini and his workshop (a **Madonna**), Titian (**Portait of Sperone Speroni***) and Lorenzo Lotto (**Portrait of a Dominican Friar***). There is also a fine *bust of Marianna Angeli Pascoli* by Antonio Canova.

Museo Etnografico Provinciale "Case Piavone" 17

This ethnographical museum 17th-century Case Piavone has a collection of 150 weighing instruments from all over the world, some unique or extremely rare. It also contains documents and iconographic material about the history of weights and measures, with a particular focus on the Veneto.

ÀSOLO [32 km]

Àsolo, which has been awarded the TCI's "Bandiera Arancione" (Orange Flag), once an important Roman town with a theater, baths and an aqueduct, played a key role over the centuries as the seat of a bishop (6th to 10th centuries), and, from 1337, came under Venetian rule. After the year 1000, the urban fabric was laid out in two main areas: Borgo S. Caterina on the side of Bassano del Grappa and Borgo Novello on the side of Castelfranco Veneto. The Da Carrara, lords of Padua (1381-88), built a set of walls linking the fort on the top of the hill to the castle below. When it ceased to be a center of political and administrative power, Àsolo – which became a center for high-quality embroidery and silk fabrics – remained a cultural center, attracting artists and intellectuals (Henry James, Ernest Hemingway, Gabriele D'Annunzio). A staircase leads down from *Piazza Maggiore* to the **Duomo**, dedicated to the Assumption (1747), with a fine 15th-century atrium on the right of the church. Inside, it has a nave and two side-aisles, paintings by Lorenzo Lotto (**Madonna and Saints***, 1506) and Jacopo Bassano (*St Mary of the Assumption and Saints*). The 15th-century **Loggia del Capitano** on the same square has a portico and a facade with frescoes (1560). It houses the **Museo Civico**, with an extensive collection of paleontological and archeological material, mementoes of Caterina Cornaro, Gabriele D'Annunzio and Eleonora Duse (her house is in Via Canova, her grave in the town cemetery), paintings by Bernardo Strozzi, Il Pordenone, Canaletto and Luca Giordano, and statues by Antonio Canova. Much of the **Castello della Regina** was demolished in 1820; part of the garden is occupied by the 19th-century Villa Beach, built by the English poet, Robert Browning. Nearby, on Piazzetta D'Annunzio, **Palazzo Beltramini** (now the Town Hall), has an 18th-century facade. The imposing **Rocca** (fort) looks rather like a huge ship (58 m long, 15 m high, with walls 3.5 m thick). Already a fort in the late Imperial period, it was rebuilt after 1100. The chemin-de-ronde, the merlons and parts of the walls were restored in 1993. Beyond the town center, a path leads down through the Foresto Vecchio (Old Wood) past the **house of Gian Francesco Malipiero**. Beyond the little 14th-century church of S. Angelo or S. Gottardo, and the 16th-century Villa Zen, it reaches **Borgo Casella** (1.5 km). Here, on the road to Masèr, stands the 17th-century **Villa Rinaldi***, built in the flamboyant Baroque style. Another walk leads from the Town Hall to **Borgo S.**

Peaceful atmosphere in the center of Àsolo

Caterina. On the left it passes the house that belonged to Eleonora Duse and, beyond the church of S. Caterina, **Casa Longobarda**. Here the road forks. Signs lead to the *church of S. Anna* and the cemetery where Eleonora Duse is buried. The **Museo Civico** has paleontological and archeological finds, paintings and sculpture (by Luca Giordano, Canaletto and Antonio Canova) and an interesting collection of mementoes, personal effects and portraits of famous people, including Eleonora Duse, Antonio Canova, D'Annunzio and Caterina Cornaro.

CASTELFRANCO VENETO [28 km]

Founded between 1195 and 1199 as a military outpost of Treviso, its name stems from its role as a fortified town and its exemption, since its foundation, from paying taxes. A bone of contention between the neighboring powers of Treviso, Padua and Vicenza for more than a century, in 1339 it came under Venetian rule, remaining loyal until Napoleon's arrival in 1797. This improved its status as a trading town. As a result, the Venetian nobility began to invest in local farmland. In the 18th century, civic buildings were erected and large public squares were laid out. The town's most famous son is Giorgio di Castelfranco, "Giorgione", the revolutionary Renaissance painter of the Venetian School, who died young and about whose life very little is known.

The **Castello** is the square set of walls surrounded by a moat which encircles the old town. Built in the late 12th century, most of its red-brick curtain walls (on average c. 17 m high) and four high corner towers are still standing. Around the castle is the *Bastia Nuova*, with buildings dating from the 16th to 18th centuries, the vast square where the market used to be held (now Piazza Giorgione) and the *Loggia del Grano*, built in the 15th century for storing corn and restructured in 1603. The **Duomo** was built within the castle walls in the 18th century. *Inside*, in the chapel right of the presbytery: the famous **altar-piece by Giorgione**** depicting the *Madonna and Child Enthroned with St Francis and St Liberal*, an early work (1505) by the local master. In the *sacristy*: on the walls and ceiling, fragments of **frescoes*** (allegorical figures, 1551) attributed to Paolo Veronese, brought here from a villa in Soranza, and paintings by Palma il Giovane, Jacopo Bassano and Annibale Carracci.

The **House of Giorgione**, next to Piazza del Duomo, was thus called because of the **band of chiaroscuro decoration*** on the first floor attributed to the painter (*Symbols of the Liberal and Mechanical Arts*).

The **Teatro Accademico** is a 19th-century theater with a brick facade, an interior with stucco decoration, and an elegant auditorium with three tiers of boxes. The **Museo Agricolo** (Farming Museum) and the **Museo dell'Arte**

Conciaria "Chiminelli" (Tanning Museum) are housed in the 16th-century Villa Corner-Tiepolo (now Chiminelli), at S. Andrea, 5 km south of Castelfranco. The farm buildings west of the villa house a collection of tools and machines from tanning workshops in the Bassano area, and there is a barn with a collection of more than 2,000 objects illustrating the life of the Veneto farming community.

CONEGLIANO [28 km]

A castle, built before the year 1000 (and dismantled in the 18th century) on the first hill north of the Veneto plain, was the origin of the town, which has gradually spread down into the plain. We can see the same light, colors and atmosphere portrayed in the paintings of Giovanni Battista Cima (" Cima da Conegliano", c.1459-1517), who was born, lived and worked here for many years. The **Duomo** has a fine Gothic doorway with nine arches (14th to 15th centuries) and a bell tower (1497). The *interior*, now restored to its 14th-century lines, has a painting of (St Francis (1545), corner of the right aisle) and, at the high altar, an **altar-piece*** (*Madonna Enthroned with Saints*) by G.B. Cima (1493). The adjacent guildhall, **Sala dei Battuti***, dates from the late 14th century and is entirely frescoed by early 16th-century artists. The **Casa-Museo Giambattista Cima**, birthplace of Cima da Conegliano, is an interesting example of early domestic architecture. Recently restored, it is now the headquarters of the G.B. Cima Foundation, which exhibits reproductions of Cima's works. The museum also has archeological finds (fragments of terracotta pots) from the late Bronze Age, found during excavations under the house. It is used for temporary exhibitions and organizes visits related to local cultural events.

Spianata di Castelvecchio is a formal Italianate garden laid out above the town on the site of the ancient fort. Some of the medieval walls (partly reconstructed) and the towers of the medieval castle remain, with the *Oratory of St Ursula*. The *Torre della Campana* houses the **Museo Civico del Castello**, with archeological finds ranging from the late Paleolithic period to the Roman period, detached frescoes from various locations, paintings of the School of Cima da Conegliano,

Palma il Giovane and Jacopo Amigoni, also sculptures by Giambologna and Arturo Martini, and collections of coins and armor. On the top floor is a permanent exhibition illustrating the development of the town's fortifications.

FANZOLO [24 km]

The focal point of this village in the municipality of *Vedelago* is **Villa Emo*** (built for a Venetian noble, Leonardo Emo), a Palladian masterpiece. On each side of the elegant main part of the villa, built on a square plan, is a rustic wing for agricultural purposes. The rooms of the villa are decorated with frescoes on mythological themes (1565) by G.B. Zelotti, a colleague of Paolo Veronese.

MASÈR [32 km]

Approaching Masèr, **Villa Barbaro***, now Villa Volpi, appears on a slight rise, a splendid country-house built by Palladio in c. 1557 for the Barbaro family. The central part projects from the rest of the house, transforming the former family castle into a sort of temple, its architrave resting on huge columns, with a porticoed wing on each side. The stucco decoration is by Alessandro Vittoria (1525-1608), the **frescoes*** by Veronese (1528-1588). On the slope behind the villa is a semi-circular *nymphaeum* decorated with statues; a *Carriage Museum* occupies a nearby farm building. The last feature of the complex is the **Tempietto***, completed in the year of Palladio's death (1580). Stone statues adorn the outside of this small church built on a central plan; the stucco decoration inside is by Alessandro Vittoria.

ODERZO [28 km]

In the 13th century, this ancient town (founded 1st century BC) resumed its historic role as a market town, and was surrounded by fortifications. By the 16th century, they were already too small to contain urban expansion.
Framed to the north by the River Monticano, the central Piazza Vittorio Emanuele II, formerly Piazza del Mercato, is surrounded by the facades of public and private buildings, some with frescoed porticoes. The **Duomo**, altered in the 16th century, has a sloping roof, a Renaissance doorway and a Gothic bell tower, an adaptation of one of the town's defensive towers. Inside, it has a single nave, a

raised presbytery, and paintings by Palma the Younger. In Via Mazzini is a Roman archeological site with part of the forum, the basilica and some private houses. The **Museo Civico Archeologico "Eno Bellis"** has prehistoric finds and valuable pre-Roman and Roman exhibits found in the Oderzo area (inscriptions, steles and amphoras). It also has some 3rd- and 4th-century mosaics depicting hunting scenes. The **Museo di Storia Naturale "Brandolini-Rota" e "Giol"**, founded in 1938, has archeological finds, ethnographic material, an ornithological collection, and minerals, fossils and geological specimens.

PARCO NATURALE REGIONALE DEL SILE [7-15 km]

The park incorporates the entire course of the River Sile, from its source to its mouth at Portegrandi. The river flows through three main types of landscape: wetlands and marshes near its source, the winding section before it reaches Treviso, and the lagoon landscape near its mouth. The area is interesting from the point of view of plants and wildlife, and also from the historical and architectural point of view (patrician villas and gardens). There are also some notable examples of industrial archeology. The area can be explored by bike and there are boats for hire in the lower reaches of the Sile.

VITTORIO VENETO [42 km]

Created in 1866 by merging two historically separate, independent towns: Serravalle (of Roman origin) and Cèneda (medieval). The town was named after King Vittorio Emanuele II to mark the Veneto's inclusion in the Kingdom of Italy. **Serravalle**. Entering the town from the north, you pass the 13th-century **church of S. Giustina**, radically altered in the late 16th century. Inside is the tomb of **Rizzardo VI Da Camino***, (1336-1340), supported by some early statues of warriors. Further on is the 14th- to 15th-century **church of S. Giovanni Battista**, with a remarkable early 15th-century *fresco cycle* (1st chapel on right). Further on, the cobbled Via Roma leads into the area of the old Roman castrum. On *Piazza Flaminio*, its early 16th-century layout, the **Loggia Serravallese** is the old seat of political power, rebuilt in 1462 on foundations which may date from the

13th century. Since 1938, this has housed the **Museo del Cenedese**, with archeological finds from the paleo-Veneto, Roman and Lombard periods (delightful bronze figurines), sculpture (a Madonna and Child by Sansovino) and paintings. The square leads beyond the river to the **Duomo**, rebuilt in the 18th century but never finished. The bell tower is all that remains of the previous Romanesque church (12th to 13th century). Inside the Duomo, a frescoed ceiling, and a **Madonna and Child with Saints*** by Titian (1547) at the high altar. A footpath starts at the monumental staircase behind the *Cathedral* (1931), leading up to the *Santuario di S. Augusta*, originally 15th-century, rebuilt in the 17th, with some 15th-century frescoes.
Via Martiri della Libertà starts at Piazza Flaminio. Giuseppe Segusini designed the street in the mid-19th century, also the *Teatro Sociale* (theater) (1879). A fine series of noble palaces lines the street.

the original 4th-century church. In Viale della Vittoria, which leads into Piazza del Popolo with its neoclassical Town Hall, Palazzo Croze will soon house the works of the **Galleria d'Arte Vittorio Emanuele II**, mainly by 20th-century Venetian artists. Via Petrarca, Via Virgilio and Via Dante run parallel to Viale della Vittoria, joining the two parts of the modern town. At the end of Via Dante is the **church of S. Maria del Meschio**, with an **Annunciation*** by Andrea Previtali over the high altar.
Piazza Giovanni Paolo I is a broad square with a Renaissance fountain in the center, dominated by the **Cathedral** (built in the 13th century but rebuilt in the mid-18th century, with a facade dating from 1912). The adjacent portico belongs to the former town hall, **Loggia del Cenedese** which, according to local tradition, was built in 1538, to a design by Sansovino. It is now the **Museo della Battaglia** with reminders and testimonials from WWI.

The castle of S. Martino in Vittorio Veneto

Opposite the Baroque facade of the *little church of S. Paolo al Piano*, the 16th-century *Bishop's Seminary* (recently rebuilt) houses the **Museo Diocesano d'Arte Sacra Albino Luciani**, a museum of sacred art created by the man who became Pope John Paul I when he was bishop of Vittorio Veneto (1959-70). The collection includes silverware, vestments and sacred furnishings, and many paintings (*Deposition* and a *Madonna of the Rosary*

One of them is the 16th- to 17th-century **Palazzo Minucci-De Carlo**, which has a collection of furnishings and *objets d'art* belonging to the last owner. Next to the *clock-tower*, (built in the 19th century to replace the old town gate of Porta S. Lorenzo), is the 15th-century **Oratorio di S. Lorenzo**, built onto the 14th-century hospital of the Scuola dei Battuti and now part of the Museo del Cenedese. Altered in 1835, the whole interior is decorated with a cycle of Gothic **frescoes***.
Cèneda. The **church of S. Andrea**, on the east bank of the Meschio, has preserved its late-Gothic features (15th- 16th century) and is the result of alterations to

by Palma il Giovane, *triptych of the Madonna and Child with St Peter and St Paul* by Titian, *Legend of St Tiziano* by Pompeo Amalteo, a triptych by Cima da Conegliano, and paintings by Tintoretto, De Pisis, Guidi and others).
The **Museo di Scienze Naturali "Antonio De Nardi"**, also located in the Bishop's Seminary, has sections on botany, zoology, minerology, petrology and geology.
The road to the left of the Loggia leads up to the **Castello di S. Martino**, (at 211 m). Rebuilt by the Lombards and again in the early 15th century, it is now the Bishop's Palace.

Built on piles, it has more than 100 islands, more than 400 bridges, and one piazza, Piazza S. Marco (the others are 'campi' or 'campielli'). Its glorious political and artistic history lasted 1,000 years. Settlements in the lagoon date from Roman times. Venice is laid out differently to mainland towns: there is no central focus but clusters of islands separated by canals. Each island has a square ('campo') with a church. In the 13th century, Venice was much as it is today. In the 14th century, it had a population of more than 130,000, roughly the population at the end of the Venetian Republic. During the intervening centuries, Venice set out across the sea, its main concern being that its ships should have free transit in the Adriatic when Pisa and Genoa posed a constant and serious threat. After the political and military victory of the Sack of Constantinople in 1204 by a Crusader fleet, the Republic became master of "a quarter and a half of the (Byzantine) empire". In the early 13th century, Venetian power in the Levant was at its height. For at least a century, from 1381 until 1498, Venice traded all kinds of goods: gold and silver from Africa, pepper and other spices, cotton and silk. For security, in the 15th century, Venice expanded into the mainland, adding Padua, Vicenza, Verona, Belluno and Udine to its possessions around Treviso. In the 16th century, its status was confirmed for ever: on the mainland by the alliances formed by European and other Italian states against Venice; at sea by the wars against the Turks; with regard to trade, by the forging of new trade routes, shifting the focus from the Mediterranean to the oceans. In the 16th century, Venice invested part of its wealth in a new image. A great fire destroyed the Rialto in 1513 and the whole area was rebuilt, including the Rialto Bridge (1588-1591). In S.Marco, in 1514, work started on the Procuratie Vecchie; in 1582, on the Procuratie Nuove; in 1537, on the Zecca (mint) and the Libreria. In the second half of the 17th century, Venice began to decline. It reacted to the decline of its productive, mercantile and military role by becoming a center for festivals and theater. After many carnivals, Napoleon arrived in 1797, ending an aristocratic republic which had outlived its purpose. For Venice, no longer a capital, a period of transition began under Austrian rule, until it joined Italy in 1866. After Unification, between 1868 and 1871, a broad new street, the Strada Nuova, was laid out parallel to the Grand Canal, linking the Rialto to the station. Between 1880 and 1882, large hotels sprang up on the Riva degli Schiavoni and the Lido. In 1922, work began on the pavilions of the Biennale.

Piazza S. Marco and Campanile ➊

Symbol of the city and center of its public life throughout, this famous square has slowly adapted to the functional and representational needs of Venice. Not quite a rectangle, its backdrop is *St Mark's Basilica* with its tall, free-standing *bell tower*. The **Procuratie Vecchie** on its north side were built in the 12th century and re-built after 1514. To the east is the **Torre dell'Orologio** (clock tower), built in 1496-99. On the south side stand the **Procuratie Nuove**, begun in 1582 by Vincenzo Scamozzi and completed in about the mid-17th century by Baldassarre

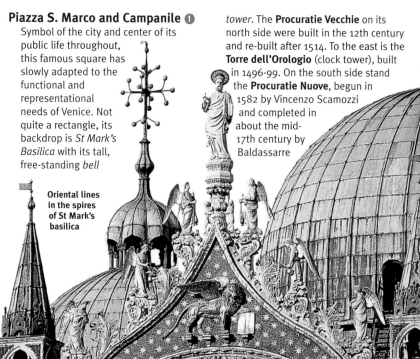

Oriental lines in the spires of St Mark's basilica

Gold mosaics adorn the interior of St Mark's basilica

Longhena. Under the portico is the 18th-century *Caffè Florian*, refurbished in the 19th century. The **Campanile** is 96.8 m high. Built in the 12th century on the base of an old lookout tower and restructured in the 16th century, it was rebuilt completely in 1912 after it collapsed on July 14, 1902 (fortunately with no victims or serious damage). The *view* over the lagoon from the top is stunning. The elegant marble **loggetta*** below the tower is by Jacopo Sansovino (1537-49).

Basilica di S. Marco and Tesoro della Basilica ❷

Fulcrum of the religious and public life of the city, the place where its doges were consecrated, the basilica is one of the symbols of Venice. Founded in the 9th century to enshrine the body (stolen from Alexandria in 828) of Mark the Evangelist, adopted as the city's patron saint, it has a complex structure. Gothic and Renaissance features were added to its early Byzantine and Romanesque forms. Rebuilt several times, it eventually took on the characteristic profile of Byzantine churches: a large central dome and four semi-spherical domes, capped by onion-shaped domes. The atrium in front of the main doorway has a marble mosaic floor from the 11th and 12th centuries. The walls are adorned with marble and columns, the vaults and domes with gleaming **mosaics*** (stories of the Old Testament) in the Venetian Byzantine style of the 12th and 13th centuries. Three doorways with bronze doors from the 11th and 12th centuries lead into the Basilica. The **interior**** is typically Byzantine: a Greek-cross plan, with three aisles in each arm separated by rows of columns supporting the matroneums; mighty arches support the five domes.

The **mosaics**** on a gold background decorating the upper walls and domes, executed by Byzantine and Venetian artists in the 12th to 14th centuries, are one of the Basilica's main treasures. Many were replaced in the 16th and 17th centuries based on cartoons by Titian, Tintoretto, Veronese and others. A marble balustrade with statues (1396) divides the raised **presbytery** over the crypt from the rest of the church. Four alabaster **columns*** decorated with 12th-century capitals support the high altar above St Mark's tomb. Behind is the famous **Pala d'Oro**** (Golden altar-piece), a masterpiece of Byzantine and Venetian craftsmanship (10th to 14th centuries). Made of silver, gold and gemstones, its small enameled panels depict religious scenes. Left niche of the apse: the bronze **door*** of the sacristy, Jacopo Sansovino's last work (1546-69).

The **Treasury** housed in the Basilica is a sumptuous collection of sacred art, mainly objects from the east from the 6th to 10th centuries, brought to Venice after the 1204 Sack of Constantinople, but also later works by gold- and silversmiths from Venice and Western Europe. The Treasury, (about 300 objects), occupies three rooms: the Anteroom (a silver statue of St Mark, 1804), the Sanctuary (110 reliquaries and a rare back to an alabaster altar-piece decorated in the Eastern style), and the Treasury proper (restored 1938).

The exhibits include Egyptian, Roman, Byzantine and Asian vases, amphorae, and bowls; Byzantine icons; glass and rock- crystal chalices; reliquary caskets from the 13th to 18th centuries; sacred furnishings; a 13th-century back altar-piece by a Venetian goldsmith; bindings for sacred books (St Mark's Gospel is particularly elaborate). At the entrance, the 6th-century marble *Chair of St Mark* is decorated in the Eastern style.

VENEZIA
IN OTHER COLORS...

■ ITINERARIES: page 128, 130
■ FOOD: page 141, 146, 153, 159, 168
■ SHOPPING: page 178, 181, 183
■ EVENTS: page 186, 189
■ WELLNESS: page 195
■ PRACTICAL INFO: page 218

La Basilica di San Marco (St Mark's Basilica)

Founded in the 9th century, the plan of the original church consisted of a nave with two side-aisles. The basilica's current shape is the result of alterations begun in 1060 which, with the addition of the two lateral wings, made it into a Greek cross, with a huge central dome and four smaller domes above each of the four branches of the cross. Almost contemporary with these structural changes, mosaicists began to decorate the inside of the church with colorful mosaics on a gold background (12th – 15th century). A narthex was then added, initially to the three sides of the front of the building. The right-hand part of the narthex was later removed to make room for the Baptistery and the Zen Chapel. In the 13th century, the profile of the church was altered yet again by raising the height of the domes, and adding wooden superstructures covered with lead.

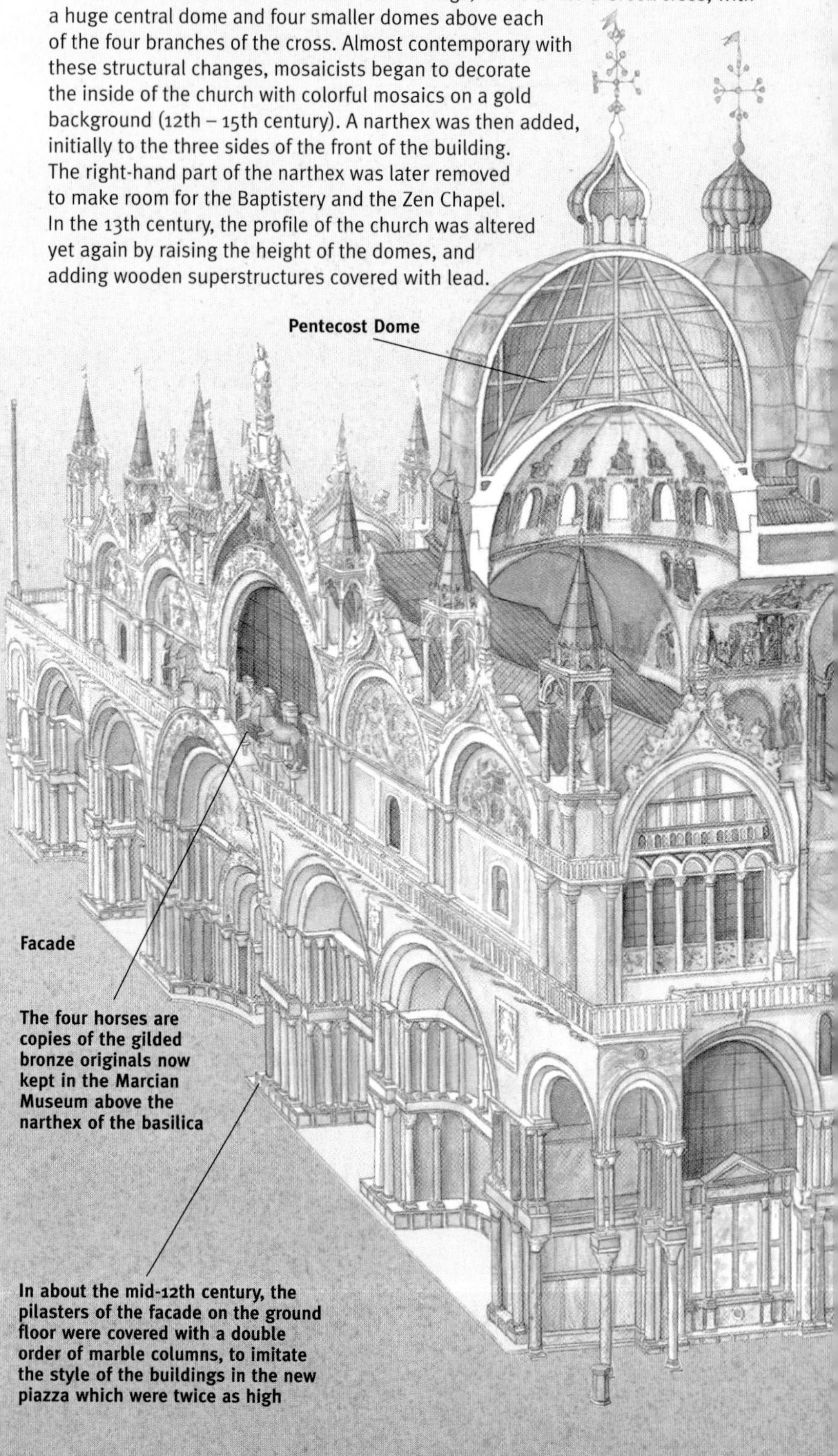

Pentecost Dome

Facade

The four horses are copies of the gilded bronze originals now kept in the Marcian Museum above the narthex of the basilica

In about the mid-12th century, the pilasters of the facade on the ground floor were covered with a double order of marble columns, to imitate the style of the buildings in the new piazza which were twice as high

Ascension Dome with 13th-century mosaics. Those on the wall below depict the Wedding at Cana

Bulb-shaped wooden superstructure

Presbytery Dome

Apse with mosaic dated 1506 by Pietro di Zorzi. The mosaics between the windows are the oldest in the basilica

The "Pala d'Oro", or Golden Altar-piece, situated behind the main altar, consisting of 250 gold panels decorated with enamels and precious stones

Doorway of the Baptistery

The Tetrarchs: a porphyry relief dating from the 4th C

Iconostasis with 4th-century reliefs

Palazzo Ducale ❸

The Doge's residence and the highest seat of the magistracy, the Doge's Palace is the symbol of the power and splendor of the ancient Republic. Founded as a 9th-century castle, it gradually assumed its current appearance in the 14th and 15th centuries, resulting in one of Venice's finest examples of Gothic architecture. The *Porta della Carta* (1438), a Gothic arch linking the palace to St Mark's Basilica, leads into a beautiful **courtyard****, with two 16th-century bronze well-heads. To one side is the *Arco Foscari*, a Gothic arch (1470); opposite, the late 15th-century **Scala dei Giganti*** (Giants' Staircase), with Jacopo Sansovino's statues of Mars and Neptune (1554), where newly-elected doges swore allegiance to the city's laws.

Interior. A staircase on the south-east side of the portico leads up to the Gothic loggia. From it, the **Scala d'Oro*** (1559) leads to the "piano nobile" and the private apartments of the doge, decorated by Giovanni Bellini, Titian and Carpaccio. On the floor above, the first room is an atrium: on the wooden ceiling (16th century), paintings by Jacopo Tintoretto; on the walls, paintings by Veronese. *Sala delle Quattro Porte*: a famous work by Titian: **Doge Grimani kneeling in front of Faith*** (1556). In the Anticollegio: four **wall panels*** by Tintoretto; **Rape of Europa*** by Paolo Veronese. *Sala del Collegio*: on the walls, works by Tintoretto and Veronese; the elaborate wooden ceiling (1577) has **panels*** by Veronese. *Sala del Consiglio dei Dieci*: the gilt wooden ceiling has **panels*** by Veronese and his assistants. *Sala dei tre Capi del Consiglio dei Dieci*: a ceiling decorated with **panels*** by Veronese and his assistants. Stairs lead down to the *Andito del Maggior Consiglio*, the *Sala della Quarantia Civil Vecchia*, and the *Sala dell'Armamento*, where the remains of Guariento's famous fresco of Paradise, ruined by a fire in 1577, is displayed; in the loggia, the original **statues*** of Adam and Eve by Antonio Rizzo (1464) for the Arco Foscari. *Sala del Maggior Consiglio* (Hall of the Great Council): on the walls, paintings by Tintoretto and assistants (including

A staircase inside the Doge's Palace

Paradise), and a frieze of portraits of 76 doges (that of Marin Faliero, executed for treason in 1355, has been obscured), by the Tintoretto; in the center of the ornate ceiling, **Triumph of Venice*** by Veronese. By descending to the Loggia, you can see part of the Prigioni Vecchie (old prisons), with their small, dark, damp cells. Across the **Ponte dei Sospiri** (Bridge of Sighs) the *Prigioni Nuove* date from the late 16th century.

Piazzetta S. Marco ❹

This square overlooks the quay facing the island church of S. Giorgio. Near the water, two 12th-century granite columns support the lion of St Mark and St Theodore, Venice's first patron saint. The space between was once used for public executions. On the square is the **Museo Archeologico Nazionale**, founded in 1523 to house a bequest by Cardinal Domenico Grimani. The museum is based on donations from important Venetian families: in 1593, Giovanni Grimani donated a group of original Greek statues (mainly female statues of the 5th and 4th centuries BC); Piero Morosini donated his medal collection in 1646 and Gerolamo Zulian left his famous cameo of Jove to the museum. In addition to numerous Greek sculptures, the collection contains Roman architectural fragments and sculpture, inscriptions, marbles and busts, bronze figurines, pottery, jewelry, Etruscan, Egyptian and Mesopotamian artifacts, as well as precious stones, ivories and a coin collection (3rd to 1st century BC). The museum, owned by the State, also houses part of the Museo Correr's archeological collection (Neolithic and Bronze-Age finds; Egyptian, Assyrian and Babilonian artifacts; Greek, Etruscan and Roman art). Next-door is the **Libreria Sansoviniana**, a masterpiece of 16th-century Venetian architecture, designed by Jacopo Sansovino and completed after his death (1570) by Vincenzo Scamozzi. This airy building with a portico and a loggia crowned by a fine balustrade once housed the Biblioteca Marciana (St Mark's Library); a monumental staircase leads to the vestibule, with a frescoed ceiling by Titian (**Wisdom***). The Zecca (mint), just off the Piazzetta, with rusticated decoration, designed and built by Sansovino (1537-66), now houses the *Biblioteca Nazionale Marciana*. Created to house a bequest from Cardinal Bessarion in 1468 of about a thousand Greek and Latin manuscripts, it was enlarged by incorporating the libraries of suppressed convents and monasteries; its most precious possession is the late 15th-century illuminated Grimani Breviary.

Across Piazza S. Marco the **Museo Correr** occupies the Ala Napoleonica and part of the Procuratie Nuove. Created from the collection which Teodoro Correr left to the city in 1830, it offers various options: rooms in the neoclassical style with important sculptures by Antonio Canova (1757-1822); historical exhibits associated with Venice's institutions; the city's development over the centuries; aspects of daily life; its art gallery, one of the finest collections of Venetian painting, from its beginnings to the early 16th century, with works by the Bellini, Carpaccio, Cosmè Tura, Antonello da Messina, and Lorenzo Lotto, in an imaginative setting by Carlo

Scarpa. Annexed to the museum: the Biblioteca d'Arte e Storia Veneziana, with its fine collection of manuscripts and historical documents, the famous *Gabinetto di stampe e disegni* with its print and drawing collection, a Photographic Archive, and a Centre for Catalogues and Multimedia Products.

From Campo S. Moisè to Palazzo Grassi ❺

The square is overlooked by the **church of S. Moisè** (1668), a fine example of the luxuriant Venetian Baroque style. Another example of exuberant decoration is the facade of the **church of S. Maria del Giglio**, built in 1683, in the eponymous square, with paintings by Rubens, Sebastiano Ricci and Jacopo Tintoretto. Close by is **Teatro La Fenice**, one of the world's most famous opera-houses, destroyed by fire on January 29, 1996. Reconstruction work was completed in 2004. Sansovino's masterpiece, **Palazzo Corner della Ca' Granda,** (c. 1533-53), with a classical three-storey facade, is now the police headquarters for the Venice area. The **church of S. Stefano**, with a flamboyant Gothic-style doorway, dates from the 14th and 15th centuries. The vast interior has a nave and two side-aisles separated by columns, a ship's keel ceiling and many funerary monuments. In the sacristy: *Crucifix* by Paolo Veneziano; *polyptych* by Bartolomeo Vivarini; *Holy Family* by Palma the Elder and three large works by Tintoretto (*The Last Supper*, **Washing of the Feet***, **Prayer in the Garden***).

Palazzo Grassi with its imposing classical forms, built in the 18th century, used for major exhibitions, is now the headquarters of the Palazzo Grassi Foundation. Close by, the 11th-century **church of S. Samuele**, with its small, picturesque Venetian Romanesque 12th-century bell tower, is used for temporary exhibitions.

A detail of the facade of S. Maria del Giglio

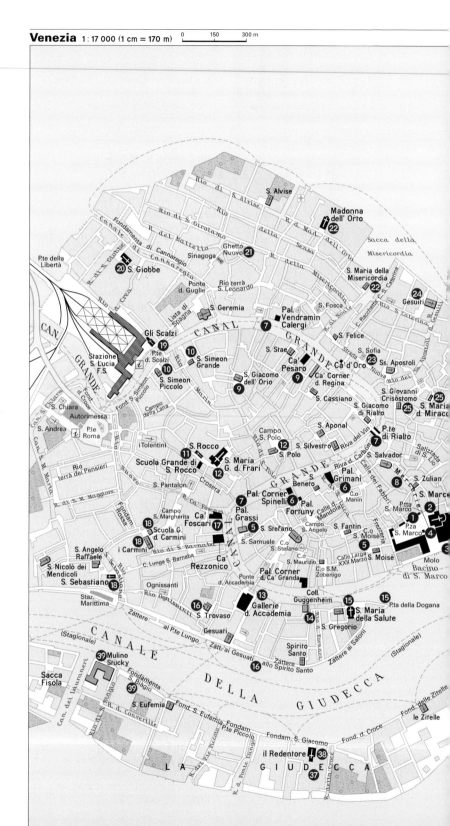

Venezia 1 : 17 000 (1 cm = 170 m)

0   150   300 m

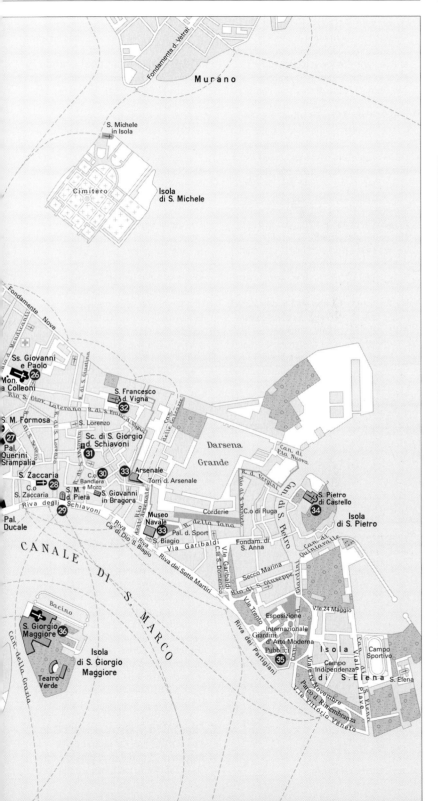

Palazzo Corner Spinelli, Palazzo Fortuny and Palazzo Grimani ⑥

Palazzo Corner Spinelli is an early Renaissance building with two storeys of two-light windows, designed by Mauro Codussi (late 15th century). The Gothic facade of this 15th-century palazzo overlooks Campo S. Beneto. It houses the **Museo Fortuny**, converted by the Spanish painter and interior designer Mariano Fortuny y Madrazo (1861-1949) from his studio (used for photography, designing stage sets, stage machinery, textiles and painting). The museum also hosts exhibitions on the ground floor and the "piano nobile".
Palazzo Grimani is an imposing three-storey Renaissance building with broad arches supported by pilaster strips and columns. A masterpiece of Michele Sanmicheli (1556-75), it is now the seat of the judiciary.
Not far away is **Campo Manin**, dominated by the offices of the Cassa di Risparmio di Venezia, a new building noted for its flexible interior design features and its facade, which employs traditional Venetian motifs in a modern context. Just behind the square is the late-Gothic **Palazzo Contarini del Bòvolo**, famous for its external spiral staircase ("bòvolo" in local dialect), connecting several storeys of superimposed loggias.

Ponte di Rialto and Canal Grande ⑦

Antonio da Ponte rebuilt Venice's most famous bridge in 1591. 48 m long and 22 m wide, it has a single arch 7.5 m high and a maximum width of 28 m. Until the 19th century, it was the only bridge linking the two sides of the city. Three parallel staircases lead from one side to the other, the central one lined by arcades with shops. The sides of the bridge are adorned with 16th-century reliefs.
The **Canal Grande**, Venice's main internal waterway, flows through the city uniting its various parts. 3,800 m long and between 30 m and 70 m wide, the shape of an upturned S, it owes its current form to the continuous alignment and consolidation of its banks since the 14th century. Originally used to transport goods between the port and the Rialto market, in the 16th century, the Venetian nobility chose it as a site for their luxurious mansions. It is lined with a virtually uninterrupted sequence of palaces dating from the 13th to 18th centuries.

S. Salvador and Mercerie ⑧

This church with its white Baroque facade (1663) overlooks the eponymous square. In the right aisle: *monument to Doge Francesco Venier* by Sansovino (1561) and a late work by Titian (**Annunciation***) (1566); above the high altar, another Titian (**Transfiguration***) (1560) hides a precious 14th-century silver altar-piece.
Divided into several parts, the **Mercerie** runs between Piazza S. Marco and Rialto. One of Venice's busiest streets, the shops on either side sell all kinds of goods. At the end of the first section (Merceria dell'Orologio), the ancient **church of S. Zulian** overlooks the square named after the church. Rebuilt in its present form (1553-55) by Jacopo Sansovino, it has paintings by Paolo Veronese and Palma the Younger.

Ca' Pesaro to S. Giacomo dell'Orio ⑨

Near Ca' Pesaro, **Ca' Corner della Regina** is an impressive building with classical motifs by Domenico Rossi

Palazzo Contarini del Bòvolo

The imposing stone arch of the Rialto Bridge

(1724) and a facade decorated with two tiers of loggias. It houses the *Archivio Storico della Biennale di Venezia*.

Ca' Pesaro, one of the most important palazzi on the Grand Canal, has an open courtyard with a well-head attributed to Jacopo Sansovino and a splendid entrance-hall. The first and second floors house the **Galleria internazionale d'Arte moderna***, the city's 19th- and 20th-century painting and sculpture collections, including works by Klimt, Chagall, Kandinsky, Klee, Matisse and Henry Moore, as well as works by Italian artists and a graphic art display. The third floor, the **Museo d'Arte orientale*** has one of the world's largest collections of Japanese Edo art (1614-1868). Other sections focus on China and Indonesia, with an important collection of weapons from the 12th to 19th centuries.

Nearby, **Campo S. Maria Mater Domini**, named after the **church of S. Maria Mater Domini** (1502-40), has a facade attributed to Jacopo Sansovino and a harmonious interior with a Greek-cross plan. It has a *Martyrdom of St Cristina* by Vincenzo Catena (1520) and an early Tintoretto, **Invention of the Cross***.

To the west, **Palazzo Mocenigo** is a noble residence with original 18th-century furnishings and paintings. It houses the Centro Studi di Storia del Tessuto e del Costume, a rich and varied display of exhibits from several different collections. Of these, the **Museo di Storia del Tessuto e del Costume** has some particularly rare pieces (fabrics and costumes). The museum also allows

scholars access to its library of specialized books on the sector.

Overlooking the Grand Canal, the **church of S. Stae** (St Eustace) has an imposing facade by Domenico Rossi (1709), a single nave and fine works by some of the foremost artists of the early 18th century (Tiepolo and Ricci). On the same side of the canal, the **Fondaco dei Turchi** (heavily restored in 1858-69) with its Venetian Byzantine motifs, was used by Turkish traders. Today it houses the **Museo di Storia Naturale**, an important institution, with many collections and a large library. It also monitors and collects information about the lagoon and its fauna.

A long, narrow street leads to **Campo S. Giacomo dell'Orio**, one of the few planted with trees. The eponymous church, one of the oldest in Venice, contains precious artworks, including Lorenzo Lotto's **Madonna and Saints*** (1546) in the presbytery.

S. Simeòn Grande and S. Simeòn Piccolo ⑩

A cemetery once preceded the facade of the old **church of S. Simeòn Grande**, heavily restored in the 18th century. Inside, it has a basilica plan, a nave and two side-aisles separated by ancient columns with Byzantine capitals, a *Presentation in the Temple* by Palma the Younger and a *Last Supper* by Tintoretto.

The **church of S. Simeòn Piccolo**, built in 1718-38 by Giovanni Scalfarotto, has an elegant Corinthian pronaos at the top of a flight of steps. Its design combines several themes: the Pantheon in Rome, Palladian influences and the church of the Salute.

S. Rocco and Scuola Grande di S. Rocco ⑪

Not far from from S. Rocco stands the **Scuola Grande di S. Giovanni Evangelista.** Suppressed by Napoleon in 1806 and deprived of its most precious artworks, and altered several times from the 14th to 18th centuries, it reflects various architectural styles. Restored between 1969 and 1974, it has a splendid monumental staircase (1498) and frescoes by G.D. Tiepolo and Tintoretto. In the *Sala dell'Albergo*, four paintings by Palma the Younger depict the *Apocalypse*. The **church of S. Rocco**, rebuilt in the 18th century, has six remarkable **paintings*** by Tintoretto. The **Scuola Grande di S. Rocco**, begun in 1478, was completed in 1560. The interior is decorated by Tintoretto: his **cycle of paintings** (1564 to 1587) includes more than 60 canvases. To follow the chronological sequence, start upstairs in the Sala dell'Albergo, begun in 1564, with the enormous Crucifixion, one of the few works signed and dated by Tintoretto; the others depict the Passion. The 21 canvases on the ceiling and walls of the upper hall, painted from 1575 to 1581, depict scenes from the Old and New Testaments. A double flight of stairs leads to the lower hall (1583-1587), where Tintoretto painted the last eight scenes from the Life of Mary: the *Annunciation*, the *Flight into Egypt*, *St Mary of Egypt* and *St Mary Magdalene* are particularly fine. Other works in the Scuola include *Christ carrying the Cross*, attributed to Giorgione.

S. Maria Gloriosa dei Frari and Campo S. Polo ⑫

Marked by its massive 14th-century bell tower, one of the tallest in Venice, this is one of Venice's most important churches, together with Ss. Giovanni e Paolo. Built by Franciscans in 1340-1443, its majestic Gothic forms end in a complex apse. The vast **interior**, a long nave with two aisles separated by pointed arches resting on massive columns, contains many monuments to doges and illustrious Venetians of the 14th to 19th centuries, and other treasures. In the center of the nave: the **choir***, decorated in the Renaissance and Gothic styles, with a marble choir-screen (1475) and carved

wooden choirstalls with fine marquetry (1468). In the *sacristy*: Giovanni Bellini's **triptych of the Madonna and Saints**** (signed and dated 1488). In the chapel to the right of the high altar: a fine sculpture of **John the Baptist*** by Donatello (c.1450). In the *presbytery*: behind the high altar, Titian's famous altar-piece of the **Assumption**** (1518); on the right wall, the *monument to Doge F. Foscari* (c.1457); on the left wall, the marble *tomb of Doge Niccolò Tron* (c.1476). Left aisle: 2nd altar, the **Pesaro**

The apse of the Frari: above the altar, Titian's "Assumption"

Altar-piece** by Titian (1526); in the last bay, the pyramidal monument to Antonio Canova, to his own design (1827).
In a narrow lane near Campo S. Polo, Palazzo Centanni is the **birthplace of Carlo Goldoni**, the comic playwright. It is now a small museum about his life and work, with a famous puppet theater, an extensive archive and a library of scripts and theatrical sketches with more than 30,000 original manuscripts.
Campo S. Polo, one of Venice's largest squares, was once used for popular festivals. Around it are palaces from the 14th to 18th centuries and the apse of the **church of S. Polo**, of Byzantine origin, with important works by Tintoretto and Stations of the Cross (1747-49) by G.D. Tiepolo.

Ponte dell'Accademia and Gallerie dell'Accademia ⑬

The Accademia Bridge was built in 1934 as a "temporary" measure to replace a 19th-century metal bridge built by the Austrians. On one side of it, the **Gallerie dell'Accademia**, founded in 1807 to house paintings from churches and ecclesiastical foundations suppressed by Napoleon have grown as a result of donations and acquisitions. The first rooms have panels and polyptychs of the 14th and early 15th centuries (Paolo and Lorenzo Veneziano, Gentile da Fabriano, Pisanello). The next rooms contain eight canvases depicting the **Miracles of the True Cross** (1494-1501) by Gentile Bellini and Vittore Carpaccio and nine huge paintings by Carpaccio depicting the **Legend of St Ursula** (c.1490-1495). Giovanni Bellini's unforgettable Madonnas, Giorgione (*The Tempest*), Cima da Conegliano, Mantegna (*St George*), Piero della Francesca and Cosmè Tura mark the progression from the 15th to the 16th century, represented by Titian (*Pietà* and *Presentation of the Virgin*), Veronese (**Christ in the House of Levi**), Lorenzo Lotto, Palma the Elder, Palma the Younger and Tintoretto. Bernardo Strozzi and Luca Giordano represent the Baroque and Rococo periods. The 18th century is represented by G.B. and G.D. Tiepolo, Sebastiano Ricci, the "vedutisti" Francesco Guardi and Canaletto, pastels by Rosalba Carriera, domestic scenes by Pietro Longhi and sketches by Antonio Canova.

The Gabinetto di Disegni is next to the main gallery.

Palazzo Venier dei Leoni ⑭

Designed in 1749, Palazzo Venier dei Leoni was bought in 1949 by American heiress Peggy Guggenheim to house the **Peggy Guggenheim Contemporary Art Collection**, associated with the Salomon R. Guggenheim Foundation in New York. It has paintings and sculptures of the leading art movements of the 20th century. Artists represented include Pablo Picasso, René Magritte, Giorgio De Chirico, Gino Severini, Marcel Duchamp, Georges Braque, Fernand Léger, Piet Mondrian, Paul Klee, Max Ernst, Juan Miró, Constantin Brancusi, Giacomo Balla, Henry Moore, Salvador Dalí, Marc Chagall, Yves Tanguy, Paul Delvaux, Victor Brauner, Jackson Pollock, Francis Bacon, Graham Sutherland and Jean Dubuffet. The museum organizes temporary art exhibitions. Just beyond the gallery is the Renaissance-style **Palazzo Dario** (1487) with a triple loggia, four-light windows and an elaborate marble facade.

S. Maria della Salute and Punta della Dogana ⑮

This masterpiece of Venetian Baroque by Baldassarre Longhena (1631-87) was built by the Senate in thanks for deliverance from the plague. This imposing white marble church built on an octagonal plan is decorated with a statues and topped by a huge semi-

The Punta della Dogana, with the church of the S. Maria della Salute

spherical dome; above the presbytery, a smaller dome and two bell towers. Visually flamboyant, it dominates the Venetian landscape. Inside, the slender dome rises above the vast round central area with a circular aisle. A passage leads to the Great Sacristy: above the altar, **St Mark and Saints***, an early work by Titian (1512), who also painted the three **canvases*** in the ceiling; to the right of the altar, a large painting by Tintoretto depicts the **Wedding at Cana***.

The Patriarchal Seminary, built by Baldassarre Longhena in 1671, houses the **Pinacoteca Manfrediana**, created from the bequest of Marquis Federico Manfredini (1743-1829). It has works by Italian and Venetian painters (15th to 18th centuries), sculpture (13th to 17th centuries) and illuminated manuscripts (14th to 16th centuries). The **Museo Lapidario** (in the cloister) has archeological finds from the Roman period, and architectural features from churches, monasteries and convents suppressed by Napoleon.

The **Punta della Dogana** juts out between the end of the Grand Canal and the Canale della Giudecca, opposite the island of S. Giorgio. This long, low building shaped like a ship's prow was the **Dogana da Mar** (1677), and already existed in the 15th century as the customs post for all goods arriving in Venice by sea.

Top of the high altar of the church of the S. Maria della Salute

The Zattere ai Gesuati is named after the church of the **Gesuati**. Built in 1724-36, it incorporates Palladian features. Inside, beyond the rectanguar nave, is a light-filled oval apse.

The **church of S. Trovaso** is the result of reconstruction begun in 1585; two almost identical facades conceal an interior with a single nave and a broad presbytery, with works by Tintoretto.

Ca' Rezzonico and Ca' Foscari ⑰

This imposing Baroque palazzo on the Grand Canal (1649-1750) houses the **Museo del Settecento Veneziano***. Its luxuriously decorated rooms (some frescoed by G.B. Tiepolo) give a fascinating insight into the life and customs of 18th-century Venice: tapestries, furniture, lacquer furniture, costumes, furnishings, paintings (P. Longhi, Rosalba Carriera, Canaletto, F. Guardi) and **frescoes*** by G.A. Guardi and G.D. Tiepolo.

Palazzo Giustinian and **Ca' Foscari** (begun in 1452), now the main offices of the University, are some of the best examples of architectural uniformity in large 14th-century patrician residences on the Grand Canal. The long facades of the two buildings form a single block overlooking the Grand Canal.

Zattere and S. Trovaso ⑯

The Zattere is a long promenade running beside the Canale della Giudecca, the waterway separating the city from the island of the Giudecca. The long (almost 2 km) "fondamenta" (running alongside a canal) is divided into four sections, each named after its most salient feature: Zattere al Ponte Lungo, Zattere ai Gesuati, Zattere allo Spirito Santo and Zattere ai Saloni.

Cà Rezzonico, now the Museum of 18th-century Venice

Scuola Grande dei Carmini, i Carmini and S. Sebastiano ⑱

The Scuola was built by the confraternity of the Carmelites, founded out of devotion to St Mary of Carmel: the facade (1668-1670) is attributed to Baldassarre Longhena. It contains works by G.B. Tiepolo, who, between 1739 and 1749, decorated the nine sections of the ceiling of the Sala del Capitolo. Next to it stands the 14th-century church of **Carmini**, with a Renaissance facade, a curved pediment (early 16th century) and a 14th-century doorway (left of the church). The works by Cima da Conegliano, Francesco di Giorgio Martini and Lorenzo Lotto are particularly fine.

The **church of S. Sebastiano**, rebuilt in the first half of the 16th century in the elegant Renaissance style, is famous for the spectacular decoration executed between 1555 and 1565 by Paolo Veronese (buried here in 1588). A fine series of canvases and frescoes adorns the ceiling, the walls of the nave, the sacristy and nun's choir. The canvases by Titian are also remarkable.

The Ten Commandments written in Hebrew

Ponte degli Scalzi and gli Scalzi ⑲

The stone Ponte degli Scalzi, rebuilt in 1934 (the first iron bridge dated from 1858), is one of three bridges spanning the Grand Canal.
Baldassarre Longhena began building the church in 1654 for a barefooted Carmelite community which had moved to Rome. The exterior is Baroque, the interior has a single nave with three chapels on each side: the vaults of the 2nd chapel on the right and the 1st chapel on the left were frescoed by G.B. Tiepolo.

S. Giobbe ⑳

The church, built in the Gothic style in 1450, was finished by Pietro and Tullio Lombardo in the Renaissance style. The beautiful doorway, the marble decoration in the presbytery and the two niche chapels on either side of it are by Pietro Lombardo.
At the other end of the same fondamenta, facing the Grand Canal, is **Palazzo Labia**, a luxurious 18th-century residence, now the seat of the RAI. The interior was frescoed by G.B. Tiepolo, who left an extraordinary testimonial of his artistic genius here. Assisted by Girolamo Mengozzi Colonna, between 1745 and 1750, he painted two great scenes: *The Arrival of Cleopatra* and *The Banquet of Anthony and Cleopatra*.

Ghetto Nuovo ㉑

The Ghetto Nuovo is part of the ghetto where, from 1516 until 1797, Venetian Jews were forced to live. A small island surrounded by canals and fringed by tall buildings, it is now the location of the **Museo Ebraico di Venezia**, opened in 1953. Recently restored, the museum has a collection of ritual and household objects, sacred furnishings, tapestries, precious bindings for books, manuscripts, silverware, containers for scrolls, curtains for the doors of the Holy Ark, pulpit drapes and old manuscripts of marriage contracts.

Madonna dell'Orto and S. Maria della Misericordia ㉒

Built in the 15th century, the **church of Madonna dell'Orto** overlooks a charming little square. Statues and a doorway with Renaissance and Gothic features adorn its brick facade. The interior, with a nave and two side-aisles, has **paintings*** by Jacopo Tintoretto (buried in 1594, in the chapel to the right of the presbytery): in the right aisle, 1st altar, **John the Baptist*** by Cima da Conegliano (1493). Fondamenta dell'Abbazia leads to the quiet square before the abbey, where the original terracotta pavement lends it a particular old-worldly charm. It is overlooked by the **church of S. Maria della Misericoria**, founded with the abbey in the 10th century and restructured several times, and, in the corner, with a Baroque facade, the 14th-century *Scuola Vecchia di S. Maria della Misericoria*, one of the largest confraternities in Venice.

Marble loggias on the facade of the Cà d'Oro on the Canal Grande

Strada Nuova and Ca' d'Oro ㉓

Before you turn into into Strada Nuova, the elegant Renaissance-style **Palazzo Vendramin Calergi** was designed by Mauro Codussi and completed by the Lombardo (1509). The composer Richard Wagner died here on February 13, 1883; it is the winter seat of the Casinò Municipale (in summer it moves to the Lido).
Strada Nuova is a wide street laid out in 1871 to link the station to the Rialto. Many buildings were demolished to make this possible. It runs along behind the rear facades of the palazzi overlooking the Grand Canal.
Built in the Gothic style (1422-40), the name **Ca' d'Oro** (Golden House) refers to the gold decoration of the facade overlooking the Grand Canal; it has a handsome portico on the ground floor supported by columns, two open loggias with intersecting arches and balconies on the upper floors, and a distinctive row of merlons. This and the adjoining Palazzo Giusti are now the **Galleria "Giorgio Franchetti"**. In 1916, this musician from Turin donated his private collection and the Cà d'Oro to the State. The collection includes paintings by Italian and foreign artists, marbles, bronzes, and Venetian ceramics from the 15th to 18th centuries. Highlights include, on the 1st floor: works by Alvise Vivarini (**polyptych of the Passion***), Andrea Mantegna (**St Sebastian****), Vittore Carpaccio, Giovanni da Rimini,

Luca Signorelli and Carlo Braccesco. The sculptures include bronzes and marble busts by Tullio Lombardo (*Double Portrait*). A fine 14th-century wooden staircase leads to the second floor: works by Titian and Tintoretto, and views of Venice by Francesco Guardi.

Gesuiti ㉔

The original church, S. Maria dei Crociferi, was rebuilt for the Jesuits (1715-30). The elaborate Baroque facade is based on Roman models. The interior is a riot of Baroque. Above the altar left of the entrance, the **Martyrdom of St Laurence*** is by Titian (1558).

S. Giovanni Crisostomo and S. Maria dei Miracoli ㉕

The Renaissance church of S. Giovanni Crisostomo was built by Mauro Codussi (1497-1504). Inside, 1st altar on the right, **St Christopher, St Jerome and St Augustine***, a masterpiece by Giovanni Bellini (1513).
This small, isolated **church of S. Maria dei Miracoli** is one of the most eloquent expressions of the early Renaissance in Venice. The masterpiece of Pietro Lombardo, aided by his sons Antonio and Tullio (1489), polychrome marble decoration enhances its elegant sides and facade, crowned with a semi-circular pediment. The interior is also faced with marble, with an extraordinary marble tribune by Tullio Lombardo.

Campo and chiesa dei SS. Giovanni e Paolo 26

Situated in front of the great church dedicated to St John and St Paul is Venice's second-finest monumental square. In the center is a well-head dating from the 16th century. Its focal point is the **equestrian monument to Bartolomeo Colleoni****, a masterpiece of Renaissance sculpture. Modelled by Andrea Verrocchio in 1481-88, the statue of this Venetian mercenary general was cast by Alessandro Leopardi. From the mid-15th century onwards, the church of **Ss. Giovanni e Paolo**, built by the Dominicans between 1246 and 1430, was used for the funeral ceremonies of the Doges. Note the polygonal **apses*** in the right side of the church. The high slender Gothic *interior* is similar to that of the church of the Frari, and, like it, contains innumerable funerary monuments of doges, captains and illustrious figures of the Venetian Republic from the 14th to 17th centuries. Back of the main facade: *monument to Doge Pietro Mocenigo* by Pietro Lombardo (1481). *Right side-aisle*: 2nd altar, *polyptych of St. Vincenzo Ferrer*, an early work by Giovanni Bellini (c.1465). At the end of the aisle, the Chapel of St Dominic (1716), with a carved gilt ceiling and a *St Dominic in Glory* by G.B. Piazzetta (1727). On the walls of the *presbytery*, on the left, *monument to Doge Andrea Vendramin* by Pietro and Tullio Lombardo (15th century), and the Gothic *monument to Doge Marco Corner*, with statues of the Madonna and saints by Giovanni Pisano. At the end of the left transept is the 16th-century **Cappella del Rosario*** (Chapel of the Rosary): the ceiling was rebuilt after a fire and has **paintings*** by Veronese. Next to it, the building which once housed the Scuola Grande di S. Marco is the city hospital. The masterpiece of Pietro, Antonio and Tullio Lombardo and Giovanni Buora (1487-90), its long facade with

The monument to Colleoni in Campo Ss. Giovanni e Paolo

polychrome marble decoration dates from the early Renaissance. The curved pediments were added by Mauro Codussi in 1495.

S. Maria Formosa and Palazzo Querini Stampalia 27

According to tradition, the church was built in 639 after a miraculous apparition of the Virgin Mary and rebuilt in 1492 by Mauro Codussi. The **interior*** has numerous treasures, including a famous polyptych by Palma the Elder of *St Barbara and Saints* (right transept). The bell tower (1678-88) stands on the side facing Campo S. Maria Formosa. Behind the church, **Palazzo Querini-Stampalia** is accessed by a metal bridge by Carlo Scarpa, who also designed the ground floor (it had to be waterproof) and the garden (1959-63). The palazzo was built in about 1528 and, since 1869, has been the seat of the Querini Stampalia Foundation. (As well as a library, it has a fine art gallery with art-works from the 14th to 18th centuries.) The **garden** has a lawn with a series of pools and fountains, an original well-head, a stone lion, capitals and fountains, creepers and various flowering shrubs.

Campo and chiesa di S. Zaccaria 28

Situated near Campo S. Zaccaria, the **Museo Diocesano d'Arte Sacra di S. Apollonia** is worth a visit. The museum belongs to the Diocese of Venice and was created by Pope John Paul I (Albino Luciani, 1912-1978) when he was Patriarch of Venice. It includes restored art-works from churches in Venice. One room is devoted to silverware; another has objects donated by priests working in Venice (statues of the Virgin Mary in traditional Venetian costume).

Quiet **Campo S. Zaccaria** is dominated by the facade of the church and, to the right, its 13th-century brick bell tower. To the left of the church, the arcades (now occupied by shops) belong to the 16th-century cloister of the old convent.

The **church of S. Zaccaria** was built in the Gothic style in the 15th century and completed by Mauro Codussi (1483-90), who designed the white stone tiered facade. It is one of the finest examples of early Venetian Renaissance architecture. The *interior* has a nave and two side-aisles separated by vast columns; the walls are decorated with large canvases from the 17th and 18th centuries. The most significant work graces the second altar on the left: Giovanni Bellini's famous altar-piece of the **Madonna Enthroned with Saints*** (1505). In the apse of the *Cappella di S. Tarasio* are some important **frescoes*** by Andrea del Castagno and Francesco da Faenza (1442). There are also three *polyptychs* in the Gothic style by Antonio Vivarini and Giovanni d'Alemagna (1443).

Riva degli Schiavoni ㉙

The name of the broad, busy promenade beside the Basin of St Mark refers to the sailors from Schiavonia (now eastern Croatia), who used to moor their ships and do business here. Walking towards St Mark's Basilica, you pass the 18th-century **S. Maria della Visitazione** or *Pietà*, the interior of which was designed partly with the performance of concerts in mind. Beyond the *Ponte del Vin*, the promenade is thronged with tourists and souvenir-sellers. Overlooking it is the Gothic *Palazzo Dandolo* (15th century), now the exclusive Danieli hotel.

Nearby, the **church of S. Giorgio dei Greci** is part of the complex which belonged to the Greek Orthodox community of Venice, the city's largest ethnic group during the Renaissance. The tall, narrow facade of the church, divided into two levels overlooks the center of the area - almost a courtyard - acquired in 1526. Behind it, a harmonious, solemn rectangular interior, richly decorated with Byzantine paintings and icons, separated from the presbytery and its triple apse by a marble iconostasis with late-Byzantine paintings on a gold background. Next to the facade stands the **bell tower** (1587-92), which has been leaning ever since it was built. Other buildings of the Greek community include the Istituto Ellenico di Studi Bizantini e Postbizantini (a research institute) and, in the former **Scuola di S. Nicolò dei Greci**, the **Museo dei Dipinti sacri bizantini** (Icon Museum). The museum has illuminated manuscripts,

S. Francesco della Vigna watches over the houses of Castello

embroidered sacred vestments and small craft objects, and the most important collection of icons in Western Europe (14th to 18th centuries), many of them by Greek artists who settled in Venice, from Constantinople, or from the workshops of painters from Crete.

Campo Bandiera e Moro ㉚

Tucked away from the busier streets in Campo Bandiera e Moro is the Gothic **church of S. Giovanni in Bràgora**, rebuilt in 1475, with an unusual brick facade. The interior, with a nave and two side-aisles, has important **paintings*** by Alvise Vivarini, Bartolomeo Vivarini and Cima da Conegliano.

Scuola di S. Giorgio degli Schiavoni ③

The little Scuola di S. Giorgio degli Schiavoni was built in the early 16th century by the confraternity of the Dalmatian community ('Schiavoni'). It's famous for the **paintings by Carpaccio**** which adorn the ground floor. The cycle of paintings, regarded as one of Carpaccio's masterpieces (1501-11), depicts scenes from the life of St George, St Jerome and St Tryphone.

The land entrance of the Arsenale

S. Francesco della Vigna ③

This large 16th-century Franciscan church, designed by the Tuscan architect, Jacopo Sansovino, has a classical temple-front facade by Andrea Palladio (1564-70). The left transept leads into a chapel with a **Madonna and Child with Saints*** by Giovanni Bellini.

Arsenale and Museo Storico Navale ③

A high merloned wall surrounded by canals marks the perimeter of this great shipbuilding complex from the 12th and early 13th centuries. It was enlarged several times and continued to develop over the centuries. From this ancient center of maritime power, the Venetian

fleet used to set sail. The land entrance to the Arsenale is a **gateway*** (1460), often regarded as the earliest work of the Venetian Renaissance. Above the gateway is a splendid lion of St Mark, attributed to Bartolomeo Bon.

The **Museo Storico Navale (**Naval History Museum), owned by the Italian Navy since 1923, is housed in the former granaries of the Venetian Republic, a 15th-century building close to the Arsenale. The collection includes a 'human torpedo' used very successfully by the Italian Navy during WWII. One section of the museum focuses on the achievements, the vessels and the men of the Serenissima and the Italian Navy. A highlight on the first floor is the model of the Bucentaur, the ceremonial barge used by the Doge during the ritual marriage with the sea. The third floor houses a collection of traditional wooden boats of the Venetian lagoon. One room focuses on the gondola (Peggy Guggenheim's was donated to the museum after her death). The Ship Pavilion contains Venetian vessels and ships belonging to the Italian navy.

S. Pietro di Castello ③

At the eastern end of *Via Garibaldi*, the only "via" in the city, lies the island of S. Pietro and the church of S. Pietro di Castello. Its simple facade has a majestic doorway. The broad flat ceiling inside is decorated with 17th-century frescoes.

Giardini pubblici ③

The Public Gardens were laid out during the Napoleonic period and altered in the mid-19th century to suit the romantic tastes of the time. They are the setting for the pavilions of the *Biennale d'Arte*, the two-yearly international exhibition of painting, sculpture and decorative arts held here since 1895. The pavilions of the individual countries reflect the architectural trends of different nations over the course of almost a century (1907-95).

The island of S. Giorgio Maggiore, owned by the Cini Foundation

S. Giorgio Maggiore 36

This church designed by Andrea Palladio stands on the island of S. Giorgio opposite Piazzetta S. Marco. The church, with its noble, classical-style facade, was begun by Palladio in 1566 and completed in 1611. Its somber gray and white interior is composed of a nave and two side aisles. On the walls of the presbytery are two works by Tintoretto: a **Last Supper*** and the *Shower of Manna* (1594). Above the altar of the winter choir: a painting by Vittore Carpaccio: **St George killing the Dragon*** (1516). From the top of the campanile, built in 1791 to replace a 15th-century tower, there are magnificent **views*** over the city and the lagoon.

The **Monastery of S. Giorgio Maggiore** is now the headquarters of the Fondazione Giorgio Cini. The complex surrounds two lovely **cloisters***. Some of the greatest architects of the late 14th- to 17th centuries worked here: Andrea Palladio, Giovanni and Andrea Buora, and Baldassarre Longhena.

Giudecca 37

The name of this long, narrow island situated between the Canale della Giudecca and the southern part of the lagoon may derive from the fact that some Jews ("giudei") established a settlement here in the Middle Ages. Thanks to its position, removed from the city center yet close to the Basin of St Mark, from the 16th century onwards, it became a place of leisure, where noble residences alternated with orchards, monasteries and gardens. In the 19th century, when the Venetian nobility had declined and the convents and monasteries had been suppressed, it was increasingly used for military and naval barracks, prisons, housing for factory workers and factories. The sole remaining testimonial, located in the far east of the island, is the neo-Gothic Mulino Stucky (1896). On April 16, 2003 a fire destroyed some of the building, causing the collapse of a tower.

Il Redentore 38

The votive church on the Giudecca was built at the wishes of the Senate to give thanks for deliverance from a serious Plague. It was conceived as the culminating step in the solemn procession of the Redentore (Redeemer) which crossed the canals each year on a bridge of boats. One of Andrea Palladio's masterpieces, it was begun in 1577 and completed after the architect's death by Antonio da Ponte in 1592. Its noble facade is based on classical lines. The somber, majestic interior has a colonnade running down the single nave and round the back of the presbytery, crowned by a dome. Above the altar, paintings from the Venetian School of the 16th and 17th centuries.

lace-making has been an important industry, and received encouragement from the wife of Doge Marino Grimani, Morosina Morosini. The lace-making school, opened in 1872, ensured the survival of a dying art.

The **Museo del Merletto** has about 200 rare and precious pieces illustrating the development of local lace-making from the 16th to the 20th centuries. The museum also has an archive of the famous lace-making school founded by Andriana Marcello in 1872, an important center of culture and business for more than a century.

CÀORLE [66 km]

You will see Venetian words like "calle", "campiello" and "rio" in the names of the streets, squares and canals of the old town, protected from the sea by a high dyke. The descendants of refugees from the Roman town of Concordia Sagittaria, who possibly founded the town in late Antiquity, cultivated vegetables and went hunting and fishing. Today it is still a fishing town. The town's round campanile is a landmark for homeward bound sailors and fishermen, marking the site of the harbor. Càorle is the third-largest fishing port in the region in terms of the catch. A modern seaside resort has grown up along the sandy beaches east of the town. The Romanesque **Cattedrale** of St Stephen, situated in the heart of the old town, dates from 1038. Pilaster strips divide its facade into three sections; on each side of the central doorway, a high relief from the Byzantine period (12th century). Opposite the cathedral stands the tall, round **bell tower*** typical of churches in the Ravenna area. In the remarkable *interior*: a nave and two side-aisles separated by pilasters and columns (with Byzantine capitals); frescoes from the 14th to 17th centuries; above the high altar, a 15th-century crucifix; in the apse, a fine **pala d'oro*** (golden altar-piece), made of gilt silver with tiny Byzantine panels, from the 12th and 13th centuries, and other examples of Venetian 14th-century gold- and silver-ware. Since 1975, the priest's house next-door has housed the **Museo Sacro del Duomo**, with sacred furnishings, vestments from the 14th to 17th centuries, gold- and silverware (including three reliquaries, a crucifix from 1534 and

Fondamenta di S. Biagio and ex Mulino Stucky ㊴

Fondamenta San Biagio is lined with low buildings dating from the 15th century to the end of the Republic, and was consolidated to enable the large ships of the late 19th-century to moor when factories began to spring up here. The high merloned walls belong to a former beer and liqueur factory, while the Tessuti Fortuny textile factory (No. 805), built in 1919, is still operating. The fondamenta peters out at a metal bridge now closed to the public. In a scenario which is reminiscent of the fog-bound cities of the north, across the Canale della Giudecca is the imposing neo-Gothic **Mulino Stucky**. It was built to the design of the German architect Ernest Wullekopf (1896) at the wishes of a Swiss entrepreneur, Giovanni Stucky.

DAY TRIPS

BURANO

Burano is a flat island in the lagoon lying north-east of the city center, less than 10 km from St Mark's. Its four tiny islands have brightly-painted houses and canals with fishing boats. Painters have always loved coming here. To the delicate colors of the walls, the water and the sky, they added the colors of sails and the ladies making lace sitting on the fondamenta, in the style of Canaletto. Since the early 16th century,

some chalices); six late 14th-century panels of the Apostles, a fine collection of Byzantine icons and a collection of manuscripts from churches in the area. The museum collects, conserves and safeguards sacred objects and also tries to raise public awareness of the Church's cultural assets.

CHIOGGIA [53 km]

The *piazza* is a wide street with porticoes on one side and public buildings on the other, bisecting the town from its lagoon entrance on the Bacino di Vigo to the land entrance, Ponte Lungo. Parallel to the main street, Canale della Vena, the brightly-painted houses overlook the sails of the fishing boats moored below the quay. Perpendicular to the piazza and the canal is a dense network of narrow streets, dotted with little squares and courtyards straight out of a Goldoni play. Tucked away in the southern corner of the Venetian lagoon, the town has a large fishing fleet. Although you see cars here, this miniature version of Venice is still an important fishing town and, with the nearby beaches of Sottomarina and Isola Verde, also a popular seaside resort. The **Duomo**, which already existed in the 11th century, was rebuilt in the Baroque style by Baldassarre Longhena in the first half of the 17th century. Its tall campanile (64 m high) dates from the mid-14th century. Inside, there is a marble pulpit (1677), a high altar with marble inlay and, in the **chapel*** to the left of the presbytery, an 18th-century painting of the Venetian School.

Corso del Popolo, known as the *piazza*, with an average width of 24 m, crosses the town from north to south, parallel to Canale della Vena. Walking in this direction, note: on the left, the Baroque church of *S. Andrea*, with its Veneto-Byzantine bell tower; the Gothic building with a portico is the **Granaio** (granary), dating from 1322, with a *Madonna* by Jacopo Sansovino in a tabernacle on its facade; the 19th-century *Palazzo Comunale* (Town Hall); the 16th century *Loggia dei Bandi* with a colonnade in the Doric style, and the church of *S. Giacomo*, with an 18th-century interior. Further down, on the right, is the Gothic oratory of **S. Martino**

dating from 1392, built entirely of bricks and crowned with a polygonal lantern; inside, a **polyptych*** dating from 1349 attributed to Paolo Veneziano.

The **church of S. Domenico**, altered in the 18th century, has a 14th-century bell tower; inside, a *St Paul*, the last known work of Vittore Carpaccio (1520), half-way up the right aisle; a wooden 15th-century *Crucifix* above the main altar; and a Crucifixion and Saints attributed to Jacopo Tintoretto, left of the presbytery. The **Museo Civico della Laguna Sud "S. Francesco Fuori le Mura"**, housed in a former monastery, traces the historical and environmental development of the area since Roman times and during the Venetian Republic. One section of the museum is devoted to marine activities, fishing and the shipyards, a feature of Chioggia since the 18th century. The display shows how boats have evolved, especially the 'bragozzo', the typical boat of this area. Finally, there is a section for temporary exhibitions.

JÈSOLO [41 km]

Jèsolo is a modern town of Roman foundation. The most important remains of the ancient town are the foundations of two *basilicas*, situated in the area of Le Mure. One basilica is covered and dates from the 8th and 9th centuries; the second 11th-century church, reconstructed after WWII, was erected over an earlier paleo-Christian oratory dating from the 5th and 6th centuries, of which a few fragments of floor mosaic still remain. 3.5 km away, right on the sea, **Lido di Jèsolo** is one of the largest and best-known resorts in the northern Adriatic. Begun in 1928, it has spread along the coast. This is where the long, straight Canale Cavetta, built between 1595 and 1601 to carry the floodwaters of the River Piave away from the northern entrance to the lagoon, flows into the sea.

LIDO DI VENEZIA

With Pellestrina and the Cavallino peninsular, the island of the Lido, about 12 km long, separates the lagoon from the open sea. Although now mainly residential, there is evidence that it was a once a famous cosmopolitan holiday resort: its splendid beach, its grand hotels and villas, its casino and the premises of the annual film festival. The old towns of S. Nicolò and Malamocco complete the historical picture of the lagoon. The main **jetty of the Lido** stands next to Piazzale S. Maria Elisabetta. From it, Via Sandro Gallo heads south, and the broad Viale S. Maria Elisabetta, the heart of the modern town, leads off to the far side of the island. The residential area of the town is built mainly on avenues parallel to the main avenue. From the jetty you can see the **island of S. Lazzaro degli Armeni**, the Armenian monastery which has been a center of Armenian culture since the island, formerly the 12th-century leper hospital of St Lazarus, was given to the monks in 1717. The monastery, with a lovely

(1898-1908), built in the eccentric but now familiar Moorish style. The recently restored old **Jewish Cemetery**, on Riviera S. Nicolò, dating from 1389, is one of the oldest in Europe. The new Jewish cemetery on Via Cipro beyond the Roman Catholic cemetery was founded in the 18th century. The **church of S. Nicolò** stands at the far end of the island, close to the northern Lido entrance to the lagoon, the main access route to Venice from the open sea. You can still see the remains of the 17th-century fort of S. Nicolò (or Castel Vecio), which used to defend it, and the fort of S. Andrea (or Castel Nuovo) alle Vignole (1545-50) on the far side. In the south of the island, **Malamocco** was one of the first areas of the lagoon to be settled. Destroyed by a tidal wave

The Hotel Excelsior on the Lido di Venezia

garden, has a library, a printing press, a museum with paintings, archeological finds (including a 15th-century BC Egyptian mummy) and other relics. The other main streets lead off from Piazzale del Bucintoro: Lungomare Gabriele D'Annunzio runs north-east and ends at the Ospedale al Mare (town hospital); Lungomare Guglielmo Marconi runs south-west. No. 52 is the Yacht Club with its Residence (1979-81). Further along are the **Grand Hotel des Bains** (1900), the **Casino** (1936-38), the **Palazzo della Mostra del Cinema** (1937 and 1952), site of the annual film festival, and the **Grand Hotel Excelsior**

in 1106-1107, it began to recover from the 14th century. Between the front facing the lagoon and Piazza della Chiesa stand the *Palazzo del Podestà* and the church of *S. Maria Assunta* (both 15th century). **Alberoni** is a small residential resort at the southern end of the Lido; it has a broad pleasant beach and sand dunes fringed by trees. On the other side of the strait, the small towns of S. Piero in Volta and Pellestrina on the **island of Pellestrina** have always been inhabited by fishermen. The towns face the lagoon while, on the sea side of the island is the huge dyke (11 km long) built between 1774 and 1782.

MESTRE [9 km]

This bustling modern town has a long history. Situated on the west side of the lagoon, where the causeway bearing the road and the railway to Venice begins, in the 18th century, its villas and gardens attracted wealthy visitors. Together with Marghera and Porto Marghera, on the other side of the railway (built in the 1920s), it is Venice's industrial zone and main port. The **parish church of S. Lorenzo**, with its neoclassical facade, dates from the 18th century. The bell tower belonged to the original Romanesque church. On the right, the *Scuola dei Battuti* is a small 14th-century building with trefoil windows. The **Torre dell'Orologio** (clock-tower) (1108), with its Ghibelline merlons, is all that remains of the town's medieval fortifications.

MURANO

In 1291 the Signoria of Venice transferred the already flourishing glass factories of the city to these five small islands behind Venice, about 1 km from the Fondamenta Nuove, to reduce the risk of fire. A small Grand Canal divides the town, lined by elegant houses, formerly holiday villas for the nobility, modest-looking houses, palazzi of the old merchant bourgeoisie, shops, workshops and glass factories.

The **Museo del Vetro** is located in Palazzo Giustiniani. The collection is displayed chronologically. The archeological section has some remarkable Roman artifacts from the 1st and 3rd centuries. Upstairs is a vast collection of fine Murano glass from the 15th to 20th centuries. The **church of Ss. Maria e Donato** is a splendid example of Venetian Byzantine architecture. The *apse*, with intricate arcading, loggias and niches, dates from the 12th century, as does the free-standing bell tower. Inside, the capitals of the columns and the mosaic floor (1140) are remarkable. In the vault of the apse is a 13th-century Byzantine mosaic of the Madonna, with frescoes from the early 15th century. The top floor of Palazzo Contarini, now the main office of the Vetrerie Barovier & Toso glass factory, houses the **Museo Barovier & Toso**, with about 250 pieces of glass, most produced in the factory between 1880 and 1970. The museum archive contains more than 22,000 original drawings, old catalogues and books containing recipes for making glass. The **church of S. Pietro Martire**, rebuilt in the 15th and 16th centuries, contains art-works from churches and religious institutions suppressed by Napoleon:

The apse of Ss. Maria e Donato on Murano

on the right wall, two paintings by Giovanni Bellini (1488 and 1510-13); above the door of the sacristy, St Jerome in the Desert by Paolo Veronese (c.1566). The **Museo Parrocchiale S. Pietro Martire** was founded in 1815. It has sacred furnishings, chalices, silverware from the 12th to 19th centuries, paintings and tapestries from the 14th to 19th centuries from churches and monasteries suppressed by Napoleon.

The Barovier Marriage Cup in the Glass Museum on Murano

PORTOGRUARO [66 km]

Now 19 km from the sea, this was once a flourishing port. **Corso Martiri della Libertà** is the busiest street in the old town, lined with fine Venetian-style palaces. Immediately on the left is the early 19th-century **Duomo**, dedicated to St Andrew, with a solid Romanesque leaning bell tower with three-light windows. Inside, 16th-century altar-pieces of the Venetian School. Further on is the 15th-century *Palazzo Muschietti*, with large, pointed terracotta arches, followed by *Palazzo Moro* of the same date. No. 23 is *Palazzo de Götzen* (15th century) and No.1 is *Palazzo Dal Moro*, decorated with two- and three-light windows. The gateway at the end of the street, *Porta S. Gottardo*, was rebuilt in the 16th century. The **Loggia Comunale**, now the Town Hall, is a building from the 14th to 16th centuries, with a facade topped with merlons, Gothic windows and an outside staircase. In front of the palazzo is an elegant *well-head* with two elegant bronze cranes, the symbol of the town. In **Via del Seminario** is former *Palazzo Marzotto*, now the *Villa Comunale*. It houses the **Museo paleontologico "M. Gortani"**, with its fine collection of fossils from the Veneto and the Carnia region. Just beyond the museum is *Casa Fabrici*. The lower part of the building is Romanesque with Renaissance frescoes. Today it houses the **Museo Nazionale Concordiese**, created in 1885, with inscriptions, sculptures and various objects (a rare collection of stone weights, coins, and a 4th-century glass bowl) from excavations at the nearby Roman site of Concordia Sagittaria.

S. DONÀ DI PIAVE [38 km]

This old town criss-crossed by canals, situated in the plain on the left bank of the River Piave about 15 km from the Adriatic, was hit hard by WWI. Reconstructed in the 1920s, all the most important buildings were concentrated in one part of town. In the **Town Hall**, the "Map of the Battle of the River Piave" depicts the event which destroyed the town. The display at the **Museo della Bonifica** shows how the area of the lower Piave was reclaimed (through a display of tools, information panels and photographs). Other sections of the museum: an ethnographical collection (local traditions and customs before and after the land was reclaimed), military history (documents from WWI) and archeological finds (from the nearby Roman site of Eraclea).

STRA [30 km]

It was the success of the shoe factories of the Brenta area which brought wealth to the town. The many stately homes in the town include **Villa Pisani***, now Villa Nazionale, originally built for the family of Doge Alvise Pisani in 1740; in 1807, his indebted heirs sold the property to Napoleon. He passed it on to the Habsburgs who were succeeded by the House of Savoy and, 16 years later, the villa passed to the Italian State. Finally, in 1934, it was chosen by Mussolini as the setting for his first meeting with Adolf Hitler.
The facade facing the canal, which has a very regal air, is a splendid example of the architectural revival of the Palladian style in the Veneto in the mid-18th century. A row of caryatids supports the central balcony, above which half-columns with Corinthian capitals support the cornice, pediment and statues. The *park* can be seen through the railings on each side of the villa. Inside, little remains of the original furnishings. The central part of the villa has an atrium with rusticated columns and a splendid ballroom, with the best frescoes, with much use of trompe l'oeil to lengthen perspective. The fresco on the ceiling (*The Triumph of the Pisani Family*) is by G.B. Tiepolo

Villa Pisani at Stra

(1760-62). In the park is a **maze** (1721) of box hedges, with a central tower surrounded by two external spiral staircases. Just beyond the exedra, a narrow lane on the left leads to a moat surrounding an old ice-store. A gate and a fence divide the park from the glasshouses and the orangery, decorated with 18th-century statues. Finally you come to the elegant **stables***, with stalls for 24 horses, each marked by a column with horse rampant. Villa Pisani is the setting for the **Museo Nazionale**.

The **Museo Rossimoda della Calzatura d'Autore** is in Villa Foscarini-Rossi, built between 1617 and 1635 by Vincenzo Scamozzi for the Foscarini family. The museum has 1,500 examples of shoes produced by the Rossimoda company from the 1950s to the present day. Other rooms in the same villa house the *Collezione d'Arte Moderna* (including works by Jim Dine, David Hockney, Man Ray and Victor Vasarely), collected over many years by Luigino Rossi, who owned the villa until 2002. There is an interesting series of Pop Art designs for ladies' shoes created by American designer Andy Warhol in the 1950s, when he worked as a stylist for a shoe factory in New York.

TORCELLO

This once important town developed steadily between the 5th and 10th centuries and was gradually abandoned due to the silting up of its canals. Miraculously, only its monumental buildings have survived. A broad path leads from the landing-stage along the side of a canal past Ponte del Diavolo (Devil's Bridge) to a grassy square, the piazza of Torcello, where the buildings are a testimonial to the island's former economic and artistic wealth. In the center of the square is a stone chair called the *Throne of Attila*. The **Cattedrale**** dedicated to the Assumption is connected by a portico to the **Baptistery** and the **church of S. Fosca**. The original church dates from 639, was enlarged in 824 and partially rebuilt in 1008. In front of the cathedral, the ruins of the 7th-century *Baptistery*; a narthex begun in the 9th century but extended in the 14th and 15th centuries. An extra aisle was added to the left of the church in the 15th-century. At the back is a beautiful apse (the central apse is part of the 7th-century building, the side-apses were added in the 9th century). Next to it, the massive bell tower (11th century), one of the tallest in the lagoon. The interior, built on a basilica plan, has a nave and two side-aisles, with marble columns and a polychrome marble floor. The wooden rood-screen (depicting the twelve Apostles, 14th and 15th centuries) separates the rest of the church from the area dominated by the apse with its fine mosaic in the vault.

The iconography used in the apse is of extraordinary stylistic and thematic unity: the *Virgin* stands, holding the Child making the sign of benediction, alone on a gold background. Below, are the twelve Apostles (12th to 13th centuries). *S. Fosca* is linked to the cathedral by the narthex, its complex features culminating in a round drum which, together with the pentagonal portico, may be based on the plan of a 7th-century 'martyrium'. However, the church was built in about 1100. The interior, which reflects the complexity of the external architectural features, is built on a Greek-cross plan, one arm of which extends into the presbytery.

VERONA

Roman from 49 AD, Verona became an important hub of consular roads and a defensive outpost of primary importance, a role it continued to play for centuries. The rise to power of the Della Scala (or Scaligeri) family, in 1262, marked the start of a new building phase, with the construction of Castelvecchio and new fortifications (1283 to 1329). As a result of the town's newfound prosperity, Piazza delle Erbe and the nearby Piazza dei Signori were laid out: the former symbol and center of commercial power, the latter of political power. The Scaligeri were driven out by the Visconti (1387), who, in turn, were ousted by the Venetians (1405), under whom, in the 16th century, the city's fortunes generated a wave of artistic excellence. The first major changes came in the 18th century due to increasing friction between the local nobility and the Venetian overlords. After the French interlude (1796-1814), a brief period of "co-existence" with the Austrians (1801-1805) under Habsburg rule (1814-66) restored Verona's defensive role: the city was encircled with a massive set of fortifications. When Verona became part of Italy in 1860, its military role diminished, and disappeared entirely in the 20th century. WWII caused serious damage to the city's historical, artistic and monumental assets. In 1945, and again in the 1970s, the administration embarked on an ambitious reconstruction plan.

Piazza delle Erbe ❶

Piazza delle Erbe occupies the site of the old Roman forum. The rectangular square is surrounded by medieval houses and towers: the **fountain*** (1368) in the center incorporates a Roman statue. On the right is *Palazzo del Comune* with the high *Torre dei Lamberti* and the *Arco della Costa* (1470), so called because of the whale's rib dangling from its vault.
The arch leads into Piazza dei Signori.

Piazza dei Signori ❷

This square surrounded by monumental buildings joined by arcades, once the seat of the city's public civic institutions, looks more like a courtyard. **Palazzo del Capitanio**, with a tower built by the

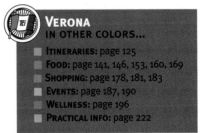

VERONA
IN OTHER COLORS...
■ **ITINERARIES:** page 125
■ **FOOD:** page 141, 146, 153, 160, 169
■ **SHOPPING:** page 178, 181, 183
■ **EVENTS:** page 187, 190
■ **WELLNESS:** page 196
■ **PRACTICAL INFO:** page 222

Scaligeri and a doorway by Michele Sanmicheli, was altered in the 19th century. **Palazzo della Prefettura**, formerly called *Palazzo del Governo* or *di Cangrande*, is an early residence of the Scaligeri (both Dante and Giotto stayed here). Built in the 14th century, restored in 1929-30, the doorway is by

Aerial view of Verona, built on a loop of the River Adige

Sanmicheli (1533). **Loggia del Consiglio**, built in the late 15th century as the Town Hall, is an elegant expression of Renaissance architecture. An arch joins it to the *Casa della Pietà*, rebuilt in 1490.

Arche Scaligere ❸

The little Romanesque *church of S. Maria Antica* (12th century) and the *Arche Scaligere* (the monumental tombs of the lords of Verona) are situated in Piazzaletto delle Arche. A 14th-century wrought-iron grille with the heraldic symbol of the Della Scala family ("scala" means "ladder") surrounds the tombs. They are portrayed as recumbent or equestrian figures covered with elaborate carved stone canopies. Inside the grille (on the left) is the **tomb of Mastino II** (died 1351), the sumptuous **tomb of Cansignorio**, the richly decorated **sarcophagus of Albert I** (died 1301) and, at the back, the hanging *memorial tablet of Giovanni della Scala* (died 1359). Above the doorway of the little church is the **tomb of Cangrande I** (died 1329). The equestrian statue of Cangrande is a copy of the original.

S. Anastasia ❹

The church of St Anastasia was built between 1290 and 1481 (restored late 19th century); it has an unfinished facade with a 14th-century **doorway*** and a bell tower (1481). *Inside*, the holy-water stoups date from the 16th century; the 1st altar on the right is by Sanmicheli (1565); in the first chapel of the right apse, a large fresco, *The Cavalli family being presented to the Virgin by Three Saints* by Altichiero (c. 1370); in the 2nd chapel, two Gothic tombs and some terracotta low reliefs (1435); in the presbytery, a large 14th-century fresco (*Last Judgment*), and the tomb of Cortesia Serego, attributed to Florentine Nanni di Bartolo (1429). The left transept leads into the *Cappella Giusti*, with a detached fresco of **St George at Trebizond***, an early work by Pisanello.

An unusual holy-water stoup in S. Anastasia

Galleria d'Arte Moderna e Contemporanea Palazzo Forti ❺

The Gallery of Modern and Contemporary Art was created in 1938 to house the bequest of Achille Forti. Housed in 18th-century Palazzo Emilei-Forti, it has about 1,000 works by Italian 19th-century artists (Hayez, Fattori, Bianchi, Savini et alia) and 20th-century artists (De Pisis, Birolli, Casarini, Casorati, Boccioni, Vedova et alia).

Duomo ❻

Dedicated to S. Maria Matricolare, the cathedral is Romanesque with 15th-century and Renaissance additions. The front has a two-tiered monumental **porch*** decorated with reliefs (1139); the 16th-century bell tower (Romanesque at the base) is unfinished. The 12th-century **apse*** is made of tuff. In the chapels and the presbytery: sculptures and paintings from the 14th to 16th centuries.

Left of the cathedral is the Romanesque **cloister** (c. 1140), with part of the mosaic floor of a paleo-Christian basilica; from it you enter the little church of *S. Elena* (a Romanesque church built on paleo-Christian foundations) and the old *baptistery of S. Giovanni in Fonte* with its 13th-century octagonal **marble font***, both 12th-century. Behind the cathedral, *Palazzo del Vescovado* has a Renaissance facade (1502).

Biblioteca Capitolare and Museo Canonicale ❼

The Chapter Library, housed in *Palazzo del Canonicato* (built 1673, rebuilt 1948) is one of the finest ecclesiastical libraries in Europe. It also houses the *Museo Pinacoteca Canonicale*, with sculptures and paintings from the 12th to 19th centuries: highlights include a relief of *St Hermagorus and St Fortunatus* (c. 1120), a *Madonna allattante* (mid-13th century) and an edicule with *Christ giving the Blessing and Saints* (15th century). The collection focuses on the Verona School of the 15th and 16th centuries, with enamels, ivories, bronze figurines, coins, medals and musical instruments from the Roman period.

S. Giorgio in Braida ❽

The church of St George and its majestic dome by Michele Sanmicheli dominate the loop of the Adige. Built between 1477 and 1536, the white marble facade was added in the 17th century. Inside

The charming cloister of the Duomo

are many fine paintings: **Baptism of Christ*** by Jacopo Tintoretto, **Madonna appearing to Saints*** by Moretto da Brescia, **Martyrdom of St George*** by Paolo Veronese. Opposite is Sanmicheli's *Porta S. Giorgio* (1525).

S. Stefano ⑨

The church, one of Verona's most important paleo-Christian buildings, was seat of a bishop until the 8th century. The facade and apse date from the 12th century. The **interior*** has a nave and two side-aisles separated by massive pilasters, with a raised presbytery and transepts. The apse has paleo-Christian and medieval features: the 10th-century ambulatory, and the capitals from the 5th- and 6th-century church; the bishop's throne (8th-century) with 12th-century decoration. The 10th-century crypt has an apse and an ambulatory.

Area archeologica del Teatro romano ⑩

Built into the hillside of Colle di S. Pietro is the Roman *theater* (early 1st century) and the little *church of Ss. Siro e Libera* (rebuilt in the 14th century and altered since). The theater is used for summer performances.

Museo Archeologico al Teatro Romano ⑪

The Archeological Museum, founded in 1924, is housed in the former convent of St Jerome (15th century). It has Roman finds from Verona and the surrounding area, and Greek and Etruscan finds from private collections and acquisitions.

S. Giovanni in Valle ⑫

The church dates from the 8th and 9th centuries, was rebuilt in 1120 and has been altered since. The interior has a nave and two side-aisles with traces of 14th-century frescoes. Below the church is a crypt with two paleo-Christian sarcophaghi: one is the *tomb of St Simon and St Jude* (4th century). Next-door to the church is the 12th-century *Canon's house*

Palazzo Giusti del Giardino ⑬

Palazzo Giusti del Giardino, built after 1572 on a U-shaped plan, is decorated with 18th-century frescoes. It has a magnificent Italianate garden, laid out like a stage set, with beautifully tended beds edged with box-hedges. An *avenue of ancient cypresses* crosses the garden to the rock-face below the *Colle di S. Zeno*. Near the rock, the garden becomes wilder: on the right is a box-hedge *maze* surrounded by pollarded cypresses and there is a wild *wood* traversed by a winding path running below the hill. By following the avenue and climbing some steps you come to a **grotto** originally decorated with stalactites, shells and mirrors, creating optical illusions. Finally, a steep winding staircase leads up to a small bell tower on the summit of the hill, with a *viewpoint* on the top, with wonderful views over Verona. A valuable collection of *Roman finds* is scattered around the beds of the garden.

S. Maria in Organo ⑭

The present church dates from 1481, but is the result of additions to the original 8th-century church. The lower part of the **facade*** was re-designed by Michele Sanmicheli, who covered it with marble and added the three arches; the top still has its original 14th-century blind arcading in tuff and brick. The interior, built on a Latin-cross plan, with a nave and two side-aisles separated by columns, has beautiful Renaissance frescoes: in the nave, stories from the Old Testament; in the apse, frescoes by Giolfino, and magnificent inlaid wooden **choir-stalls*** by Fra' Giovanni da Verona, who also carved the *panelling* in the sacristy. Below the church, a rare example of a pre-Romanesque crypt with a nave and two side-aisles, and the remains of an early medieval church.

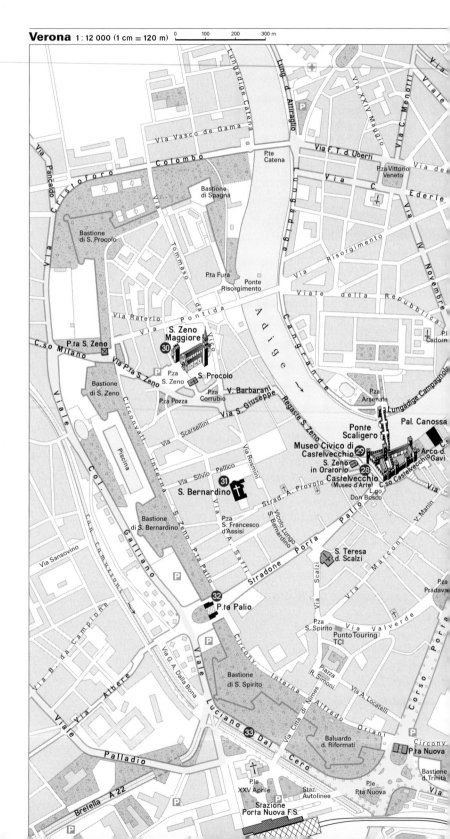

Verona 1 : 12 000 (1 cm = 120 m)

0   100   200   300 m

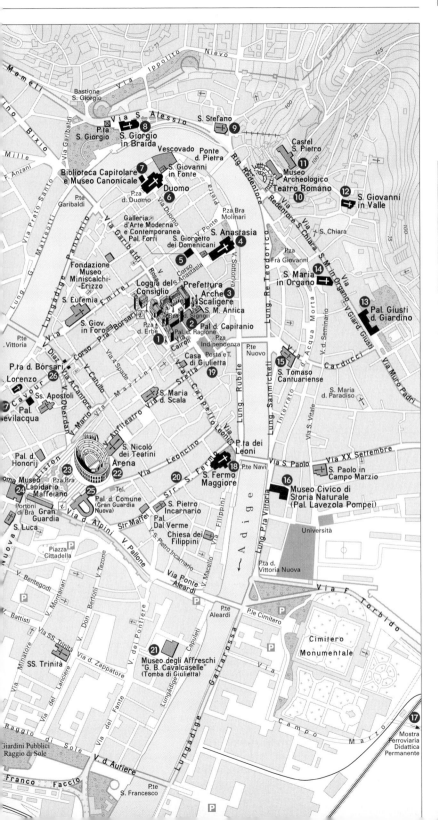

S. Tomaso Cantuariense ⑮

The church of St Thomas Becket lies on the far side of the *Ponte Nuovo*. Begun in the first half of the 15th century, consecrated in 1504, a marble doorway adorns its unfinished facade. Nearby, the church of *Ss. Nazaro e Celso* (1483) contains some fine paintings by Venetian Renaissance painters. In the left transept is the Renaissance-style *cappella di S. Biagio*.

Museo Civico di Storia Naturale ⑯

Since 1926, the 15th-century *Palazzo Lavezola Pompei*, a masterpiece by Sanmicheli, has housed the town's scientific and natural history collections. Its sections on botany, geology and paleontology, prehistory and zoology give visitors an insight into the evolution of our planet. They include a fine zoological collection and remarkable finds, such as numerous fossils from Bolca and prehistoric artifacts from early settlements around Lake Garda.

Mostra Ferroviaria Didattica Permanente ⑰

Housed in Porta Vescovo station, this railway museum has a collection of parts of 20th- century Italian and Austrian railway superstructure, prototypes of locomotives, models of steam trains, locomotives and carriages, and scale models of the Brennero railway line and other major railway networks.

S. Fermo Maggiore ⑱

The church of St Fermo is really two superimposed buildings: the lower church dates from the 11th and 12th centuries, the upper one from the 14th century. The *apses* (the smaller ones are Romanesque and the larger one is Gothic) are remarkable. The *interior* of the **upper church** has a single nave with a ship's

Verona:
S. Fermo
Maggiore

keel ceiling (1314), frescoes from the 14th and 15th centuries and sculptures from the 15th and 16th centuries; next to the ambo, a detached fresco by Stefano da Verona of *Angels with Scrolls*; halfway up the left side of the church, a Baroque chapel dedicated to the Virgin Mary with a fine altar-piece (*Madonna and saints*) (1528). 1st altar on the left, an altar-piece by Battista dal Moro and the *Brenzoni tomb* by Florentine Nanni di Bartolo (1439) are framed by a famous fresco of the **Annunciation*** by Pisanello. The right transept leads into the remains of the old Romanesque *cloister*. From here, steps lead down to the **lower church**, with frescoes dating from the 11th to 13th centuries.

Casa di Giulietta ⑲

The 13th-century house labeled *Casa di Giulietta* stands on Via Cappello. Its only connection with Shakespeare's heroine is the famous balcony overlooking the courtyard, added during restoration work in 1935. The building is also interesting because it is a fine example of Gothic domestic architecture in a Roman part of the town.
If you proceed from here into Via Leoni, you come to the remains of the Roman **Porta dei Leoni***, dating from the 1st century BC and restored in 1959.

Stradone S. Fermo ⑳

This street is lined with fine buildings from the 16th to 19th centuries, some partly rebuilt. At the end of the street, the church of *S. Pietro Incarnario*, founded in 955 but subsequently rebuilt, has Roman foundations.

Museo degli Affreschi "Giovan Battista Cavalcaselle" ㉑

Named after an art historian, Giovan Battista Cavalcaselle (1819-1897), this fresco museum is housed in the monastery of S.

Francesco al Corso. It includes architectural fragments and about 50 frescoes removed during the 19th century from palaces and churches in Verona. Highlights include the *sinopias* by Altichiero, paintings of the Verona School of the 16th to 18th centuries, Roman amphoras, medieval and modern marbles and inscriptions.

The famous balcony associated with Juliet

Arena ㉒

The third-largest amphitheater in Italy (with a seating capacity of 25,000), the "Arena" is one of the symbols of the city. Since 1913, it has been the venue of a highly prestigious international opera festival. Built in the 1st century BC, only four arches of the north wing of the outermost arcade of the amphitheater are still standing. The 2nd tier of the inner arcade is almost intact.

Piazza Bra' ㉓

Once a suburban field ("braida"), today, this square is the most popular meeting-point of the city. Part of it is laid out as a garden: to the north-east is the Arena; to the south-east, the neoclassical **Gran Guardia Nuova** or

Palazzo Municipale (1848); to the south, the *Gran Guardia* (begun in 1610, completed in 1836) and the two archways, joined to a pentagonal tower, of *Portoni della Bra'* (c. 1480). Nearby are the headquarters of the *Accademia Filarmonica* and the **Museo Lapidario Maffeiano**. Porticoed palaces line the north-west side of Piazza Brà and the *Listón*, the elegant and lively paved street where the people of Verona like to stroll.

Museo Lapidario Maffeiano ㉔

This museum is one of the oldest in Europe. Created in 1732 by Scipione Maffei to house his vast collection of inscriptions, it was donated to the city in 1882. The collection, completely reorganized in 1982, has Latin inscriptions, milestones from the Via Postumia, carved stone material, mainly from the Greek and Roman periods, but also of Etruscan and paleo-Venetian origin, including steles, funerary reliefs and small funerary urns.

Palazzo del Comune ㉕

Palazzo del Comune (or *Palazzo della Ragione*) dates from the late 12th century, but was considerably altered in the 16th century. The **courtyard***, Mercato Vecchio, is Romanesque. The palazzo incorporates the *Torre dei Lamberti*, 84 m high, begun in 1172 and completed in the mid-15th century.

Porta dei Bórsari ㉖

Porta dei Bórsari, built in the mid-1st century, was the main entrance to the Roman town. Its current medieval name refers to the "bursarii", who collected taxes for the bishop.

Corso Cavour ㉗

Corso Cavour is one of the most elegant streets in Verona. It stretches from Piazzetta di Castelvecchio, from the reconstructed arch of **Arco dei Gavi** (1st century) to Porta dei Bórsari. Palaces once owned by Verona's nobles line the street: No. 44, *Palazzo Canossa* by Michele Sanmicheli (1537); No. 19, **Palazzo Bevilacqua***, a masterpiece by Sanmicheli with an interesting facade (c. 1534). Opposite, the 12th-century church of S. Lorenzo with a Gothic archway over the entrance.

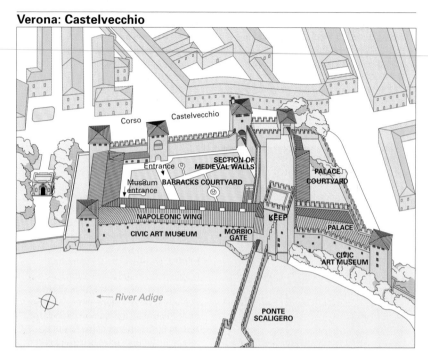

Castelvecchio 28

Castelvecchio is the most important
example of civic medieval architecture
in Verona. It was built by Cangrande II
della Scala as a residence-cum-fortress
in 1354-57. The keep dates from 1375.
An imposing brick building with towers
and merloned walls, it is bisected
by the bridge: the rectangular part on
the right, with towers at the corners and
a courtyard, was the parade-ground; on
the left, the residence of the Scaligeri
is surrounded by a double set of walls,
with two courtyards and drawbridges.
A section of walls (first half of the
12th century) incorporated within
the structure runs between the two
parts of the castle. The gate of *Porta
del Morbio* (12th century) leads onto
the bridge. Inside the castle, the
**Museo Civico Fondazione Museo
Miniscalchi-Erizzo**, inaugurated in 1990,
still feels like a noble residence.
The 16 rooms of the museum house
the collections of the Miniscalchi-Erizzo
family, including drawings, especially
by artists of the Venetian School
of the 16th and 17th centuries,
Renaissance bronzes, sacred art,
archeological finds, early weapons
and armor, examples of the decorative
arts, coins and paintings.

Museo Civico di Castelvecchio 29

The museum is housed in the rooms of
the castle (mid-14th century), the Torre
Maggiore and the Napoleonic wing,
restructured in 1957-1964 by Carlo
Scarpa. The entrance to the museum,
accessed from the courtyard, leads to
the ground-floor rooms where early
medieval and Romanesque reliefs and
inscriptions are kept, with sculptures
from the Verona area from the 14th and
15th centuries. The exhibits in the rooms
of the noble residence include detached
frescoes, paintings from the medieval
and Renaissance periods, 14th-century
sculptures and jewelry. Highlights
include the separated parts of the
Polyptych of the Holy Trinity by Turone,
the *Madonna of the Rose-garden* by
Stefano di Francia, the **Madonna of the
Quail** by Pisanello, and works by
Giovanni Bellini, Carpaccio, Crivelli,
Mantegna and Rubens. The Torre del
Mastio (keep), where the armory is
situated, leads into the Napoleonic
wing, with large paintings by Venetian
painters from the 16th to 18th centuries,
including works by Tintoretto and
Veronese. The last room concentrates
on 18th-century works, with works by
Luca Giordano, G.B. Tiepolo, Francesco
Guardi, Pietro Longhi and others.

On your way around the museum, note the equestrian statue from the tomb of Cangrande I della Scala (14th century) on a pedestal, moved here from the Arche Scaligere.

S. Zeno Maggiore ㉚

A masterpiece of Italian Romanesque architecture, the church dedicated to Verona's patron saint stands in a large, quiet square between a tower (13th to 14th centuries) of the old abbey and the bell tower (12th century). Built in the 9th century to enshrine the remains of the city's first bishop (died 380), it was rebuilt in the 12th century after the earthquake of 1117 (the apse dates from 1398). Its elegant tuff facade, decorated by an early 13th-century rose-window, has an elegant **porch*** with reliefs (1138) and a west *door* decorated with 24 12th-century bronze **panels*** (Stories from the Old and New Testaments and the Life of St Zeno). The simple, majestic *interior* has a nave and two side-aisles separated by columns, with a raised presbytery over the crypt and a ship's keel ceiling (1386). On the inner wall of the west facade: a *Crucifix* (c.1360); at the top of the right aisle, an octagonal late 12th-century *baptistery*; in the right aisle and the presbytery, frescoes from the 13th to 15th centuries; above the balustrade of the presbytery, 13th-century statues of Christ and the Apostles; above the high altar, a triptych of the **Madonna and Saints**** by Andrea Mantegna (1459); wooden choir-stalls (15th century). In the left apse: a polychrome statue of St Zeno laughing. The 13th-century **crypt** houses the (modern) tomb of St Zeno. The left aisle leads into the Romanesque *cloister* (13th to 14th century). A door on the left leads into the 12th-century *Oratorio di S. Benedetto*.

S. Bernardino ㉛

The church was built in the mid-15th century; a cloister surrounded by small columns precedes the facade, with a doorway dating from 1474. Inside the church, the two naves are decorated with paintings of the Verona School from the 15th and 16th centuries; the organ dates from 1481. Upstairs is the **Sala Morone***, an old frescoed library (1503).

Porta del Palio ㉜

Porta del Palio (1561) refers to the horse-race, the "Palio", which used to pass under it. It is the most beautiful of the gates designed by Sanmicheli.

Viale Dal Cero ㉝

On the right-hand side of Viale Luciano Dal Cero is the *Baluardo dei Riformati* and the *Bastione di S. Spirito*, built by the Austrians in the 19th century to replace sections of the 16th-century Scaligeri walls, which still encircle the town and are approximately 10 km long.

DAY TRIPS

GARDA [45 km]

This popular holiday resort shares the name of the lake (possibly from the German "*Warte*" referring to a fortress, which has since disappeared). The town has an atmosphere of days gone by and is worth visiting not only for its lake-side promenade but also for its 18th-century church, S. Maria Maggiore. A clock-tower marks the entrance to the old town with its fine palazzi.

LAGO DI GARDA

The largest of the Italian lakes, its Roman name was Benacus. At 65 m above sea-level, it has an area of 2,370 km2, is 51.6 km long, between 2.4 km

Lago di Garda, promontory of S. Vigilio

and 17.5 km wide (the southern part is wider) and 346 m deep. Of glacial origin, it occupies a long, broad valley with Lombardy to the west, the Veneto to the east and the Trentino to the north. The Sarca flows into it from the north and the Mincio, a tributary of the Po, flows out of it at Peschiera. The south of the lake has low-lying shores and is divided into two large bays by the Sirmione peninsula. The northern part is long and narrow. The west side of the lake is dominated by steep rocky cliffs, the east shore by Monte Baldo (2,218 m high). The vegetation is typically Mediterranean. Because of the mild micro-climate, olives, citrus fruits, oleanders, agaves and palm-trees thrive. It has attracted tourists since the 18th century.

The Madonna della Corona seems to be suspended in mid-air

PESCHIERA DEL GARDA [18 km]

Built on the south-eastern shore of Lake Garda, where the Mincio flows out of the lake south towards the Po, in Roman times, the town was famous for its plentiful supply of fish. Its role as a military stronghold dates from the 6th century, although Venice did not build a fortress here until 1556. Much later, under the Austrians, it became part of the Austrian "Quadrilateral", a system of fortresses built to guard the valley of the Adige. The Venetian walls now surround Piazza Betteloni, down by the harbor. In Piazza Ferdinando di Savoia, the long building is a military prison. The *parish church of S. Martino* dates from the 18th century.

S. BONIFACIO [24 km]

The modern industrial town stands on the site of the early medieval Castle of Sambonifacio, destroyed in 1243. On the edge of the town is the little church of S. Abbondio (1491). On the main road leading out of town is the **Abbazia di S. Pietro Apostolo***, founded in the 8th century, rebuilt in the 12th and altered several times. The bell tower dates from 1139. Inside the abbey, there are 14th-century frescoes.

SANTUARIO DELLA MADONNA DELLA CORONA [42 km]

This Romanesque abbey lies on a road which, even in medieval times, connected the valley of the Adige to the plain. It was built in the 16th century on a rocky spur to celebrate the apparition of a statue of the Madonna while the Turks were capturing the island of Rhodes (1522), where the holy statue was kept.

SOAVE [22 km]

The town walls form a rectangle and stretch up to the castle on the hill above the plain of Verona, on the edge of the Monti Lessini. The medieval fabric of the town, which has been awarded the TCI's "Bandiera Arancione" (Orange Flag), has some Venetian features. The vineyards around the town are justly famous. Soave is also the name of the white wine made here. The Swabians (or "*soavi*" in local dialect), came here after the Lombards and refounded the town on a Roman site.

VILLAFRANCA DI VERONA [22 km]

The architecture of the town dates mainly from the 19th century, but it was founded by the city of Verona in 1185, for agricultural and military purposes. The *Museo del Risorgimento* is housed in the 14th-century castle built by the Scaligeri (the tower is open to the public). The collection illustrates the period of uprising during the 19th century which led to independence, with weapons, prints and memorabilia. The *Museo "Nicolis" dell'Auto, della Tecnica e della Meccanica* is a collection of vintage cars, motor-bikes, bicycles, type-writers, musical instruments, cameras, engines and planes showing how techniques and engineering have evolved in transportation.

VICENZA

A Roman town in 49 BC, modern Vicenza dates from the 12th century. In 1266 it came under the rule of Padua, and was subject to the lords of Verona until 1387. In 1404 it submitted to Venice. Industry and trade flourished, and the town expanded, remaining unchanged for centuries. Between the mid-15th century and late 16th century, the town's public and private buildings were replaced, permanently altering its appearance. This period of renovation culminated in the work of Andrea Palladio (1508-80). The Basilica, Palazzo Chiericati, the Teatro Olimpico and La Rotonda are prototypes of a classical style of architecture which, continued by Vincenzo Scamozzi after Palladio's death, was to prevail until the 19th century. After WWII, new suburbs grew up so fast around the existing town that its area doubled in the space of a few decades.

Piazza Castello ❶

Piazza Castello is dominated by *Palazzo Piovini* (1656-58) and the unfinished *Palazzo Porto*, by Vincenzo Scamozzi, to a design by Palladio (late 16th century), distinctive for the three tall columns on its facade. At the end of Corso Palladio is an imposing tower, the remains of the medieval castle. Beyond the castle is *Giardino Salvi*, a park, with the Loggetta Valmarana (1592) in the Palladian style.

Corso Andrea Palladio ❷

Corso Palladio passes monumental palaces and churches from the 14th to 18th centuries. No. 13 is *Palazzo Thiene*, later Palazzo Bonin-Longare, attributed to Palladio and completed by Vincenzo Scamozzi. No. 45 is *Palazzo Capra-Clementi* (late 15th century). No. 47 is *Palazzo Thiene* (15th century), with a beautiful five-light window. No. 67 is elegant *Palazzo Braschi-Brunello* (15th century), with a portico on the ground floor. No. 147 is **Palazzo Dal Toso-Franceschini-Da Schio***, a.k.a. Ca' d'Oro. It dates from the 14th and 15th centuries.

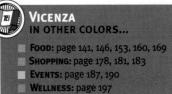

VICENZA
IN OTHER COLORS...

■ FOOD: page 141, 146, 153, 160, 169
■ SHOPPING: page 178, 181, 183
■ EVENTS: page 187, 190
■ WELLNESS: page 197
■ PRACTICAL INFO: page 224

Piazza dei Signori ❸

Piazza dei Signori is the hub of the town. On the south side is the Basilica, next to the tall, slender *Torre di Piazza* (12th to 15th centuries) (82 m high). At the far end are two fine *columns* supporting a lion of St Mark (1520) and a statue of the Redeemer (1640). On the north-west side is **Loggia del Capitaniato*** with three arches on the facade, an unfinished work by Palladio (1571-72). The long facade of the 16th-century *Palazzo del Monte di Pietà* incorporates the facade of the *chiesa di S. Vincenzo* (1389).

The solemn classical facade of Palladio's Basilica in Vicenza

Basilica ❹

The Basilica, built between 1546 and 1614, is a masterpiece by Palladio, who surrounded the medieval *Palazzo della Ragione* (15th century) with two open marble colonnaded galleries. He used the term "basilica" with the classical meaning of a place where justice is administered. A staircase on the right leads up to the loggia and the Gothic hall, which occupies the whole top floor of the building. Behind it, in Piazza delle Erbe, the medieval *Torre del Girone* is joined to the Basilica by an arch (1494).

S. Maria in Foro ⑤

The 15th-century church has an 18th-century facade; inside the Gothic building, an altar-piece by Benedetto Montagna (1st altar on the right) and a late 16th-century altar (2nd on the left).

Pinacoteca Civica di Palazzo Chiericati ⑥

Palazzo Chiericati by Palladio (1551) houses one of the region's most comprehensive art collections. The medieval section includes works from the 13th to 16th centuries, including a *Dormitio Virginia* by Paolo Veneziano, a *Crucifixion*, the central panel of the "Jan Crebbe Triptych" by the Flemish artist Hans Memling and **The Three Ages of Man** by Van Dyck; a fine collection of paintings of the Venetian School of the 15th to 18th centuries, including works by Paolo Veronese, Jacopo Tintoretto, and an *Immaculate Conception* and **Time discovers the Truth** by G.B. Tiepolo. The *Gallery of Drawings and Prints* has 33 works signed by Palladio. There is also a *coin collection* and a *sculpture collection*; works by masters such as Alessandro Vittoria, Jacopo Sansovino and others. A contemporary collection was donated to the gallery in 1988-1989, with works by Carrà, De Pisis, Tancredi et alia.

Teatro Olimpico ⑦

Palazzo del Territorio was part of the medieval Castle of S. Pietro, built c. 1266, and transformed many times over the centuries until it incorporated Palladio's last work, the Olympic Theater, begun in 1580 and finished by his son Silla in 1583. Porta dell'Armamentario (1600) leads into the courtyard where the theater was built over the palace prisons. The *theater* is a Renaissance version of a Roman theater. Almost half the space is occupied by the semi-circular auditorium, with 13 rows and surrounded by an elegant colonnade and a balustrade with statues (added 1751). The orchestra is lower than the stage. The fixed scenery is based on the "frons scenae" of a Roman theater. There are three openings in the stage set, designed with perfect perspective by Vincenzo Scamozzi to look like real streets. The wood and stucco scenery has two tiers of Corinthian columns and is decorated with niches with statues, friezes, columns and pilasters. The stage set was designed in 1584 for a production of "Oedipus Rex" by Sophocles and has remained in situ since the 1585 performance. Scamozzi also designed the Odeon (1608), the largest of the three rooms once used for meetings of the Accademia Olimpica, one of the town's most active associations.

Gallerie di Palazzo Leoni Montanari ⑧

The gallery of Palazzo Leoni Montanari houses one of the Banca Intesa's finest art collections. On the first floor is an important collection of 18th-century Venetian paintings. The highlights are Pietro Longhi's 14 canvases depicting the Venetian society at the time; urban landscapes and *capricci* by Canaletto, Francesco Guardi and Luca Carlevarijs. On the top floor is a display of 130 *Russian icons*, one of the most important collections in Western Europe (13th to 19th centuries).

S. Corona ⑨

The church of S. Corona, with its marble doorway and elegant bell tower, was begun in 1260. It has a nave and two side-aisles and a long, raised presbytery (1489). Above the 3rd altar on the right is an **Adoration of the Magi*** by Paolo Veronese (1573). In the apse are wooden choirstalls (late 15th century) with fine marquetry. The chapel to the left of the high altar contains a fine 14th-century reliquary with *a thorn from Christ's Crown of Thorns*, donated by St Louis IX of France and only displayed on Good Friday. In the left aisle, at the 5th altar is a **Baptism of Christ**** by Giovanni Bellini (1435-1516). The adjoining cloister houses the *Natural History Museum* and the *Archeological Museum*.

The brick bell tower of the church of S. Corona

Museo Naturalistico e Archeologico ⑩

The natural history and archeological museums founded in 1855 occupy the monastic complex adjoining the church of S. Corona. The former focuses on the wildlife of the nearby Colli Bèrici (Bèrici Hills). It studies the environmental changes during the various geological periods, as well as the local flora and fauna. The archeological collection has finds from numerous excavations in the area. The exhibits from the Paleolithic and Neolithic are particularly interesting, and include Neolithic **vases with a square rim***. Pre-Roman culture is also well-represented, with a collection of **small bronze plates*** depicting male and female figures. The collections also contain exhibits from the Roman and early medieval periods.

Contra' Zanella ⑪

Contrà Zanella has some remarkable buildings. No. 2 is Palazzo Sesso-Zen (14th and 15th centuries). No. 1, on the corner of Piazzetta S. Stefano is the merloned Palazzo Negri De Salvi (late 15th century). On the left, the *church of S. Stefano* has a **Madonna with Child and Saints*** in the left transept by Palma the Elder.

Contra' Porti ⑫

Some splendid palaces overlook this street. No. 11 is the grand **Palazzo Barbaran-Porto**, by Palladio (1571) which will shortly open as a museum about the life and work of the architect. No. 12 is *Palazzo Thiene*, commissioned in 1545, based on a design by Palladio: the east front (1490) of the palace has a terracotta doorway; the courtyard and the rear facade looking onto Contrà Zanella are by Palladio (1558). No. 14 is the Gothic *Palazzo Trissino-Sperotti* (1450-60), with an elegant balcony. At No. 19, *Palazzo Porto-Colleoni* dates from the late 14th century. No. 21 is an unfinished work by Palladio, *Palazzo Iseppo da Porto* (c. 1552), later *Palazzo Festa*.

S. Lorenzo ⑬

The facade of this imposing 13th-century brick church has a marble **doorway*** with sculptures (1344). Inside, various funerary monuments date from the 14th to 16th centuries: at the end of the right transept, the *altar of the Pojana family* (1474), with a 16th-century *Crucifixion*. The cloister dates from c. 1492.

Romanesque decoration in the doorway of S. Lorenzo

Duomo ⑭

The cathedral was built between the 13th and 16th centuries. Its facade, with elegant polychrome marble decoration and blind arcading in the lower tiers, dates from 1467. Across the road from the elegant apse (1482-1508) is an 11th-century *bell tower*. Inside, there is cross-vaulting above the single nave. The side-chapels contain various paintings: an Adoration of the Magi by Francesco Maffei (3rd altar on the right). There are Roman remains below the cathedral.

Casa Pigafetta ⑮

The facade of the house (1444) is richly decorated with carved columns and reliefs with a recurring spiral motif. This is the birthplace of famous navigator Antonio Pigafetta, who accompanied Magellan on the first circumnavigation of the globe (1519-22) and kept a diary of his epic voyage.

Palazzo vescovile ⑯

Erected in 1818 and partly rebuilt in 1947-52, the courtyard features the splendid **loggia Zeno*** (c. 1485). On the south side of Piazza del Duomo, next to *Palazzetto Roma* (1599, now the Tourist Information Office), is the entrance to the **Roman cryptoporticus**, probably part of a 1st-century BC house.

Ss. Felice e Fortunato ⑰

The basilica of St Felix and St Fortunatus, based on the original 4th-century church, stands on the site of a cemetery, supposedly the burial place of the Christian martyr Felix. Around the year 1000, the crypt was built, and

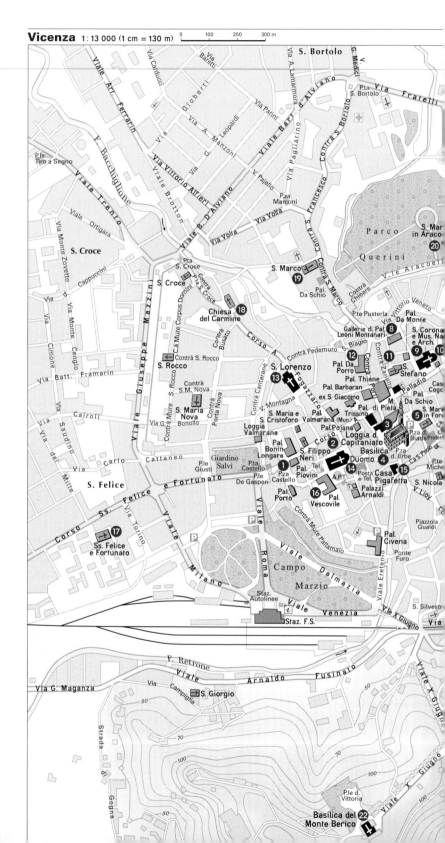

Vicenza 1:13 000 (1 cm = 130 m)

0   100   200   300 m

86

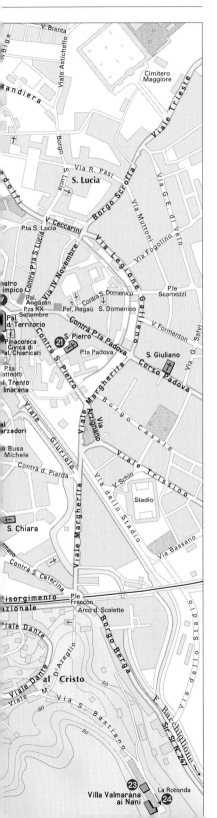

modified in the 12th century. The doorway (1154) has the remains of some 11th-century frescoes. The *Romanesque bell tower* to the left has an octagonal top from the 15th century. Inside, votive inscriptions and pieces of mosaic floor. The high altar was originally a 2nd-century Roman sarcophagus. A doorway on the right of the presbytery leads to the *martyrion* where the remains of the martyr are kept. Built in the early 6th century, the arches and the pendentives of the dome are decorated with mosaics on a gold background.

Chiesa del Carmine ⓲
The church incorporates doorways and other features from the church of S. Bartolomeo (14th to 15th centuries), now demolished. Inside, above the 3rd altar on the right, *Eternal Father and the Dead Christ* by Paolo Veronese. Above the 2nd altar on the left, a *Deposition* by Jacopo Bassano.

S. Marco ⓳
The church (1727) has a splendid facade. Above the 2nd altar on the right, **St Theresa in Ecstasy** by Sebastiano Ricci.

S. Maria in Aracoeli ⓴
One of the few Baroque monuments in Vicenza, it was possibly designed by Guarino Guarini and completed in 1680. Built on an elliptical plan, it has an elaborate high altar.

S. Pietro ㉑
This Gothic church (15th century) has a late 16th-century facade. The nearby hospice (on the right of the atrium is a *monument to the founder* by Antonio Canova) has a 15th-century **cloister*** with a portico, a loggia, and arches with terracotta decoration. A doorway off the cloister leads to the *Oratorio di S. Pietro* (1414), with a remarkable 18th-century statue of the Virgin.

Basilica del Monte Bèrico ㉒
A monumental portico with 18th-century chapels lines the road leading up to the **church of Monte Bèrico***. The present church, built on a Latin-cross plan (1687-1703), incorporates the original church founded in 1428 on the site where the Virgin Mary once appeared

(in 1426). Inside, the presbytery is formed by the early oratory, with a much revered statue of the Virgin (1430) above the altar; above the altar on the right, a **Pietà** by Bartolomeo Montagna (1500). In the Refectory is a magnificent painting by Paolo Veronese of the **Supper of St Gregory the Great**** (1572).

Villa Valmarana ㉓

Villa Valmarana*, also known as *Villa ai Nani* because of the statues decorating the garden wall, dates from 1665-70. The interiors of the villa and the guest quarters are decorated with extraordinary **frescoes*** by G.B. and G.D. Tiepolo (1757).

La Rotonda ㉔

The beautiful villa of **La Rotonda****(1567), the most famous of all Palladio's villas, can be reached by a footpath from Villa Valmarana. Finished by Vincenzo Scamozzi in 1606, it was built on a square plan. It has four symmetrical pronaoi and is topped by a dome, the underside of which is decorated with frescoes.

La Rotonda, Palladio's masterpiece

ASIAGO [62 km]

This modern town was completely rebuilt after the destruction resulting from WWI. Now a center for tourism and winter sports, it is situated on the Asiago Plateau (a.k.a. the *Plateau of Seven Towns*), of which it is the chief town and after which it is named. On Colle Leiten is the *war cemetery*, inaugurated in 1938 in memory of the soldiers who died in WWI: above the large ossuary-crypt stands an imposing four-sided stone portico. Inside, the **Museo del Sacrario Militare** has exhibits from the war and a scale model of the area reconstructing the events which, from 1916, for more than two years, dominated the Asiago Plateau. The **Museo Naturalistico Didattico** has reconstructions of typical local Alpine environments and information about local wildlife.

BASSANO DEL GRAPPA [35 km]

The architectural fabric of Bassano, which belonged to Venice from 1404, has traces of medieval buildings. **Piazza Garibaldi** is dominated by the tall *Torre civica* (13th century) and the **church of S. Franceso**, of the same date. Inside the church are fragments of *frescoes* (1400), a Baroque altar in the chapel on the left and, in the apse, a wooden *Crucifix*, a late work by Guariento (14th century). Since 1840, the **Museo Civico** has occupied the former monastery of St Francis. It has an archeological section and a fine art collection with works mainly from the Venetian School, from the 12th to 19th centuries.There are several particularly fine works by Pietro Longhi and G.D. Tiepolo; a fine collection of 18th-century Italian paintings, by artists ranging from Francesco Hayez to Medardo Rosso. The *print collection* traces

Designed by Palladio, the bridge across the Brenta has always been the symbol of Bassano del Grappa

the history of the city and the *drawing collection* includes 2,000 of Antonio Canova's works. Other highlights include a lapidary collection, prehistoric and Roman finds, a collection of Greek vases from the 4th to 3rd centuries BC, an extensive pottery section and a coin collection.

On **Piazza della Libertà** is the small *Loggia del Comune*, with its characteristic loggia, *Palazzo del Municipio* (18th century), and the church of **S. Giovanni Battista**, founded in 1308 and rebuilt in the late 18th century. During the Middle Ages, **Piazzotto Monte Vecchio** was Bassano's main square, overlooked by *Palazzetto del Monte di Pietà* (15th century), with inscriptions and coats-of-arms on the facade.

Palazzo Pretorio, built in 1275, has a doorway from 1543. From the 14th to 18th centuries it was the Town Hall. The beautiful 18th-century patrician residence of **Palazzo Sturm** houses the **Museo della Ceramica**, a collection of Bassano's famous ceramic ware, with hundreds of objects from local ceramic workshops, ranging from early fragments of medieval ceramics with sgraffito decoration to valuable examples of modern ceramics. **Ponte Vecchio** is the name of the pretty wooden bridge spanning the River Brenta, designed by Andrea Palladio in 1569, destroyed eight times by floods and war (last rebuilt in 1948). On one side of the bridge, the **Museo degli Alpini** overlooks the

river. It contains mementoes and photographs from both World Wars and tells the story of the bridge. There are finds from excavations as well as material from the battle-fields and an interesting reconstruction of a WWI trench. On the other side, **Villa Veggia-Bonaguro** is decorated with frescoes by pupils of Veronese and holds exhibitions of ceramics and craft products. The **Museo della Grappa "Jacopo Poli"** is located in 15th-century Palazzo delle Teste. The museum was created by the Poli family, who own the distillery (dates from 1898). The exhibitions focus on the history of grappa-distilling since it first began, showing how methods have changed; the production cycle of grappa, from the grape-harvest until the grappa comes out of the still. The *library* has a fine collection of antique and more recent specialist books on the subject. One of the most important is a volume entitled *Liber de arte distillandi* by Hieronymus Brunschwig (1500), the first book ever printed on the subject of grappa. The **Duomo** stands within the precinct of the *Castello superiore* (the entrance is a doorway under a 13th-century tower). The old church of S. Maria dates from before the year 1000, but has been altered several times. It has a sturdy campanile with a 13th-century tower. The **Tempio Votivo dei Caduti** is a large, modern war memorial containing the remains of many soldiers who died in WWI.

MARÒSTICA [28 km]

A merloned wall built by the Scaligeri in the 14th century connects the castle on the hill (Castello Superiore) above the town with the castle (Castello Inferiore) below. Because there were two castles, the town could be defended more easily and it had complete control over local trade routes. The town, which has been awarded the TCI's "Bandiera Arancione" (Orange Flag), is famous for a human chess tournament (held on the second Sunday of September but only in even years), commemorating a "duel" which took place here in 1454 for the hand of the Lionella, daughter of the local Venetian governor. The **Museo dei Costumi della Partita a Scacchi** is an exhibition of the costumes used in the

Maròstica, the traditional chess game with humans as the pieces

game of chess. A few meters away from Castello Superiore is the **Museo Ornitologico "Angelo Fabris"**, with one of the largest collections of birds in Europe, (more than a thousand specimens). It organizes flying demonstrations with specially trained birds of prey and guided tours of important bird sites in the area. The **Museo "Cappelli di Paglia di Maròstica"** is an exhibition about the local tradition of making straw hats. The craft skill of plaiting straw to make hats and bags was so important by the mid-17th century that the town's products were exported all over Italy, to Europe and North America.

RECOARO TERME [44 km]

In the upper reaches of the Agno, this spa town is set against the backdrop of the rocky Piccole Dolomiti. In 1689, Count Lelio Piovene discovered the properties of the ferruginous spring water here. A few decades later, Venice declared that it was a "public asset", and had the first spa establishment built. There are several mineral water springs and two spa complexes, Fonti Centrali and Fonti Staccate.

SCHIO [24 km]

Situated in an area crossed by key communication routes for three millennia, the town rose to importance after 1123. It became a textile town under Venetian rule (1406-1796). Schio's importance in the wool trade increased when Vicenza granted a concession in 1701, permitting the town to produce "refined cloth". Later, the business zeal of nobleman Niccolò Tron improved the town's reputation even further. In 1873, a branch of the Lanificio Rossi woollen mill, one of the largest woollen companies in Italy, opened its doors here.
On the town's main square, the **Duomo**, the old church of St Peter was altered in the 18th and 19th centuries and extended in 1879. Not far away, **Palazzo Da Schio**, is decorated in the neoclassical style. A plaque on the wall recalls that a member of the family was a pioneer of airships. On the top of the hill are the ruins of the **Castello**, destroyed in 1514. The **church of S. Francesco***, built on a central plan in 1436, was extended by adding a Gothic nave and bell tower (1520-22). Inside the church, a fresco cycle depicting the *Order of the Franciscans* (15th to 16th centuries) and remarkable wooden choir-stalls (1509). The **Fabbrica alta** is a large, six-storey building with 330 windows and 125 cast-iron weight-bearing columns completed in 1862. Opposite is the *garden* (1859-78) named after the inventor of the Jacquard weaving technique.

THIENE [20 km]

This little town at the foot of the Asiago Plateau is a farming town and industrial center. A cast-iron and copper town in the Middle Ages, it became a textile center in the 16th century. In the center of the town is the heavily fortified **Villa Da Porto-Colleoni***, now called *Villa Thiene*, completed in 1476, with a portico of pointed arches on the facade.

GORIZIA

Scene of conflict between different peoples and cultures, its language and culture are Italian. Its past is mainly Austrian and its territory stretches from the Friuli plain to the Slovenian mountains beyond a border which, since 1947, has run around its town center. It owes its medieval development to the fortunes of the Counts of Lurngau who, as the protectors of the Patriarch of Aquileia (from 1125), controlled access to the peninsula. As a cross-roads of trade with Central and Eastern Europe it grew fast. The opening of the railway in the 19th century brought further growth. Gorizia also discovered its vocation as a health resort. Rich members of the Austro-Hungarian bourgeoisie and nobility flocked to its hotels and villas with gardens. During WWI, the town was destroyed by bombing. Reconstruction under Fascism was rapid, but other problems arose at the end of WWII, when the border decided in 1947 with Yugoslavia, which ran around part of the town, proved to be an "iron curtain" between the Soviet and Western blocks. Gorizia lost nine-tenths of its territory, with serious repercussions on the economy. Since 1948, because it was left without a center, the Slovenian town of Nova Gorica has grown up beyond the border.

Bridge over the Isonzo near Gorizia

Duomo ❶

Dedicated to the Christian martyrs Hilary and Tazianus, patron saints of the town, the cathedral is an amalgamation of the churches of St Hilary, recorded in 1342, and St Acazio. It became a cathedral (1752) and was restored in the late 19th century and again between 1925 and 1928, to repair damage from the bombs of WWI. Inside, the eye is drawn to the high altar, masterpiece of Giovanni Pacassi (1706), with an altar-piece by Giuseppe Tominz depicting the Madonna, the town's patron saints and S. Carlo (1823). The choir with two bays belongs to the original church of St Hilary.

Via Rastello ❷

The town's main street (14th century), now a pedestrian precinct, leads from Piazza della Vittoria towards the Duomo and way up to the castle. The buildings on either side date from various periods.

Borgo Castello ❸

Borgo Castello dominates the town center from its hill and is encircled by a ring of defensive walls built by the Venetians in 1508-09. It includes the *Castello*, built within a second circle of walls, and the *Borgo*, accessed through *Porta Leopoldina* (1606). This was the original nucleus of the town. It grew up within the medieval walls, reaching its height between the 14th and 16th centuries. Of the medieval town, half-destroyed in WWI and restored in 1938, few buildings survive: some museums and the Gothic *church of S. Spirito* (1398), with a small belfry and a terracotta rose-window.

Musei Provinciali di Gorizia a Borgo Castello ❹

The museum complex, located in 16th-century palaces, has several parts. Works of art from various periods are housed in one art gallery and another focuses on 20th-century art. There is an exhibition of pieces from the Palazzo Attems-

Petzenstein museum, closed for many years. The *Museo della Moda e delle Arti Applicate* has exhibits including yarns, fabrics and costumes from the 18th and 19th centuries, tools and looms. Casa Formentini has other exhibitions on folk traditions and customs in the basement, with reconstructions of domestic rooms and craft workshops. The *Museo storico della Grande Guerra* describes in detail the 12 battles fought on the Isonzo (1915-1917) to capture Gorizia. The reconstruction of a trench and a room dedicated to General Armando Diaz (1861-1928), supreme commander of military operations from 1917 are impressive.

Castello ⑤

The castle dates from the 11th century and was rebuilt after WWI. It houses collections of medieval furniture and objects, some paintings of the Venetian School and fragments of 16th-century frescoes. The Sala della Didattica on the second floor is devoted to Gorizia's medieval history.

Piazza della Vittoria ⑥

Below the castle on the hill, the square was used for markets and civic ceremonies. On one side is the Baroque *church of S. Ignazio*. The 18th-century *fountain* with Neptune and the Tritons is by Nicolò Pacassi. In the center, the *colonna di S. Ignazio* (1640-88) marks the spot where masses were held during the Plague.

Chiesa di Sant'Ignazio ⑦

This is one of the most important Baroque buildings in the Gorizia area. The church was begun in 1654 and almost a century to complete. Its imposing facade has two domed bell-towers. The complex marble decoration includes a statue of St Ignatius. In the left-hand niche: a statue of Joseph. In the right-hand niche: a statue of John the Baptist. Inside, the single nave has a barrel vault. The length and height of the nave and the presbytery are identical, adding to the grandeur of the church. At the far end is a trompe l'oeil fresco of the Glory of St Ignazius by Christoph Tausch. The Baroque interior, with its marble altars with columns, has remained virtually intact.

Sinagoga and Museo ebraico ⑧

Built in 1756, the synagogue fell into disuse when the Jewish community was exterminated. Restored in 1984, and situated on the first floor, it is open to the public. Its 18th-century interior is perfectly preserved, with a fine women's gallery and a tabernacle supported by black twisted marble columns. On the ground floor, the *Museo Gerusalemme sull'Isonzo* (1998) tells the story of Gorizia's Jewish community.

Palazzo Coronini Cronberg ⑨

The garden of Palazzo Coronini Cronberg is one of many gardens and parks which give Gorizia the appearance of a "garden-

View of Piazza della Vittoria and the church of S. Ignazio

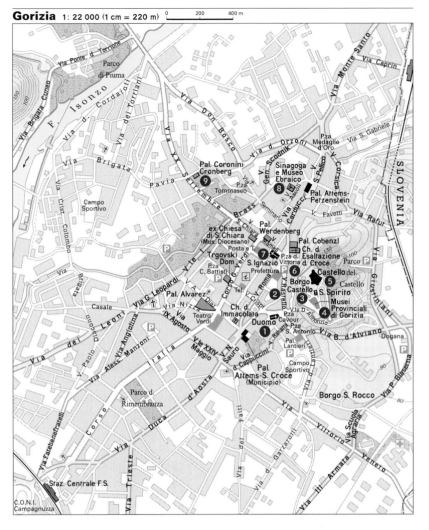

Gorizia 1: 22 000 (1 cm = 220 m)

city". A plan drawn up at the end of the 19th century was to have transformed Gorizia into a kind of Austro-Hungarian version of Nice. In 1870, Count Alfredo Coronini designed the garden at the palazzo, using the lie of the land to create romantic view-points, and perspectives which reflected the tenets of the English garden in vogue at the time. In 1990, the last owner, Count Guglielmo Coronini, left his assets to the town. The late 16th-century palazzo contains paintings, furniture, porcelain, jewellery, silverware, carpets, prints, drawings, coins and period costumes. The palazzo has an impressive archive with thousands of documents dating from the 13th to 20th centuries, and a library of more than 16,000 books.

DAY TRIPS

CORMÒNS [13 km]

The Collio hills are covered with vineyards where the excellent Collio Doc wines are made. The town of Cormòns has always been the center of its wine industry. The oldest part of the town is its medieval walls, around which the town developed in the 17th and 18th centuries. Apart from wine, small and medium-size companies make chairs and furniture. The **Duomo*** (1736-70) is worthy of note. The interior has a single nave with six altars in niches and a barrel vault. Next to the cathedral, the *Casa dell'antica Pieve* houses the **Museo del Duomo**, with documents, sacred vessels and some fine wooden sculptures.

Gorizia Castle

The imposing silhouette of the castle dominates the town. It has always been the symbol of the town, and, in fact the town began within its walls. Having received the territory of nearby Salcano (now in Slovenia) from Emperor Otto III, the Count of Friuli decided to build a fort here to control the surrounding area. In 1202, the counts of Gorizia replaced this primitive building with a castle, adding the Palazzo dei Conti (Counts' Palace) soon after. This became the administrative center of the county of Friuli. The three-storey-high structure with merloned battlements and wooden towers lasted until the 16th century, when the introduction of firearms necessitated the modernization of the fortifications. In the four centuries of Hapsburg rule which followed the fall of the local counts, the castle shed its medieval appearance and, by the 17th century, had become a barracks and a prison. But, after nine hundred years of history, it was finally destroyed by the bombing raids of the WWI. Restoration work carried out in the 1930s tried to recreate the lines of the 16th-century castle.

1 Granary
2 Count's room
3 Palace entrance
4 Count's dining-room
5 Kitchen
6 Loggetta of the Madonnina
7 Base of an 11th-C tower
8 Small portico
9 Guest quarters
10 Wooden balcony
11 Chemin-de-ronde
12 State Hall
13 Knights' Banqueting Hall
14 Cell
15 Entrance to the torture chamber
16 Prison corridor
17 Internal balcony
18 Palatine Chapel
19 Well
20 Corte dei Lanzi (courtyard)
21 Corridor leading to the guard-room, the old Salcano Gate and the Bastion
22 Veranda

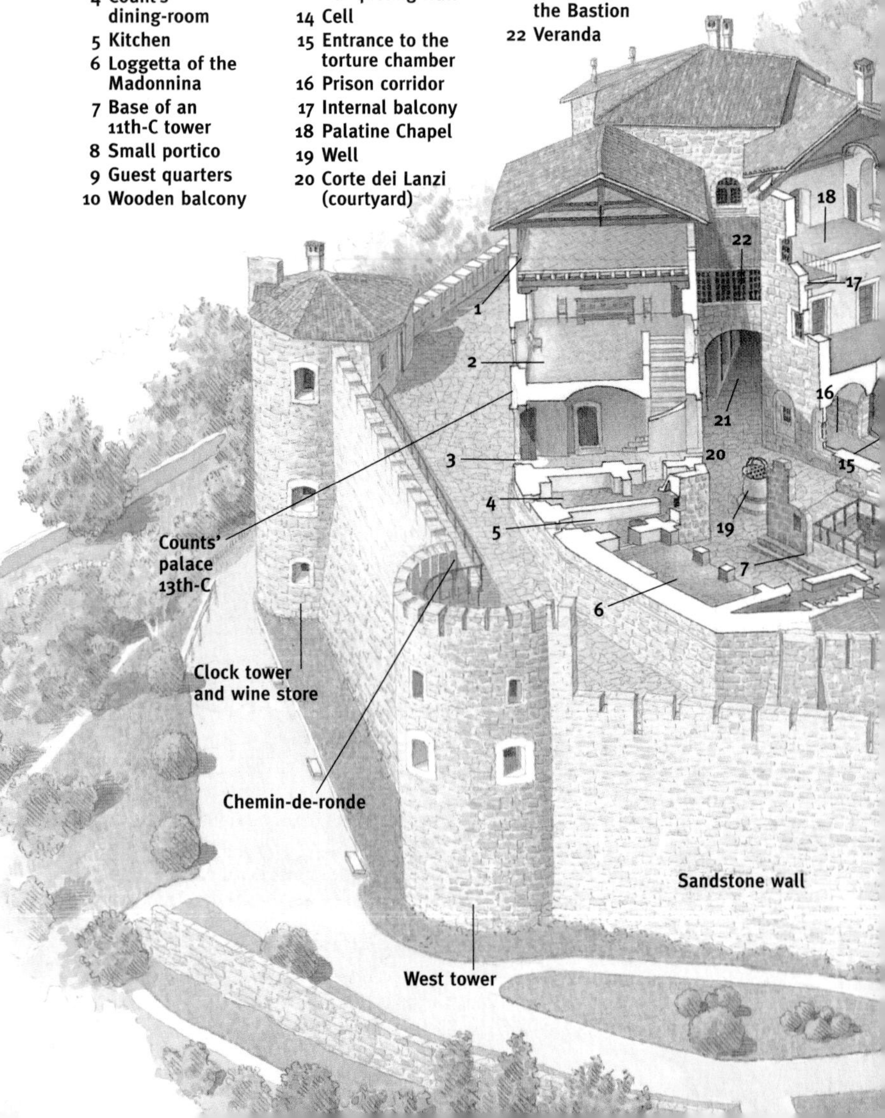

Counts' palace 13th-C

Clock tower and wine store

Chemin-de-ronde

Sandstone wall

West tower

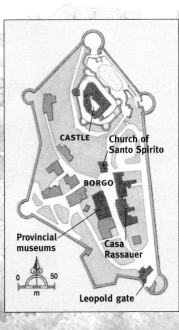

CASTLE

Church of Santo Spirito

BORGO

Provincial museums

Casa Rassauer

0   50
m

Leopold gate

Palazzo degli stati provinciali 15th-C

Piazzale delle Milizie

South-east tower

12

11

4   13

10

9

8

Castle entrance-gate with the lion of st Mark

Machicolation for pouring boiling oil or tar

Venetian palace (16th-17th-C)

South tower

GRADISCA D'ISONZO [12 km]

Sections of wall, bastions, gates and towers encircle the old town center. This is what remains of the 15th-century fortress built by the Venetians on the right bank of the Isonzo, where it was built in a "fortified place" and which, from the 10th century, had to be defended against the Turks and the counts of Gorizia. Leonardo da Vinci consulted on the building of the fortress. The Habsburgs altered it during their long rule (1509-1918). The **Duomo** dedicated to St Peter and St Paul derives from the extension of an earlier building (1656-59). The Baroque facade (1752) was altered in the 1990s. Inside, the high altar dates from 1690, its 16th-century altar-piece framed with a fake red-marble drape.

Close to the cathedral, the **Casa Corona** complex (16th and 17th centuries) was converted into a hospital and a home for the elderly in 1627 and includes the 18th-century *cappella di S. Giovanni*.

The **Museo Documentario della Città** is housed in a wing of Palazzo Torriani (1644-1705), now the Town Hall, at various times residence of the rulers of the county of Gradisca, headquarters of the Viceroy of Italy, Eugenio di Beauharnais, and seat of military command during WWI and WWII. The museum has exhibits from various periods, from archeological finds to old photographs, which reconstruct the history of the town and its Jewish community. Next-door, the **Galleria Regionale d'Arte Contemporanea "Luigi Spazzapan"** has works by the artist who born here, an exponent of the Julian Futurist Movement, and by other contemporary artists from Friuli.

GRADO [99 km]

Narrow streets and noisy squares form the background for Grado's rare paleo-Christian buildings. The inhabitants of Aquileia fled from Attila the Hun and the Lombards to this island between sea and lagoon. The modern part of the town is an elegant seaside resort, a well-known spa. In the early days, visitors eager for sea and sunshine flocked here from Central Europe by carriage and ferry. In the town center stands the **Basilica di S. Eufemia**. Built on a classical basilica plan, the cathedral was built in the 6th century over a small 4th- to 5th-century church. Above the 15th-century bell-tower is a statue of St Michael (1462). Inside the church, Roman columns with fine capitals separate the nave and two side-aisles. It has a broad apse and a magnificent 6th-century *floor mosaic*. The 11th-century ambo has reliefs with the symbols of the Evangelists, while the presbytery is delineated by 6th-century plutei. The silver altar-piece on the high altar dates from 1372. The apse has 15th-century frescoes and panels. At the sides and at the entrance to the sacristy are more floor mosaics. To the right of the basilica is a **Museo Lapidario**, with Roman and early Christian fragments: Latin inscriptions, pieces of 2nd- and 5th-century Roman sarcophagi, paleo-Christian and early medieval architectural fragments, a 5th-century sarcophagus and part of a 6th-century paleo-Christian sarcophagus from the atrium of the Baptistery. Roman sarcophagi line the path leading

The Lion of Venice on a column in Piazza dell'Unità d'Italia in Gradisca

S. Maria di Barbana, in the lagoon off Grado

The Lido on the south side of Grado, facing the open sea

Giulia. Two rooms are on the ground floor, while upstairs, the Sala Marangoni is devoted to the work of the xylographer who lived and worked here, and whose engraving skills were known all over Europe.

The *Rocca* (fort) on the hill dominates the town.

The *Museo paleontologico cittadino della Rocca* in the tower belongs to a local caving association, which had the rooms of the pre-Roman fort specially restored to house the exhibits. Opened in 1970, it has paleontological, historical and natural exhibits. They include fossilized fish from Palazzo (Gorizia) from the Cretaceous period (85 million years ago).

to the **Battistero**, left of the basilica. Built in the 5th century on an octagonal plan, it has a hexagonal font. Further left is the little church of **S. Maria delle Grazie** (4th and 5th centuries, altered in the 6th century) with a mosaic floor and a restored sculpted marble transenna, both 6th- century. Grado is famous for its **beach**. In fact, in 1873, when the local climate and environmental conditions were found to be beneficial for treating certain ailments in children, a children's seaside hospice was built based mainly on heliotherapy. Grado became a tourist resort in 1892, when the Austrian government added Grado to the list of Austro-Hungarian health spas. From then on, the town's roles of health spa and resort merged, and the town expanded. To improve the accommodation facilities, hotels were built, often becoming treatment centers in their own right.

REDIPUGLIA [21 km]
The village below Monte Castellazzo is the site of an early Venetian castle with Roman, Lombard and Frankish features. The town is famous for its **sacrario*** (war cemetery), begun in 1936, inaugurated by Mussolini in 1938 and completed in 1940. The graves contain the remains of 100,000 soldiers of the 3rd Army, its commander, the Duke of Aosta, and known and unknown soldiers who died during WWI and were brought here from other cemeteries. The *Museo Storico-Militare del Sacrario Militare,* created in 1971, contains weapons, uniforms and memorabilia of soldiers who fought in the battles of the Isonzo. Pieces of artillery decorate the nearby Parco della Rimembranza.

MONFALCONE [25 km]
This town, one of the largest shipyards in the world, began its industrial vocation in the second half of the 19th century, when spinning-mills and chemical industries were built in this area: the port and shipyards boosted the town's growth. The *Galleria Comunale d'Arte Contemporanea di Monfalcone "La Comunale"*, in the town center, is the result of the imaginative restoration of a covered market, the largest and most original gallery of contemporary art in Friuli-Venezia

SACRARIO DI OSLAVIA [5 km]
The war memorial was built in 1938 to honour the soldiers who died in the WWI. A flight of steps leads up to the triangular monument with its massive central tower and three smaller towers at the corners. Vaguely resembling a fort, it contains the bodies of almost 60,000 soldiers, brought here from the Isonzo cemeteries. From the surrounding terraces, there are views over the valley of the Isonzo, and Monte Sabotino, northern stronghold of the defences of Gorizia during WWI.

The Noncello (ancient Naone) has been navigable since ancient times and a key means of communication, explaining why the area is documented as early as 897. In 1192-94 it is cited as Portus Naonis. Pordenone began its ascent, goods were unloaded here and proceeded to Austria. Venice conquered it in the early 16th century. Since 1866 it has been part of Italy, and soon discovered the business flair now shared by most of the companies in the Province. But for much of the 20th century, times were hard in an area where livelihoods depended on farming. Towns and villages in the Alpine foothills and the plain were long to feel the impact of emigration. After the WWII, the rise of industry in the plain increased the status of Pordenone in the local economy. In 1968, it became a Province and was granted special autonomy with regard to the administration of the city and the surrounding territory.

Corso Vittorio Emanuele ❶

The main axis of the old town, Corso Vittorio Emanuele is lined by buildings in the Gothic, Renaissance and Baroque styles. Starting from *Piazza Cavour*, the focal point of growth in the 19th century, notice *Casa Simoni* (13th century); on the left, *Casa Odozzilli* with terracotta two-light windows (14th century) and *Casa Pittini* also 14th century. On the left, Via del Cristo leads to the *church of S. Maria degli Angeli*, founded in 1309, with a marble doorway (1510) and a fine side door (1551). Inside are fragments of 14th-century frescoes and a 16th-century wooden crucifix. Further along the main street is *Palazzo Tinti* (18th century) and, opposite, the monumental *Palazzo Gregoris* (18th century). At the end of the street is *Casa Vianello*, with 14th-century frescoes, and the 18th-century *Palazzo Montereale-Mantica*, now the Chamber of Commerce, whose rooms are decorated with stuccoes. To the left of the Palazzo Comunale, the 17th-century *Palazzo Ricchieri* is now the Museo Civico d'Arte.

Pordenone 1 : 17 000 (1 cm = 170 m)

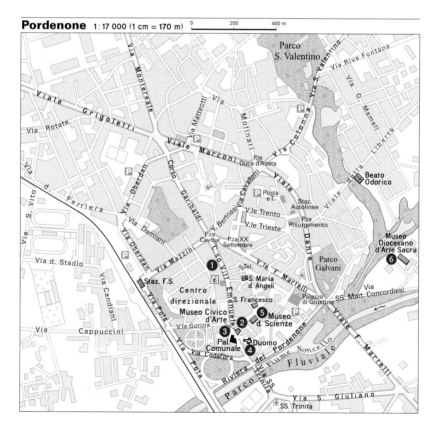

HERITAGE

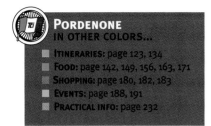

PORDENONE
IN OTHER COLORS...

■ ITINERARIES: page 123, 134
■ FOOD: page 142, 149, 156, 163, 171
■ SHOPPING: page 180, 182, 183
■ EVENTS: page 188, 191
■ PRACTICAL INFO: page 232

Museo Civico d'Arte ❷

Since 1971, this museum, restructured in the 1960s, has housed the town's art collections. Some of the rooms have late 14th-century *frescoes*. Most of the collection consists of works by artists from Friuli and the Veneto (13th to 20th centuries). It has a fine sculpture collection. A special section on the *Tesoro del Duomo di S. Marco* (Treasury of St Mark's Cathedral) has one of the most best collections in the area of Gothic and Renaissance reliquaries. The modern and contemporary art collection is in a separate gallery, with works by Italian and foreign artists of international standing (De Pisis, Guttuso, Manzù, Messina, Pizzinato, Savinio, Sironi, and others).

Palazzo Comunale ❸

The Gothic Town Hall at the end of Corso Vittorio Emanuele was built between 1291 and 1365. It has a portico and three-light windows and a projecting 16th-century tower with a large astronomical clock.

Duomo ❹

The cathedral, built between the late 14th and mid-15th centuries, has an unfinished facade (1840) with a Renaissance doorway. To the left is a slender Romanesque **bell tower*** (more than 70 m high) with Gothic features (1219-1417). The *interior* has one broad nave. To the right of the entrance: a Renaissance holy water stoup. In the first chapel on the right: an altar-piece by Il Pordenone (**Madonna of Mercy***). Above the altar of the 2nd chapel: a *St Jerome* by Domenico Tintoretto.

Museo delle Scienze ❺

The museum is housed in the 16th-century Palazzo Amalteo. Its permanent displays include the bird room, with Italian and exotic species, the diorama room, with reconstructions of local habitats and environments and the little *Theatrum Naturae*, with natural wonders and curiosities from the 16th and 17th centuries: a calf with two heads and a hen with three legs. Finally, the pre-historic section traces the course of Evolution with environmental reconstructions.

Museo Diocesano d'Arte Sacra ❻

The museum housed in the Centro Attività Pastorali has a collection of sacred objects: silver-ware, bronzes, glass, wooden statues, paintings on canvas and wooden panels, sinopias and frescoes of the 13th to 19th centuries from local churches.

DAY TRIPS

ABBAZIA DI S. MARIA IN SYLVIS [22 km]

All that remains of the 8th-century **Abbey of St Mary in Sylvis***, suppressed in 1790, is the former *church* (12th to 13th centuries), now restored. Beyond the doorway (1400) is a vestibule with frescoes from the 11th to 15th centuries and a Romanesque aisled atrium with a 15th-century wooden ceiling. The interior of the church was once covered with frescoes: fragments survive on the walls of the presbytery and the central apse. The *crypt* under the presbytery contains the **urn of St Anastasia*** (8th century) and a late 13th-century low relief.

The church of the abbey of S. Maria in Sylvis

AVIANO [14 km]

The *Duomo di S. Zenone* (18th century) has a Madonna and Child with Saints (1514). Since the 1950s, there has been a NATO base at the airfield of the Aeronautical Academy founded here in 1911. During WWI, courageous young men took off from here in early planes, with wings made of fabric and wooden propellers.

MANIAGO [24 km]

Caves on the rocky slopes of Monte S. Lorenzo were inhabited in Neolithic times. The knife-making industry, for which the town is still famous, dates from the Middle Ages. The **Museo dell'Arte Fabbrile e delle Coltellerie** (Museum of Blacksmithing and Cutlery) illustrates methods used for working steel. The Wood- and Iron-processing section of the **Museo Provinciale della Vita Contadina "Diogene Penzi"** – (Provincial Museum of Farming Life) has a display of inlaid wooden objects, tools and documents showing how iron is worked to make knives.

The Palazzo dipinto in Spilimbergo

SACILE [9 km]

The "Garden of Venice" and a "Second Padua": the dignified churches and palaces of the town, which began on two islands in the River Livenza, and its longstanding artistic, scientific and cultural enterprise earned the town these nicknames. Its noble palaces overlooking the water are very reminiscent of Venice.

SAN VITO AL TAGLIAMENTO [21 km]

The walls and gates are reminders of the past of this once farming, now industrial community. The collection of the *Museo Provinciale della Vita Contadina "Diogene Penzi"* (Provincial Museum of Farming Life) illustrates traditional local activities (silkworm farming, weaving, wine- and cheese-making). Torre Raimonda (13th century) is now the *Museo Civico "Federico de Rocco"*, with archeological finds from pre-history to the Roman period.

SPILIMBERGO [30 km]

It dominates the Tagliamento valley, whose fords it controlled from Roman times. A flourishing trading center in the 15th and 16th centuries, it reached its literary and artistic height under Venetian rule. On the edge of the town, the **Duomo*** was begun in 1284 and completed in the mid-14th century. The left-hand and central apses have 14th-century frescoes. The **organ***, rebuilt in 1981 to an original design, has organ-doors by Il Pordenone (16th century). The crypt contains more 14th-century frescoes and some 15th-century statues and sculptures. Left of the cathedral stands the *castle*. Restored after the 1976 earthquake, it has Renaissance and Gothic features, including the *Palazzo Dipinto*, with late 15th-century frescoes on the facade.

VALCELLINA
[35-105 km]

The top of the River Cellina passes below the Dolomites: rock spires, high rock-walls and endless peaks, (Cima dei Preti is 2,703 m high), then through the foothills near Claut. It forms a broad loop before flowing into the Friuli plain near Maniago. Small towns in the valley include **Barcis**, reflected in the green Lake Aprilis, created in 1954 by a hydro-electric power dam also built for irrigation; **Claut**, a mountain resort where the *Museo Casa Clautana "Eugenio Borsatti"* illustrates the history of the local community; and, finally, **Cimolàis**, on the road to the pass of Sant'Osvaldo, starting-point for many walks and climbs in the area.

VALVASONE [22 km]

This town on the Tagliamento, with a fascinating **historic center*** was the seat of a feudal lord from the 10th century. A *gate-house with a tower* leads into the 13th-century *castle*: a circle of tall buildings around a courtyard. The neo-Gothic *parish church* contains a rare Venetian organ (1532).

TRIESTE

Trieste's origins date from the Roman colony of Tergeste, founded 2,000 years ago. In 1382 it submitted to the Habsburgs. Three and a half centuries passed in obscurity before Emperor Charles VI declared the city a free port in 1719, giving Trieste a competitive advantage. This measure was renewed by the more systematic reforms implemented by Charles VI's daughter, Maria Theresa, whose reign (1740-80) was a turning-point for the mercantile fortunes of the city. In Trieste, the crisis of the Habsburg Empire in the 19th and 20th centuries was manifested as a growing desire to be freed from Austria rule. Fascism, with its expansionism towards the Balkans, worsened relations between Italians and Slavs. The Italo-German Axis declared war on nearby Yugoslavia (April 1941) and invaded it. As a result, Istria and Trieste itself were occupied (May-June 1945) by Tito's partisans. The Trieste area did not return to Italy until 1954.

Having welcomed about 60,000 refugees from Istria after WWII, between the end of the 20th century and the dawn of the 21st, the city concentrated on reviving its former role as mediator between cultures and markets in the fields of services for research, commerce and finance.

Castello di S. Giusto ❶

The present castle of St Justus was built between 1470 and 1630 over an earlier fort, which, in turn, was probably erected above a pre-Roman stronghold. Restored in the 1930s it was converted into a museum and a setting for outdoor performances. There are marvelous views over the city and the Bay of Trieste from itsts bastions. The **Civico Museo del Castello di S. Giusto** has a valuable collection of chests, furniture, paintings and weapons dating from the 14th to 19th centuries from private collections. Highlights include 12th-century swords, suits of chain-mail, late 16th-century Venetian halberds, crossbows, rifles from the Napoleonic period, sabers and bayonets. Works of art include a 15th-century wooden statue. The recently restored Bastione Lalio of the Castle of St Justus houses the *Lapidario Tergestino*: limestone

> ### TRIESTE
> ### IN OTHER COLORS...
> ▪ **ITINERARIES:** page 120, 127, 129
> ▪ **FOOD:** page 143, 149, 156, 163, 171
> ▪ **SHOPPING:** page 182
> ▪ **EVENTS:** page 188
> ▪ **PRACTICAL INFO:** page 234

material from the Roman period including inscriptions from monuments and tombs, low reliefs, full reliefs and architectural fragments

S. Giusto ❷

The church of St Justus is the symbol of the city. It was created by amalgamating (in the 14th century) two Romanesque basilicas (5th to 11th centuries) dedicated to St Justus (on the right) and the Assumption (on the left). The simple brick *facade* and sloping roof is enhanced by a magnificent 14th-century rose-window.

Trieste: the city's architecture belies its cosmopolitan culture

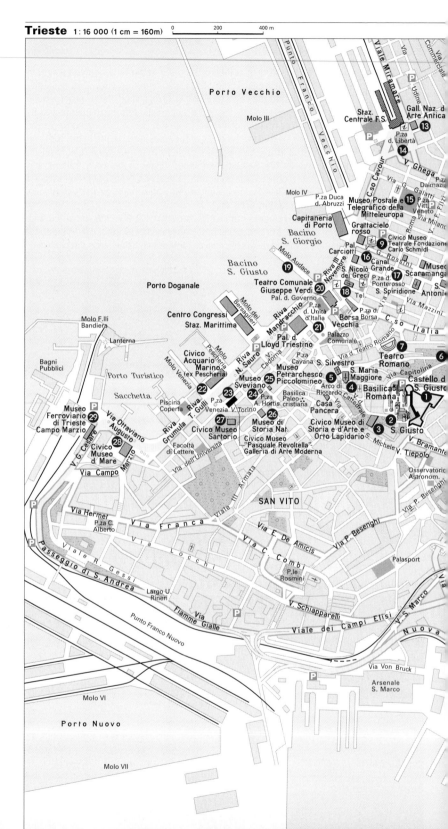

Trieste 1 : 16 000 (1 cm = 160m)

0   200   400 m

Porto Vecchio

Molo III

Staz.
Centrale F.S.

Gall. Naz. d.
Arte Antica

Viale Miramare

Via Commerciale

Via C.so Cavour

P.za
d. Libertà

Udine

Via Ghega

Via G. Galatti

P.za
Vitt.
Veneto

Dalmazia

Via Milano

Roma

Molo IV

P.za Duca
d. Abruzzi

Capitaneria
di Porto

Bacino
S. Giorgio

Museo Postale e
Telegrafico della
Mitteleuropa

Grattacielo
rosso

Civico Museo
Teatrale Fondazione
Carlo Schmidl

Pal.
Carciotti

Canal
Grande

Museo
Scaramanga

Via G. Rossini

Bacino
S. Giusto

Porto Doganale

Molo Audace

Bacino
S. Giusto

Teatro Comunale
Giuseppe Verdi

Pal. d. Governo

Riva III Novembre

S. Nicolò
dei Greci

P.za
Ponterosso

S. Spiridione

Antoni

Via Mazzini

C.so Italia

Molo F.lli
Bandiera

Lanterna

Centro Congressi
Staz. Marittima

Molo dei
Bersaglieri

Riva Mandracchio

P.za
d. Unità
d'Italia

Borsa
Vecchia

Borsa

P.za d.
Borsa

Via d. Teatro Romano

Bagni
Pubblici

Porto Turistico

Sacchetta

Molo Venezia

Civico
Acquario
Marino
(ex Pescheria)

Molo
Pescheria

Riva N. Sauro

Via Cadorna

Pal. d.
Lloyd Triestino

Palazzo
Comunale

P.za
Cavana

Museo
Sveviano

Museo
Petrarchesco
Piccolomineo

S. Silvestro

S. Maria
Maggiore

Teatro
Romano

Via Capitolina

Castello d.
S. Giusto

Piscina
Coperta

Riva Grumula

Riva T. Gulli

P.za
Venezia

Museo di
Storia Nat.

P.za
A. Hortis

Basilica
Paleo-
cristiana

Arco di
Riccardo

Via Cattedrale

Casa
Pancera

Basilica
Romana

Museo
Ferroviario
di Trieste
Campo Marzio

Via Ottaviano Augusto

Civico Museo
Sartorio

Civico Museo
"Pasquale Revoltella":
Galleria di Arte Moderna

Civico Museo di
Storia e d'Arte e
Orto Lapidario

S. Giusto

V. Michele

V. Tiepolo

V. Bramante

Civico
Museo
d. Mare

Via G. Cesare

Via Campo Marzio

Facoltà
di Lettere

Via dell'Università

Osservatorio
Astronom.

Via P. Besenghi

SAN VITO

Via Hermel

P.za C.
Alberto

Via Franca

Via Locchi

Via E. De Amicis

Via C. Combi

Via P. Besenghi

Palasport

Passeggio di S. Andrea

Viale R. Gessi

Viale III Armata

P.le
Rosmini

V. Schiapparelli

Viale dei Campi Elisi

V. S. Marco

Nuova

Largo U.
Rineri

Via Flamme Gialle

Punto Franco Nuovo

Via Von Bruck

Arsenale
S. Marco

Molo VI

Porto Nuovo

Molo VII

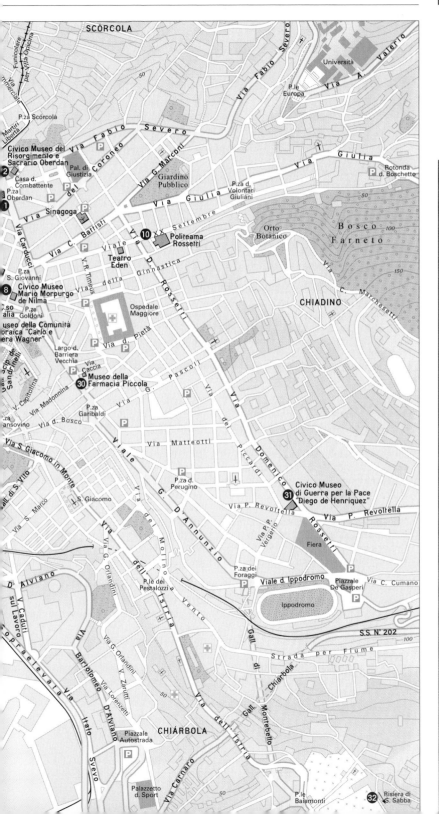

Trieste: the cathedral of St Justus

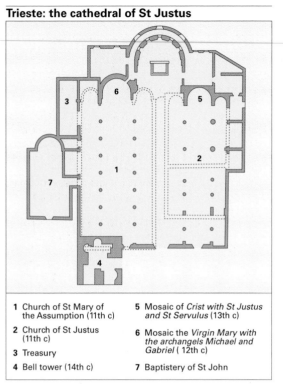

1 Church of St Mary of the Assumption (11th c)

2 Church of St Justus (11th c)

3 Treasury

4 Bell tower (14th c)

5 Mosaic of *Crist with St Justus and St Servulus* (13th c)

6 Mosaic the *Virgin Mary with the archangels Michael and Gabriel* (12th c)

7 Baptistery of St John

The jambs of the main doorway are from a Roman funerary stele. The bell tower (14th century) left of the church was built over the remains of a Roman temple. There is a Romanesque statue of St Justus in a niche on the right-hand side of the bell tower. The *interior* of the church comprises five asymmetrical naves and aisles separated by columns with fine capitals. The central nave has a 16th-century painted ship's keel ceiling, replaced in 1905. The right apse has blind arcading and 13th-century frescoes; in the vault, a fine late 13th-century mosaic. In the floor are remains of a mosaic from the 5th-century basilica. In the vault of the left apse is a Madonna between the Archangels Michael and Gabriel and, below, the Apostles, both 12th-century **mosaics***. On the wall of the left aisle is a *Virgin and Child with Saints*, by Benedetto Carpaccio (1540). The left aisle leads to the **Baptistery**, where there is a 9th-century font for total immersion.

Civico Museo di Storia e Arte and Orto Lapidario ❸

The museum, created in 1925, contains collections of finds from Egypt, Magna Grecia, Africa, Etruria and Greece, and Maya exhibits from El Salvador. There is also material from Trieste itself, Aquileia and Istria: bronze artifacts from the Tolmino necropolis (8th to 5th centuries BC), marble statues and busts, glass- and earthenware, gold, silver and amber from the Roman period and Greek pottery. The *Orto Lapidario* outside, formerly a cemetery, contains architectural fragments and inscriptions from Trieste and Aquileia.

S. Maria Maggiore ❹

Behind the Town Hall, from the hill of S. Giusto the church of St Mary the Greater overlooks an area where many buildings were demolished in the 1930s. Built in 1627-82, it has a fine Baroque facade. The altar to the right of the high altar has a revered image of the *Madonna della Salute*. To the right of the church, slightly lower down, is the little 11th-century **church of S. Silvestro**, restored to its original lines in the 1920s.

Arco di Riccardo ❺

Behind S. Maria Maggiore, the arch, erected in 33 BC, was once one of the gates of the Roman town. Restored by FAI (the Italian Fund for the Protection of the Environment), it has a single arch, decorated with pilasters.

Museo della Comunità Ebraica "Carlo e Vera Wagner" ❻

The museum, opened in 1993, has examples of Jewish culture and art of the Jewish community of Trieste, and religious fabrics from its synagogues. The collection includes richly-decorated 18th-century Venetian silver-ware, books and documents.

Teatro Romano ❼

In 1938, the cavea and the stage of an early 2nd-century Roman theater were discovered below the hill of S. Giusto. The theater had a seating capacity of 6,000.

Civico Museo Mario Morpurgo de Nilma ❽

Ceramics, glassware, porcelain, exotic furnishings, silverware, crystal, books, prints, drawings and paintings were donated to the city in 1943 by Mario Morpurgo de Nilma, a passionate collector. They are displayed in part of a beautiful late-19th century palace, now the Municipal Morpurgo Museum. Sadly, much of the collection was lost during WWII.

Civico Museo Teatrale Fondazione Carlo Schmidl ❾

The Carlo Schmidl Municipal Theater Museum has recently been created on the second floor of Palazzo Gopcevic, as the result of a bequest by a local music publisher (1859-1943) and, in terms of the sheer size, is second only to the La Scala Theater Museum in Milan. It includes costumes, posters, photographs, prints, librettos, scores and musical instruments from Europe and further afield.

Viale XX Settembre ❿

Viale XX Settembre is crossed by Via Carducci, created in 1850 by covering the river carrying the springwater from the hills above Trieste to the sea, and Via Battisti, which leads to the 19th-century *Giardino pubblico*. On Viale XX Settembre, an elegant promenade lined with cafés, theaters and cinemas, is **Teatro Eden**, now a cinema, a notable example of Art Nouveau decoration, and the **Politeama Rossetti** (1878), important in the theatrical and patriotic life of Trieste.

Piazza Oberdan ⓫

Conceived as a dramatic entrance to the city in the 1930s, Piazza Oberdan lies on the site where, in 1882, Trieste patriot Guglielmo Oberdan was hanged by the Austrians. It is also the terminus for the popular *Opicina tram*, a rack tramway dating from 1902.

Civico Museo del Risorgimento and Sacrario Oberdan ⓬

The museum has a collection of historical memorabilia, photographs, documents, uniforms and paintings illustrating local events of the Risorgimento from 1848 up to WWI. Outside is the *Sacrario*, a monument to patriot Guglielmo Oberdan, and the cell where he was detained.

Galleria Nazionale di Arte Antica ⓭

The main nucleus of the gallery is the Mentasti collection, about 50 paintings dating from the 15th to 19th centuries, including works by Giovanni Antonio and Francesco Guardi, a series of drawings by Canaletto and some paintings attributed to Lucas Cranach the Elder and Jacopo Tintoretto.

Piazza della Libertà ⓮

Piazza della Libertà has retained its monumental late 19th-century appearance. Surrounded by elegant buildings of eclectic style, including *Palazzo Economo,* it is dominated by the broad facade of the *Stazione Centrale* (1878). To the left, the former *grain depot* (1890) has been converted into the main bus terminus (1986-1989).

Museo Postale e Telegrafico della Mitteleuropa ⓯

Inaugurated at the end of 1997, the Central European Post and Telegraph Museum has an interesting collection of objects associated with early postal services, including a reconstruction of a late 19th-century post office and a military field post office.

Canal Grande ⓰

Dug in 1750-56, the Canal Grande provided a safe haven for sailing ships and enabled them to unload their cargoes, destined for the warehouses of the newly-emerging *borgo teresiano* in the 18th

The Roman theater below the hill of S. Giusto

The "red skyscraper" and Palazzo Carciotti from Bacino di S. Giorgio

century, created by filling in the salt-pans west of the old city. On the right of the sea end of the canal is **Palazzo Carciotti** (1802-05), one of the city's best examples of neoclassical architecture, with a facade decorated with six columns, a balustrade and statues. Close by is the former *Hôtel de la Ville* (1839). At the top of the canal stands the neoclassical **church of Sant'Antonio Nuovo**.

Piazza Ponterosso ⑰

Piazza Ponterosso ("red bridge") was named after a wooden drawbridge, replaced in 1840, which spanned the Canal Grande. This square, adorned by an 18th-century fountain, and nearby Piazza Sant'Antonio Nuovo are dominated by the shining **church of SS. Trinità e S. Spiridione Taumaturgo**. Built by the Serbian Orthodox community and opened in 1868, its interior has silver furnishings and mosaics with a gold background.

S. Nicolò dei Greci ⑱

The church of St Nicholas, built in 1784-87 for the Greek Orthodox community, has a facade with twin bell towers (1819-21). Inside, the iconostasis is richly decorated with worked silver.

Molo Audace ⑲

This quay where the people of Trieste like to stroll takes its name from the torpedo boat which brought the first battalions of Italian soldiers on November 3, 1918.

Teatro Comunale Giuseppe Verdi ⑳

Overlooking Piazza Giuseppe Verdi, the theater is a neoclassical building (1801), whose facade is reminiscent of La Scala in Milan. In 1850, Giuseppe Verdi staged the first performance of *Stiffelio*, conceived and written in Trieste.

Piazza dell'Unità d'Italia ㉑

Heart of the old town, Piazza dell'Unità d'Italia faces the sea (the buildings on the front were knocked down) like a sort of enormous stage, with the facade of the **Palazzo Comunale** (Town Hall) (1875) as a backdrop.

Civico Acquario Marino ㉒

Opened in 1933, the acquarium has 26 tanks fed with sea water, containing various species of fish, most of them native to the Adriatic, but also brightly-colored tropical fish, turtles, and, in a special environment, a family of penguins from South Africa.

Civico Museo "Pasquale Revoltella" - Galleria di Arte Moderna ㉓

The Civic Museum and Modern Art Gallery, founded in 1872, is housed in the palazzo built by Baron Pasquale Revoltella (1852-1858). There are three main parts to the collection. The first is the palazzo itself, with many works from the early 19th century, including neoclassical sculptures by Antonio Canova; the second consists of works from the second half of the 19th and early 20th centuries; finally, the third part, designed in the 1960s by Carlo Scarpa, focuses on 20th-century art.

Museo Sveviano ㉔

Created in 1997 by the daughter of writer Italo Svevo, the museum is a place where the work of the writer can be studied through an exhibition of manuscripts, photographs, books and letters, which are available for consultation along with translations of his work.

Museo Petrarchesco Piccolomineo ㉕

The museum houses art and book collections relating to two great men: Francesco Petrarca (Petrarch) (1304-1374) and Enea Silvio Piccolomini (1405-1464). The collection includes 5,500 printed books, 79 manuscripts, about 700 examples of iconography and ancient documents.

Civico Museo di Storia Naturale ㉖

The museum, opened in 1846, is divided into two main parts: the function of the first is primarily educational, with

collections of animals and plants, while the second is only open to scholars. The paleontological and mineral exhibits come from caves and breccia of the Carso and Istria, like the fossil remains of a dinosaur found at Duino. A Mammal Room has recently opened, focusing on local mammal species.

Civico Museo Sartorio 27

Housed in a villa where the Sartorio family lived from 1838 to 1947, the museum offers the chance to see rooms with their original furnishings and some very fine art collections, including a collection of Italian ceramics from the 16th to 19th centuries. The museum, which is constantly being restored, contains a magnificent triptych attributed to Paolo Veneziano (**Triptych of St Clare***), and a valuable collection of drawings by G.B. Tiepolo. The Quadreria (picture gallery) has more than 1,200 paintings from Trieste's Municipal Museum of History and Art. There is also a plaster-cast collection of more than 350 works (sculptures and busts of plaster, marble and different types of stone) from the 16th to the mid-20th centuries.

Civico Museo del Mare 28

The museum provides a complete picture of Trieste's maritime history, with models of boats and ships, scale models of the harbors of Trieste and Dalmatia, nautical maps, photographs and prints.
The museum began in 1904, when the School of Fishing and Fish-farming set up a permanent marine exhibition, subsequently enriched with other material.

Museo Ferroviario di Trieste Campo Marzio 29

Housed in the old station of Campo Marzio (1887-1907), the museum contains documents, scale models,

locomotives and carriages of the trains which crossed the Alps to Vienna, some trams, a large collection of photographs and a scale model of the Trieste area with an electric model railway track.

Museo della Farmacia Piccola 30

The museum has seven rooms containing a collection gathered over 200 years which traces the history of this old, family-run city pharmacy (1799). It includes more than 2,000 pharmaceutical objects, 800 scientific books and documents. Since 1999 it has belonged to the Associazione Europea Musei delle Arti Medicali in Paris.

Civico Museo di Guerra per la Pace "Diego de Henriquez" 31

The Museum of War for Peace, created in 1997, contains the collection of Diego de Henriquez (1909-1974), comprising military objects, early and modern weapons, tanks, uniforms, photographs, prints, scale models and a collection of paper soldiers.

Risiera di S. Sabba 32

This former rice refinery, built in 1913, was converted by the Fascists and Nazis after September 8, 1943, into a depot for confiscated possessions and a prison camp for partisans, political prisoners and Jews. Thousands of people were deported from here to the death camps in Poland. Many were eliminated here, the only place on Italian soil with a cremation oven, between June 1944 and April 1945. In 1965 S. Sabba was declared a national monument and, now restored, houses the *Museo della Resistenza* (Museum of the Resistance).

DAY TRIPS

CASTELLO DI MIRAMARE [7 km]

Surrounded by a huge 19th-century, Italian-style garden, with many rare species of trees, Miramare Castle was built between 1856 and 1860 for Maximilian Habsburg and is remembered by Giosuè Carducci in his ode, *Miramar*. Archduke Maximilian lived there until 1864; from 1931 until 1936 it was the home of Amedeo di Savoia-Aosta. The castle is situated on a promontory jutting out into the sea. Its rich collections of furniture, paintings, porcelain and ivories, and lavish interior decoration make this one of the finest examples of a princely residence of the second half of the 19th century. Built in a similar style, the *Castelletto*, occupied by the Archduke and his wife Charlotte of Belgium while the new castle was being built, is now the *Centro di Educazione all'Ambiente Marino di Miramare*, with an exhibition on the marine environment and teaching laboratories. The surrounding area of sea has hydrological and biological characteristics which are unique in the Mediterranean, and has been a Marine Reserve since 1986.

DUINO-AURISINA [22 km]

Surrounded by Mediterranean maquis, the silhouettes of the **Castelli di Duino** become clearer as you approach. Only a tower and one arch remains of the *original castle* (11th century). Below the vertical cliffs, the white stone known as the *dama bianca* (white lady) was named after a beautiful occupant of the castle who committed suicide for love. Close by, the *new castle*, begun in the 14th century, is encircled by 15th-century walls. Rebuilt several times, it is now the residence of the descendants of the Thurn-Hofer Valsassina family, who have owned it since 1660, and the Thurn und Taxis family, who invited the poet from Prague, Rainer Maria Rilke, to stay here in 1911 and 1912. His *Duino Elegies*, published in 1923, were inspired by his stay here. The rooms of the castle, its luxurious halls full of art-works and historical memorabilia and the fine garden are open to the public.

GROTTA DEL GIGANTE [13 km]

This immense natural cave, elliptical in shape (130 m by 65 m) and 115 m high, is one of 2,000 in the area, and was formed as a result of water penetration and erosive phenomena. Explored for the first time in 1840, it has many beautiful limestone formations. Near the entrance is a *Speleological Museum* with geological exhibits and finds from the cave.

MUGGIA [14 km]

The modern center of Muggia is dominated by the old part of the town, Muggia Vecchia: the *church of S. Maria Assunta* (9th century but altered several times since) contains frescoes from the 12th and 13th centuries. In 1420 the town came under the rule of Venice, which influenced its architectural appearance. The historic center focuses on **Piazza Marconi***, where the town's most interesting buildings are located. The *Palazzo Comunale* (Town Hall), rebuilt several times (latterly in 1934), incorporates Palazzo dei Rettori, begun in the 14th century. The most striking architectural feature is the little **Duomo**, erected in 1263 on the site of a church built in the previous century. The facade is most unusual. Above the doorway is a low relief depicting the Trinity and the saints to whom the cathedral is dedicated, John and Paul. The **Mostra Permanente del Presepio**, housed in the church of S. Francesco, contains hundreds of cribs from all over the world. The **Museo di Muggia e del Territorio** contains local finds dating from the Bronze Age to the Early Middle Ages.

OBELISCO DI OPICINA [8 km]

The Opicina Obelisk, built in 1830 to mark the opening of the new Trieste-Llubljana road, has a *belvedere* with **views*** over the city. This is the starting-point of the *Strada Napoleonica*, a footpath 5.5 km long which runs along the edge of the karst to the *Santuario di Monte Grisa* (1960). From the obelisk, a road leads to the village of *Trebiciano* (3 km). Nearby is the **cave of Trebiciano**, one of the deepest in the area (319 m).

View of the coast and the Carso hills between Sistiana and Duino

UDINE

The castle was probably built to defend the area during the Hungarian incursions (5th century). In a document of 983, Emperor Otto II ceded the castle of *Udene* to the Patriarch of Aquileia, Rodoaldo, for this purpose. In the 13th century, Patriarch Bertoldo of Andechs moved back to Udine, abandoning Cividale. For Udine, this was the start of a period of growth of which little remains, apart from the little church of S. Maria di Castello. From now on, Udine was the capital of Friuli. The original set of defensive walls proved to be insufficient and, in the first half of the 14th century, a second set of fortifications was built (destroyed in the 19th century). In 1420, Udine and the rest of Friuli became part of the Republic of Venice. The loss of its independence was compensated by considerable autonomy and by dramatic development in art, culture and town-planning. Piazza della Libertà with the Palazzo del Comune and the Portico di San Giovanni, together with the current structure of the castle, all date from the 15th and 16th centuries. In the 18th century, the town was enhanced by G.B. Tiepolo (1696-1770), who executed paintings in the Duomo and frescoed

the Palazzo Patriarcale and the Oratorio della Purità. After the fall of the Venetian Republic and the short period of Napoleonic rule, Udine became part of the Austrian region of Lombardy-Veneto and was then incorporated in the Kingdom of Italy (1866). Only after WWI did the town begin to expand beyond the old walls, and only very recently has it begun to spread in terms of urban development.

Piazza della Libertà, with the Loggia del Lionello on the left and the Porticato di S. Giovanni

Piazza della Libertà ❶

Situated below the castle hill, Piazza della Libertà, the focal point of the town, is surrounded by Venetian-style buildings. Formerly Piazza Nuova, and then Piazza Contarena, it has changed little since the 16th century. Notice the Loggia del Lionello and the Portico di S. Giovanni: to the left of it, an archway marks the way up to the castle.

Porticato di S. Giovanni ❷

This beautiful Renaissance portico (1533) supported by slender columns is overlooked by an elegant *clock tower* of 1527 with a lion of Venice and two moors which strike the hour. In the center, a broad archway leads into the *chapel of S. Giovanni*, now a war memorial.

Civici Musei and Galleria di Storia e Arte Antica ❸

Udine's Municipal Museums were inaugurated in 1865. In addition to the town's art collection, there was also a library and a natural history museum.

Since 1906, they have all been housed in the castle. There are five main parts: the Donazione Ciceri (a private collection donated to the town), the Archeological Museum, the Gallery of Early Art, the Gallery of Drawings and Prints, and the Friuli Museum of Photography. Finally, the town's cultural heritage includes an Art Library of 30,000 volumes about the area's historical and artistic heritage – and the Fototeca, which has tens of thousands of photos of the region. The *Galleria d'Arte Antica* has a collection of paintings by Friuli artists from the 14th to 19th centuries, but also works by Carpaccio (*Blood of Christ*), Caravaggio (*St Francis in Ecstasy*) and G.B. Tiepolo

UDINE
IN OTHER COLORS...

- ITINERARIES: page 121, 123, 126
- FOOD: page 143, 149, 156, 163, 171
- SHOPPING: page 180, 182
- EVENTS: page 188, 191
- WELLNESS: page 198, 199
- PRACTICAL INFO: page 236

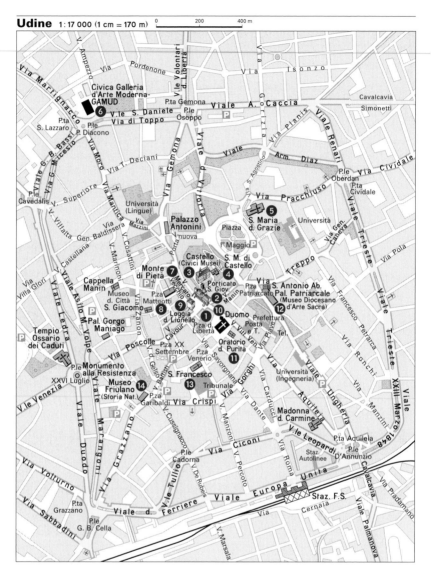

Udine 1 : 17 000 (1 cm = 170 m) 0   200   400 m

(*Consilium in arena*). The *Galleria dei disegni e delle stampe* contains several thousand drawings and prints, especially by Venetian artists (Antonio Guardi, Palma il Giovane, G.B. and G.D. Tiepolo).

S. Maria di Castello ④

Originally a small Christian oratory, re-built in the 8th century, the church was enlarged and altered in the 12th and 13th centuries. The interior, restored to its original Romanesque lines in 1929-31, has fragments of 13th-century frescoes under the broad arches and in the apses.

S. Maria delle Grazie ⑤

Overlooking Piazza 1 Maggio, an oval square planted with trees, today, the famous 15th century church of the Serviti has 18th-century lines.
A neoclassical pronaos was added later (1838-51). Inside, above the high altar, is a Madonna and Child (1522).

Civica Galleria d'Arte Moderna ⑥

The gallery contains more than 4,000 works dating from the late 19th century to the 20th century (Modigliani, Arturo Martini, Fontana) and the present day (Vedova). The *Collezione Astaldi* includes masterpieces of Italian 20th-century painting by De Chirico, Savinio, Severini, Carrà, Sironi, Morandi and others, and also works by foreign painters such as Dufy, Ben Nicholson and De Kooning. One part of the collection contains architectural drawings and designs by Friuli designers.

Via Mercatovecchio 7

This street claims to be the site of Udine's first market in 1223. It is curved and lined with porticoed buildings.

Piazza Matteotti 8

This is possibly the oldest square in Udine. In 1248, it was known as the "Forum novum" (New Forum). The square, surrounded by buildings with low porticoes, dates from 1486.

Loggia del Lionello 9

The Loggia del Lionello is the *Town Hall*. Built between 1448 and 1456 in the Gothic style, it has alternating stripes of white and pink stone with a large loggia on the ground floor. The first floor is decorated with two-light windows and windows with several lights.

Duomo 10

The cathedral has retained its Gothic, 14th-century appearance, particularly the central doorway and the **doorway*** on the left (1390). The interior contains altar-pieces by G.B. Tiepolo. A door on the left of the presbytery leads to the **Museo del Duomo**, which includes the 14th-century *chapel of S. Nicolò* with frescoes (*Life of St Nicholas*, 1348-49) the old *Battistero* (Baptistery), situated below the campanile, with fine Gothic arches, and the tomb of the Blessed Bertrando, with reliefs dating from 1343.

Oratorio della Purità 11

Situated opposite the right doorway of the cathedral, this 18th-century oratory has frescoes by G.B. Tiepolo, above the high altar (**Immaculate Conception***) and on the ceiling (**Assumption***) (1759). The monochrome frescoes on the walls are also by G.B. Tiepolo.

Palazzo Patriarcale 12

The complex was built in the early 16th century, when Venetian governors came to live in the castle. Most of the palace is 16th century, but it wasn't completed until the early 18th century, when young G.B. Tiepolo was summoned to decorate it. The main entrance leads into the atrium and a staircase embellished with the first fresco executed by Tiepolo on his arrival in Udine in 1726, the *Fall of the Rebel Angels*. The first floor of the palace houses the **Museo Diocesano d'Arte Sacra***, with a collection of wooden sculptures carved in Friuli between the 13th and 18th centuries. A spiral staircase leads up to the second floor and the reception rooms: the Blue Room, the Yellow Room (named after the stucco decoration on a gold background), and the Red Room, formerly the old ecclesiastical courtroom. This theme features in the huge ceiling fresco by Tiepolo (1729): *The Judgement of Solomon*. Next is the **Throne room***, or Portrait Room (containing portraits of the bishops, patriarchs and archbishops from the foundation of the church of Aquileia to the present day). A door leads into the Palatine Chapel, the altar of which has a painting by Palma il Giovane (Madonna and Child). Back in the Throne Room, the **Galleria degli Ospiti**** is Tiepolo's masterpiece. After completing his work in the Gallery, Tiepolo was recognized as one of the greatest painters of his time.

S. Francesco 13

The left side, apse and bell tower are all that remain of the original Romanesque church of St Francis (12th century), restored after incurring damage in 1945. It has fragments of frescoes from the 14th and 15th centuries.

Palazzo Patriarcale, fresco above the main staircase

Museo Friulano di Storia Naturale ⑭

In 1949, the Friuli Natural History Museum was housed in Udine's Old City Hospital. Damage sustained during the earthquake of 1976 led to the removal of the collection to Palazzo Giacomelli, since when it has been in temporary premises. The collection has sections on earth science, pre-history, botany and zoology, all with a local focus. The museum also has a huge library of more than 38,000 volumes.

DAY TRIPS

AMPEZZO [70 km]

A charming atmosphere pervades the old town center, its narrow streets lined with porticoed buildings with long wooden balconies. The **Museo Geologico della Carnia** has collections of rocks and fossils dating from 450 to 40 million years ago.

AQUILEIA [41 km]

The Romans founded the town in 181 BC. Its strategic geographical position at a place where roads set off across the Alps towards the valley of the Danube, helped to transform it into an important trading center, together with the marine commercial traffic which sailed up the river from the Adriatic to moor here. A set of walls was built in the late 4th century to defend the town. Protected behind its fortifications, it resisted the attacks of the Goths of Alarico (in 401 and 408) but finally yielded to Attila the Hun in 452. One of the most important religious Romanesque buildings in Western Europe, the present **Basilica** still reflects the lines decided by Patriarch Poppo in the 11th century. The first building dates from 313. It continued to expand until 1021, when Patriarch Poppo started a major reconstruction program which lasted until 1031. The basilica was damaged in the earthquake of 1348, but was restored in the Gothic style between 1350 and 1381. The Renaissance architectural features date from the Venetian period. In front of the facade is a portico connecting the basilica to the *Chiesa dei Pagani* (an unusual, rectangular, 9th-century building) and the remains of the 5th-century *Baptistery*. To the left of the basilica is the solid 11th-century bell tower. It was restored in the 14th century and a belfry was added in the 16th century. The interior of the church has a nave and two side-aisles. Built on a Latin-cross plan, with a raised presbytery, the nave and aisles are separated by 13th-century arches supported by columns. The **mosaic floor****, from the early 4th century, was rediscovered in 1909-12. Divided into 9 large squares, it depicts various themes. This is the largest paleo-Christian mosaic in Western Europe. In the Gothic *Cappella di S. Ambrogio* lie the large tombs of four of the patriarchs of Aquileia. In the center of the steps leading up to the *presbytery*:

Detail of the mosaic floor of the basilica at Aquileia

an elegant Renaissance **tribune***; on the vault and walls of the apse, majestic 11th-century Romanesque frescoes; right of the main altar: part of a 5th-century mosaic. Below the presbytery is the *crypt*: the walls and vaults are entirely covered with **frescoes***, probably from the late 12th century. At one end of the left-hand aisle, near the round 11th-century Santo Sepolcro, is the entrance to the **crypt of the excavations***. It contains three levels of **mosaic floors*** found in excavations of a 4th-century paleo-Christian basilica, another 5th-century basilica and a 1st-century BC Roman house. Behind the bell tower and the apse of the basilica, the **war cemetery** contains the graves of soldiers who died in 1915 and the *tomb of 10 unkown soldiers* whose remains were brought here from battlefields of WWI. A marble slab on the apse of the basilica has verses by Gabriele D'Annunzio.

In the **Museo Civico del Patriarcato** most of th material consists of religious inscriptions and sacred vestments, showin the artistic side of the Patriarchate of Aquileia (4th to 18th centuries).

The **Museo Archeologico Nazionale** has an impressive collection of Roman artifacts The museum was opened in 1882, but wasn't properly organized until after WWII Highlights include the Head of an Old Man (1st century BC), a fine collection of Roman glass and a coin collection. The marble collection in the garden includes architectural fragments, inscriptions, mosaics and a marine section with the remains of a Roman ship. Aquileia has many Roman remains: a complex of **Roman houses and paleo-Christian oratories**, with the remains of mosaic floors, drain-pipes and wells; the ruins of two sma paleo-Christian oratories

Aquileia: the basilica

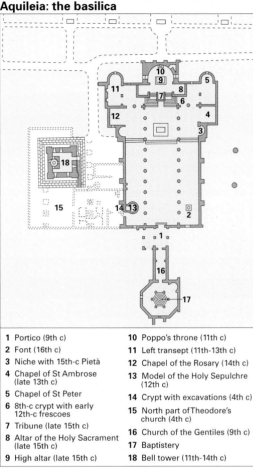

1. Portico (9th c)
2. Font (16th c)
3. Niche with 15th-c Pietà
4. Chapel of St Ambrose (late 13th c)
5. Chapel of St Peter
6. 8th-c crypt with early 12th-c frescoes
7. Tribune (late 15th c)
8. Altar of the Holy Sacrament (late 15th c)
9. High altar (late 15th c)
10. Poppo's throne (11th c)
11. Left transept (11th-13th c)
12. Chapel of the Rosary (14th c)
13. Model of the Holy Sepulchre (12th c)
14. Crypt with excavations (4th c)
15. North part of Theodore's church (4th c)
16. Church of the Gentiles (9th c)
17. Baptistery
18. Bell tower (11th-14th c)

with apses; a small **Roman necropolis**, used from the 1st to 4th centuries, containing five family tombs (part of the material has been transferred to the Archeological Museum). Close to the large 1st-century mausoleum 17 m high, reconstructed in 1955, are the excavations of the **Roman forum**. The 2nd-century forum and the forum basilica complex includes some of the columns and part of the floor of the portico.

The **Port** was discovered in the late 19th century. The current layout dates from the 1st century AD. A pleasant path lined with cypresses, signposted as *Via degli Scavi del Porto fluviale*, leads past architectural features and marbles with Latin inscriptions from excavations in the area. On the quay of the ancient harbor are the remains of some 3rd-century walls.

Since 1961, the **Museo Paleocristiano Nazionale** has been housed in the 18th-century building in front of a 5th-century paleo-Christian basilica. The collection dates from the early years of Christianity: sarcophagi and mosaics from the 4th and 5th centuries which possibly belonged to churches or private oratories, the remains of the 5th-century mosaic floor which once decorated the floor of the presbytery of a basilica that has since been destroyed, and 11th-century low reliefs.

CIVIDALE DEL FRIULI [16 km]

After the Roman period, the history and art of Cividale document the medieval Patriarchate of Aquileia and the period of Venetian dominion, but, more importantly, they include the most important testimonials left by the Lombard tribes who came down into Italy (568), held the area for 200 years and then disappeared. Construction of the

Duomo began in 1457 in the Gothic style. In the 16th century, Renaissance features were added. There are three doorways in the stone facade, the central one by Jacopo Veneziano (1465). Next to it, the bell tower dates from the 17th and 18th centuries. The *interior* is composed of a nave and two side-aisles. Below the organ in the 4th bay on the right, is the fragment of a standard (Annunciation, 1536). At the high altar: the **altar-piece of Pellegrino II***, with gilded embossed silver decoration (1195-1204). On the walls of the chapel in the apse: two paintings by Palma the Younger, a Last Supper and a Martyrdom of St Stephen. The 3rd bay of the right aisle leads into the **Museo cristiano** and the **Tesoro del Duomo** (the Cathedral Museum and Treasury), which contains the octagonal shrine with columns of the **Battistero di Callisto**** (Baptistery of Callistus) (8th century), the *altar of the Lombard king Ratchis* (8th century) and fragments of frescoes from the Tempietto Longobardo. Founded in 1817, the **Museo Archeologico Nazionale** is housed in the 16th-century Palazzo dei Provveditori Veneti, the design for which is attributed to Andrea Palladio. The collection is arranged on two floors: the lapidary collection (ground floor) has splendid mosaics from a *domus* (house) from the Roman settlement of *Forum Iulii* as well as fragments from the early medieval, Romanesque and Renaissance periods.

The first floor has Lombard exhibits with grave-goods from necropolises around Cividale. The permanent collection of gold Lombard ducats is rated the second-largest in the world. On the top floor is a precious library containing volumes from the Lombard period and the early centuries of the patriarchate (7th to 15th centuries).

The **Tempietto longobardo** (Lombard temple) is an unusual example of early medieval art (8th and 9th centuries). It consists of a small square chamber with a cross-vaulted ceiling. The modern entrance is from the sacristy which has frescoes detached from the inner walls of the church (12th to 14th centuries) and leads into the area of the apse.

On the right is the so-called Piltrude sarcophagus, made with re-used material from an 8th-century bishop's throne. The main part of the temple has splendid 8th-century **stucco decoration**** with a frieze of vines above six female figures. Steep steps lead down to the **Ipogeo celtico** (Celtic Hypogeum), an underground complex of chambers and tunnels. The Romans used it as a prison but it was probably used earlier as a Celtic burial site. The 14th-century *church of S. Francesco* has frescoes dating from the 14th to 16th centuries. The 18th-century *Palazzo Pontotti-Brosadola* looks onto the same square. To the left is the *church of S. Pietro ai Volti*, with a fine altar-piece by Palma the Younger.

LIGNANO SABBIADORO [61km]

The sea, a fine sandy beach, 8 harbors, a funfair, umbrella pines and the charming landscape of the lagoon. Situated on the peninsula enclosing the Marano lagoon, this *holiday resort*, which has sprung up fairly recently, consists of the three towns of Sabbiadoro, Pineta and Riviera.

PALMANOVA [31 km]

This well preserved example of a fortified town still has the layout established by the Venetians in 1593. Built on a polygonal plan in the shape of a nine-pointed star, it is surrounded by curtain walls and a deep moat. The design combined the military need to create a defensive stronghold on its eastern boundary and the Renaissance dream of building the perfect city. Napoleon seized it in 1807, reinforced

The River Natisone at Cividale del Friuli, spanned by the Ponte del Diavolo

it even further and changed its name from Palma to Palmanova. **Piazza Grande** is the hexagonal square in the center of the town. It contains some 18th-century statues of the town's governors and is overlooked by the *Duomo* (1602). Six streets lead off at regular angles from the central square, three to the monumental gates of *Porta Udine, Porta Cividale* and *Porta Aquileia*, attributed to Vincenzo Scamozzi (1605).

Created in 1987, the **Museo Storico Militare** has a collection of documents relating to the military garrisons stationed in the fortress from 1600 until WWII. From it you can access the chemins-de-ronde of the fortifications. The **Civico Museo Storico** was created in 1926 as the result of a private initiative. Since 1974, it has been housed in Palazzo Trevisan. It contains documents and weapons illustrating the town's history from the Venetian Period until WWI.

collection includes archeological finds, fragments of frescoes, wooden sculpture, paintings and objects which were associated with local craft industries and farming methods.

TARCENTO [19 km]
From the holiday resort of Tarcento, a road leads up into the valley of the River Torre to Villanova. The **caves**** here are of morainic origin and consist of 14 km of chambers and tunnels. There are three main chambers. The *Grotta Nuova* is the only one that is open to the public. The other caves (only for experts) are the *Grotta Dóvizza* and the *Grotta Egidio Feruglio*.

TARVISIO [95 km]
This holiday resort, which is a popular skiing center in winter, is also a center for industry and international commerce. The parish church (1400), with frescoes from the same period, is one of the

Villa Manin at Passariano

PASSARIANO [25 km]
A few farms **Villa Manin****, a country house set in the Friuli countryside, was built in the mid-17th century by the powerful Manin family. Ludovico Manin was the last Doge of the Venetian Republic. The villa houses the *Centro regionale di Catalogazione* (Regional Cataloguing Center) and a *Scuola di Restauro* (Restoration School). It is also the setting for the new **Centro d'Arte Contemporanea**.

SAN DANIELE DEL FRIULI [27 km]
This town was damaged in the earthquake of 1976, but has been rebuilt at the foot of the hill. Here, the **Museo del Territorio** has a collection of treasures from towns damaged during the earthquake. The

town's few old buildings. The **Laghi di Fusine** (Lakes of Fusine) are about 10 km away: the *bottom lake* (it has greeny-blue water), is at 924 m. The *top lake*, at 929 m, is only a short walk away.

TOLMEZZO [48 km]
This small town with its old, narrow streets, set in the valley of the Tagliamento, also has a long history as an industrial town. The **Duomo** dedicated to St Martin dates from the 18th century. It contains some 16th-century sculptures, and 18th-century altar-pieces and paintings. The **Museo delle Arti e Tradizioni Popolari "Michele Gortani"** is an ethnographical museum opened in 1937. Its collection illustrates the life, the traditions and early farming methods of the area.

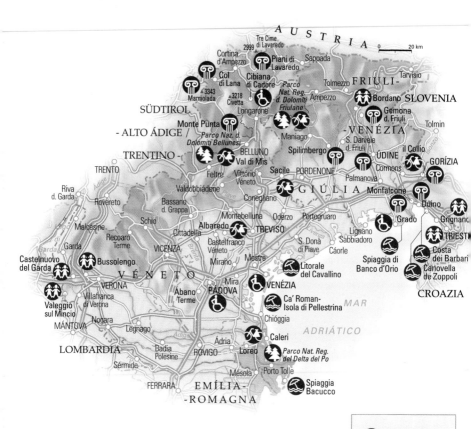

The long and, at times, troubled history of this land has shaped a multiform landscape where the scars of the Great War, the numerous land reclamation efforts, the fortifications from the Middle Ages and the structures from the Roman era stand side by side. Yet, this is much more than a land of history, with countless sandy beaches, various wonderful nature reserves and some notable amusement parks, including the well-known Gardaland with its attractions for children and parents. These itineraries combine all of these features,

Itineraries

from the remnants of trenches on Mt Grappa to the pristine and unique nature of the Po Delta. The well-marked roads and bike paths make exploring this zone both easy and enjoyable, allowing you to find some unusual gems, like the highest museum in Europe.

Highlights

- The areas of Belluno related to the Great War; the Roman era castles and forts in Friuli Venezia Giulia
- Gardaland and the other main amusement parks, and the museums for children
- The well-equipped and welcoming beaches on the Adriatic, an ideal holiday for families with children
- The three biggest parks: Dolomiti Bellunesi, Dolomiti Friulane and Delta del Po
- Five lovely bike trails that explore the natural surrounds

Inside

WORLD WAR I IN THE BELLUNO AREA

Between 1915 and 1917, a war within the War was fought on the Belluno Dolomites, the likes of which had never been seen before, nor since. The deep marks that that war made on these mountains left traces that can still be seen today.

The Dolomite Front

Starting from the north, the plains of Lavaredo (2,350 m) are the first place we encounter related to the history of the Great War. Amidst the peaks of some of the world's most beautiful mountains you can still visit the remains of Italian bases on the road from the Auronzo refuge to the Longeres mountain pass, south of the Three Peaks. Moving on, we come to the Lavaredo mountain pass, from which the Locatelli/Drei Zinnen refuge can be seen to the north. From the Auronzo refuge, it is easy to reach the area of the Arghena mountain pass (2,036 m), with remnants of trenches, and the Val de l'Aga, along which we come across an Italian fort built in the late 19th century.

The heroic dimension of the battles

The majestic Three Peak of Lavaredo are outstanding even in the mythical Dolomites

around the Three Peaks of Lavaredo withered on Mt Piana, where more than a thousand soldiers died in the vain attempt to occupy the mountain dominating the access to the Val di Landro. Today, the peak is reached by a shuttle from Lake Misurina, and you travel along the ring that linked Mt Piana to Mt Piano through tunnels and posts. The route then moves to the area of the Falzàrego Pass and the Val Travenanzes.

Be sure to visit the open-air museum at Cinque Torri (2,255 m), reached by a chairlift from Bai de Dones up to the Scoiattoli refuge, from where a signed route leads visitors through trenches, artillery stations, barracks and lookouts. Another open-air museum is at Piccolo Lagazuoi (2,778 m), one of the theatres of battle. A favorite target of the Italians, who were clinging to the Martini Ledge, was the Austrian fort, Tre Sassi (2,197 m), which defended the Valparola Pass and Val Badia. Today a museum is housed in the fort (built between 1897 and 1901), displaying objects from both fronts. Trips can be taken from the fort through trenches and tunnels and two cemeteries. From Valparola Pass, you can also reach a place that evokes the bloodiest images of the conflict on the Dolomites at the Col di Lana (2,209 m), or as the soldiers called it, the "Mountain of Blood". This was a mountain which, despite its low height, the Italian state (perhaps mistakenly) considered, from the start of the war, essential to have full dominance of the area. For almost a year, from July of 1915 to April of 1916, Italian troops were sent to the attack on the mountain's grassy slopes, where Austrian machine guns mowed them down. Thousands of soldiers were killed, until it was decided to blow up the mountaintop and the Austrian positions with an enormous mine placed under the southern peak. This also proved futile as the Austrians were entrenched on the nearby Sief peak to the north where they continued to block the pass to the Alps.

The history museum at Seràuta-Marmolada (2,950 m) (the highest in Europe) is full of documents of the battle fought on the "Queen of the Dolomites", one of the rare places in which Italians enjoyed an advantageous position, dominating the entire glacier. This is why the Austrians adopted an extraordinary solution, digging dozens of kilometers of tunnels under the glacier. The remains of this incredible "city of ice" are shown in the museum.

Grappa

After Caporetto, at the end of October of 1917, the Italians abandoned the Dolomite front. The troops retreated beyond the Piave and to Mt Grappa,

The Dolomite Front and Grappa

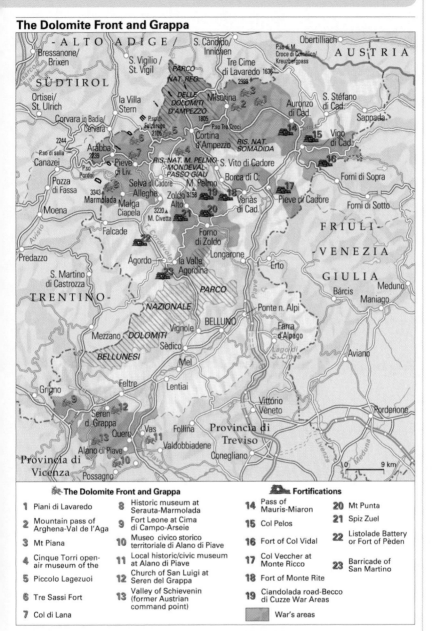

🌿 The Dolomite Front and Grappa

1 Piani di Lavaredo
2 Mountain pass of Arghena-Val de l'Aga
3 Mt Piana
4 Cinque Torri open-air museum of the
5 Piccolo Lagezuoi
6 Tre Sassi Fort
7 Col di Lana
8 Historic museum at Serauta-Marmolada
9 Fort Leone at Cima di Campo-Arseie
10 Museo civico storico territoriale di Alano di Piave
11 Local historic/civic museum at Alano di Piave
12 Church of San Luigi at Seren del Grappa
13 Valley of Schievenin (former Austrian command point)

🏰 Fortifications

14 Pass of Mauris-Miaron
15 Col Pelos
16 Fort of Col Vidal
17 Col Veccher at Monte Ricco
18 Fort of Monte Rite
19 Ciandolada road-Becco di Cuzze War Areas
20 Mt Punta
21 Spiz Zuel
22 Listolade Battery or Fort of Pèden
23 Barricade of San Martino

🟩 War's areas

where they successfully fought off two major Austrian offensives in the following months and then went on to a victorious counterattack that ended at Vittorio Veneto. The entire area affected by these events is part of the "Museo Diffuso del Grappa dal Brenta al Piave" project. In the Province of Belluno, parts of this museum include Fort Leone at the Campo di Arsiè peak, a mighty fortress built between 1908 and 1912; the Museo Civico Storico Territoriale at Alano di Piave, with an impressive photographic collection; the Museo Storico della Madonna del Piave at Vas, which has pieces from the conflict as well as items related to the river; the church of San Luigi at Serèn del Grappa, where a viewpoint on the Grappa is now located; and finally, the former Austrian point of command, which has been restored in the valley of Schievenìn near Quero.

119

CASTLES AND FORTIFICATIONS

For many centuries, from the Roman Age to the Modern Age, the Friuli and Giulia areas were the site of profuse fortification building. It was vital to defend travel routes and the rivers' fords. The situation was highly diversified and grew increasingly complex. Structures with military functions were joined by abbeys, villages and walled cities, growing to today's total of over 300 structures. The Romans built the first systems of fortifications and watchtowers. Castles in Gemona, Venzone and Udine were built between 1077 and 1420. The city of Palmanova (1593) is the sole example of a fortress built from scratch. Many other sites were adapted, expanded and renovated. After the 16th century, the importance of castles diminished. Those in isolated areas were often abandoned, while those near main roads became mansions.

In Venezia Giulia

The region's most famous castles are on the coast of Trieste. The castle of San Giusto overlooks Trieste. It was built in the early 15th century and renovated after World War I, adapted into a museum. The nearby 19th-century Miramare castle was built at the behest of Archduke Maximilian of Habsburg. In keeping with the fashion of that era, every room is inspired by a different style. The dining room features Rococo furniture; the chapel is Gothic; the sitting rooms are Japanese and Chinese;

Castles and fortifications

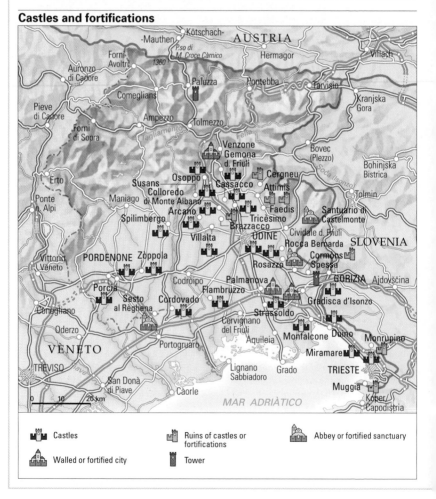

	Castles		Ruins of castles or fortifications		Abbey or fortified sanctuary
	Walled or fortified city		Tower		

Miramare castle: the surrounding water is part of a marine reserve

and the archduke's bedroom is set up like a ship cabin. A similar variety is seen in the park. Its romantic scenery includes a lake of swans, mountain pavilions, grottos, Greek statues, a Sphinx and hundreds of plant species. Moving west, we come to the castle of Duino: a group of buildings from various eras distributed within a courtyard that includes a tower partly built by Romans. There are nearby ruins of an earlier castle, destroyed by the Turks in the 15th century.

Gorizia is also loomed over by a hulking fortress, originally from the 11th century and expanded many times. The complex fell into disrepair starting in the 17th century, was bombed during World War I and rebuilt with its 16th century features, rendering it today sort of a castle/museum. The fortification works in Gradisca date from the 15th century. The Venetians fortified this city as a bulwark against Turkish raids; it fell into the hands of the Habsburgs in the early 16th century. The fortress at Monfalcone was the stronghold of the d'Aquileia patriarchate. Surviving is a square tower within circular walls, which are surrounded by the remains of pre-Roman *castelliere* settlement. It holds a paleontological museum about Karst geology. In Spessa (Capriva del Friuli), underground passages dug into the rock are all that remains of its 13th-century fortress. Ruins of a 7th-century fortification are found near Cormòns.

In Friuli

On the way to Carnia, the first castle is the Bernarda (Premariacco) fortress, turned into a residence in 1567. Today, it holds a wine producer, as does the nearby abbey of Rosazzo, a fortified medieval complex. The fortified sanctuary, Castelmonte in Cividalese, is the grandest of its kind. Continuing northwest, the rises controlling the valleys and roads were extremely well fortified. A visit to the Attimis medieval archeological museum is well worthwhile, illustrating the nature of the settlements, their construction types and the military needs that the castles of this area met. A short ways to the northeast, the fort of Osoppo, the castle of Gemona and the walled city of Venzone clearly announce their importance given their position in the valley of Tagliamento on the road to Austria.

The hills surrounding Udine are no less important. The castle of Udine, already documented in 983, sits atop the hill over the city. It was destroyed by an earthquake in 1517 and rebuilt with residential and diplomatic functions; it is currently home to the Civici Musei. Castles around the city include Tricesimo, Cassacco, Colloredo di Monte Albano, Susans, Arcano and the ruins of the upper castle of Brazzacco. Villalta boasts one of Friuli's most majestic medieval castles, which includes a residence, a crenellated wall, towers and a keep. On the plain, the fortress city of Palmanova is noteworthy; and there are two 14th-century castles in Strassoldo.

The greatest example of a fortified construction in the Pordenone Friuli area is the abbey of Santa Maria in Sylvis at Sesto al Reghena, first documented in 762. It was destroyed in 889 and then rebuilt. The travails of history have brought it to us in its current form, slowly developed since the 15th century. Other important sites include the castles of Porcìa, Cordovado and Zòppola (with a 15th-century tower and an 18th-century chapel) and the castle of Spilimbergo, consisting of a series of structures gathered around a courtyard, is of particular interest.

PARCO NAZIONALE DELLE DOLOMITI BELLUNESI

PROVINCE OF BELLUNO

AREA: 31,512 HECTARES. MOUNTAINOUS AREA WITH STEEP ROCKY PEAKS, GLACIAL AND FLUVIAL EROSION FEATURES, WOODS AND HIGH ALTITUDE PASTURES.

HEADQUARTERS: ENTE PARCO NAZIONALE DOLOMITI BELLUNESI, PIAZZA ZANCANARO 1, FELTRE (BL), TEL. 04393328, E-MAIL: ENTE@DOLOMITIPARK.IT

VISITORS' CENTERS: IN PEDAVENA, PIAZZA 1° NOVEMBRE 1, TEL. 0439304400; IN VINCHETO DI CELLARDA, RISERVA NATURALE-ZONA UMIDA, TEL. 043989520.

WEB SITE: WWW.DOLOMITIPARK.IT

On the southern edge of the mountain chain, groups of varying types of mountains run from southwest to northeast. The first are the Alpi Feltrine with craggy, steep slopes, glacial cirques and grassy peaks next to the Dolomitic plateau structures of the Cimonega subgroup and the Karst of Erera-Brendol and the Piani Eterni. Beyond the gully of the Canale del Mis, the Pizzon-Feruch-Monti del Sole group rises. Separated by another valley gully are the Schiara-Pelf group and then the Monte Talvena-Cima di Pramper ridge.

Plant and wildlife

Its plant life is the area's most interesting aspect. There are true rarities among its 1,500 identified species of plants, such as the Moretti bellflower, the park's symbol, the extremely rare Alpine scurvy grass and the alyssum of Obir. There are four large hoofed animal species (chamois, roe buck, deer and mouflon), and the carnivores include the wolf, the marten and the beech marten. Dominant bird species include day (the golden eagle, the buzzard and the kestrel) and night raptors (royal owl and dwarf owl), the tetraonidae (mountain pheasant and capercaillie) and the woodpeckers. A resurgence of large carnivores such as the lynx and brown bear evidence the area's great natural value.

A stunning view of the imposing Castello del Mochesin (2,500 m)

The golden eagle (Aquila chrysaetos) can grow to 84 cm and have a wingspan of 2 m. Once it was nearly absent from the Alps, but it is now protected and can be found in just about every valley

A mighty, mountainous bulwark rises above the plateau of Western Friuli. The Friuli Dolomites are difficult to navigate and considered an area with a high degree of wilderness. The slopes have deep creases, faults and surfaces smoothed by the sliding of rocky layers. Nature has worked on the rock, contrasting pyramids of earth with ancient ice deposits and a wide range of Karst forms with rock piles. Its relative proximity to the sea, heavy rains and the mountains' orientation mean the vegetation bands occur at lower altitudes than normal. Up to 1,000 m, thermophilic woods dominate, followed by red fir forests mixed with beech and white fir trees, which give way to larch and dwarf pines at higher altitudes.

Animal life is another precious wealth of the area. Chamois, capercaillie and rock goat live here on a permanent basis. Also on hand are the European honey-buzzard, the black woodpecker, all kinds of tetraonidae and the golden eagles. Of special paleontological significance is the discovery in 1994 of theropod dinosaur prints in the Casera Casavento area, impressed on a mass of Dolomia Principale deposited in the Late Triassic Age (approx. 210 million years ago).

Key to symbols

Ⓢ Park headquarters

Ⓥ Visitors' center

Human history and the park

Archeological digs have brought to light prehistoric traces dating back 40,000 years and the discovery of an Epigravettian grave (around 12,000 years ago). In more recent times (the 18th and 19th centuries), miners, mountaineers and foresters were the main figures active on the land. There are fascinating mines in Val Imperina, with a mining village over five hundred years old. There are many huts and cottages, abandoned for decades, which have been renovated and are ready to be given a second life under the park's management.

PARCO NATURALE REGIONALE DELLE DOLOMITI FRIULANE

PROVINCES OF PORDENONE AND UDINE

AREA: 36,950 HECTARES. VALLEYS, SLOPES AND MOUNTAINOUS MASSIFS OF THE WESTERN ALPS.

HEADQUARTERS: VIA V. EMANUELE II 27, CIMOLAIS (PN), TEL. 042787333/877404, E-MAIL: CIMOLAIS@AGEMONT.IT

VISITORS' CENTERS: L'AVIFAUNA DEL PARCO (ANDREIS), TEL. 0427764416; LA VEGETAZIONE DEL PARCO (FORNI DI SOPRA), TEL. 043388080. GUIDED VISITS AND EDUCATIONAL ACTIVITIES (TEL. 042787333).

WEB SITE: WWW.REGIONE.FVG.IT/BENVENUTI /BENVENUTI.HTM

PARCO NATURALE REGIONALE DEL DELTA DEL PO

PROVINCE OF ROVIGO

AREA: 12,592 HECTARES. COMPLEX OF WETLANDS IN THE PO DELTA.

HEADQUARTERS: ENTE PARCO, VIA G. MARCONI 6, ARIANO NEL POLESINE (RO), TEL. 042637220, E-MAIL: INFO@PARCODELTAPO.ORG

VISITORS' CENTERS: CENTRO TURISTICO CULTURALE SAN BASILIO, TEL. 042671200; RIFUGIO PARCO DEL DELTA DEL PO, VIA GORINO SULLAM 43, TAGLIO DI PO, TEL. 042688254.

WEB SITE: WWW.PARCODELTAPO.ORG

An oystercatcher

The Park includes one of Italy's most biologically dynamic environments, formed by sedimentation from the Po and the wandering of its branches. The environment has the features of a wilderness but a landscape strongly conditioned by human presence. Ongoing efforts to direct it, drain it and consolidate it have proved sometimes effective, sometimes useless and with disastrous results (breaches, floods and so forth). The agricultural landscape features stretches of corn, alfalfa and soy crops, broken up by dams. Towns, villages, neo-Classical villas, industrial and hydraulic systems are distributed along the waterways and historic roads. Despite the many marks of human activity, this is still a frontier landscape which melds into a natural landscape near the river mouths. The features of the area's spatial organization are lost in a tangled mosaic of valleys, inlets and sandy strips. These are the reproductive habitats of countless species of birds, which attract droves of devoted bird-watchers. The areas of typical lake and halophyte plant life create a great environmental variety. The coexistence of fresh and salt water diversify the animal species as well, with common coastal species such as gray mullets, surmullets, sole, and inland water species such as carp and catfish. Also of interest are the fragments of fossil dune shoals, partly forested and now far from the sea.

Scardovari. The shoal with the same name is the largest in the delta (3,800 ha) . It has no riverine vegetation, except for some southern reed-beds

GARDALAND

Castelnuovo del Garda (Verona)

FACILITIES: Many refreshment points, picnic areas, shops, photo service, nursery, and stroller rental.

GETTING THERE
By car: from Milan, A4 Milano-Venezia highway, Peschiera del Garda exit; from Venice, Sommacampagna exit; A22 Modena-Brennero highway, Affi exit.
By train: Peschiera del Garda train station; free shuttle bus to park.

INFO: Gardaland, Località Ronchi, Castelnuovo del Garda (Verona), tel. 0456449777, web: www.gardaland.it

OPENING TIMES: 23 March – 30 September, daily; October, only weekends; special openings at the end of October (Halloween) and during Christmas season. 9.30 a.m.–6 p.m.; summer (22 June – 10 September) 9 a.m.–Midnight.

ADMISSION: full-price € 22; discounted (over 1 meter tall – 10 years old) € 18.50, free under 1 meter tall; 2 consecutive days € 35 and € 29; 3 days of your choice € 46 and € 37; evenings after 8 p.m. (summer) € 15 and € 13; season ticket € 75 and season evening ticket € 40.

and the Kingdom of Tunga.
For bigger kids, there are the Colorado Boats carved out of tree trunks, the Jungle Rapids and the Valle dei Re. Kids more than 1 meter (about three and a half feet) tall can enjoy the Magic Mountain roller coaster. There are also age and height restrictions for the dynamic cinema of the Isola dei Dinosauri and the heart-challenging attractions, such as Space Vertigo and Blue Tornado. One of the newest attractions is Fuga da Atlantide, a trip on a 20-seater boat through fabulous scenery with two 10- and 15-meter drops. Palablu, a dolphin aquarium, is also part of the park. If you love entertainment, you'll enjoy the Torneo Medievale and Fantasy on Ice, with ice skaters acting out fairy tales.

Gardaland is Italy's largest and best-known amusement park

Opened in 1975 and expanded to become Italy's largest and best-known amusement park, Gardaland is at the top of the list for families with children as well as young people and adults. Its mascot is Prezzemolo, a little dragon; his house is near the entrance in the area reserved for little kids. Its trunk leads to the Magic House, a fun house where everything is topsy turvy, and a stairway between its branches leads up to a scenic viewpoint. Other kids' attractions include the Doremifarm, the Volaplano kiddie airplane, Baby Pilota carousel and the Puppet Theatre. Elsewhere there are plenty of attractions suited for kids, such as Trans Gardaland Express, the Flying Island orbiting station and the Panoramic Tour cable railway. Popular attractions include the Orto Bruco caterpillar ride

PARCO GIARDINO DI SIGURTÀ

Valeggio sul Mincio (Verona)

GETTING THERE
By car: A4 Milano-Venezia highway, Peschiera or Sommacampagna exits; Bologna-Brennero highway, Mantova or Verona exit.

INFO: Parco Giardino Sigurtà, Valeggio sul Mincio (Verona), tel. 0456371033, web: www.sigurta.it

OPENING TIMES: March – early November: 9 a.m.–6 p.m. (exit 7 p.m.).

ADMISSION: full price € 8; discounted (6–14 years old) € 5.50; free to 6 years old; train ride € 2 per person, free for 0 to 5 years old; bicycle rental € 3 an hour; electric golf-cart rental € 12 weekdays, € 15 Sundays and holidays

The park is considered among the most beautiful in the world, covering 50 hectares near Lake Garda. It can be visited along two routes to enjoy its flowers and buildings. The yellow route starts from the Eremo lakes with their dwarf water lilies and continues towards the small neo-Gothic church and the dog cemetery. The red route starts at the avenue of roses and continues with a walk and

Parco Natura Viva includes an animal and a safari park

visit through the water gardens, a garden of medicinal plants and a religious grotto. The garden is perfect for visitors of all ages, and particularly for enthusiasts of botany and nature photography. At the ticket office you are provided with a map that illustrates the most interesting points, which can be reached walking on one of the two routes (each takes about 50 minutes) or with the trains that cross the 7 km of the Route of the Magical Spells. With this option, the scenic tour takes about 30 minutes with no stops. Bicycles and golf-carts can also be rented in the park.

PARCO NATURA VIVA

BUSSOLENGO (VERONA)

FACILITIES: PLAYGROUND FOR CHILDREN, SNACK BAR, PIZZERIA, PUB, BUFFET, RESTAURANT.

GETTING THERE

BY CAR: A4 MILANO-VENEZIA HIGHWAY, PESCHIERA DEL GARDA EXIT; A22 HIGHWAY, VERONA NORD EXIT, IF YOU ARE COMING FROM VENICE OR BOLOGNA, AFFI EXIT IF YOU ARE COMING FROM TRENTO; SS 11 PESCHIERA-VERONA, CASTELNUOVO-PASTRENGO DIRECTION.
BY TRAIN: VERONA PORTA NUOVA TRAIN STATION.

INFO: PARCO NATURA VIVA, LOCALITÀ FIGARA 40, BUSSOLENGO (VERONA), TEL. 0457170052, WEB: WWW.PARCONATURAVIVA.IT

OPENING TIMES:
FEBRUARY–NOVEMBER: IN FEBRUARY ONLY HOLIDAYS AND HOLIDAY EVES; WEDNESDAYS IN NOVEMBER. FEBRUARY–MAY AND OCTOBER–NOVEMBER 9 A.M.–4 P.M.; JUNE, JULY, SEPTEMBER 9 A.M.–5 P.M.; AUGUST 9 A.M.–6 P.M.

ADMISSION: ANIMAL PARK, FULL PRICE € 9, DISCOUNTED (3-12 YEARS OLD) € 7; SAFARI FULL PRICE € 9, DISCOUNTED € 7; PARK + SAFARI, FULL PRICE € 13, DISCOUNTED € 10.50

Nestled in the green of the hills, the park includes two sections, an animal park and a safari park. Rare animals and some endangered species live in the animal park area. The route gives visitors close up views of monkeys, bison, camels, leopards, pumas, lynx, bears and many species of birds and wild animals. There is also a dinosaur park and tropical birdhouse in this area. Plus, there's a small aquarium with fish, amphibians and reptiles. The safari park may be visited only by car or bus. The route is 7 km long and takes about 90 minutes.

CASA DELLE FARFALLE

BORDANO (UDINE)

The Butterfly House has some of the largest specimens in the world

GETTING THERE
BY CAR: A23 HIGHWAY, GEMONA-OSOPPO EXIT, TAKE SS 13, AT THE GEMONA-CAMPAGNOLA TRAFFIC LIGHTS, TURN LEFT AND CONTINUE FOR ABOUT 2 KM TOWARDS TRASAGHIS, CROSS THE BRAULINS BRIDGE, AND TURN RIGHT FOR BORDANO.

INFO: CASA DELLE FARFALLE, VIA CANADA, BORDANO (UDINE), TEL. 0432988049, WEB: WWW.CASAPERLEFARFALLE.IT

OPENING TIMES: MARCH–OCTOBER 9.30 A.M.–12.30 P.M. AND 2 P.M. – 5.30 P.M. (UNTIL 4 P.M. IN MARCH AND OCTOBER); HOURS CONTINUE THROUGH SPRING HOLIDAYS.

ADMISSION: FULL PRICE, HOLIDAYS AND WEEKENDS € 6.50, WEEKDAYS € 5.50; DISCOUNTED (4-12 YEARS OLD), HOLIDAYS AND WEEKENDS, € 3.50, WEEKDAYS € 3.20

The center includes the Butterfly House and the Entomological Trail. Colorful butterflies fly free in the Butterfly House in exotic gardens with three settings: one Amazon garden, one African tropics and one Indian/Australian setting. Visitors can see the butterflies' development stages, learn the difference between diurnal butterflies and moths, and observe their insect behavior. The largest butterflies in the world are part of the collection.

SCIENCE CENTRE IMMAGINARIO SCIENTIFICO

GRIGNANO (TRIESTE)

GETTING THERE

BY CAR: TAKE COASTAL ROAD (SS 14) FROM THE CITY CENTER, PASS TWO TUNNELS AFTER THE MIRAMARE INTERSECTION, GO LEFT IN THE DIRECTION OF GRIGNANO MARE: FROM A4 HIGHWAY, SS 14 IN THE DIRECTION OF TRIESTE, AFTER ABOUT 5 KM, AND BEFORE THE TWO MIRAMARE TUNNELS, TURN RIGHT IN THE DIRECTION OF GRIGNANO MARE.

The Science Centre has interactive games and multimedia attractions

BY TRAIN: TRIESTE RAILWAY STATION.

INFO: SCIENCE CENTRE IMMAGINARIO SCIENTIFICO, RIVA MASSIMILIANO E CARLOTTA 15, GRIGNANO (TRIESTE), TEL. 040224424, WEB: WWW.IMMAGINARIOSCIENTIFICO.IT

OPENING TIMES: YEAR ROUND. FROM OCTOBER TO MAY, SATURDAY–SUNDAY (10 A.M.– 8 P.M.); FROM JUNE TO SEPTEMBER, FRIDAY (7 P.M.–11 P.M.), SATURDAY AND SUNDAY (10 A.M.–9 P.M.).

ADMISSION: FULL PRICE € 4, DISCOUNTED € 3

The Science Centre Immaginario Scientifico is a science museum that combines interactive play and multi-media entertainment with the pleasure of learning and discovery. The Elis space features theme-based exhibits updated with multiple scenes on jumbo screens, hypertexts and interactive exhibits. The Area space contains a collection of interactive stations, organized in six theme-based routes with items to touch and play with. The inflatable Starlab planetarium is in the latter area. The exhibits and shows are supported by many educational events, planned for groups and individuals of different ages.

MUSEO DEL MARE

TRIESTE

GETTING THERE

BY CAR: A4 VENEZIA-TRIESTE HIGHWAY, LISERT TOLL STATION, SISTIANA EXIT.

BY TRAIN: TRIESTE RAILWAY STATION.

INFO: MUSEO DEL MARE, VIA CAMPO MARZIO 5, TRIESTE, TEL. 040304987.

OPENING TIMES: 8.30 A.M.–1.30 P.M., YEAR ROUND, CLOSED MONDAYS, CIVIL AND RELIGIOUS HOLIDAYS.

ADMISSION: FULL PRICE € 2.58; DISCOUNTED € 1.55; FREE TO 5 YEARS OLD

The Museo del Mare [Museum of the Sea] lets visitors discover the history of boating, with an exhibit of ship models and instruments. Theme-based spaces are related to historical figures and events. One hall is entirely dedicated to Guglielmo Marconi with the radio equipment that was on the Elettra (the yacht that he turned into a floating laboratory). Another hall is dedicated to Frantisek Ressel, considered the inventor of the propeller applied to steamboats. On the ground floor, there are models of Columbus's three ships, and the first floor is dedicated to 19th-century sailing in Trieste. The second floor has functional models of steam engines. The outside courtyard has a cross section of the hull and an anchor of the Elettra.

The regions of Veneto and Friuli Venezia Giulia have some of Northern Italy's most beautiful and famed beaches with wide, sandy coastlines, blue seas and well-furnished, comfortable seaside resorts. Most beaches on the Upper Adriatic Sea are very long with wide sandy stretches, sloping gently towards the sea for easy access to the water. Seaside resorts in these regions are exceptional for their high quality services and many special events, and can be reached quickly from cities of extraordinary historic and artistic interest. The most notable beaches in the Veneto and Friuli Venezia Giulia are listed below.

Spiaggia di Boccasette

(Province of Rovigo) Located in the Po delta, it is reached on a diversion of the Romea state road at Contarina, in the direction of Ca' Venier. Passing Po di Maistra, continue to Boccasette, from where you can reach the sea by following the road through the valleys for 1 km. From June to September, a floating footbridge connects the bank to the shoal on which, other than a bar and a *trattoria* for dining near the bridge, there is only a narrow strip of sand with sparse vegetation. The tips of the shoal are home to colonies of oystercatchers, which must not be distrubed.

Scano Boa

(Province of Rovigo) Perfect visitors to Scano Boa are those who embrace nature's unpredictability and limits to their mobility imposed by the biological cycle of different animal species; those who appreciate a beach with no colorful umbrellas or barbecues. This is the Po Delta's historic sandbar, the longest in the Adriatic Sea. Its boundaries (which are sadly often ignored by those tramping through the park areas) are dictated by rules for conserving a fragile environment, with limits changing from season to season based on the erosion and re-filling of the delta's coasts. They are also set by the reproduction cycle of the oystercatchers, which live here from June onwards.

Spiaggia di Bacucco

(Province of Rovigo) To get to Bacucco beach, after getting off the Romea state road between Mesola and Taglio di Po, turn on the road for Porto Tolle. At Ca' Vendramin, follow the road that runs parallel to the Po di Gnocca to reach Gorino Sullam. After you pass the town, continue to the riverbank at Bacucco point. From here, take a boat to an island very close to the coast. During the summer, frequent ferries take you to the sandy shore that marks the edges of a land sculpted by wind and tides.

Ca' Roman – Island of Pellestrina

(Province of Venice) To reach the Ca' Roman beach from the Lido di Venezia, take bus 11 in Piazzale S. Maria Elisabetta and continue by ferry to the Lido di Pellestrina. When you get to the Pellestrina cemetery, you can walk along the "Murazzo" wall or take a motorboat straight to Chioggia. Another option is to rent a bike at the Lido di Venezia and ride along the entire coast. It is easiest to reach the island directly from Chioggia, where you take a motor boat to Pellestrina. Ca' Roman is the first stop; the history of this beach began when an off shore dyke was built around the turn of the 19th century. The sea current then favored the accumulation of sand which gradually formed the beach. The absence of beach resorts or tourism facilities allowed the environment to evolve absolutely naturally, forming many dunes and a wood behind the dunes. The area is full of plant and wildlife. Birds nesting here include puffins, various species of sparrows, royal seagulls and, especially in the summer, Sandwich terns and oystercatchers.

Laguna del Morto

(Province of Venice) This large, wide open beach is close to a small coastal lagoon formed by the accumulation of lime and sand brought by the sea current and the Piave River. It is one of the few non-urbanized stretches of the Venetian coast, well protected thanks to the many environmental battles that brought up the risk of damages caused by years of negligence. The entire area is filled with native plant and wildlife. To get here, exit the A4 at the San Donà di Piave toll station, and take the state road to San Donà, continuing to Eraclea Mare. From here, continue on the municipal road towards the Marina di Eraclea basin. After parking, walk along the path that runs along the lagoon, entering in a large, beautiful pine forest amidst the dunes. Go through the wavy hills of sand to come to the seashore.

Litorale del Cavallino

(Province of Venice) From Punta Sabbioni, take a short stretch of road running along the dyke and come, to the left, to Via Montello, on which you find several entrances to the Del Cavallino beach, passing through a thicket of mixed conifers and broad-leafed trees. The sea can also be reached from the opposite side, from the Lido di Jesolo. When you get to the town center of Cavallino, follow Via Ca' Savio until you reach Via Adige. At the end of this street, from which other sea entrances branch off, you take Via Spealto to the left, and then, at the intersection to the right, Via Montello, which takes you to the sea through some thick plant growth. The abundance of green areas is caused by the nearby mouths of the Rivers Sile and Piave, and the area's geographic biology which includes both Mediterranean maquis and a steppe area. Three separate natural areas can be identified. In the first area there are maritime pines, black alder and bushes surrounded by heather, sea fennel and sea holly. The second area features dunes with lichen, moss and reeds. Finally, we find the area most affected by the sea, full of sea rocket and clot bur; from here, stretch a sandy beach and a foreshore coated with countless pieces of shells.

Litorale di Valle Vecchia or Spiaggia della Brussa

(Province of Venice) The Brussa beach has no tourist services, which means that it is almost forgotten in favor of the more well-known beaches of Lignano Sabbiadoro. It is reached by getting off the A4 at the Portogruaro toll station, about 25 km away. When you get off the highway, follow signs to Caorle; after 9 km, turn in the direction of Latisana. After another 8 km, follow the road going south to Brussa-Valle Vecchia. The road ambles through the beautiful landscape of the fishing valleys nestled in an area of reclaimed land to eventually reach its destination. The beach is sandy and protected on the sides by a wonderful, fragrant pine thicket near the dunes, a perfect place for resting after taking a dip.

Spiaggia di Banco d'Orio

(Province of Gorizia) The Banco d'Orio beach is part of the municipality of Grado, and it is located beyond the long beach at the end of the island. It is a large area formed by a shoal on the lagoon's

The Banca d'Orio beach consists of a sandy shoal on the southern shore of the lagoon

southern edge. The area, Banco d'Orio, is part of a coastal area for which environmental protection and nature reserve projects are planned. On the southern side, the sea soaks the sand; while to the north the lagoon's muddy depths prevail. On these banks, filled with lush plant life, gulls and many other lake birds fly in peace. The area can be reached by motor boat from the port of Grado.

Spiaggia di Canovella de' Zoppoli

(Province of Trieste) Take state road 14 from Trieste towards Monfalcone to get to the Canovella beach. Park your car about a half kilometer from the area's only natural tunnel. Not far away is a lovely pebbly beach named after the traditional, rough-hewn boats made of hollowed tree trunks, in the tradition of this ancient mooring for tuna fishers. You get to the seashore through a convenient, though long and winding stairway that descends from the coastal road amidst large vineyards and thick Mediterranean maquis.

Costa dei Barbari

(Province of Trieste) Coming from Monfalcone, you reach the sea a short way past the town of Sistiana. Once you arrive, leave your car in a bend that has been closed to traffic and turned into a parking lot. The beach stretches the considerable length from the Sistiana bay to the Aurisina marina. The rocky beach is gorgeous and framed by Mediterranean plant life. There are no buildings or places to eat in the area, which makes it perfect for those in pursuit of quiet and nature.

MUSEO DELLE NUVOLE

Cibiana di Cadore (Belluno)

GETTING THERE
BY CAR: A27 highway, Pian di Vedoja exit; take SS 51 and SS 347 to Cibiana di Cadore to reach the town of Forcella Cibiana.

VISITORS' CENTER: tel. 043531315, www.museonellenuvole.it

OPEN from 1 June to the first snow of October.

The highest museum in Europe (at 2,181 m) is built on a World War I fortress on the peak of Mt Rite. The famous climber Reinhold Messner conceived the idea for a museum "above the clouds". The fortress was restored to become home to archeological finds, drawings, photographs, minerals and other pieces made available by Messner. The museum is reached with a shuttle bus and has no architectural barriers. Audiocassettes are available.

MUSEO CIVICO CORRER

Venice

GETTING THERE
By boat: public boat services from Venice's San Lucia station: lines 1, 82 and 51, 41.

VISITORS' CENTER: Piazza S. Marco 52, tel. 0412405211, www.museicivicivenezian.it

OPEN from November to March (9 a.m.–5 p.m.), from April to October (9 a.m.–7 p.m.).

The museum offers a fascinating exploration of Venice's art and history. It includes interesting clues to what life was like in Venice between the 14th and 18th centuries. The entrance for disabled visitors is located in Calle del Salvadego. The first floor can be reached by elevator. An exhibit for blind visitors has been installed, equipped with an audio guide. A special handrail runs through the four exhibit halls for the tactile exploration of small bronzes and sculptures in openable cases. The exhibit pieces are also provided with Braille captions. A tactile map at the entrance describes the entire area.

ORTO BOTANICO DELL'UNIVERSITÀ DI PADOVA

Padua

GETTING THERE
Located near the Basilica of Sant'Antonio. By bus: 8, 12, 18.

VISITORS' CENTER: Via Orto Botanico 15, tel. 0498272119, www.ortobotanico.unipd.it

OPEN from 21 March to 31 October, daily (9 a.m.–1 p.m., 3 p.m.–6 p.m.). From 1 November to 21 March, from Monday to Saturday (9 a.m.–1 p.m.).

Created in 1545, it is the oldest university botanical garden in the world. There was an adjacent research center for cultivating medicinal and exotic plants; the potato, the sunflower, the rhubarb and the lilac were cultivated here for the first time. The garden has been declared a UNESCO World Heritage Site, and holds important historic plant collections. There is also a large collection of medicinal, poisonous and insectivore plants and rare and endangered species. About 6,000 plants are grown in the garden. There is an educational tour through the garden for sight-disabled visitors.

THE OLD CENTRE OF GRADO

Grado (Gorizia)

GETTING THERE
BY CAR: A4 highway, Palmanova exit; continue to Cervignano and Aquileia.
BY TRAIN: Monfalcone or Cervignano station.
BY BUS: APT Gorizia, tel. 800955957.
BY PLANE: Ronchi dei Legionari airport.

VISITORS' CENTER: AIAT Grado, Via Dante Alighieri 72, Grado, tel. 0431877111, www.grado.turismo.info

Grado is an accessible city. The historic center is a pedestrian zone paved with stone slabs; it can be traversed in a wheelchair. It has reserved parking places, and handicap-designated cars may also park in areas for residents. There are steps to the Cathedral that can be passed with a platform. Footbridges render the ruins of the Basilica of San Giovanni open to visitors. Piazza Biagio Marin is connected to the boardwalk by a ramp.

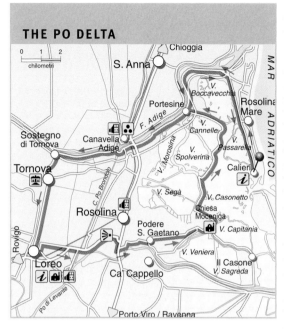

THE PO DELTA

ROUTE 50 KM: PORTO CALERI - ROSOLINA MARE - PORTESINE - LOREO - SAN GAETANO FARM - VIA DELLE VALLI - PORTESINE CROSS-ROADS - ROSOLINA MARE - PORTO CALERI. ON PAVED ROADS, NOT ALWAYS IN GOOD CONDITIONS. THE STARTING POINT IS 25 KM FROM CHIOGGIA. IT IS REACHED BY GETTING OFF THE SS 309 ROMEA AT THE INTERSECTION WITH SP 65 IN THE PORTO CALERI DIRECTION.

DIFFICULTY: THE ROUTE IS NOT DIFFICULT IN TERMS OF HILLINESS. HOWEVER, THE 50 KM REQUIRE A MINIMUM LEVEL OF TRAINING. THE SUN IN SUMMER AND WIND ALL YEAR ROUND CAN CREATE SOME DIFFICULTIES.

BIKE + TRAIN: THE LOREO TRAIN STATION IS ON THE CHIOGGIA-ROVIGO LINE.

BIKE SERVICE: CRIVELLARI GIUSEPPE, STRADA DEL SUD 218, ROSOLINA MARE, TEL. 042668462.

TOURIST NFORMATION
APT ROVIGO, VIA J.H. DUNANT 10, TEL. 0425386290, WWW.APT.ROVIGO.IT
ENTE PARCO DELTA DEL PO, VIA MARCONI 6, ARIANO NEL POLESINE, TEL. 0426372202, WWW.PARKS.IT/PARCO.DELTA.PO.VE/; WWW.PARCODELTAPO.ORG

From Loreo to Caleri

The Po Delta is a place of delicate balances where

Key to symbols

🔴	Point of departure and arrival
⚪	Stop en route
i	Tourist Information Office
🚉	Train station
🏰	Castle
⛪	Church
🏛	Museum
🏛	Monastery, abbey
🏛	Villa, palace, park
🔭	Viewpoint
💧	Spring
⁝⁝	Ancient monuments, ruins

land and water team up with human intervention to form a unique landscape. Start biking from the botanical garden in Porto Caleri where you take the SP 65 and continue straight. The road runs through a pine forest and the valleys of Boccavecchia and Passarella. Go left at the intersection for Casoni, staying on SP 65, and then turn right on Via Ca' Diedo, which passes over a canal and, past a pizzeria, goes up the banks of the Adige River. Cross Via Romea taking care at the dangerous intersection, and continue along the river bank (Via Adige). Pass a lock with a drawbridge on the Po Brondolo canal. Shortly thereafter, on the left, you come to the houses of Corte di Cavanella where Roman-age archeological remains have been discovered. Come to the Loreo Canal and leave the river bank to turn left on Via Tornova, which runs along the canal. Past the village of Tornova, go right at the crossroads and continue to follow the canal to Loreo, which was an important river port for the Venetian Serenissima Republic, as witnessed by the beautiful Venetian-style houses overlooking the canal. At the bridge over the navigable Loreo Canal (Piazza Matteotti), turn left and take Via Roma. After 250 m, you reach a roundabout where you turn left on Via XXV Aprile. Cross a level crossing and then, shortly thereafter, turn left on SP 45. Then turn right to Rosolina Mare and take the bridge over the Romea road and continue towards Albarella. After a few kilometers, near the San Gaetano farm, leave Via delle Valli and turn left onto the road of the reclaimed land, to the abandoned Moceniga church.

Right before the church, you pass near the Veniera barn, a testament to the history of Veneto barns, once a common sight in the delta, where fish were chosen and sorted out for the markets.

Continue to the left on Via delle Valli along the bank going through the Segà, Spolvetina and Cannelle valleys where you have a good chance of catching glimpses of wildlife. Come to the Portesine junction and turn right following SP 65, a fairly heavily trafficked road which leads to the crossroads to Porto Caleri where you go right on Via Boccavecchia. At the detour to the left for Rosolina Mare, continue straight following signs for the Giardino Botanico [botanical garden] of Porto Caleri and come to the parking lot.

Fishing weels, Porto Calieri

BIKE + TRAIN: RETURN IN TRAIN FROM ALBAREDO TO TREVISO ON THE VICENZA-TREVISO LINE.

BIKE SERVICE: PINARELLO, BORGO MAZZINI 9, TREVISO, TEL. 0422543821. CONTE, VIA XI FEBBRAIO 28, QUINTO DI TREVISO, TEL. 0422379227.

TOURIST INFORMATION APT TREVISO, VIA TONIOLO 41, TEL. 0422540600, WWW.SEVENONLINE.IT/TVAPT PARCO DEL SILE, VIA TANDURA 40, TREVISO, TEL. 0422321994, WWW.PARKS.IT/PARCO.FIUME.SILE/

ALONG THE SILE

ROUTE 28 KM: TREVISO - QUINTO DI TREVISO - CORNAROTTA - ONGARIE - BADOERE - SPADA - TORRESELLE - LORENZONI - SORGENTI DEL SILE - CASACORBA - ALBAREDO. RETURN TO TREVISO BY TRAIN. IF YOU WISH TO RETURN BY BIKE: AT THE CHAPEL OF CASACORBA, GO RIGHT ONTO VIA SILE AND TAKE THE BIKE PATH THROUGH VICILIEGIE AND CORRIVA, WHERE YOU GO RIGHT TO CAVASAGRA. THEN, GO STRAIGHT TO QUINTO AND MADONNA DELL'ALBERA; 300 M AFTER THE CHAPEL, TURN RIGHT ONTO VIA MUNARA TOWARDS THE SILE RIVER. TAKE VIA BASSA, THEN RIGHT ONTO VIA BARBASSO AND LEFT ONTO VIA PESCATORI. AT THE BRIDGE, GO STRAIGHT TO QUINTO DI TREVISO, AND TAKE VIA NOALESE FROM HERE TO TREVISO.

DIFFICULTY: SUITABLE FOR ALL RIDERS. NO MAJOR HILLS.

From Treviso to Albaredo

A peaceful ride along the course of the Sile, a rare spring-water river (the largest in Italy) whose sources are in the plain.

To leave the center of Treviso, take Via Calmaggiore, Via XX Settembre, Corso del Popolo and, after crossing the bridge, the Mattei Lungosile, which is closed to motor traffic. Turn to the left in Via dei Cacciatori, and after passing a level crossing, take Via Sant'Angelo under the bypass road and continue to the intersection with SS 515 to Quinto di Treviso. Cross the state road and continue towards Ongarie and Badoere. Now you are riding outside the urban area, in a countryside where you can see many farmhouses and pools formed by the waters of the Sile. A little later, you come to the entrance of the Cervara nature oasis. The ride continues along Via Cornarotta, and after passing through a residential area of Ongarie, you turn right and come to Piazza Indipendenza in the center of the village

of Badoere. The village has an unusual city plan, having been a market center since 1689.

You leave Badoere turning right on Via Palazzo, and then left on Via Marcello and left again on Via Rialto, which passes the Zero River and takes you through an area with asparagus fields, meadows and poplar groves.

You come out onto Via Levada, where you turn right. After about 200 m, turn right on Via Menaredo and right again on Via Foscolo, then left onto Via Munaron. The road ends in Via Piave in Spada. Continue right passing near the houses of Torreselle and Lorenzoni, where, at a flashing traffic light you turn right on Via Montegrappa, which winds through the countryside.

Go 2,2 km on Via Montegrappa and turn towards the Sile's sources. Turn right on the dirt road and left at the next junction. Turn on Via Montegrappa, which becomes Via Santa Brigida, and ride on to the small chapel of Case Seccafien. Here, turn right towards another chapel in Casacorba, where you turn left towards Albaredo and the railway station to take the train back to Treviso.

A stretch of the Sile River at Quinto di Treviso

PARCO DELLE DOLOMITI BELLUNESI

ROUTE 52 KM: ÀGORDO - PONTE DELLA MUDA - LA STANGA - CANDATEN - PERON - MAS - LAGO DI VEDANA - PASCOLI - LAGO DEL MIS - GENA BASSA - FORCELLA FRANCHE - RIVAMONTE AGORDINO. ON A PAVED ROAD AT ALTITUDES BETWEEN 360 AND 990 M.

DIFFICULTY: THE ROUTE INCLUDES ONLY ONE LONG UPHILL TOWARDS TITELE, WHERE IT GETS MORE DIFFICULT NEAR THE FRANCHE FORCELLA. THE MOST CHALLENGING PART IS IN THE 11 KM BETWEEN GENA BASSA AND THE CROSSING OF THE FRANCHE FORCELLA. THE LAST PART IS ALL DOWNHILL.

BIKE SERVICE: FREE TIME, PIAZZA IV NOVEMBRE 10, CENCENIGHE AGORDINO, TEL. 0437580118.

TOURIST INFORMATION
UFFICIO INFORMAZIONI TURISTICHE, VIA XXVII APRILE 5/A, ÀGORDO, TEL. 043762105.
PARCO NAZIONALE DELLE DOLOMITI BELLUNESI, PIAZZALE ZANCANARO 1, FELTRE, TEL. 04393328, WWW.DOLOMITIPARK.IT
VISITORS' CENTER, PIAZZA 1° NOVEMBRE, PEDAVENA, TEL. 0437304400.

The Val di Mis

A trip through the wilderness of the Belluno Dolomites following the magic of the waterways through the Val del Mis, full of crystal-clear waterfalls. Start in Àgordo, the main town of Valle del Cordevole. From Piazza della Libertà take Via Battisti (which soon becomes SS 203).

Go 3,3 km downhill from Àgordo and pass near Valle Imperina, a historic town that once lived on an intensive mining activity. The descent continues along the Àgordo canal to the tunnel of Castei where you should take the abandoned road that passes from the other side of the Cordevole stream, with a scenic bridge over the ravines. Get back onto the state road and, soon thereafter, pass La Stanga, accompanied by the sight of the wild Val de Piero. At Candaten, pass by the park's equipped area and continue to Ponte Mas where you turn right following signs for Sospirolo and then, immediately to the right, pass the bridge over Cordevole to Vedana Lake. Come to the Certosa and go left, riding along the outside walls. A short detour to the left leads to Lake Vedana. The road continues to Mis, following the signs for Val del Mis to the right, and at Volpez you make another right turn to get onto the SP 2 that goes along Lake Mis through short tunnels.

Short after the bridge over Valle Falcina, an equipped rest area is to the left. The artificial area ends at Gena Bassa. Ride on along SP 2 climbing the Val del Mis. To the right, you can see a small abandoned village on the Stua, and on the left you can see falls diving into the Mis's river bed.

The route follows the valley that becomes narrower as the road tunnels through the rock. Not far from there, the road climbs and winds through some villages. Take SP 3 at Tiser to the Franche Forcella at its 990 m height, the highest point on the route. The descent becomes steeper at Rivamonte Agordino where a series of curves winds towards the bottom of the valley, displaying a beautiful view of the deep gorge of the Àgordo canal. When you get to the bottom, cross the bridge over Cordevole and turn left onto SS 3 to go to Àgordo.

THE LIVENZA

ROUTE 34 KM: SACILE - POLCENIGO - GORGAZZO - SARONE - CANEVA - FIASCHETTI - NAVE - SACILE. THE STARTING POINT CAN BE EASILY REACHED FORM PORDENONE (12 KM), CONEGLIANO VENETO (17 KM) AND VITTORIO VENETO (17 KM).

DIFFICULTY: NOT VERY DIFFICULT, WITH ONLY ONE CHALLENGING, SHORT UPHILL BETWEEN SARONE AND CANEVA.

BIKE + TRAIN: THE SACILE TRAIN STATION IS ON THE TREVISO-PORDENONE RAIL LINE.

BIKE SERVICE: **BRAVIN MAURO**, VIA POLCENIGO 30, GORGAZZO, TEL. 0434748751.

TOURIST INFORMATION
APT DI PIANCAVALLO CELLINA LIVENZA, PIAZZA DUOMO, AVIANO, TEL. 0434651888, WWW.PIANCAVALLO.COM
MUSEO DEL CICLISMO "TONI PESSOT", C/O AUDITORIUM COMUNALE, CANEVA, TEL. 0434797411.

From Sacile to the river's sources

The bike ride borders on the hills of the woodland of Cansiglio and follows the clear waters of the Livenza, a historic river that transported much of the logs that support Venice. Ride from the center of Sacile to Nave, from where you continue for about 10 km to Polcenigo. Continue towards Gorgazzo, the perfect place to see one of

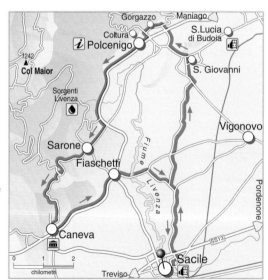

the Livenza's most charming sources. The route follows the mountain-foot road towards Sarone and Caneva. Short way, you come to the detour to the Chiesa della Santissima and the Livenza's sources. A path starts at a small bridge in front of the church and takes you on a brief tour of the sources.

Returning to the road at the foot of the mountain, ride up a small uphill section, followed by a crossroads where you keep right to Sarone. Cross the town and take the road to Cansiglio, on which you will face a challenging uphill section that leads to another crossroads. Go left downhill to Caneva, where you take a break. The Museo del Ciclismo Toni Pessot cycling museum is worth a visit, with exhibits of jerseys and possessions of famous cyclists (open Monday to Friday, 2 P.M.–6 P.M.). From the church, continue left, riding to Fiaschetti, a little village that heralds the last part of the tour. At the intersection with traffic lights, turn right and follow directions to Fontanafredda. A little later, take Via Deciani (on the right) and continue to Nave, where you turn right for the last short run to Sacile.

TOURIST INFORMATION
AZIENDA REGIONALE PER LA PROMOZIONE TURISTICA, VIA ROMA 9, GORIZIA,
TEL. 0481386225, WWW.REGIONE.FVG.IT

From Gorizia to Cormòns

The hilly area of Collio borders Slovenia and provides bikers a very relaxed environment where noble vineyards stretch between majestic woods of beech and oak trees. Leave Gorizia to the north, following directions for San Floriano. After a few kilometers, pass the Isonzo River and reach Parco Piuma, which is full of pleasant paths winding along the Isonzo River. Continue on an uphill cycle-path section to Oslavia (2 km) and its impressive memorial chapel. Continuing a slight uphill, come to San Floriano del Collio, overlooking stretches of vineyards. Leave the parish and the complex of Castello Formentini and ride through varied scenery along the road that follows the Collio from east to west.

On this part of the route, you can stop at charming cellar-shops and buy wine. Ride through the towns of Uclanzi, Valerisce, Giasbana and Zegla. Right before Plessiva, which features a beautiful natural park, turn left to Cormòns on the SS 409 that crosses the Preval, a valley marked by land reclamation projects in the past decades. At Cormòns, near the barracks, continue left to the villages of Capriva del Friuli, Mossa and Pubrida. At this point, continue easily to Gorizia and enter the town center. Optional variation by train: the bike route can be shortened by stopping at Cormòns and taking the train to Gorizia, instead of riding the last 13 km.

THE COLLIO

ROUTE 37 KM: GORIZIA - OSLAVIA - SAN FLORIANO DEL COLLIO - UCLANZI - VALERISCE - GIASBANA - ZEGLA - CORMÒNS - CAPRIVA DEL FRIULI - MOSSA - PUBRIDA - GORIZIA. ON PAVED ROADS. GORIZIA IS REACHED ON A4 TORINO-TRIESTE HIGHWAY, VILLESE EXIT, AND EXPRESSWAY (20 KM).

DIFFICULTY: MEDIUM DIFFICULTY WITHOUT PARTICULARLY CHALLENGING SECTIONS, THOUGH THE FIRST PART (UNTIL CORMÒNS) IS QUITE HILLY. SUITED TO THOSE USED TO REGULAR PHYSICAL ACTIVITY, THOUGH NOT NECESSARILY SPECIFICALLY TRAINED.

BIKE + TRAIN: THE GORIZIA TRAIN STATION IS WELL CONNECTED WITH FREQUENT TRAINS FROM UDINE AND MONFALCONE.

BIKE SERVICE: CICLI CUK ELIA, PIAZZA CAVOUR 9, GORIZIA, TEL. 0481535019;

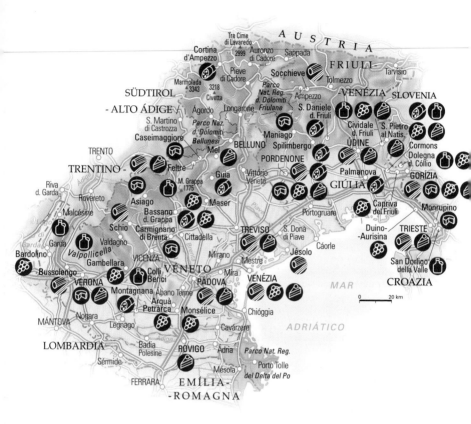

🌀	PASTA	🍶	OIL
🥓	HAMS AND SALAMI	🍇	WINE
🧀	CHEESE	🍰	CAKES

The enormous diversity of quality foods in the Veneto reflects its landscape: Montasio cheese from the mountains of Cadore, fresh fish from the Adriatic, Prosciutto San Daniele ham, polenta, olive oil from Lake Garda and 20 DOC wines. Whether you are exploring Venice or the lesser-known parts of the Veneto, you can count on a memorable gastronomic experience. Food in Friuli-Venezia Giulia derives partly from the Veneto (polenta, risottos) but also reflects Habsburg, Slavic and Oriental influences.

Food

Try iota, the Trieste soup of beans, cabbages and potatoes, flavored with cumin, cialzons (ravioli filled with meat and aromatic herbs), gulasch or cevapcici (spicy Slavic sausages). A unique range of tastes and smells awaits you: sit down and enjoy!

Highlights

- Veneto and Friuli Venezia Giulia have an exceptional range of typical foods, including Asiago and Pandoro; Montasio and Prosciutto San Daniele.

- In both regions, the gastronomic tradition has been affected by outside influences: Venetian cuisine uses Middle Eastern ingredients, while Friuli Venezia Giulia cuisine has Slav and Germanic elements.

- 20% of all Italy's wine is produced in the Veneto. Some of the best-known wines are Merlot, Bardolino, Soave and Valpolicella. Friuli produces Tocai friulano and grappa.

From the Dolomites to the Adriatic

The cuisine of the Veneto is inspired by the cuisine of the aristocracy and of the common people. In Venice, this is particularly true. Here, this was reflected in the splendor of the Serenissima (the Most Serene Republic of Venice) at the banquets which were immortalized in the canvases of Veronese, of the 16th-century Venetian school, but it also reflects the simple fare of sailors and farming folk. It is the cuisine of the luxurious villas of the Veneto, of *risi e bisi* (rice cooked with peas), which was traditionally served to the Doge (the highest authority of the Venetian Republic) on St Mark's feast day (April 25), but also of country dishes like *polenta* and *pasta e fagioli*, the delicate Venetian biscuits called *baicoli* and the drink called *rosolio*, not to mention cake called the *fugassa* and honest, straightforward wines.

up, these give way to chestnut woods and the first mountain pastures. Finally, there are the mountains, stretching from Monte Baldo, on the east side of Lake Garda, to the limestone slopes of the Monti Lessini, and the wood-covered plateaus and rocky heights of the Dolomites. Cattle farms and dairy farms are common everywhere, the emphasis being on cheese production. With such a varied landscape, the region has one of the richest bread-baskets in Italy. The fish-markets of Chioggia and Venice always astonish visitors because of the sheer variety of fish on sale. In the plain, the main emphasis is on cereals: in addition to maize, rice-farming is important, especially the *Vialone Nano Veronese* rice variety, which carries the Igp label. In the sphere of fruit- and vegetable-production, the area is home to the *radicchio rosso di Treviso* Igp (a kind of dark-red chicory with white striations, a crunchy texture and a distinctive bitter taste). White asparagus is grown around Bassano del Grappa. Other products worthy of protection are the apples, pears and vegetables of various kinds grown in the valley of the River Adige and in the lower part of the Province of Verona. Poultry dominates the livestock-farming scene, especially an early breed of hen known as the *antica gallina padovana*. Special salami is made in Valeggio sul Mincio, while Saonara is famous for its cured horse-meat products. The Province of Rovigo is famed for its truffles.

Typical Veneto landscape: because it is so diverse, many different types of farming are possible

Many different landscapes, many different flavors

The landscape of the Veneto is very diverse and well-defined. Starting from Venice, the first type of landscape we encounter is that of the *valli* (inlets) of the lagoon, where acquaculture is practiced. Then there is the plain of the Po Valley: closest to the sea, the more monotonous landscapes of recently-reclaimed land, then, further inland, the hedge-bordered fields where cereals, vegetables and fruit are grown. In the hills, the landscape is one of vineyards are interspersed with olive-groves and cherry orchards. Higher

The hills and mountains of the Veneto

The Veneto produces 20% of all Italy's wine. Famous names such as Bardolino, Soave and Valpolicella are made here along with lesser-known wines made in the hills of the Colli Bèrici and the Colli Euganei. The Veneto also produces distillates, with Bassano del Grappa as its main center. As far as olive oil is concerned, the extra-virgin olive oil made on the shores of Lake Garda is one of the best in Italy. Natural products include truffles in the area of the Monti Lessini and on the Bèrici hills, and mushrooms, for which the Montello Hills are famous. Snails are traditional in the upper Province of Verona and around Vicenza. The lower slopes of Monte Grappa and the Belluno Dolomites are famous for their chestnuts, walnuts and honey. Pig-farming in the region has produced two specialties: *Prosciutto Veneto Bèrico-Euganeo* Dop and *soprèssa*, which is made all over the Veneto. Livestock farming is particularly geared to cheese production, from *Asiago* Dop to *Monte Veronese*.

The fascinating landscape of the Friuli hills

The traditions of the Serenissima in the kitchen

Veneto cuisine is associated with two things in particular: polenta and the use of ingredients from countries bordering the Eastern Mediterranean, such as spices and raisins. One of the main dishes is fish. Often it is served cold but there are also dishes such as *baccalà alla Vicentina*, salt-cod made according to the traditional Vicenza recipe. Fresh-water fish are also eaten a great deal, such as eels from the River Sile and trout from the region's rivers and Lake Garda. Game dishes are a typical feature of cuisine in the mountains, with dishes of hare and roe deer. One of the favorite past-times of the people of the Veneto is wandering from one osteria to another in search of an *ombra*, namely, a glass of wine, preferably with a snack.

FRIULI VENEZIA GIULIA

This region, a land of vivid contrasts in terms of landscape, is a symbol of the transition from a culture based on that of the Po Valley and Italy in general, to a kind of Central European culture, with Austrian influences on the one hand and Slavic influences on the other.
Our journey begins in the Carnia mountains, where there is a long-standing tradition of livestock-rearing and especially geared to cheese production, notably *Montasio* Dop. Then there are the Alpine foothills and the circle of hills which accompanies the

River Tagliamento and the River Isonzo down towards the plain. They are home to another star of the gastronomy of this area, of world-wide renown, the *Prosciutto di San Daniele* Dop, and to wines which have made the region justly famous, such as Tocai, Merlot, Picolit and Ribolla, to name but a few. Finally there are the endless, bare, flood-prone plains of the *magredi*, now taken over by vines and orchards. Finally, there is the sea, with the reflections of the Adriatic lagoons and, behind, those of the wild and fascinating landscape of the Carso.

A multi-ethnic cuisine

The gastronomy of Friuli Venezia Giulia is as varied as its landscape. On the one hand, it reflects the cuisine of the Veneto. On the other, it reflects a bewildering number of Austrian, Hungarian and Slavic influences, as well as other influences from further east, such as the widespread use of spices and a penchant for sweet and sour foods. Stars of the gastronomy of the Carnia area include bean and barley soups, *cialzons*, ravioli filled with meats and aromatic herbs, and game. Risottos are typical fare in the plain. The sea is the inspiration behind the fish soup of Grado known as brodetto di pesce bianco, and fish dishes such as the Venetian dish *in savor* and other dishes from the Dalmatian coast. In Trieste and around Gorizia, we find the *iota*, a soup made with beans, crauti and potatoes, seasoned with cumin. Other dishes of the region include *goulash*, the spicy stew of Hungarian origin, and *cevapcici*, spicy sausages from the Slavic tradition. Polenta is the unifying factor. It is eaten with everything, from cheese to fish and often replaces bread. It is served with *muset con la brovada*, a cotechino made with parts of the pig's head, accompanied by turnips which have been pickled in grape-pressings. This typical dish can be found at any hour of the day or night in the many osterias which are still the mainstay and the strength of this area's finest gastronomic tradition.

FOOD

In the Veneto, the tradition of *primi piatti* is associated mainly with rice, eaten either in a broth or dry, together with *zuppe di pane* and *polenta*. However, pasta is also a mainstay of the local food. *Bìgoli* are the local, rustic, rough-textured, hand-made cousins of *spaghetti*, made with a special press. In addition to the many different types of *gnocchi*, made from potatoes or breadcrumbs, we find numerous variations on the theme of *tagliatelle*. One example is *tirache trevigiane*, which are ideal for making *pasta e fagioli* (the typical bean soup of the area), or the sammler *paparele veronesi*, typical of the Verona area, which are often served with a chicken-liver sauce, but which also form the basis for a famous dessert, the *torta di paparele*. There are also local recipes for savory cakes and timbales, such as the exquisite *pasticcio di radicchio*, where slender pancakes are interspersed with red chicory from Treviso, and the *pasticcio di maccheroni*, which is flavored with parmesan cheese and mushrooms. Finally, in the mountains of Belluno, we find the typical *casonziei*, outer casings of shortcrust pastry filled with all the special flavors of the Dolomites, from herbs to cheese.

Bìgoli

Bìgoli are really home-made spaghetti made with a machine called a *bigolaro*, which is basically a rudimentary kind of extruder. According to local legend, the bigolaro was invented by a pasta chef in Padua in the 17th century, but, in actual fact, *bìgoli* has been a feature of Veneto since as early as the 14th century. The dough is made with hand-sieved wholemeal flour, eggs, olive oil and butter. In the Veneto they are served with onions and sardines or anchovies. Traditionally, this recipe, known as *bìgoli in salsa*, was the dish usually served on Fridays during Lent and on the eve of important religious festivals. In the Lake Garda area, *bìgoli* are served with a small lake fish called *àole* (or alborelle). In Chioggia, *bìgoli* are served *in cassopipa* (the name comes from the word *casso*, meaning the terracotta pot in which they are cooked). In this recipe, the *bìgoli* are served with a seafood sauce, to which small octopus or squid are sometimes added.

Casonziei

These large semi-circular *ravioli* have different fillings, depending on the area. The base of the filling is either spinach or pumpkin with cooked ham, seasoned with cinnamon. In Cortina, the filling consists of beetroot, smoked ricotta cheese and breadcrumbs. The beetroot variety is an Austro-Hungarian dish. They are usually served with melted butter and grated cheese.

Tirache can be cooked whole or broken into short lengths

Lasagne da fornèl

This is a sort of local *pappardella* (like *tagliatelle*, but broader and thicker), traditionally made on Christmas Eve in the Valle del Biois, in the Province of Belluno. First they are boiled in water and then they are cooked in the oven, interspersed with round apple slices and seasoned with melted butter.

Paparele

These are the rather narrow *tagliatelle* made in Verona. They are usually served with a sauce made of chicken livers. The livers are boiled in beef or hen stock and then tossed in butter. Paparele are also used to make a dessert called *torta di paparele*.

Tirache (tagliatelle)

Tirache (the dialect word for *braces*) are roughly-cut *tagliatelle*. They are used with various seasonings to make the famous dish of *pasta e fagioli*, which is common throughout the Veneto, especially in winter, and particularly around Treviso.

BELLUNO

FELTRE

Pastificio Feltrino Casalingo
Via Tancredi Parmeggiani 17
tel. 043989229
Fresh pasta is the main specialty of this pasta shop. All the pasta is made by

hand. In addition to shapes of pasta which are common all over Italy, it makes the classic casonziei from the Veneto, with beetroot, mushrooms, cheese, nettles, red chicory or pumpkin.

PADOVA

Nuovo Pastificio Orso di Condomitti & C.
Via Tiziano Aspetti 152, tel. 0498645672
This pasta shop makes fresh artisan pasta. The many shapes of pasta made here include bìgoli, gnocchi and tortelloni with many different fillings: red chicory, artichokes, speck, crabmeat and shrimps.

Ovosfoglia
Via F. Petrarca 23, tel. 049663693
This pasta workshop makes fresh pasta by hand, using wheat flour. It has a wide range of pasta shapes, including bìgoli and canederli alla tirolese. The chefs here also make the pasta shapes which are common throughout Italy, such as tortellini, gnocchi di patate, tagliatelle and tortelloni with many different fillings.

TREVISO

Bottega del Tortellino
Via Palestro 23, tel. 0422549953
An artisan pasta workshop which sells fresh pasta made with egg. Long shapes of pasta include bìgoli, tagliatelle and tagliolini, pappardelle and spaghetti alla chitarra.

CORNUDA
Pastificio Montello di Condutta Silvio
Via Matteotti 29, tel. 0423639810
Only fresh artisan pasta is made here, with flour and eggs. The workshop also makes colored pasta and wholemeal pasta.

VENEZIA

La Dispensa di Ventura & C.
Castello, Via San Paolo 376
tel. 0415231700
The fresh artisan pasta made here includes casunzei ampezzani, with a filling of beetroot and smoked ricotta cheese. Their colored pasta is also excellent.

JÈSOLO
Casa della Pasta
Piazza Aurora 7, tel. 0421972018
This artisan pasta workshop makes fresh pasta. The shapes of pasta are those commonly found all over Italy: tortellini, ravioli and agnolotti. The chefs here also make pasta colored with spinach and cuttlefish ink.

VERONA

Pastafresca La Spiga
Via XXIV Maggio 29, tel. 0458344133
This company produces fresh artisan pasta made with egg, wheat flour and durum wheat flour. In addition to the classic pasta shapes, this workshop makes bìgoli and filled-pasta shapes, with different fillings depending on the season (pumpkin, ricotta and red chicory, and so on).

BUSSOLENGO
Nonna Mary
Via Borgolecco 38, tel. 0457150663
This artisan workshop produces both fresh and dried pasta. The dried variety is made using traditional drying equipment. The chefs here make various kinds of filled pasta, including tortellini, ravioli and crespelle filled with meat, prosciutto crudo, grana padano cheese and so on.

VICENZA

LONIGO
I Giovani Leoni
Via Damiano Chiesa 26/c, tel. 0444830759
This artisan pasta workshop makes fresh pasta, using semolina, white flour, or egg pasta. The shapes of pasta include bìgoli, fusilli, sedanini, spaghetti, fettuccine, lasagne, and so on. It also makes a wide range of filled pasta shapes.

SCHIO
Gianbon Tortellini di Schiavon Luigi & C.
Via Francesco de Pinedo 10
tel. 0445521843
This artisan workshop specializes in fresh pasta, especially tortellini. It also makes tagliatelle, tortelloni and bìgoli al torchio using the cold extrusion method.

FOOD

141

East and West blend in the cuisine of Friuli. The gastronomic culture of the Veneto and Padua blend with rich Austrian, Hungarian and Slavic influences, creating an unbeatable variety of flavors. The traditional dishes of farming folk have blended with the gastronomy of the aristocracy, and the result is an extraordinarily rich heritage of recipes which is unusual in Italian cuisine. Friuli cuisine often mixes flavors, adds generous doses of sugar, together with cheese, butter and even jam on first courses, main courses and desserts. Along with the soups (including the famous *iota*, a typical soup with sauerkraut as the base ingredient, from Trieste), *polenta* and bread *gnocchi*, *primi piatti* include puff-pastry filled with fruit compotes, cheese or spinach, seasoned with sugar or cheese. Two of the most typical *primi* in this area are *biechi* and *cialzons* (read on!).

Biechi
(also called blécs, bléchi)

Biechi are the typical pasta shape of the Carnia region. The dough is made of buckwheat flour and wheat flour, and is rolled and cut into irregular triangles with sides approx. 4-5 cm long. First they are cooked in boiling water. Then they are tossed in a pan with butter and maize flour, and served with a sprinkling of grated cheese.

Cialzons

This is a local kind of filled pasta, semi-circular in shape, with a diameter varying between 6 cm and 8 cm. *Cialzons* are common throughout Friuli and resemble *agnolotti*. The dough is made with flour and a few eggs. The filling varies, depending where you are. In Carnia, the filling usually consists of smoked, salted ricotta cheese, eggs, rye-breadcrumbs, sugar, sultanas, chocolate, cinnamon and aromatic herbs, to which spinach (sometimes replaced by boiled potatoes), and chopped apples and pears are added.

Chocolate is one of the ingredients of the filling for cialzons

The *cialzons* made in Carnia (also called *ciargnei* or *agnolotti carnici*) are served dry, and seasoned with melted butter, ricotta or another matured Carnia cheese and a dusting of cinnamon. The *cialzons* made on the plain, typical of the flatter areas of Friuli, are filled with roast chicken meat, cow's brains, eggs, Parmesan cheese and nutmeg and are served in broth. Formerly, *cialzons* was a typical Easter dish.

Gnocchi

There are many different ways of preparing *gnocchi* in Friuli cuisine. Besides the medieval recipes, which include bread, raisins, spices and aromatic herbs, *gnocchi all'uso della Carnia* are made in the old-fashioned way. In this recipe, the basic dough of boiled potatoes, flour and cheese is stuffed with a mixture of sausage meat, rye bread and eggs.

GORIZIA

Pasta & Pasta
Via Giovanni Boccaccio 19
tel. 0481534385
Shop specializing in fresh egg-pasta made by hand in a local workshop. The shop also sells colored pasta and tagliatelle colored with spinach, salmon or chocolate on request.

PORDENONE

Casa del Tortellino
Corso Giuseppe Garibaldi 5
tel. 0434522748, www.casadeltortellino.it
This pasta workshop sells its own artisan machine- and hand-made pasta.

The pasta dough is made with semolina made from durum wheat.

Pastificio Tomadini
Via Benedetto Marcello 7
tel. 0434541424
www.tomadini.com
This pasta workshop produces dried pasta on an industrial scale in approximately 100 different shapes. The most unusual ones are farfalle grosse and pennoni. They also make pasta with organic semolina.

Cialzons have a characteristic half-moon shape

pappardelle, as well as filled pasta with different vegetable fillings according to the season, meat, speck and cooked ham. There is no shortage of colored pasta using the natural ingredients of mushrooms, salmon, basil, and so on. The workshop will accept orders for any shape of pasta.

SACILE

Antica Fabbrica di pane e pasta Brisotto
Via Villorba 7, tel. 0434780985
www.antichisapori.ws/index.html
This artisan pasta workshop produces pasta with the Antichi Sapori brand-name. It makes both fresh pasta and dry pasta, dried slowly in ovens for 24 hours. Their more unusual pasta shapes include filled pastas, such as ravioli, margherite and mezzelune, filled and scored gnocchi di patate, red and green pasta and dark pasta colored with mushrooms.

TRIESTE

Pastificio La Casalinga
Largo della Barriera Vecchia 4/b
tel. 040774245
Fresh pasta from this workshop is made with many different kinds of flour: wheat, durum wheat, wholemeal and organic flours. It produces many different kinds of pasta: fusi, strozzapreti, trofie, pappardelle, maccheroni alla chitarra, tagliatelle and orecchiette. It also makes pasta shapes filled with vegetables in season, mushrooms, basil and pumpkin and wholemeal tagliatelle. The workshop makes a whole range of gastronomic dishes.

Pastificio Mariabologna
Via Cesare Battisti 7, tel. 040368166
Fresh and dried artisan pasta made with Sicilian and wholemeal durum wheat flour. The workshop makes various shapes of pasta with egg-pasta including tagliatelle, linguine and

UDINE

Pastificio Artigiano De Luisa
Via Poscolle 16, tel. 0432501674
www.cuorediudine.it
This artisan workshop produces some very unusual types of pasta, including green tagliatelle made with *sclopit* a grass local to the region. The shop also sells the traditional cialzons, ravioli made from dough colored with cocoa or pistachio, cappelletti to serve in broth or tortellini filled with ham, and panzerotti made by hand and filled with the produce of the season. The shop's delicatessen section is a riot of Friuli specialties: wines, liqueurs, grappas, olive oil, *brovada* (a turnip marinaded in grape pressings and sold in jars, rather like crauti), gelatines for cheeses and jams made with the fruit typically grown in the area.

SOCCHIEVE

Sapori antichi
Via Nazionale, tel. 0433749244
www.zanier.it
An artisan workshop which produces fresh pasta and dried pasta (dried slowly for 24-36 hours) made with durum wheat semolina. The pasta is extruded through bronze dies to give the pasta a rougher texture (which helps the sauce to stick). There are various shapes of local pasta including crespelle, trombette, conchiglioni, elmetti, fisarmoniche, stelle alpine and trucioli. The company also produces special types of pasta with unusual aromas and flavorings, such as paglierini flavored with cuttlefish ink, lemon, saffron, red chicory, basil, spinach and parsley.

FOOD

Bondòla, *figadei oco in onto*, *sacol mat*, *brasolara* and *luganega* are just some of the specialties in the Veneto art of charcuterie. The Prosciutto Veneto Bèrico Dop made here is the product at the top of the range, along with two other products carrying the Dop label, namely the Soprèssa Vicentina and the Soprèssa Veneta. The area of the Bèrici and Euganean Hills has developed a high level of quality industrial production, but, in rural areas and in the mountains, the quality of cured meats and salami is excellent. Areas where these products are typically made include the plateau of Asiago, and the areas around Vicenza, Padua and Belluno. Here, artisans produce salami with a definite hint of spices. They are usually smoked over a fire of wood which is rich in essential oils wherever the humid climate makes this treatment necessary. The Veneto is a land of famous wines, and wine is one of the ingredients in more than one type of local salami.

Prosciutto Veneto Bèrico Euganeo Dop

This *prosciutto crudo stagionato* is produced with the legs of adults of valuable breeds such as Large White and Duroc, reared on local farms. These hams must be made in the territory of a specific region comprising 15 municipalities in the Bèrici and Euganean Hills, on the boundary with the Provinces of Padova, Vicenza and Verona. When it has been matured for more than ten months, the ham is hung by passing a cord through a hole in the top of the shank. Once the ham reaches the minimum amount of aging required by the Law, the *Consorzio di tutela* conducts quality controls and the hams which pass are fire-branded with the symbol of the Lion of St Mark and the word *Veneto*, a seal which guarantees the characteristics safeguarded by the Dop protection laws.

Soprèssa Vicentina Dop

This pure pork salami is round and slightly curved, and is broader at one end. It is 25-40 cm long and has a diameter of 10-12 cm. It is made with pork meat from locally-farmed pigs of the Large White, Duroc or Landrace breeds which have reached a weight of at least 160 kg. The most valuable cuts — the leg, the shoulder, the neck and the belly — are used, and are minced to a medium-rough grain. The mixture is then seasoned with salt, crushed peppercorns, sugar, garlic and, if desired, cinnamon, cloves and rosemary.

Bondòla

This salami is typically round and tied with string which marks the surface into *slices*. It is produced in the south part of the region known as the Polesine and in other areas of the Province of Rovigo. Soft pork-fat is added to the leaner cuts of quality pork. The ingredients are seasoned with salt, pepper, garlic and red wine, after which the mixture is put into a pig's bladder or the skin of the neck of a turkey so that it forms a large, rounded salami.

Bondòla co'l lengual

This pure pork salami is made around Vicenza and Padua and in the Province of Venezia. The bones are removed from the pig's head, and it is minced together with the skin and cheeks so as to obtain a uniform mince which is then seasoned with salt, pepper, bay leaves, juniper berries and Marsala.

Bresaola di cavallo

Many provinces in the Veneto produce this cured horse-meat specialty, although the key production centers are around Padua, Venice and Treviso. Made from pure horse-meat, bresaola is dark-red and made with the finest cuts of meat. These are dry-seasoned with salt, pepper and spices, and then pickled in brine for 20 days.

Carne di pecora affumicata

Production of this smoked lamb is small-scale and done entirely by hand. This smoked salami is made from the meat of mature lambs, preferably of the indigenous Lamon breed.

The cuts of meat are seasoned with salt and pepper and smoked for 5-6 hours in special stoves in which juniper leaves, and hornbeam and beech shavings are burnt to produce aromatic smoke.

Carne sfilata

This typical salami of pure horse meat is made around Padua using the top-quality, leaner cuts. The meat is sliced, seasoned with salt and pepper, beaten with a mallet and then shredded into tiny strips.

Figadei

This pure-pork product is made in small quantities all over the Veneto. The liver of a freshly-butchered pig is used, together with the lungs and a small quantity of the minced pork normally used for making salami. The mixture is spiced with salt, pepper and sugar and, occasionally, with raisins, candied citron-peel and pine-kernels.

Ossocòlo

This pure-pork product is made all over the Veneto, but in tiny batches at a time. The muscles of the pig's neck situated along the vertebrae are used. These *ossocòli* are cut from the bone and seasoned with cinnamon and cloves. Then the pieces of meat are stuffed into a piece of pig's intestine and each one is then enveloped in a mixture made of ham, and meat from the shoulder, top of the neck, throat, belly and loin which has been finely minced and seasoned with salt and peppercorns.

Salame d'asino

A typical salami of the Vicenza area made with animals of the Furlana breed with top-quality donkey meat from the leg and shoulder which has been marinated in red wine. To make this kind of salami, about 60% of the meat used is pork belly. The ingredients are minced and seasoned with salt, pepper, garlic and nutmeg.

Salame di cavallo

This salami is made in various provinces, including Padua, Rovigo, Venice and Treviso, using top-quality horse meat combined with about 40% of pork belly. All the ingredients are minced together to a medium grain and the mixture is then seasoned with salt and pepper.

BELLUNO

CORTINA D'AMPEZZO
Macelleria Salumeria Caldara
Corso Italia 71-73, tel. 04362360
This pork butcher's offers a range of artisan products made with local game and meats. The animals are butchered on the premises and the products are naturally matured in the shop's own cellars.

Salamis and sides of bacon during the maturing process

PADOVA

Fratelli Franchin Specialità Alimentari
Via del Santo 95, tel. 0498750532
www.franchin-pd.it
This shop sells most of the gastronomic specialties of the Veneto. The artisan hams and salami sold here are personally selected by the owners, in recognition of the great gastronomic tradition of this region.

MONTAGNANA
Attilio Fontana Prosciutti
Via Campana 8, tel. 042981010
www.fontanaprosciutti.it
The Fontana family has been running this business for 83 years, and has built up impressive experience in the processing of raw hams. Their production of prosciutto veneto Dop remains faithful to the strict discipline imposed by the Dop label.

TERRASSA PADOVANA
Salumificio Bazza
Z. A., tel. 0499501066
This small pork butcher's sells salami with and without garlic, coppa, s"opr`essa veneta, cotechino and pancetta. All the products are hand-made using only natural ingredients.

FOOD

ROVIGO

Bondòla di Adria: typical Veneto charcuterie

Salumeria Fratelli Piva
Piazza Garibaldi 15
tel. 042524845
A shop run by experts in gastronomy who also have a real passion for food. It sells the best products made locally or elsewhere in Italy.

TREVISO

Gastronomia Danesin
Corso del Popolo 28
tel. 0422540625
The cured meats and hams sold here are selected and matured specially for this shop, which also has a delicatessen counter of excellent, ready-made Veneto gastronomic specialties.

GUIA DI VALDOBBIADENE
Emporio Carni
Via Madean 5, tel. 0423901079
www.salumidestefani.it
In the area which is home to Prosecco wine, it is only natural that it should be used to flavor some of the local salami and cured meats. Here, it is used to make soprèssa and filettino di maiale, which is matured naturally.

VENEZIA

Aliani Gastronomia
Ruga Rialto, San Polo 654
tel. 0415224913
This shop has been the leading delicatessen in Venice since 1933 and sells a range of typical dishes and selected gastronomic products.

SALZANO
Salumificio Zampini
Via Villatega 5, tel. 041437200
This pork butcher's makes its own soprèssa veneta, porchetta and a specialty called castradina. Castradina is the true specialty of this shop and it is possibly the last one that still knows how to make it.

VERONA

Salumeria Da Adriano
San Massimo, Piazza Risorgimento 19/20,
tel. 0458900066
This is a compulsory stop for lardo enthusiasts. Here you can choose from six different varieties.

Macelleria equina Avesani
Piazzetta Monte 4, tel. 0458033693
The Verona area has a long tradition of producing horse meat, and this horse-butcher's is no exception.

PASTRENGO
Macelleria Gemmo Aldrighetti
Pol 15, tel. 0457170404
This pork butcher's makes its own salami, pancetta steccata (belly pork with garlic) and soprèssa veneta. The shop sells its artisan range of exclusively local products made on the premises.

VICENZA

BASSANO DEL GRAPPA
Enogastronomia Antonio Baggio
Via Roma 33, tel 0424522500
This shop has a special room where it matures its hams and salami, all of which have been carefully selected.

MARÒSTICA
Casa del Parmigiano
Piazza Castello 25, tel. 042475071
The range sold by this shop includes non-industrial salami, soprèssa, ossocollo, prosciutto, speck, filetto and pancetta di Sauris, mocette and cured meats and salami made with game, as well as Italian and foreign specialties, including American buffalo steaks.

VALDAGNO
Al Ranch di Davis Pasin
Via Bernardi 10, tel. 0445412387
This farm-holiday establishment up in the mountains feels as if it was made for producing cured meats and salami. It uses the meat from animals reared on the farm to make traditional Veneto cured meats and salami, which are served in the restaurant or sold in the farm shop.

HAMS AND SALAMI IN FRIULI VENEZIA GIULIA

As a crossroads of the Latin, Slavic and Germanic cultures, Friuli Venezia Giulia is a border region which is still very wild. From the Alpine foothills to the Adriatic, between karst formations and valleys, the area has countless typical indigenous specialties. The jewel in the crown is the area where Prosciutto di San Daniele Dop—served on tables throughout Italy—is produced. Along with Prosciutto di Sauris, this is an expression of the art of processing hams and salami where the old methods are used alongside modern technology. In addition to these pure pork products, in Friuli, cured meats, sausages and salami tend to be eaten freshly-made or matured, often with different sizes of minced meat, together with the various kinds of salami made from goose meat, which is processed in small quantities to make salami and hams. In the hefty local gastronomy, hams and salami are used to flavor traditional soups, like the *iota* of Trieste and the *minestrone alla triestina*. They are also used to make dishes like muset (a local sort of *cotechino*), which is served with *polenta* and boiled turnips.

Prosciutto di San Daniele Dop

Prosciutto crudo stagionato is made with the haunches of the Large White and Landrace pigs, which are sometimes crossed with pigs of the Duroc breed, from farms in Friuli and other areas of Italy. The pigs must be at least 160 kg when they are butchered and are fed according to a strict diet sanctioned by the production regulations. The whole cycle must take place on farms located on the territory of San Daniele, which nestles among the Alpine foothills, not far from the River Tagliamento. The haunches are treated with sea salt and pressed. Then they are transferred to rooms where they await the final maturing process. While they are maturing, the tops of the legs are smeared with a natural paste made of pork fat or lard and cereal derivatives. At this point the San Daniele ham is tested by the *mastro stagionatore* (maturation supervisor) who pokes a needle made of horse bone into the ham. The needle becomes impregnated with the aroma of the meat, which is the key indicator of its organoleptic characteristics (mainly taste and smell). When it has passed quality control, the special brand is stamped on the ham by the quality control institute.

Cevapcici

Freshly-made spicy sausages of minced pork, beef and lamb, seasoned with salt, pepper and chilli. Originally a Slavic dish.

Guanciale cotto affumicato

This salami is made in Palmanova with animals from pig-farms in Friuli. The cheek is seasoned with salt, spices and sugar, after which it is trussed and transferred to smokeries where it is smoked over a beech-wood fire.

Marcundela

A fresh cured meat prepared with a minced paste of pork giblets and pork fat seasoned with salt, pepper, and, sometimes garlic and wine. This is used to make a kind of rissole which is then put into a casing of natural pig gut.

FOOD

The climate of San Daniele del Friuli is fundamental for maturing hams in special ventilated sheds

Muset

Cotechino made with the less valuable parts of the pig, such as the head, the skin, shin-meat and minced pork meat. The minced meat is seasoned with salt, pepper, garlic, wine and cinnamon. Muset is served hot.

Prosciutto carsico

Production of this ham is very small-scale and limited to the Carso area. The legs of locally farmed pigs are used. First they are salted in brine and then they are seasoned by hand with a mixture of salt, pepper and paprika.

Prosciutto di Sauris

This ham is a local specialty with a very ancient tradition, and is typical of the area of Sauris, in the north of the Carnia area. Once it was produced with the meat from the Black Friuli Pig, whereas, now, heavier white pigs are used. When they have matured, the hams are transferred to the smokeries, to be smoked over fires of wood from resinous trees such as beech, juniper and pine.

Prosciutto cotto d'oca

This special ham made from pure goose meat is typical of Lower Friuli. The whole animal is used. The goose is de-feathered and cleaned. The meat is removed from the legs and dry-salted. Then it is stuffed into the goose carcass. The ham is then sewn into the skin by hand, cooked in the oven and smoked.

Prosciutto crudo d'oca

This recipe from the 15th century is the typical raw ham of Lower Friuli. The raw materials include top-quality meat from the legs of the romagnola breed of goose. The meat is seasoned in a dry mixture of salt, pepper, nutmeg, bay leaves and various spices for about six weeks. Then it is dried, covered with roughly ground black pepper and transfered to well-ventilated store-rooms.

Prosciutto cotto d'oca

Salame d'oca friulano

This is the typical raw salami of Lower Friuli. It is made from top-quality goose meat and shoulder of pork. Meat from the legs and wings of the goose is cleaned and trimmed. Then it is minced finely together with the pork meat. The minced meat is then seasoned with salt, pepper, cloves, garlic, wine or Marsala and stuffed into the skin of the goose's neck.

Salame friulano

Pure-pork salami made with the meat from local animals. The meat is minced together with pieces of belly and lard, then seasoned with salt and pepper and put into a casing of natural gut. The salamis are smoked over a fire of bay, pine or juniper wood.

Sasakà

This local specialty is made with belly of pork, and lard from geese and pigs. It is produced in the area of Canal del Ferro, on the border-line between Carnia, Carinthia and Slovenia. First the pork meat is seasoned with salt and pepper, after which it is marinaded in white wine. A week later, the lard and belly are smoked, added to the goose lard and minced. Sasakà should be eaten just after it has been made, usually spread on bread.

Speck di Sauris

This cured meat is produced in Sauris using meat from the legs of locally reared pigs. First the meat is dry-salted and left to mature in tubs. The pieces of speck are then taken to special smokeries where they are smoked over a fire of beech, juniper and pine wood. Finally they are left to mature for 4-6 months.

GORIZIA

Vinicio Cargnel
Lucinico, Piazza S. Giorgio 9/a
tel. 0481392322
The owner learned his trade from his grand-father, who founded this pork butcher's shop with an emphasis on Middle European wines and gastronomy. Hence the use of Austrian and Hungarian influences such as cinnamon, paprika and other spices.

Prosciutto di Sauris, a ham with a very ancient tradition

CORMÒNS
Salumificio Lucia Grion in D'Osvaldo
Via Dante 40, tel. 048161644
A small shop which still uses time-honored methods, treating all the meat by hand. The ham is smoked slightly using a cold-smoking process. The perfume from the burning cherry wood gives it an unusual, balanced taste.

MOSSA
Azienda Agricola Simone Turus
Via Campi 6, tel. 048180471
Simone Turus is a young man with innovative ideas, who has chosen the poetic life of the countryside and prefers to use artisan methods. His small range of cured meats and salamis is all made with meat from animals he has reared himself which have been fed with cereals produced on the farm.

PORDENONE

CAVASSO NUOVO
Macelleria Bier
Via Diaz 1, tel. 042786189
This shop belongs to an artisan who has helped to save a type of salami that was threatened with extinction. In his products, the flavor of the finest quality raw materials is enhanced by a restrained use of spices and aromatic herbs.

CLAUT
Macelleria Giordani
Via Toti 15, tel. 0427878012
The smokery of this butcher's is fired with beech, juniper and pine wood. His products are smoked in a special stone building. His strips of dried meat—the food of travelers in ancient times and now the trendy food at fashionable pubs and wine-bars—should not be missed.

SPILIMBERGO
Salumificio Lovison
Via U. Foscolo 18, tel. 04272068

A pork butcher's whose products are famous and popular all over Friuli, thanks to the use of time-tested artisan techniques, such as the *punta di coltello* technique.

TRIESTE

Salumeria Masé
Via C. Battisti 5, tel. 040370886
This pork butcher's has five shops in the city where you can buy all the best artisan products in terms of hams and salami, cheese and other typical products of the local gastronomy.
Salumificio Sfreddo
Via Giarrizzole 37, tel. 040817357
www.sfreddo.it
Here you will find a vast range of cooked hams processed in various ways, some on the bone, according to the Trieste tradition, which are gradually earning a reputation all over Europe.

UDINE

PALMANOVA
Jolanda de Colò
Via I Maggio 21, tel. 0432920321
www.jolandadecolo.it
Here they make an unusual salami according to an old Jewish recipe which has survived unchanged since the 16th century. This company, which rears and butchers its own animals, organizes tastings for groups, but you are advised to book beforehand.

SAN DANIELE DEL FRIULI
La Bottega del Prosciutto
Via Umberto I 2-4, tel. 0432957043
A fascinating shop, whose owners, in their untiring quest to find the best-quality artisan products, use their business to promote the safeguarding of local gastronomic specialties.

Prosciutti Coradazzi di Rino Coradazzi & C
Via Kennedy 128, tel. 0432957582
www.coradazzi.it
It is certainly worth visiting the maturing rooms of this small-scale business. Here, the precious hams are hung to mature for at least 14 months. It also has an exhibition of plates signed by famous artists in honor of S. Daniele.

FOOD

A round the year 1000, the Altopiano dei Sette Comuni (Plateau of the Seven Communes), a delightful area situated under Monte Ortigara, in the north of the Province of Vicenza, was famous both for the high quality of its wool and for its excellent cheese, called pegorin (meaning sheep's cheese). Then, in the early 16th century, the demand for dairy products from cows increased, so that it became more profitable to sell calves, butter and cow's-milk cheeses. So the type of production changed. Instead of flocks of sheep, farmers kept herds of cows, and the type of milk also changed from ewe's milk to cow's milk. The Asiago cheese was born, but, even today, the older mountain people still occasionally refer to it in dialect as pegorin. Cheese is a tradition in the mountains of the Veneto, the Dolomites and the upland plateaus. On the Cansiglio plateau they make an excellent smoked ricotta which is used to fill casonzei. Thanks to the skill and imagination of some chefs, the refined cuisine of the Veneto blends happily with the culinary traditions of the mountains.

Asiago Dop

This cheese is named after the capital of the Altopiano dei Sette Comuni. The origins of this semi-cooked cheese made from cow's milk dates back to the 16th century, when livestock rearing received a great boost from the conversion of vast areas of woodland into pasture and mountain farms. Traditionally-made Asiago is referred to by the Dop regulations as Asiago *d'allevo*, that is, matured. There are two types of Asiago. It is called *mezzano* if it is more than six months old and *vecchio* if it is more than a year old. There is another kind of Asiago called *pressato*, which has a mild, delicate milky flavor. The area of production has now extended to the Province of Trento and parts of the Provinces of Padova and Treviso.

Monte Veronese Dop

The name of this very old cheese refers to the Monti Lessini, where cheese-making has always been a tradition in the higher mountain valleys, and where the practice of mountain-farming is still very much alive. Full-fat cow's milk is used to make fresh cheese, and semi-skimmed milk is used for making cheese to be matured. The former type is a mild formaggio da tavola whereas the second, known as *d'allevo*, after being matured for six months, has a consistency which lends itself to being

sliced, and, later still, to grating. The brand applied by the *Consorzio di tutela* depicts an eagle with its wings outstretched at the top of a ladder, a reference to the noble family of the Scaligeri, who were once the lords of Verona.

Piave

This is possibly the most typical cheese of the Belluno cheese-making tradition, and it is fitting that it should be named after the river which flows through the province. Piave is a cheese made with whole cow's milk, and can be semi-hard or hard, depending on how long it is matured. There are three types: *fresco*, *mezzano* and *vecchio*. The first Piave cheese was made by the Caseificio Sociale di Busche, in the municipality of Cesiomaggiore, but, with the passing of time, the typical area of production has extended beyond the provincial boundaries into the Province of Treviso and the area around Trento.

Ubriaco

This kind of cheese is obtained by leaving various types of cheese to steep under grape-pressings or grape pomace. This applies to asiago d'allevo, montasio and latteria. While the cheese is being steeped, it takes on a characteristic color: straw-yellow in the case of white grapes (Prosecco and other aromatic or passito grapes), purple in the case of red grapes (Raboso, Merlot and Cabernet). The method of *ubriacatura* (literally "making the cheese drunk") is supposed to have been invented by farmers at the time of the defeat of Italian forces at Caporetto in WW1, to hide their precious reserves of cheese from the Austro-Hungarian troops.

The curd is pressed by hand into the wooden mold

Bastardo del Grappa

A cheese made with semi-fat cow's milk. Its name refers to the fact that milk from two milkings is used to make it: the milk from the evening milking, which is skimmed, and the milk from the morning milking of the following day, which is used whole. Its mild taste becomes more intense as the cheese matures.

Caciocapra

Caciotta stagionata di capra, made with goat's milk. It is matured for between two and four months.

Caciotta misto pecora

This is a mild cheese made with full-fat cow's milk with the addition of 20% of ewe's milk, mostly from Massese sheep.

Casato del Garda

This is a product made with Monte Veronese Dop cheese, which is cut into cubes and put into jars under olive oil from the Colline Veronesi or Lake Garda for at least 90 days.

Casel

This cheese owes its name to the first dairy cooperative (called *caselo* in local dialect) which was founded at Canale d'Agordo in 1872. Today, the cheese is made with milk from Bruna Alpina cows. Casel matured for two months is mild, while the cheese matured for a year has a stronger flavor.

Grana Padano Dop

A cheese produced in many of the northern Italian regions, including the whole of the Veneto.

Misto pecora fresco dei Bèrici

This is a typical product of the area of the Bèrici Hills, once the scene of transhumance (when flocks and herds of animals were driven up to the mountain pastures to graze in the summer). Today, the custom of mixing cow's and ewe's milk is being used again in the ratio of 4:1 to make this type of cheese.

Morlacco or Morlach

This cheese is made from semi-fat untreated milk in the area of the Monte Grappa massif. Its name refers to an early people of Slavic origin who came to settle here. An unusual feature of the cheese-making process is the habit of keeping Morlacco under clay or sand from a riverbed.

Nevegal

The name comes from a mountainous area near Belluno with luscious pastures for grazing. Made with milk from Bruna and Bruno Alpina cows.

Pecorino dei Bèrici

The name refers to a cheese made from pure whole ewe's milk with the addition of rennet from a lamb's stomach.

FOOD

Although technology has contributed a great deal, the cheesemaker has the final word

151

Provolone Valpadana Dop

The vast zone where this semi-hard cheese (Lombardia) is produced includes the provinces of Padova, Rovigo, Verona and Vicenza.

Ricotta affumicata

This type of ricotta smoked with resinous wood is produced in various municipalities in the area around Belluno.

Ubriaco cheese is a common feature at autumn parties in the Treviso area

BELLUNO

CESIOMAGGIORE

Cooperativa Lattebusche
Busche, Via Nazionale 55, tel. 04393191
www.lattebusche.it
Situated on the slopes of the Parco delle Dolomiti Bellunesi (Belluno Dolomites Park), this company, which was founded in 1950, organises guided tours on request. It has a vast range of dairy products, with cheeses such as latteria, crescenza, casatella, caciotta fresca and mozzarella. Other products include piave, asiago d'allevo and asiago pressato, grana padano, mascarpone and ricotta.

CORTINA D'AMPEZZO

La Cooperativa di Cortina
Corso Italia 40, tel. 0436861245
www.coopcortina.com
This shop sells Italian cheese and cheese from the local mountains, casunzei ampezzani and smoked meats.

PADOVA

Remigio Vignato Alimentari
Via Roma 62/64, tel. 0498751320
This shop has been in the cheese business since 1925. It sells Italian and local cheeses, including asiago at various stages of maturity.

CARMIGNANO DI BRENTA

Latteria Sociale Coop. Carnazzole
Via Breda 3
tel. 0495957592
This dairy sells its own cheeses, as well as milk and butter made by other producers. It also sells products such as grana padano, asiago d'allevo and asiago pressato.

GAZZO

Latteria Sociale Coop. Centro
Via Roma 14
tel. 0499425730
This dairy was founded in 1929. It arranges visits for private individuals and groups, provided you book beforehand, and tastings are included. It sells grana padano made on the premises and a wide range of Italian cheeses.

TREVISO

Latte e...
Via S. Antonino 110, tel. 0422320716
This delicatessen sells cheeses from artisan dairies including asiago stagionato, ubriaco and morlacco. The shop also prepares selections of cheese, with wines or jams, as gift parcels.

BREDA DI PIAVE

Caseificio Tomasoni
Campagne, tel. 0422686200
www.caseificiotomasoni.com
In addition to products made on the premises, this dairy also sells grana padano and parmigiano reggiano. The dairy has almost half a century of experience in the field of traditional cheese-making.

MIANE
Cooperativa dell'Alta Marca
Combai, Via Trento 2, tel. 0438893472
This shop sells cheese made on the premises (formaggi di malga, montasio, latteria, fresh and smoked ricotta) as well as cured meats and salami, chestnut purée, fresh juices made with forest fruits, and organically-grown fruit and vegetables.

VENEZIA

Aliani Gastronomia
Ruga Rialto, San Polo 654
tel. 0415224913
This shop has a wide range of local and Italian cheeses as well as quality cured meats and salami. It takes great pride in having sold the best that Italian gastronomy has to offer for the last 30 years.

VERONA

La Bottega del Vino
Via Scudo di Francia 3, tel. 0458004535
On sale here is a vast selection of Italian, French, British and Spanish cheeses. Located in a side-street off Via Mazzini, this is one of the city's oldest enotecas. It has an astonishing range of wines to accompany its vast range of cheeses.
Retrogusto
Via F. Berni 1, tel. 0458002167
This shop has a range of 400 different cheeses from Italy, France, Great Britain, Spain and Greece. It prepares cheese-

The industry of a whole mountain community may lie behind a cheese trademark

boards for tastings accompanied by jellies, jams and wines.

SANT'ANNA D'ALFAEDO
Caseificio Giulia
Piazza Dalla Bona 4, tel. 0457532575
This dairy has been doing business for 15 years. It offers guided tours with tastings, but you must book beforehand. It sells cheeses made on the premises as well as typical local and Italian cheeses.

VICENZA

Gastronomia Il Ceppo
Corso Palladio 196, tel. 0444544414
www.gastronomiailceppo.com
On sale here: asiago d'allevo and asiago pressato, mild and strong mezzano, vezzena, and cured meats and salami. Typical regional delicacies are accompanied by Vicenza specialties.

ASIAGO
Consorzio Produttori Latte
Caseificio Pennar
Via Pennar 313, tel. 0424462374
In business since 1927, this dairy is located in an old building. Visits may be arranged beforehand. Products on sale include asiago d'allevo and asiago pressato, grana padano and ricotta.

BREGANZE
Latteria Sociale Cattolica di Breganze
Via Roma 100, tel. 0445300579
www.latteriasoligo.it
This dairy was founded in 1911. Now it also sells all the products made in the dairy next-door.

The smells of a mountain farm: the sweet smell of milk blends with the tang of woodsmoke, and the fragrant smells of cheese and soprèssa

FOOD

By definition, borders are made to keep people out or prevent them from coming in. In actual fact, for the local people, they have always been regarded as osmotic lines of exchange between different cultures, which, in the end, proved to be not so very different after all. As a result, Friuli cuisine has absorbed a wealth of influences from nearby Slovenia, dishes which are Slavic in name, with spicy flavors, which tread the interesting path between sweet and sour. This is a land of many different languages and landscapes where the scenery includes the placid lagoon at the top of the Adriatic, the poor untilled land created by flooding, the hills used for growing vines, the mountains and rivers of the Carnia region and the mountains of the Carso. Friuli gastronomy reflects all these variations in the landscape. The Carnic Alps, the Carso, the Julian Alps: their beauty lies in the thick covering of woodland and high mountain pastures and this is where many of the local cheeses are made. Some of them have been made there for centuries. Montasio was conceived at the

abbey of Moggio in the 13th century, thanks to the inventiveness of the Benedictine monks. The cheeses of the Carnia region are used to fill *cialzons*. Frico Balacin comes from the Val Cellina, above Pordenone. It is delicious grilled, but *frico* is also a dish in its own right when a wafer-thin slice of it is fried with potatoes in a pan. Often the raw materials in the local cuisine are simplicity itself—herbs of the season, left-over bread or cheese, but the interpretation is always so imaginative.

The interior of a dairy farm in the Carnia

Montasio Dop

This is the symbol of Friuli cheese-making. Its name comes from a broad plateau in the Julian Alps, near Tarvisio. The origins of the cheese date back to the 13th century, and the activities of the monks of the Abbey of San Gallo at Moggio di Sopra. The name Montasio first appeared in 1775. It is a fat, semi-hard cheese made with cow's milk. The Dop label applies to three different types, depending how long it is left to mature: *fresco* (2-5 months); *semistagionato* or *mezzano* (5-12 months); and *vecchio* (more than a year). Its texture varies from uniform to crumbly. Young cheese has a milky flavor while the matured cheese has a strong taste. Another cheese worthy of the Dop label is Montasio *ubriaco*, which is matured in grape-pressings.

Asìno

The name of this old cheese comes from Monte d'Asio, one of the foothills of the Carnia range, in the north of the Province of Pordenone. It is produced in Clauzetto and Vito d'Asio, and recently, also in Spilimbergo. It is made from cow's milk and is also known as *formadi salmistrà* because of the refining process, which

involves salting the cheeses for between 2 and 6 months in a brine solution consisting of milk, cream and salt. The unusual aspect of this process is that the salt solution is never changed, but preserves a base which absorbs the fat of the cheese. There is also a softer version of Asìno which has a more delicate flavor.

Monte Re

The name of this cheese refers to the area where the cheese was originally made, namely the pastures of Monte Re or Plesa, which is now in Slovenia. Another name for the same cheese is Nanos, which refers to the valley which runs down the mountain towards Postumia or Postojna, famous for its karst caves, again now in Slovenia. The main production area of this cheese, which has since spread throughout the Carso region, is centered on Monrupino (in the Province of Trieste). It is made from cow's and goat's milk, and is matured for at least 4 months.

Caciotta caprina

Semi-hard goat's milk cheese, made with unpasteurized or pasteurized goat's milk, with the addition of live bacteria and enzymes or starter cultures. The curds are collected in plastic baskets, salted by hand or salted in brine. Goats have been kept here for a very long time, and their milk has traditionally been used to make fresh and smoked ricotta.

Formaggio caprino a pasta morbida

Cheese made from unpasteurized or pasteurized goat's milk with the addition of natural bacteria and enzymes. It comes plain or with aromatic herbs.

Formaggio di malga

Cheese made from the partially-skimmed milk of the evening milking of cows fed on mountain pastures, mixed with full-fat milk from the morning milking, sometimes mixed with 10-15% of goat's milk.

Formaggio nel vino

A Latteria-like cheese, matured for at least 60 days, or a Caciotta-like cheese matured for a minimum of 20 days. The cheeses are put into tanks and covered with the non-fermented grape-pressings of local white or red grapes, after which they are smeared with the pressings and squeezed.

Frico

The typical crispy fried cheese of the Province of Udine. First a cheese such as Montasio is grated. A handful of the grated cheese is tossed into a pan and the excess fat is removed. It is taken out of the pan and left to cool on a piece of absorbent paper. The result is a friable, very tasty savory biscuit. Formerly it was the food of the wood-cutters. There are many other versions apart from the crispy one using onions, potatoes, apples and aromatic herbs.

Latteria

A cheese made with the milk from two milkings. The milk from the evening is partially skimmed and the milk from the morning is left whole. The cheeses are pressed, branded and salted in brine. Finally they are dry-salted. They are matured for at least 30 days.

Ricotta affumicata

Ricotta made from the whey left-over from the processing of Malga cheese, sometimes with the addition of milk or cream. When the ricotta comes to the surface, it is removed with a perforated ladle and hung up to drain in hand-made linen bags, pressed, dry-salted and smoked.

Ricotta di capra. Squete

Ricotta made from the coagulated whey of goat's milk. The fresh ricotta is collected in baskets and left to drain, while the ricotta destined for smoking is collected in linen bags and compressed to remove some of the liquid. It is then placed on rush mats in the smokery for 2 days with a fire of beech and hazel wood, with juniper branches.

Tabor

The typical cheese of the Carso around Trieste. Made with milk from cows which have been fed on local fodder. The cheeses are salted in a brine bath for 24 hours, and dried before being matured for at least 30 days.

FOOD

GORIZIA

Alimentari Mosetti
Via Crispi 6, tel. 048182004
This shop has been trading for 25 years. It sells matured montasio stagionato, ricotta affumicata, formaggio salato, and a vast range of Dop, Italian, French and English cheeses, as well as local salami and speck.

Ierman Salumi e Formaggi - da Rudy
Corso Verdi 32, tel. 0481534223
A small shop with a surprisingly broad range of cheeses and salami from all over Italy, including many rarities.

Frico, a typical Friuli delicacy

CORMÒNS
Agriturismo la Boatina
Via Corona 62, tel. 0481639309
www.paliwine.com
Set among green vineyards, this haven of peace has been opened up to visitors by a leading wine producer. Here you can taste all the typical products made locally.

PORDENONE

Salumeria Martin
Via Gemelli 31, tel. 0434571424
Located in the town center, this shop specializes in local cheese products such as montasio, formaggio salato, ricotta carnica affumicata and malga cheeses but also has pecorini and caprini (cheeses made from ewe's and goat's milk) from all over Italy.

MANIAGO
Alimentari Mauro
Via Umberto I 37, tel. 042771305
Located 100 m from the main square, this is an extraordinary cheese shop. It sells montasio in various stages of maturation, formaggio salato, ubriaco, organic cansiglio and ricotta affumicata di Sauris.

SESTO AL REGHENA
Caseificio Venchiaredo
Ramuscello, Via Ippolito Nievo 31
tel. 0434690333, www.venchiaredo.com
A state-of-the-art dairy, making high-quality traditional and organic cheeses. It also makes kosher products. You are advised to telephone before visiting.

SPILIMBERGO
Renato Tosoni
Via Barbeano 9/F, tel. 04272448
www.tosonispa.it
This dairy is at San Foca di San Quirino whereas the cheeses are matured in Spilimbergo where asìno cheese is also produced.

TRIESTE

Alimentari Salumeria Il Salamino
Villa Opicina, Via Nazionale 51
tel. 040213306, www.ilsalamino.com
This shop sells cheeses from small-scale artisan dairies in Piedmont, Friuli and Tuscany. It has an impressive tasting counter where you may even find the true, and very rare, Monte Re.
Masè
Via Genova 13, tel. 040639492
This shop sells high-quality Italian cheeses as well as local meat and salami as well as more unusual Italian foodstuffs.

MONRUPINO
Latteria Sociale di Cividale
Zolla 73, tel. 040327427
This dairy produces Monte Re, montasio and monrupino. The cheeses are matured in a cellar which protects them from the windy local climate.

UDINE

Alla Baita dei Formaggi
Via delle Erbe 1/B, tel. 0432510216
On sale here: montasio, latteria and malga, ricottas and ewe's and goat's milk cheeses, as well as hams, salami and other specialties of Friuli gastronomy.

CERVIGNANO DEL FRIULI
Casa del Formaggio di Della Vedova Ivo
Piazza Indipendenza 18, tel. 043130535
This shop has a range of more than 300 cheeses: from Friuli, Piedmont, Tuscany, Sardinia, Apulia, with formaggio di fossa and blue cheese from Moncenisio. It also sells top-quality hams, salami and olive oil.

SAN DANIELE DEL FRIULI
Enoteca Speziaria pei Sani
Via Cairoli 2, tel. 0432505061
This shop, housed in a 14th-century building, sells formaggio salato, montasio, frico made on the premises, local goat's and ewe's milk cheeses at various stages of maturation, olive oil from the Carso, as well as Friuli wines and grappas.

TARCENTO
Giorgione Formaggi di Mara e Renata Giorgione
Via Angeli 2, tel. 0432785336
www.giorgione.tarcento.com
This shop sells grana padano, latteria and montasio. Mara and Renata Giorgione also offer a gift parcel delivery service to destinations in Italy and abroad.

WINE IN THE VENETO

When it comes to Doc wines, the Veneto holds three national records: for the 200,000,000 liters of wine produced, for the 20 recognized Doc wine zones and for the 4 wines which are among the top ten in Italy in terms of production. From Verona to the area around Treviso known since medieval times as the Marca Trevigiana, vineyards are a constant leitmotif of the Veneto landscape. The merit for this goes to the monastic orders which, during the Middle Ages, set about reclaiming and making suitable for cultivation the land between the River Adda and the River Piave, thus bringing about a return to the growing of vines which had already been successfully experimented under the Romans. Vines were important during the period of the communes and at the time when wealthy citizens of the Serenissima (the Most Serene Republic of Venice) built villas in the country outside the city, when grape varietals were introduced from the colonies of the Republic. In the 19th century, the art of vine-growing underwent a profound revival with the introduction of grape varietals from France. Today, wine-production is one of the pillars of the regional economy.

The huge Merlot vineyard

Vines of the Merlot grape alone cover more than 30% of the all the vineyards in the Veneto, and the indigenous grape varietals Garganega and Prosecco are grown in more than half of the total area of vineyards. Other local grape varietals such as Corvina Veronese and Rondinella are also common, along with imported grape varietals: white grapes like Chardonnay, Pinot Bianco, Pinot Grigio, Riesling and Sauvignon, and red grapes such as Cabernet Franc, Cabernet Sauvignon and Pinot Nero. The Veneto has the highest output in Italy of Doc wines: more than 200,000,000 liters, equivalent to 20% of Italy's total production. Veneto wines are protected by 20 Doc labels, the second-highest number for an Italian region.

Prosecco

Pride of the Marca Trevigiana (around Treviso), where it has been grown since time immemorial, this grape produces one of Italy's most famous and imitated sparkling wines.

Merlot

Originally from Bordeaux, in France, this vinestock produces wines of extraordinary quality, whether used alone—when it produces a red wine which is velvety even when young with a slightly bitter after-taste, after only a short period of aging—or when used with other grape varieties such as Cabernet Sauvignon and Cabernet Franc. The Veneto was the first region in Italy where the Merlot grape became acclimatized.

Corvina and Rondinella

These two indigenous grape varieties constitute the basis of the Verona reds, Bardolino and Valpolicella. When left to wither on the vine, they result in two splendid passito wines. If the wine is made just before all the sugar has turned into alcohol, it becomes a dessert wine called Recioto dolce. If the wine is made later, the result is Recioto asciutto, better known as Amarone.

FOOD

WINE CATEGORIES

Three labels define Italian wines according to quality. Igt (Typical Geographic Indication) guarantees vine cultivation according to certain regulations. Doc (Controlled Origin Denomination) indicates conformity to regulations on area of origin, and production and maturation procedures. The top label is Docg (Guaranteed and Controlled Origin Denomination); there are around 20 Docg wines in Italy, 6 in Tuscany. Vdt (Table wine with an alcoholic content of at least 10 per cent).

Cabernet Franc and Cabernet Sauvignon

These two grape varietals from Bordeaux are often mixed with Merlot. On its own, Cabernet Sauvignon produces deep-red wines with a capacity for aging. Cabernet Franc has similarities with the previous wine, but its properties are more pronounced.

Tocai Italico

This stalwart of Friuli wines, well represented also in the Veneto, produces a fresh, dry wine. An international dispute is currently being waged with Hungary, which claims the exclusive right to use the name Tocaj. Recently, Tocai Friulano has been identified as Sauvignonasse, a grape varietal which has disappeared completely from France but is commonly grown in Chile.

Pinot Bianco

This grape of French origin produces a dry white wine with an almond-like bitter undertone and an intense perfume which can be aged for a few years. It is one of the best varieties for making sparkling wines.

Verduzzo

There are two varieties of this grape, Trevigiano and Friulano, which produces a dry, white wine with an almond-like, bitter undertone. The second type is left to wither on the vine and used to make sweet wines with a high degree of alcohol.

Raboso

Originally from the valley of the River Piave, Raboso is a wine of character, suitable for aging. A lesser-known variety, called Veronese, is grown in the western provinces of the Veneto.

Moscato

This aromatic grape is used to produce sweet-tasting dessert wines. The Bianca variety has been cultivated around the Mediterranean since ancient times. The Gialla variety, which is less common, may have been imported from Greece during the period of the Venetian Republic.

Tocai Rosso

This grape variety is grown exclusively in the Berici Hills. For a long time it was thought to have been imported from Hungary, however, recent studies show that it belongs to the Grenache family, a grape variety originating in Aragon and spread around the world by Spanish seafarers. It may have come to the Vicenza area from Provence with bishops who visited the Papal court when it was based in Avignon.

Marzemino

The grape varietal is used to produce a dry, white wine near Vicenza, at Breganze. It is used to make a passito wine in the hills around Treviso, resulting in the famous Refrontolo, the excellent wine praised in Mozart's opera, Don Giovanni.

PADOVA

ARQUÀ PETRARCA
Azienda Agricola Vignalta
Via Scalette 23, tel. 0429777225
www.vignalta.it
● Colli Euganei Rosso Gemola - Doc

Hillsides planted with vines

- Agno Tinto Veneto Rosso - Igt
- ☽ Colli Euganei Fior d'Arancio Alpianae - Doc

BAGNOLI DI SOPRA
Dominio di Bagnoli
Piazza Marconi 63, tel. 0495380008
www.ildominiodibagnoli.it
- Bagnoli Classico Cabernet - Doc
- Bagnoli Classico Friularo - Doc
- ☽ Bagnoli Classico Friularo V.T. - Doc

CINTO EUGANEO
Ca' Lustra
Via S. Pietro 50, tel. 042994128
- Colli Euganei Cabernet Vigna Girapoggio - Doc
- Colli Euganei Merlot Vigna Sasso Nero - Doc
- ○ Colli Euganei Chardonnay Passo Roverello - Doc

MONSÉLICE
Borin Vini & Vigne
Via dei Colli 5, tel. 042974384
www.viniborin.it
- Colli Euganei Cabernet Sauvignon Riserva Mons Silicis - Doc
- ○ Colli Euganei Chardonnay Vigna Bianca - Doc
- ☽ Colli Euganei Moscato Fior d'Arancio Passito - Doc

TREVISO

CONEGLIANO
Carpenè Malvolti spa
Via Carpenè 1, tel. 0438364611
www.carpene-malvolti.it
- ○ Prosecco di Conegliano Brut Cuvée - Doc

- ○ Prosecco di Conegliano Dry Cuvée Oro - Doc
- ○ Spumante Metodo Classico Millesimato – Vdt

MASÈR
Villa di Masèr
Via Cornuda 1, tel. 0423923003
www.villadimaser.it
- Montello e Colli Asolani Cabernet Sauvignon - Doc
- Montello e Colli Asolani Merlot - Doc
- Pinot Nero Colli Trevigiani - Igt

MOTTA DI LIVENZA
Tenute Aleandri
Via Collalta 52, tel. 0422765571

PIEVE DI SOLIGO
Col Sandago - Case Bianche
Via Chisini 79, tel. 0438841608
www.martinozanetti.it
- Col Sandago Camoi Rosso delle Venezie - Igt
- Col Sandago Wildbacher Colli Trevigiani - Igt
- ○ Prosecco di Conegliano Valdobbiadene Brut Vigna del Cuc - Doc
- ☽ Col Sandago Passito del Veneto - Igt

VENEZIA

ANNONE VENETO
Bosco del Merlo
Via Postumia 14, tel. 0422768167
www.boscodelmerlo.it
- Lison Pramaggiore Refosco dal Peduncolo Rosso Roggio dei Roveri - Doc
- Vineargenti Rosso delle Venezie - Igt
- ○ Priné Bianco delle Venezie - Igt

FOSSALTA DI PIAVE
Botter Carlo
Via Cadorna 17, tel. 042167194
www.botter.it
- Piave Merlot - Doc
- ○ Piave Chardonnay - Doc

FOSSALTA DI PORTOGRUARO
Santa Margherita
Via Ita Marzotto 8, tel. 0421246111
www.santamargherita.com
- Laudato Malbech del Veneto Orientale - Igt
- ○ Alto Adige Chardonnay Cà d'Archi - Doc

FOOD

○ Prosecco di Valdobbiadene Spumante Superiore di Cartizze Extra Dry - Doc
○ Luna dei Feldi Vigneti delle Dolomiti Bianco - Igt

NOVENTA DI PIAVE
Tessere
Via Bassette 51, tel. 0421320438
www.tessereonline.it

PRAMAGGIORE
Le Carline di Piccinin Daniele
Via Carline 24, tel. 0421799741
www.lecarline.com

VERONA

BARDOLINO
Cantina Fratelli Zeni
Via Costabella 9, tel. 0457210022
www.zeni.it
● Amarone della Valpolicella Classico Vigne Alte - Doc
● Bardolino Classico Superiore Vigne Alte - Doc
● Valpolicella Classico Superiore Vigne Alte - Doc
○ Soave Classico Vigne Alte - Doc
◑ Recioto della Valpolicella Vigne Alte - Doc

CASTELNUOVO DEL GARDA
Corte Sant'Arcadio
Via Ca' Brusa 12, tel. 0457575331
● Bardolino Classico - Doc
● Cortigiano Cabernet Sauvignon del Veneto - Igt
● Bardolino Chiaretto Classico - Doc

ILLASI
Trabucchi
Monte Tenda 4, tel. 0457833233
● Amarone della Valpolicella - Doc
● Valpolicella Superiore Terre del Cereolo - Doc
◑ Recioto della Valpolicella - Doc

MARANO DI VALPOLICELLA
Castellani Michele e Figli
Valgatara, via Grande 1, tel. 0457701253
www.castellanimichele.it
● Amarone della Valpolicella Classico Cà del Pipa Le Vigne - Doc
● Valpolicella Classico Superiore Ripasso I Castei - Doc
◑ Recioto della Valpolicella Classico I Castei Campo Casalin - Doc

PESCHIERA DEL GARDA
Zenato
Via S. Benedetto 8, tel. 0457550369
www.zenato.it
● Amarone della Valpolicella Classico Riserva Sergio Zenato - Doc
● Valpolicella Classico Superiore Ripassa - Doc
○ Lugana Riserva Sergio Zenato - Doc

SAN BONIFACIO
Inama
Biacche 50, tel. 0456104343
www.inamaaziendaagricola.it
● Bradisismo Rosso del Veneto - Igt
○ Soave Classico Superiore Vin Soave Cuvée Speciale - Doc
○ Vulcaia Fumé Sauvignon Blanc del Veneto - Igt
◑ Vulcaia Aprés - Vdt

VICENZA

BARBARO VICENTINO
Cantine dei Colli Berici
Via Ca' Dolfina 40, tel. 0444896521

BASSANO DEL GRAPPA
Due Santi
Viale Asiago 174, tel. 0424502074
● Breganze Cabernet Vigneto Due Santi - Doc
○ Breganze Sauvignon Vigneto Due Santi – Doc

GAMBELLARA
La Biancara
Contrada Biancara 8, tel. 0444444244
○ Gambellara Superiore La Sassaia - Doc
◑ Recioto di Gambellara – Doc

MONTEBELLO VICENTINO
Dal Maso Luigino
Via Selva 62, tel. 0444649104
○ Gambellara Classico Vigneti Cà Cischele - Doc
○ Gambellara Recioto Classico Vigneto Riva dei Perari - Doc

SAN GERMANO DEI BERICI
Villa dal Ferro - Lazzarini
Villa dal Ferro, Via Chiesa 23
tel. 0444868025
● Colli Berici Cabernet Riserva Le Rive Rosse - Doc
● Colli Berici Merlot Campo del Lago - Doc
● Rosso del Rocolo - Vdt

WINE IN FRIULI VENEZIA GIULIA

Although it represents only a small area of Italy as a whole, Friuli is a key player in the Italian wine scenario. The merit for this must go to the wine producers who have succeeded in blending tradition with the state-of-the-art culture of quality. The vineyards of Aquileia and Cividale, like those of Istria, were praised by ancient chroniclers and, today, still enjoy the same high reputation. The reason for this is to be found in the physical characteristics of the region, where the dry expanses of the higher part of the plain are complemented by land watered by underground springs in the lower part, which overlooks the lagoons of the Adriatic. There is great variation in the landscape, from the undulating Friuli hills to the jagged mountains of the Carso. It is a region where osterie (inns), the perfect haven for anyone wishing to taste a glass of the local wine, are plentiful.

From Merlot to Tocai

The vineyards of Friuli, 70% of which are situated in the plain and the rest on hillsides, are dominated by the Merlot grape, which, alone, accounts for 54% of the vines. Some way behind lies Tocai Friulano (11%), currently at the center of a legal battle being fought at Community level between Hungary, who claims the exclusive right to use the name Tokaj, and Friuli, which does not intend to relinquish its right to use it. Friuli is fighting back, pointing out the considerable diversity between the two wines: Italian Tocai is a dry wine made from a single grape varietal while its Hungarian counterpart is sweet and is made from various kinds of grapes. At present, Hungary appears to be winning the battle and Italian Tocai seems destined to be sold under the *Tocai Friulano* label.

1 Docg and 9 Doc wines for a high-quality wine-production area

Interestingly, there are several indigenous grape varietals, such as Refosco dal Peduncolo Rosso, Verduzzo Friulano, Malvasia Istriana and the rare Picolit. The original *casarsa* method of training the vines is most common here, the *sylvoz* method following close behind. Almost three quarters of the region's wines, equivalent to an area of 13,000 hectares, are Doc. Annual production amounts to approximately 68,500,000 liters, corresponding to about 6.75% of national wine-production, and placing Friuli Venezia Giulia in seventh place in the regional table. There is one Docg, recently awarded to Ramandolo, and there are 9 Doc zones: Carso, Colli Orientali del Friuli, Collio, Friuli Annia, Friuli Aquileia, Friuli Grave, Friuli Isonzo, Friuli Latisana and Lison-Pramaggiore (shared with the Veneto). One in particular, Grave Doc, has a very high level of production: it has sixth-largest output in Italy.

Merlot

Friuli was one of the first areas in Italy where this famous Bordeaux grape varietal became acclimatized. It has a deep ruby-red color and a full, fragrant scent. It is dry on the palate and goes well with dishes of white and red meat, roast meat and cheese.

Tocai Friulano

This dry white wine is the flagship of Friuli's wines. The name was already used in the 18th century, and is now at the center of a legal battle being waged at Community level with Hungary, which claims the exclusive right to use the name Tokaj. After years of large-scale production

which detracted somewhat from its reputation, Tocai Friulano is regaining its status through a return to its more traditional lines, with a typical hint of bitter almond and hay. It is excellent drunk as an aperitif, or with prosciutto crudo di San Daniele. It also goes well with *primi piatti* and white meats.

Cabernet Franc

Along with the Veneto, Friuli is the main area where Cabernet Franc is made in its purest form. It is ruby-red in color, has an intense perfume, a full-bodied taste and usually has a fairly low alcoholic content. Young wines go well with red meats and roast meat whereas more

> **WINE LEGEND**
>
> Wines are listed with symbols which indicate their type
> - ● red
> - ○ white
> - ● rosé
> - ◐ sweet or dessert

FOOD

mature wines are excellent with game and mature cheeses.

Pinot Bianco

This vinestock of exceptionally high quality produces wines with a smooth, velvety texture. Young wine has a characteristic scent of apple and apricot. Aged wine has hints of dried fruit and aromatic herbs. It is excellent as an aperitif and goes well with a vast range of lean starters and fish.

Pinot Grigio

This grape variety with medium-sized fruits results in well-structured wines. Its perfume is reminiscent of acacia flowers and it has a dry, almond-like, bitter undertone. This wine goes well with ham, fresh cheeses, *primi piatti* with tomato-based sauces and also white meat.

Refosco dal Peduncolo Rosso

This is an old Friuli grape varietal. It produces a full-bodied, ruby-red wine. It has an intense bouquet with a hint of forest fruits. Produced mainly in the hills of Friuli, although the Doc wines produced in the plain are also yielding good results. This is the perfect wine to accompany greasy meats and the typical rustic dishes of Friuli cuisine.

San Floriano del Collio: the Wine Museum

Sauvignon

This white wine is unmistakable because of its scent of yellow flowers and mature fruit. It is an excellent aperitif and may accompany *primi piatti* such as soups, slightly matured cheeses and ham.

Malvasia

Documents dating from the 14th century testify to the early presence of a vinestock of this varietal of Greek origin in Friuli. Even earlier, it was recorded in Istria, where the varietal we know today is called Malvasia Istriana. The wine is straw-colored with a light, delicate scent. It makes an excellent aperitif and goes well with *primi piatti* made with vegetables, and fish.

Verduzzo Friulano

An indigenous vinestock hundreds of years old. The wine is golden-yellow with a strong fruity scent. Made from Verduzzo grapes, which are left to wither on the vine, and made in its pure form, the result is a dessert wine with a fairly high alcohol content, which has found its maximum expression in Ramandolo Docg. More innovative wines also go well with very mature cheeses.

Pìcolit

Although the exact origin of Pìcolit is not known, it was mentioned in historical documents as early as the 17th century. The name (which means "little one") seems to derive from the small size of the grapes and the bunches on the vine. Limited production has brought this wine to the verge of extinction. Now it is only grown in a few vineyards in the Colli Orientali. The wine is a deep golden-yellow with a scent of flowers and fruit. It is smooth, sweet and velvety on the palate. It usually has a fairly high alcohol content.

Ribolla Gialla

A straw-yellow, light, dry wine with a slightly greenish tinge. It goes well with cold starters and *primi piatti* made with vegetables.

Franconia

This grape varietal arrived in Friuli in the second half of the 19th century from Austria, where it is called Blaufränkisch. It is a rustic grape variety which produces a ruby-red wine with a fruity, heady scent. It is grown most commonly on the plain. It is used to make vini da tavola and more pretentious wines which are aged for a moderate length of time.

Vitouska

This is the second most common white grape in the Carso area, the first being Malvasia Istriana. Although its origins are vague, it is probably a Slovenian variety. This fresh, dry wine is straw-yellow, and has a delicate scent with a hint of pears.

GORIZIA

Gravner Francesco
Via Lenzuolo Bianco 9
tel. 048130882
www.remedia.it/gravner
● Rosso Gravner - Igt
○ Collio Bianco Breg - Doc
○ Collio Ribolla - Doc

CAPRIVA DEL FRIULI
Russiz Superiore
Via Russiz 7, tel. 048180328
www.marcofelluga.it
● Collio Rosso Riserva degli Orzoni - Doc
○ Collio Pinot Bianco - Doc
○ Collio Sauvignon - Doc
○ Collio Tocai Friulano - Doc
◑ Verduzzo Venezia Giulia - Igt

CORMÒNS
Borgo San Daniele
Via S. Daniele 16, tel. 048160552
● Arbis Rosso Venezia Giulia - Igt
● Gortmarin Rosso Venezia Giulia - Igt
○ Isonzo Bianco Arbis - Igt
○ Isonzo Pinot Grigio - Doc
○ Isonzo Tocai Friulano - Doc

DOLEGNA DEL COLLIO
Venica & Venica
Via Mernico 8, tel. 048161264
● Collio Merlot Perilla - Doc
● Bottaz Refosco dal Peduncolo Rosso
   Venezia Giulia - Doc
○ Collio Bianco Tre Vignis - Doc
○ Collio Chardonnay Ronco Bernizza - Doc
○ Collio Rosso Rosso delle Cime - Doc
○ Collio Sauvignon Ronco delle Mele - Doc
○ Collio Tocai Friulano Ronco delle Cime - Doc

PORDENONE

CASARSA DELLA DELIZIA
Viticoltori friulani La Delizia
Via Udine 24, tel. 0434869564
www.ladelizia.com

MONTEREALE VALCELLINA
Agribene
San Leonardo Valcellina, Via Maniago 7
tel. 042775375, www.newtech.it/agribene

PORCIA
Principi di Porcia - Castello di Porcia
Via Castello 1, tel. 0434921408

www.porcia.com
○ Friuli Grave Chardonnay
   Cà Bembo - Doc
      ○ Friuli Grave Pinot Grigio
      Cà Bembo - Doc

PRATA DI PORDENONE
Vigneti Le Monde
Le Monde, Via Garibaldi 2
tel. 0434626096
www.vignetilemonde.com

TRIESTE

DUINO-AURISINA
Zidarich
Prepotto 23, tel. 040201223
www.zidarich.com
● Carso Terrano - Doc
○ Carso Malvasia - Doc
○ Carso Vitovska - Doc
○ Prulke - Vgt

UDINE

CIVIDALE DEL FRIULI
Dal Fari
Località Gagliano, Via Darnazzacco 44
tel. 0432731219, www.vinodelfriuli.com
● Colli Orientali del Friuli Rosso
   d'Orsone - Doc
○ Colli Orientali del Friuli Chardonnay -
   Doc
○ Colli Orientali del Friuli Sauvignon - Doc
○ Colli Orientali del Friuli Tocai Friulano -
   Doc

FAEDIS
Accordini
Campeglio, Via P. Diacono 12
tel. 0432711005, www.accordinivini.com

PREMARIACCO
Fiore dei Liberi
Rocca Bernarda, Via Case Sparse 21
tel. 0432716501
● Colli Orientali del Friuli Merlot Camillo
   - Doc
● Colli Orientali del Friuli Rosso
   Cassiopea - Doc
○ Colli Orientali del Friuli Chardonnay
   Flysch - Doc
○ Colli Orientali del Friuli Pinot Bianco -
   Doc
○ Colli Orientali del Friuli Ribolla Gialla -
   Doc

FOOD

The Veneto's justly famous wine-making tradition is also reflected in its range of liqueurs and distillates. Vital ingredients in any of these recipes are plants that grow locally. Local products range from the Amaro al radicchio rosso di Treviso and the Liquore Amaro del Cansiglio. On a historical note, the liqueur known as Sangue Morlacco was given its name by the poet and freedom fighter Gabriele D'Annunzio, who tasted it during his expedition to Fiume (in 1919). The name, which means "Morlacco blood", was so called because of its red color and in deference to the brave people of the Dalmatian hinterland.

Acqua di melissa

This herbal product is made with extract of lemon-balm (*Melissa officinalis*), a perennial plant about a meter high which is very common in the Mediterranean. The liqueur is pale yellow and both the perfume and the taste are dominated by lemon-balm. It is used in the food industry to make both alcoholic drinks, like vermouths and *amari* (the name given to a wide range of Italian digestifs), and non-alcoholic drinks, and is an ingredient in many different cake recipes.

Amaro al radicchio rosso di Treviso (Red chicory liqueur from Treviso)

Invented in the heart of the area around Treviso known as the Marca Trevigiana, where the Igp label Treviso red chicory is grown, this digestif is a perfect blend of the sweet ingredients and the bitter taste of the red chicory used to make it. It has an alcohol grade of 27°, an intense dark-red color and a distinctive smell. It is also a remineralizing agent, combats anemia and acts as a laxative. It is also regarded by some as a diuretic and a choleretic.

Elisir Gambrinus

This liqueur is made with Raboso Piave. The wine is produced from one of the Veneto's few indigenous grape varietals, which is commonly grown in the area around Treviso. The wine is added to infusions and blends of natural substances and the grappa obtained from the same grape, demerara sugar and high-quality alcohol. These ingredients are mixed together and are then left to mature for at least 5 years. The liqueur has an alcohol grade of 27°.

Liquore all'uovo (Egg liqueur)

Originally from Padua, the basic ingredients of this egg liqueur are eggs and sugar, plus other ingredients which vary depending on the producer. According to the oldest recipe, which dates from 1840 (known as "Vov"), the egg yolks are beaten into the sugar and flavored with Marsala. It can be drunk straight, at room temperature, or hot in winter. According to another version (known as "Zabov"), milk and egg yolks are added to sugar, brandy and natural flavorings. The two versions are strengthening liqueurs and can be used to make puddings, cocktails, and to enhance ice-cream and *panettone* (Italian Christmas cake).

Liquore Amaro del Cansiglio (Bitter Cansiglio Liqueur)

This liqueur is produced mainly from the natural extracts of the trees that grow in the Bosco di Cansiglio, a large forest occupying a plateau in the foothills of the Veneto, part of which is in the Province of Belluno and part in the Province of Pordenone. It is made by infusing 18 different plants in water and alcohol and various kinds of berries, without adding any artificial colorants or flavorings. The end-product is a liqueur with a pronounced, fragrant, herby aroma, and an alcohol grade of 25°. It should be drunk at room temperature, straight, as a digestif, or in warm weather, may be served chilled from the fridge.

Liquore Barancino

This liqueur originated in the Cadore area, this recipe is a blend of natural ingredients and old traditions, in an area where the country folk made infusions using pine cones from the dwarf pine (*Pinus mugo*), juniper berries and various natural plant extracts, to cure various ailments. It is a transparent golden brown with an alcohol grade of 38°. Because of its ingredients, Barancino helps to combat colds and bronchitis and aids digestion.

Maraschino

Typical of Dalmatia (modern Croatia) and produced by various companies, thanks to the Luxardo company, based in Padua, this has become a specialty among Italian liqueurs and is sold and enjoyed in countries all over the world. It is one of the few sweet liqueurs that involves a distilling process. Today it is still made according to the traditional method, which involves distilling

marasca cherries into alcohol. It is usually drunk at the end of a meal, straight or on the rocks, or can be diluted with chilled tonic water or fizzy orange and seerved as a long drink.

Sangue Morlacco

This is a variation on the theme of cherry brandy which is obtained by infusing marasca cherries in alcohol. The cherries are grown on the 20,000 trees belonging to Luxardo, the only company that makes it, in the company's huge cherry orchards. The liqueur is a dark red color, it has a full-bodied taste and an alcohol grade of 30°. It is usually drunk straight, at room temperature, or chilled, as a digestif or as a liqueur for meditation.

LIQUEURS IN FRIULI VENEZIA GIULIA

In this region, as in the Veneto, grappa is the product with the highest output and the highest consumption, and the quality is very good indeed. There are hundreds of grappas to choose from, each with its own peculiar characteristics, able to satisfy the most diverse palates, whether you are grappa aficionado or not. There follows a description of the most typical liqueurs of this area, for example Amaro Radis, which is made by blending 33 medicinal plants, roots and flowers, and Liquore di mugo, which is also used as a medicinal syrup.

Amaro Radis

This drink is closely associated with the area where it is made and with the medicinal plants which grow there. Unlike other more classic-style *amari* (digestifs) this one is semi-sweet. Invented in 1976, the recipe is a mixture of 33 medicinal plants, essential oils, aromatic roots and various flowers. This dark brown liqueur has a balanced taste and an alcohol grade of 32°. It is usually drunk straight, at room temperature, after a meal as a digestif.

Grappa

The word *grappa* is thought by some to come from the German word "schnapps", meaning spirit, or strong liqueur. In fact, grappa is a distillate made from fermented grape pressings. According to Italian Law, grappa must have an alcohol grade of at least 38° and not higher than 60°. The regulations of the European Union allow the Denominazione Geografica label to be applied to the

grappas of Barolo, Piedmont, Lombardy, the Veneto, Trentino-Alto Adige and Friuli. The Istituto Nazionale Grappa (National Grappa Institute) then sub-divides them into various types: *giovane* (young), *giovane aromatica* (young and aromatic), *affinata in legno* (refined in wooden casks), *invecchiata* (aged), *aromatizzata* (aromatized), and so on..., after which there are grappas made from the pressings of a single grape varietal.

Liquore di mugo

This liqueur is made by infusing the buds of the dwarf pine (*Pinus mugo*), a member of the *Pinaceae*, also called the mountain pine. In Italy, this species is typical of the Friuli Venezia Giulia region in general and of the Carnia area in particular. In Carnia it has always been used as a medicinal syrup: it is an excellent remedy for infections of the respiratory tract.

FOOD

CAKES IN THE VENETO

The Veneto plays an important role in the Italian cake- and biscuit-making scenario, and its range of biscuits is impressive: *baìcoli*, *frìtole*, *zaleti*, *bussolai*, to which a number of Jewish recipes must be added. The Veneto is on the leading edge when it comes to cakes and biscuits, one of its best-known specialties being the *pandoro*. This light cake vies with the *panettone* to be the favorite at Christmas, and has already made Verona Italy's largest outlet of the cake and biscuit industry. The Veneto is a key player when it comes to cakes and biscuits because of its enormous diversity. From the Belluno Dolomites to the Po Delta, the ingredients range from chestnuts to maize flour, from apples to jujubes. Then there are the hills: Verona and the Monti Lessini, Vicenza and the Bèrici Hills, Padua and the Euganean Hills, Treviso and the Montello Hills – with their wonderful range of sweet wines. A characteristic feature of the region is its loyalty to tradition, to the old dialect as well as to old recipes for cakes and desserts: the *pinza*, a traditional cake made with wheat and maize flour, apples and dried fruit, or the soft, leavened *fugassa*, perfect for dunking in one of the excellent local wines.

Pandoro

For the cake at Christmas, Italians marginally prefer *panettone* to *pandoro*. Its secret lies in its inimitable softness. It has no crust, is the shape of a truncated cone but is also an eight-sided star, dusted with icing sugar. It is made with the simplest of ingredients – flour, butter, sugar and egg yolk– but it is complicated to make because it has to be mixed seven times. As to its origins, the most interesting anecdote is that it dates from the time of the Venetian Republic, when there was a cone-shaped cake covered in gold leaf—hence the origin of the name *Pan de oro* (cake of gold).

The pandoro made in Verona is world-famous

Baìcoli

These are some of Venice's most popular biscuits and they keep for a long time. The name, which refers to the shape of these wafer-thin biscuits, is the same word used by fishermen to refer to the newborn fry of sea bass, which they are supposed to resemble.

Gelato artigianale del Cadore

In the history of the valleys near Belluno, the second half of the 19th century was a time of serious economic crisis. Many people from the area were forced to emigrate towards the towns further north, where they began to make ice-cream. In those days, ice-cream was made in special tubs, which were kept cold with a mixture of ice and salt. The mixture was then transferred to wooden containers which were insulated with sacks so that the ice-cream remained solid.

Biscotti bussolai or Buranei

These doughnut-shaped biscuits are a traditional specialty of the island of Burano, in the Venetian Lagoon. They are made and sold all over the Veneto, their ingredients being flour, butter, eggs and a liqueur called Mistrà.

Colomba pasquale di Verona

The origins of this traditional Easter cake in the shape of a dove date back to the time when people used to make votive offerings of bread. The modern *colomba* was invented in the late 19th century. Almonds, hazelnuts and large grains of sugar feature both inside and on the outer crust.

Dolce bissioleta

The name of these dry biscuits from Chioggia (Province of Venezia) means "little snake" in the local dialect. They are made with flour, butter and starch.

Dolce del Santo

Short-crust pastry filled with apricot jam, sponge-cake, marzipan or ground amaretto biscuits. Its shape is supposed to represent the halo of St Anthony, the patron saint of Padua.

Dolce polentina

These cakes baked in the oven contain eggs, sugar, butter and maize flour. They look and taste like a sweeter version of *polenta*.

Fave alla veneziana

Also called *fave dei morti*, these round cakes are made with almonds, pine kernels, sugar and other ingredients to give color (pistachio nuts, chocolate and hazelnuts). Originally they used to be made in November for the feast of All Saints.

Frittelle veneziane or Frìtole

These are soft fritters with raisins. Once upon a time they used to be sold in the streets by *fritoleri*. One of them features in a comedy by the 18th-century Venetian playwright, Carlo Goldoni, called *Il Campiello* (the Venetian name for a small square). This is the typical cake in the towns and islands of the lagoon at carnival time.

Fugassa padovana or Focaccia

This rounded cake leavened with yeast is made with flour, milk, eggs, sugar, butter, lemon zest and salt.

Galani

These light fritters, flavored with orange and lemon rind, white wine and grappa are typical during carnival, but are well-known throughout the Veneto as *crostoi*.

Offella di Bovolone

This soft cake leavened with yeast, is made with lots of butter, decorated with dried fruit and covered with a thin layer of sugar icing. The recipe, which is thought to be very old, may be regarded as the predecessor to the *nadalin*, or *pandoro*.

Pan del Santo

This doughnut-shaped cake from Padua contains almonds, chocolate chips and ground amaretto biscuits.

San Martino

This Venetian cake is made in the shape of St Martin, sitting astride his horse with a long sword. Each year, it is made around the time of the saint's feast day, November 11. Traditionally it is decorated with sugared almonds, chocolate and tiny silver balls made of sugar.

Torta pinza or Torta de pan

The ingredients of this old, very traditional recipe vary, but include stale bread soaked in milk, dried figs, raisins, hazelnuts, walnuts or pine kernels and wild fennel seeds.

Zaleti

Rounded, diamond-shaped biscuits which are originally Venetian and are mentioned in Goldoni's comedies. The name refers to the maize flour used in the recipe, which also includes raisins and pine kernels.

Zaleti and a glass of passito wine: the perfect end to a meal

FOOD

BELLUNO

Pasticceria Bellunese
Via F.lli Rosselli 160, tel. 0437943954
This shop sells only cakes and biscuits made on the premises: classic types of cakes and biscuits, praline chocolates and Easter eggs.

FELTRE
Garbuio
Via Tezze 16, tel. 04392316
www.pasticceriagarbuio.it
Here they make panettone, pandoro and the typical cake called polentina feltrina.

MEL
Deola Dolciaria
Via Tiago 3/A, tel. 0437747199
www.deoladolciaria.it
This tiny shop sells cakes and biscuits made from organic ingredients. The ovens in the workshop are wood-fired.

The Dolce del Santo: a delicacy with religious connotations

PADOVA

Caffè Pedrocchi
Via VIII Febbraio 15, tel. 0498781231
www.caffepedrocchi.it
This historic café has recently been restored to its former splendor, and has hosted a series of cultural initiatives. In this fascinating ambience you can taste caffè alla Pedrocchi (served with a mint cream), hot chocolate, and cakes and biscuits made by Master-chef Biasetto.

ALBASEGO
Pasticceria Sette
Via 16 Marzo, tel. 049710788
Specialties here include crostoli and caramelle fritte ripiene for carnival, and St Valentine's cakes with personal dedications.

RUBANO
Le Calandre
Via Liguria 1, tel. 049633000
The cake-shop is next to the restaurant. Temptation displayed on the counter includes pastries, croissants, cakes, mignons and biscuits.

ROVIGO

Pasticceria Mignon
Via del Sacro Cuore 17, tel. 042528117
The shop is adjacent to the workshop and the bar. Needless to say, as the name of the establishment suggests, its specialty is mignon cakes, but the ice-cream cakes and ice-cream here are also worth a try.
Dolci Tentazioni
Via Mazzini 26, tel. 042524008

Specialties here include marzipan cakes, jellied fruits, doughnut-shaped strudel and cakes and biscuits from the Polesine area near Rovigo.

BADIA POLÉSINE
L'Abbazia
Via degli Estensi 34
tel. 042551531
The shop sells the artisan products made in the workshop next-door: traditional cakes and biscuits and praline chocolates.

VILLADOSE
Schiesari
Via S. Leonardo 5, tel. 042590575
www.pasticceriaschiesari.it
A large cake-shop in the old town center. Their wide range of cakes and biscuits includes the pagnotta del Doge.

TREVISO

FONTANELLE
Pasticceria Fabris
Via Roma 258, tel. 0422809096
At Christmas they make the traditional panettone, but they also make versions with chocolate and chestnuts. Other hand-made chocolate products include praline chocolates, Christmas trees and many other good things.

MONTEBELLUNA
Offelleria Bernardi
Piazza Marconi 16, tel. 042322968
Here the crostatas are excellent but don't miss their dolce di castagne or the torta linzer.

VENEZIA

Caffè Florian
S. Marco 56/59, tel. 0415205641
www.caffeflorian.com
One of Venice's historic cafés, a must for gastronomes visiting Venice. They have four coffee blends roasted exclusively for the café, countless varieties of tea, cocoa, chocolates, cakes, biscuits and delicious home-made ice-cream.

Harry's Dolci
Giudecca 773, Fondamenta San Biagio
tel. 0415224844
This caffetteria on the island of the Giudecca in Venice has a delightful ambience and sells hand-made cakes and chocolates.

Rosa Salva
Ponte Ferai, S. Marco 951
tel. 0415210544
This pasticceria, situated close to St Mark's Square, has been selling cakes and biscuits made on the premises for many years. Their pastries, mignon cakes, traditional biscuits and cakes are all on display in the shop-window.

Fugassa padovana

PORTOGRUARO
Pasticceria Toffolo
Via Matteotti 46, tel. 042171439
This cake-shop produces traditional Venetian specialties such as pinsa, pandoro, crostoli and frittelle.

VERONA

Roma
Via Cesena 14, tel. 045505814
This café can seat 32 people inside and 48 outside. Typical Verona specialties on sale include the torta di Verona and baci di Giulietta.

Rossini
Via Trento 9, tel. 045915312
In the Borgo Trento district, here is a cake-shop which uses top-quality ingredients. Do try its torta Wanda con pasta margherita filled with Chantilly cream and tropical fruits.

COLOGNA VENETA
Casa del Dolce
Viale del Lavoro 21
tel. 044285961
This elegant shop has just been restored. It sells a vast range of sweet things. It also has a large workshop and a car-park.

SAN GIOVANNI LUPATOTO
Adami
Via Madonnina 3, tel. 0459250791
All its products are on display. In the morning, there are fresh pastries straight from the oven, and choux-pastry puffs with various cream fillings: vanilla, caramel and pistachio.

VICENZA

Offelleria Bolzani
Contrà XX Settembre 6, tel. 0444514267
Excellent chocolate puddings and a wide range of classic and traditional cakes, sweets and biscuits. They are particularly proud of their typical fugassa and frittelle.

ASIAGO
Casa del Dolce
Corso IV Novembre 124
tel. 0424462378
This elegant shop with somewhat somber furnishings has two long counters full of ice-cream, cakes and biscuits.

POZZOLEONE
Pigato
Via Chiesa 44, tel. 0444668250
www.pasticceriapigato.it
A wonderful range of coffees, cakes and biscuits and ice-cream is sold in this venue which has a garden for use in the summer. Its Easter eggs are decorated by hand.

Traditional pane all'uva: temptation for the taste-buds

FOOD

The local regional gastronomic tradition is the result of two very different cuisines—that of the ordinary people and that of the nobility—together with influences from the Po Valley, the Veneto plain and others from Central Europe. Now and again, these influences overlap, creating something very original. The *gubana*, the flagship of Friuli cake-making, started as a cake made with poor ingredients from the land and was later enhanced by the addition of dried fruit and spices. In the mountain valleys, traditional dishes for feast days and festivals include fried *polenta*, cakes made with potatoes and forest fruits, apple- and cheese-cakes. In the historic cafés of Trieste, the Viennese Sachertorte reigns supreme. All these good things are enhanced by the local wines. These range from fairly sweet wines like Verduzzo to the sheer ambrosia of Picolit.

Gubana

The name comes from the Slav word *guba*, meaning "fold", and refers to the shape of the cake, which vaguely resembles a turban. Originally, this Friuli cake "par excellence" was a rustic cake made in the valleys of the River Natisone, which lie along the Italo-Slovenian border. The cake became more sophisticated in the town of Cividale. It used to be made for Easter, weddings and other important occasions. To begin with, it was made with a leavened dough stuffed with local produce such as walnuts, hazelnuts and apples, to which sweet wine or a liqueur was added. The gubana became more sophisticated in the city: the dough became puff-pastry and other ingredients were added to the recipe, such as sultanas, candied fruits, cinnamon and cloves. Its status was such that it featured on the menu of the banquet held at Cividale to mark the visit of Pope Gregory XII in 1409.

Sachertorte

Trieste is one of the best places in Italy to try the most famous chocolate cake of all, the Sachertorte. Its history reads like a fairy-tale. In Vienna, in 1832, a young man called Franz Sacher, who was a 16-year-old apprentice chef at the court of Prince Metternich, had the idea of making a soft cake perfumed with almonds, filled with apricot jam and covered with a hard dark-chocolate icing.

Biscotto Esse della Carnia

Biscuits made with wheat flour, sugar and vanilla. An icing glove with a star-shaped nozzle is used to make flattish, S-shaped biscuits between 9 and 10 cm long.

Buiadnik or Buiarnik Resia

A typical dry cake for feast days or festivals. Once it used to be cooked wrapped in cabbage leaves under the ashes of the fire. Nowadays it is cooked on a special hot-plate in the oven from which it takes its shape. The ingredients include maize and wheat flour, cream, cooked apples and/or pears, dried figs, sultanas, wild fennel seeds and cinnamon.

Favette triestine

Small hard cakes made with skinned almonds mixed with eggs, honey, rice flour and maraschino. To make pink favette, sherry or rose essence is added, while brown favette are made by adding cocoa or rum.

Kranz

This golden-brown, soft cake with its typical plait shape is baked in the oven. The ingredients include wheat flour, butter, sultanas and milk.

Pinza triestina

These cakes are round, with three cuts across the top, and are made with flour, sugar, butter, eggs oil, honey, yeast, milk, salt and natural flavorings.

Presnitz

A soft filling with dried fruit is enveloped in a roll of pastry and is typical of the provinces of Trieste and Gorizia. The dough is rolled and folded several times, then rolled flat and filled with raisins, walnuts, hazelnuts, almonds, pine-kernels, apricot jam, cocoa and rum. The recipe dates from the Austro-Hungarian Empire.

Torta Linz

A cake with many different ingredients and flavors: its name and the raspberry-jam topping are reminiscent of cakes north of the Alps. The ingredients of almonds, chocolate, cinnamon and cloves smack of the pastry-making tradition of the Serenissima. It resembles a crostata but differs because chocolate is used to make the base.

GORIZIA

La Golosa
Viale XXIV Maggio 3/A, tel. 0481530408
A refined cake-shop with the workshop behind a large glass screen. It has an astonishing range of pralines and miniature cakes.

CORMÒNS
Giardinetto Café
Via Cancelleria Vecchia 2
tel. 0481630704
This is not only a restaurant but also a shop. Its specialties include a little cake made with cream, pears and chocolate, and walnut and caramel cakes.

Sachertorte: a legacy of the Austro-Hungarian Empire

PORDENONE

Caffè Reale
Via Cavallotti 1, tel. 043429550
An elegant cake-shop in a key position in the city center. The cakes on sale here range from croissants to cakes and pastries, all home-made and delicious.
Pasticceria Peratoner
Corso Vittorio Emanuele II 22/B
tel. 0434520014
This cake-shop prides itself on its gubana, cake, ice-cream cakes, hand-made praline chocolates, chocolate bars and Easter eggs.

TRIESTE

Bar Via delle Torri
Via delle Torri 3, tel. 040765251

A modern, trendy cocktail bar which serves light lunches and has a tempting cake and pastry counter.
La Bomboniera
Via XXX Ottobre 3, tel. 040632752
www.pasticcerialabomboniera.it
In the center of Trieste founded in 1850, run by a Sicilian pastry-chef who also specializes in Austro-Hungarian recipes, such as the Sachertorte, the pischinger, the linzer and the dobos.
La Perla
Via dei Piccardi 18, tel. 040390580
Local specialties here include fave dei morti and pinza, as well as strudels and hand-made praline chocolates.

UDINE

Pasticceria Carli
Via Vittorio Veneto 36, tel. 0432504512
www.dolcicose.com
This historic café selling cappuccino, cakes, choux-pastry filled with zabaglione and meringues occupies several rooms in the 14th-century Palazzo Tinghi.
Pasticceria Torinese
Largo dei Pecile 1, tel. 0432501763
The owners' expertise lies behind the success of this cake-shop, which produces all kinds of different specialties. At Easter they even make chocolate eggs covered with meringue: a treat not be missed.

CIVIDALE DEL FRIULI
Pasticceria Gelateria Ducale
Piazza Picco 24, tel. 0432730707
This cake-shop makes local specialties including an excellent gubana and strucchi.

MOIMACCO
Quality Bio
Via Orzano 1, tel. 0432722619
www.quality.bio.it
Only organic ingredients are used here. This shop's products contain no saccharine, animal fats, rising agents or gluten.

SAN PIETRO AL NATISONE
Giuditta Teresa
Ponte S. Quirino 1, tel. 0432727585
www.giudittateresa.com
Here the excellent gubana is made strictly according to the traditional recipe.

FOOD

Oil production in the Veneto is organized into four areas, namely Garda Dop, the Eastern Veneto, and Veneto Dop, with the sub-labels of Valpolicella, Colli Euganei Bèrici and del Grappa. According to the statistics, the region produces a total of 1,100,000 kg of olive oil a year.

East of Lake Garda and Valpolicella

The area of oil production east of Lake Garda includes the part of the riviera of Lake Garda in the Province of Verona and the area on the hydrographic right side of the River Adige, where the important center of oil production is Cavaion Veronese. Further south, it also includes the olive-oil production area around Valeggio sul Mincio. The Dop regulations state that the olive oil here must be made with Casaliva or Drizzar olives. This area of oil production is where the red Bardolino Classico wine is produced. One of the most important places where Garda Veronese olive oil is produced is the cape of San Vigilio. In the same area are the Olive-oil Museum at Cisano and the Ethnographical Museum at Torri del Benaco, which has a whole section devoted to olive oil. The second district of oil production in the Province of Verona, sold under the Veneto Valpolicella label, lies to the east of the River Adige. The olive oil produced in this area must be made from the Grignano or Favarol olive varietals.

The Colli Euganei, the Colli Bèrici and il Grappa

The Veneto plain has two adjacent ranges of hills suited to olive production: the Colli Bèrici, which are formed mainly of limestone, and the Colli Euganei, which are of volcanic origin, both of which have the Veneto Colli Euganei Bèrici Dop label. Olive oil produced in this area must be made with Leccino and Rasara olives. Finally, olive oil with the Veneto del Grappa label is produced between Vicenza and Treviso. Here, the olive groves are planted with the Frantoio and Leccino olive varietals.

Cavaion Veronese

As you enter the valley of the River Adige, the town appears on the right, set on the verdant slopes of Monte San Michele. The sides of the mountain are planted with vineyards and olive-groves. During the period of peace that came with Venetian rule, many splendid villas and farms were established here, along with their vineyards and olive groves. The vineyards occupy land on the lower slopes of the mountain, while the olive-groves are on higher ground, in a patch-work of estates criss-crossed with paths and flights of steps. One of the most popular festivals in the area is the Asparagus Festival held at Cavaion on the third Sunday of May each year, when people come not only to eat asparagus, but to taste the olive oil and wines produced locally.

Olive production in this region is restricted to various hilly areas. The first is around the edge of the Alpine foothills near the River Livenza, between Caneva and Aviano, where production is still in the early stages. On the east side of the River Tagliamento, olives are grown around San Daniele and Fagagna. Beyond the area of Pontebba, the next area of olive-oil production is the Colli Orientali where olives are grown between Ribolla and Pìcolit vines from Tarcento to Cividale, and the Collio, where Cormòns is the main center. Beyond the River Isonzo, olives re-appear below the Carso around Trieste and along the coast beyond Trieste, at San Dorligo della Valle and Muggia. Here, the quality of olive oil is excellent. At San Dorligo the old oil-mill has been convert-ed into a museum. The main olive varietals cultivated are the indigenous Bianchera, which gen-erates 40-50% of total production, the Garda varietals Casaliva and Grignan, Maurino, Leccino and Pendolino, which are native to Tuscany and Umbria, and ancient varietals like Carbonara and Torcolo. In the experimental olive-grove managed by the Agricultural Institute at Cividale, 22 local varietals are being cultivated, all grown from cuttings from mother trees which are hundreds of years old. By analyzing the genetic make-up of this range of bio-diversity, scientists hope to dis-cover the varietals that are best suited to develop olive production in an area where winter tem-peratures fall below −10°C. At present, only 170 hectares are devoted to olive-growing, but the sector is growing rapidly. It produces more than 50,000 kg of high-quality oil a year.

Food and Wine Festivals

MAY

⌇ Third Sunday of May
FESTA DEI FUNGHI DI PRIMAVERA, DELL'ASPARAGO DI BOSCO E DEL RADICCHIO DI MONTAGNA
Arta Terme (Udine)
Aiat (Tourist Welcome and Information Office) Carnia tel. 0433929290 (www.carnia.org)
Street-stalls provide opportunities for tasting forest products and specialties such as mountain chicory, wild asparagus and spring mushrooms. Stalls promoting wines and local gastronomic specialties, trattorias and restaurants prepare special menus using these special wild ingredients. There are also stalls selling other typical gastronomic products from the Carnia area: honey, *frico duro* (thin wafers of fried Montasio cheese), local sausages, *polenta* and fritters.

JUNE

⌇ First week of June
SAGRA DEL PANE
Ampezzo (Udine)
Pro Loco tel. 043380758 (www.comune.ampezzo.ud.it)
A fair focusing on the baking of the typical breads, cakes and traditional dishes of the Carnia area. Cuisine using bread as its base has resulted in a huge number of recipes which can be tasted at the fair.

⌇ Last weekend of June
SAGRA DEL PROSCIUTTO
San Daniele del Friuli (Udine)
Consorzio del Prosciutto di San Daniele tel. 0432957515 (www.prosciuttosandaniele.it)
This festival is a cultural and gastronomic event of international importance as well as a tourist attraction. The historic center of the town becomes a huge tasting fair and 10 of the companies which produce the famous, air-cured San Daniele hams open their doors to visitors.

AUGUST

⌇ From the end of August to the beginning of September
IL FORMAGGIO SOTTO IL CIELO DI ASIAGO
Asiago (Vicenza)
Comune tel. 0424464081 (www.comune.asiago.vi.it)
This regional fair is a showcase for mountain cheeses made with raw milk. Thanks to the "malghe aperte" initiative, the public can visit the *malghe* (typical mountain houses of this area) on the Asiago plateau, which is famous for its cheese.

SEPTEMBER

⌇ Last weekend of September and first weekend of October
FESTA DELLA MELA
Tolmezzo (Udine)
Aiat (Tourist Welcome and Information Office) tel. 043344898 (www.carnia.org)
This apple fair is held in the historic center, where local craftsmen and apple producers exhibit their wares. There is a strong focus on the place of apples in local gastronomy, with tastings within the fair and in restaurants in the town.

OCTOBER

⌇ Last Sunday of October
FESTA DELLA CASTAGNA
San Zeno di Montagna (Verona)
Comune tel. 0457285950 (www.baldolessinia.it/sanzeno)
This traditional festival is all about chestnuts, which once formed the basic diet of many mountain people. The festival was first held in the 1930s. After a period of decline, it was resurrected in the 1970s, and has been gaining in momentum ever since. The star feature is the *marrone* di San Zeno Dop. The fair includes shops where *marroni*, roasted chestnuts and specialties made with chestnut flour can be tasted and purchased.

NOVEMBER

⌇ Second Sunday of November
FESTA DE LE FAE
Sant'Ambrogio di Valpolicella (Verona)
Iat (Tourist Welcome and Information), tel. 0457701920 (www.valpolicellaweb.it)
Broad beans (*fave*), the pulses which are supposed to symbolize immortality, are the focus of the festival of St George. The bean festival culminates with the distribution of broad bean soup at lunch-time.

⌇ Weekend closest to November 30 (Festival of St Andrew)
ANTICA FIERA DEI BOGONI
Badia Calavena (Verona)
Comune tel. 0457810503
Bogoni are snails, which are very common in this area. Around the time of the festival of St Andrew, these snails are covered with a fine film, which means that they are ready for cooking. The fair opens at dawn with a wholesale market. The snail fair takes place in the school named after St Andrew while, in the council chamber of the town hall, there are lectures on the subject of snail-farming. In the afternoon, in the cloister of the Pro Loco, snails are cooked according to various recipes for the public to enjoy.

DECEMBER

⌇ Second Sunday of December
MOSTRA DEL RADICCHIO ROSSO
Treviso
Pro Loco Tarvisium tel. 0422549648
Treviso is one of the main production centers of *radicchio rosso* (red chicory), which has had the Igp (Protected Geographic Indication) label since 1992. This unusual fair is held just before Christmas, under the huge portico of the Palazzo dei Trecento. At dawn, stalls are set up with baskets bulging with red chicory to await the decision of the judges, who award prizes according to their esthetic appearance and taste.

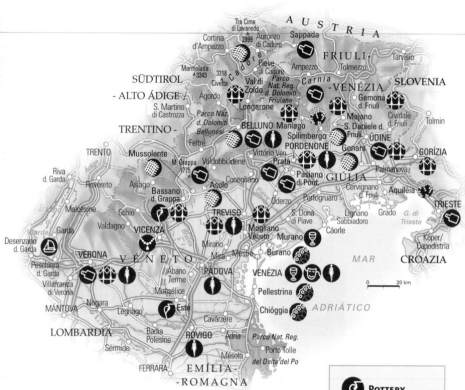

POTTERY

GOLDSMITHERY

FABRICS AND EMBROIDERY

WOOD

GLASS

LACE

MASKS

BOATS

WROUGHT IRON

MOSAICS

FASHION

History and traditions have always underpinned the development of local arts and crafts, and nowhere more so than in Veneto and Friuli Venezia Giulia. The hundreds of years of workmanship clearly visible in the Venice "palaces" bears witness to the craftsmen's skills in this enterprising area. Indeed, the wonderful traditional arts and crafts in the region reflect the entrepreneurial spirit of the small-to-medium sized family owned companies and workshops

Shopping

dotted throughout the two regions. Most famous of all is Murano glassware, but do not miss out on the lace, masks, jewellery and pottery, or even a trip to one of the many fashion outlets. The local markets simply abound with traditional handmade products.

Highlights

- ■ Among the products made by the famous Veneto craftsmen, Murano glass, Burano lace and Venetian masks
- ■ Throughout the mountain areas of Veneto wood takes centre stage with masks, toys, smokers' pipes and furniture, also the gondolas made in the historical small Venetian boat yards.
- ■ Iron, wood and copper lie at the heart of the craftwork from Friuli Venezia Giulia. Do not forger the ancient art of mosaic making.
- ■ Outlets: a chance to buy top products at competitive prices.

Inside

It was the overwhelming power and splendour of Venice over the centuries that underpinned the development of the various craftsmen's trades throughout the region; this is well highlighted by the workmanship in the wonderful Venetian "palaces". The continual demand for craftsmen's skills led to the creation of a close-knit craft system where the various trades tended to depend on each other. Often, even in our modern times, industrial production is the outcome of the development of local trades which, still today, are at the heart of sectors whose strengths lie in creativity, industriousness and the technical skills each craftsman possess.

Glasswork

The production of glassware on the island of Murano is still very much a craftsman's trade and the production processes are so spectacular that no visitor can leave the area without first visiting one of the numerous small glassmaking factories. The array of glass objects these days is indeed spectacular; apart from the classical production like "glazed" and "ice" glass, etched and filigreed glass (cups, bottles, mirrors, frames, animal figurines, chandeliers, vases, goblets), all made to traditional shapes, the small glass factories have added a range of high quality ornamental pieces that have been designed in collaboration with some of the most famous international designers. This new product range has allowed Venetian glass makers to widen their commercial horizons.

A precious and delicate Murano glass product

Weaving and embroidery

Mussolente, in the province of Vicenza, is still the heart of a thriving area where the art of weaving using hand looms is very much alive. The production includes precious silk and woollen fabrics for garments and for furnishings. The artisans from Asolo, on the other hand, have developed special skills in embroidery work and have even diversified into tapestry making. As we climb towards the mountains it is not difficult to come across small factories that still make traditional goods, such as the embroidered shawls made in Belluno or the patchwork blankets and rugs from Cadore.

Lace making

Dotted here and there among the islands in the Venice lagoon, the art of lace making is centuries old, reaching its height in the 17th and 18th centuries.

Though it has undergone moments of disaffection, the production of handmade lace has once again turned into a thriving artisan industry, especially on the island of Burano where you can still see small groups of lace makers sitting together in front of their homes. The island is also home to a museum with some of the most extraordinary pieces of local workmanship. Apart from Burano, where they use special locally made needles, the art of lace making is also carried out in Pellestrina and in Chioggia.

Venetian masks

The Venice carnival has always fuelled Venice mask production. Mask making is a very old activity where the production of the so-called *bautte* (the masks worn by the aristocracy at special festivities) goes hand in hand with the production of classical theatrical masks. Numerous small craftsmen have delved into the backs of dark old warehouses and dug out the wooden dies that had been abandoned for decades and have now started to make the original masks again in papier-mâché or leather.

Goldsmiths and jewellery making

Well entrenched in a vast range of jewellery and objects of worship, the traditions of Venetian goldsmiths have never ebbed. The art has found its firmest footing in Vicenza which, as of the early 20th century, has become the heart of Italian goldsmiths and jewellery making.

Wood

Originally only carried out in the small mountain towns, the production of handmade wooden objects is today a thriving industry. The province of Belluno is well known for wooden toys, Sappada for its carved wooden masks.

The small towns on the slopes of Monte Grappa, on the other hand, are famous for their carved and painted wooden and precious briar pipes. Though furniture making is now largely industrialised, a number of small furniture makers have recently gone back to the techniques once used in famous traditional Venetian cabinet making. This sort of furniture making is mostly to be found in the provinces of Verona and Belluno.

Metal working in an elaborate gate

Pottery

Venetian pottery production reached its height in the 16th century. Since then a very special style has made its mark, through detailed decorations, the widespread use of saints and prophets, still life and landscape scenes with Roman ruins, a typical feature of the 18th century. The old craftsmen's traditions are thriving and have produced a flourishing industry for jugs, soup tureens, large vases, ornaments and table centre-pieces. The town of Este is now the second most important production area for handmade pottery in the Veneto region. Indeed, the first pottery factories were set up in the 18th century and immediately made their mark for the wonderful decorations on a mythological background.

Boat building

From Lake Garda to the Venice lagoon the demand for traditional Venetian boats has never waned. This demand has allowed the traditional *squeri* (small Venetian boat yards) to thrive

even today, creating, based on traditional designs, the characteristic rowing boats used throughout the lagoon, of which the gondola is indisputably the most beautiful. On the other hand, the production of the traditional wooden flat-bottomed boats on Lake Garda has now been flanked with hand built boats for regattas.

Metalwork

Iron gates, balustrades and railings: this very old traditional trade is carried out throughout the region and is now also found in the production of objects such as chandeliers, branched candlesticks, furnishings, fire irons and fire sets. Most of the small workshops are to be found in the province of Verona and Treviso (the international iron academy *Accademia internazionale del ferro* is based in Mogliano Veneto). However, the use of other metals is less widespread: wrought copper is typically found in the area around Bassano del Grappa and the Val di Zoldo where they also work bronze and make *bronzini* (boilers with three feet that are put inside a fireplace). There is still a thriving industry in the province of Belluno for the production of various sorts of pewter ware, vases and containers.

BELLUNO

CORTINA D'AMPEZZO
❊ **WROUGHT IRON**
Fabbro G. Candeago
Pian da Lago 74, tel. 0436866577
Everyday items in wrought iron
❊ **GLASSWORK**
Pio Alverà
Via Alverà 126, tel. 04365147
Traditional art of glass making

PIEVE DI CADORE
❊ **FURNITURE**
Falegnameria Da Vià Angelo
Via Cortina 58, tel. 043533436
Examples of famous Veneto woodwork

Venetian gondolas, a timeless symbol of the city

PADOVA

❋ **GOLDSMITH**
Paolo Piovan
Corso Garibaldi 4
tel. 0498750709
www.paolapiovan.com
This Padua goldsmith
makes large and small gold
objects.

CITTADELLA
❋ **POTTERY**
Ceramiche Costa
Via Facca 57
tel. 0499400405
The art of pottery making:
vases, plates, jugs

GALLIERA VENETA
❋ **POTTERY**
Giorgio Ambrosi
Via Verga, tel. 0495968878
The flourishing art of pottery making

TREVISO

ÀSOLO
Ceramica Thea
Via Marosticana 37, tel. 0423529393
The art of pottery making
❋ **EMBROIDERY**
Scuola Asolana Antico Ricamo
Via Canova 331, tel. 0423952906
Embroidery and decorations: not only
linen

CASTAGNOLE
❋ **WROUGHT IRON**
Bottega del Ferro Battuto
Via Casanova 39, tel. 0422951172
www.ferrodelite.com
Wrought iron goods, chandeliers,
branched candlesticks

CONEGLIANO
❋ **WOODWORK**
Romano Moz
Calle Scoto de' Scoti 4, tel. 043834183
The craftsmanship of wood

MARENO DI PIAVE
❋ **GLASSWORK**
G.Z.
Via Strada Nuova 18, tel. 043830575
Glass making: large and small objects

Typical "sappadina" mask

VENEZIA

❋ **GLASSWORK**
Arte Vetraria Muranese
Fondamenta Vetrai 33
tel. 041739173
Famous Venetian art
of glass making
Vetreria Artistica Ballarin
Campo S. Bernardo 7/C
tel. 041736703
Artistic glass making,
precious objects
❋ **MASKS**
Mondonovo Maschere
Dorsoduro 3063
tel. 0415212633
The world of masks in the
city of masks

❋ **LACE**
Ammendola
Via S. Martino Destro 205
tel. 041735642
Traditional art of lace making
Annelie
Dorsoduro 2748, tel. 0415203277
Lace for all tastes

MURANO
❋ **GLASSWORK**
Ferro Murano srl
Fondamenta Manin 5, tel. 041736788
www.ferromurano.it
Glass in any shape or colour

VERONA

BOVOLONE
❋ **FURNITURE**
Bruno Vicentini
Via Madonna 245, tel. 0457100626
Handmade furniture from Veneto

VICENZA

❋ **GOLDSMITHS - JEWELLERY**
Giuseppe Rossi di Rossi Carlo
Viale Trieste 78, tel. 0444305845
Precious gold and silver pieces

MASON VICENTINO
❋ **WROUGHT IRON**
Corrado Micheletto
Via Roma 45, tel. 0424708192
Large and small wrought iron goods

ARTS AND CRAFTS IN FRIULI VENEZIA GIULIA

The mosaics decorating the ancient basilica of Aquileia are but one of the striking examples of the artisan artwork to be found in Friuli Venezia Giulia; the thousands of years of artwork is deeply rooted in a very rich and complex history. The local traditions developed uninterrupted from pre-Roman times to modern times, passing through the splendid classical periods, the period of the beautiful Longobard goldsmith objects, the continuous, sound work of the local population as they fashioned their everyday objects and ornaments from the basic materials at hand.

Wood

The art of making wooden objects is one of the oldest and most widespread crafts in the region. Some of the workmanship has even found its way into industrial production, such as chair and furniture making, mainly concentrated around the "furniture area" between Brugnera, Prata and Pasiano di Pordenone. There is also a more limited and more sought after production of carved and decorated furniture, not to mention a well entrenched production of wooden objects (including musical instruments), all made by the master carvers located mainly in Carnia, but also in Udine and Trieste. The traditional masks with their different shapes are of particular interest. However, the production of these masks is slowly disappearing as they are nowadays only used in the traditional carnivals in some surrounding mountain towns.

Iron

Iron is one of the most widespread materials found in traditional Friuli homes. It is used to make parts of window frames and for large fireplaces where the complex structures play a wonderful dual role: they are a marvellous decoration and have a practical purpose. The town of Maniago in the province of Pordenone is one of the towns where traditional iron working is fundamental to the local tissue (the local forge is over 400 years old and is still mainly used to make agricultural tools). Maniago became famous for its production of scissors and handmade knives with wooden, horn and mother-of-pearl handles, many of which are purpose built for special or agricultural uses. For some time now they have also been making copies of ancient armour, swords, daggers and spiked maces as collectors' pieces and for exebitions. The production of wrought iron goods is widespread throughout the region, especially in Gorizia and in the province of Udine where the output includes iron gates, railings, firedogs and branched candlesticks.

Copper and bronze

The ancient art of copper bossing, typical of the mountain areas, has found a new breath of life thanks to a typical local spirit, grappa. Indeed, grappa has to be distilled and there is a high demand for copper distillation stills by small distilleries. Traditional products are, however, still being made, especially in Ampezzano Pordenone, Gemona del Friuli and in Majano, in the province of Udine. Apart from the production of bossed copper products there is still a flourishing business in copper and bronze casting, the technique used to make branched candlesticks and traditional fireplace vessels.

Slippers

One of the many local trades that has turned into a real industry in the province of Friuli Venezia Giulia is slipper making. The small workshops that used to carry out this trade were once common throughout the region. The slippers were distributed to the surrounding regions by a handful of hard-nosed "street vendors", locals who carried out the activity when they were not working the fields. However, together with the small-to-medium sized firms there is also a thriving "cottage industry" for the typical Friulian slippers, especially around Gonars, Fagagna and San Daniele del Friuli, since these slippers are highly acclaimed for their softness, durability and traditional designs.

SHOPPING

Example of famous Friuli mosaic makers' traditions

Mosaics

Traditional mosaic making, a local art ever since Roman times, was given a new lease of life in Spilimbergo in the province of Pordenone around 1920 thanks to the *Scuola Mosaicisti del Friuli* (mosaic schools). The mosaic makers trained here use the very same techniques that were used during the Roman Empire to make the mosaics in Aquileia. Mosaics are made with tiny pieces of opaque coloured glass that are fashioned using a special hammer and then stuck to the base using a cement. Current production ranges from copies of antique mosaics to modern designs, with particular emphasis on highly personalised portraits.

PORDENONE

MANIAGO
✳ **KNIVES**
A.E. Coltelleria snc
Via Cellina 17, tel. 042771029
www.aecolt.it
Knives of all shapes and sizes
Luigi Locatello & C.
Piazza Italia 27/D, tel. 042771321
Iron knives and blades
Lion Steel
Via dei Fabbri 32, tel. 042771984
www.lionsteel.it
Knives

SAN MARTINO AL TAGLIAMENTO
✳ **MOSAICS**
Friul Mosaic
Via San Giacomo 42
tel. 0434899217
www.friulimosaic.com
The ancient art of mosaics

SPILIMBERGO
✳ **MOSAICS**
Cristina Cancian
Via 2 Giugno 4, tel. 04272084
Famous Friulian mosaics

UDINE

MOIMACCO
✳ **METALWORK**
Fonderia Rinaldo Railz
Via dei Longobardi 9, tel. 0432722116
www.fonderiarailz.com
The art of metalwork

PAULARO
✳ **TRADITIONAL COSTUMES**
Creazioni Wally
Via Roma 56, tel. 043370078
Traditions as seen through popular costumes

SAN DANIELE DEL FRIULI
✳ **SLIPPERS**
Calzaturificio Mary
Via J. Tomadini 7/9, tel. 0432957190
www.calzaturificiomary.com
World famous slippers

SAN GIOVANNI AL NATISONE
✳ **CHAIRS**
Gurisan Sedie, Dolegnano
Via Sotto Rive 26, tel. 0432756442
www.gurisansedie.com
Chairs, the craftsmanship of wood

SAURIS
✳ **WOODWORK**
Legnostile F.lli Plozzer
Sauris di Sopra, tel. 043386225
The craftsmanship of wood

TOLMEZZO
✳ **GLASSWORK**
Ente Mostra Permanente
Via Carnia Libera 1944 n. 15, tel. 043343518
Artistic glass production
✳ **WOODEN SCULPTURES**
Mecchia Legni Scolpiti
Via Grialba 30 tel. 04332801
The ancient art of artistic wood sculpture

MARKETS IN THE VENETO

Opportunities abound for anyone wanting to buy typical handmade products in the Veneto region. Indeed, the region plays host to numerous markets, antique shows, modern art collectors' markets and traditional art collectors' markets. Around Christmas these events take on an international atmosphere and offer visitors the chance to taste local food and wines and to watch past trades being practised.

BELLUNO

FELTRE
Mostra Regionale dell'Artigianato (Regional craftwork show)
Last week of June
Usually visited by some 20,000 people, this show includes wrought iron, stone, wood and glass ware. Various goods are on sale and visitors can even taste the local food.
Information: tel. 04392540, www.mostraartigianatofeltre.it

PADOVA

Mercatino in Prato (Prato street market)
Third Sunday of the month
Various things can be bought from the over 500 stalls: antiques, modern and traditional collectors' art pieces, glassware and pottery, furniture.
Information: tel. 0498767918.

ROVIGO

Mercato Fieristico Ottobre Rodigino
Second half of October
Hundreds of stalls line the streets displaying food and handmade goods.
Information: tel. 04252061, www.comune.rovigo.it

TREVISO

ÀSOLO
Mercatino dell'antiquariato (Antique market)
Second Sunday of the month, except in July and August
A hundred or so stalls with furniture, antique furnishings, silverware, clothes and other things, including modern art collectors' pieces.
Information: tel. 042355045.

ODERZO
Mercatino dell'antiquariato e artigianato (Antique and craftwork market)
First Sunday of the month, except in January, July and August
Antiques and modern art collectors' pieces: silverware, furniture, blown glass plates, old books. Information: tel. 0422812242, www.comune.oderzo.tv.it

VENEZIA

Mercatino di San Maurizio (Saint Maurice's market)
Held a number of times during the year
Some fifty antique dealers sell old prints, Murano glassware, Venetian pearl necklaces. It is held on Palm Sunday and the two following days, the first weekend of June, third weekend of September and the weekend before Christmas.
Information: tel. 335382839.

VERONA

Fiera di Santa Lucia (Saint Lucy's fair)
From 10 to 13 December
National toy show with entertainment, stalls and irresistible goodies.
Information: tel. 0458077111, www.comune.verona.it

VICENZA

MARÒSTICA
Mercatino dell'Antiquariato (Antique market)
First Sunday of the month
About 130 stalls with antiques, cameras, typewriters, magazines, pottery and old furniture. Information: tel. 0424479200, www.comune.marostica.vi.it

Cane, wood, pottery and leather goods, wicker baskets, food and wines from the Carnic Alps and Austria, local craft products in stone, iron and wood; concerts, folklore shows, displays of bygone customs, these are but some of the ingredients at the heart of the local fairs and markets held throughout the region of Friuli Venezia Giulia. With very old traditions, some of these markets date back to the late Middle Ages.

PORDENONE

Mercatino di Natale (Christmas market)
Corso Vittorio Emanuele II
Sunday before Christmas
Antique market, craftwork and flea market. Some seventy stalls with things for Christmas and other items. There is usually a group of antique dealers and paintings by local painters can be bought.
Information: tel. 0434520381,
www.pordenone-turismo.com

POLCENIGO
Sagra dei Sést (Sést festival)
Historical town centre
First weekend of September
This festival is over 300 years old and is probably the most traditional of local festivals. Lots of local goods to look at and buy: wicker baskets, cane, wood, pottery and leather goods.
Information: tel. 0434749622,
www.comune.polcenigo.pn.it

TRIESTE

Fiera di San Nicolò e Fiera di Natale (Saint Nicholas market and Christmas fair)
Viale XX Settembre
From the week of 6 December to 24 December
This is the oldest Christmas fair in the region. When the street market is over the Christmas fair begins, and lasts until 24 December. The street market and the fair both exhibit all sorts of goods, from food to costume jewellery, from clothes to tools.
Information: tel. 04067961,
www.triesteturismo.com

UDINE

Fiera di Santa Caterina (Saint Catherine's fair)
Piazza I Maggio
Last weekend of November
This fair dates back to the 15th century. Today it has about 300 stalls selling all sorts of craftwork and there is even a funfair. The fair attracts hundreds of Italian and foreign visitors.
Information: tel. 0432271111,
www.comune.udine.it
Mercatino di Natale (Christmas market)
Piazza Duomo
Second half of December
Located in a framework of wood houses, this traditional Christmas market lasts about two weeks. It offers numerous ideas for handmade gifts, all local art, as well as Christmas and floral decorations. There are a number of local products to be tasted, including Christmas sweets and local drinks. There is also a marquee that hosts a number of exhibitions: wool preparation, engraving and decoupage.
Information: tel. 0432295972,
www.udine-turismo.it

PALUZZA
Sagra di Place
Historical town centre
First Sunday of September
This is one of the oldest markets in the Carnic Alps. It is held in the town's winding streets and hosts between 50 and 200 stalls with typical products from the Carnic Alps and Austria and local handmade goods in stone, iron and wood.
Information: tel. 0433775344.

SUTRIO
Natale a Sutrio (Christmas in Sutrio)
Historical town centre
From the Sunday before Christmas to 6 January
An exhibition of handmade Christmas cribs along a street route that unveils old courtyards, arcaded loggia, cellars and the older homes. Concerts, folklore shows, exhibitions of bygone customs, food and live wood carving.
Information: tel. 0433778921.

FASHION

The outlets, managed by firms specialised in choosing the merchandise, are "villages" where a number of manufacturer's shops are gathered together. Beside the shops, which are designed to the letter, there are parking spaces, restaurants, bars and other services such as play areas for young children. Apart from being a wonderful destination for bargain shopping they are places where people can gather and where entertainment is often put on. The following places are to be found in Veneto; Pordenone is the only location in the region of Friuli Venezia Giulia with this sort of outlet.

BELLUNO

SAN VITO DI CADORE
Factory Store
Via Nazionale 47, tel. 04369264
Stock and end-of-season top brands for men, women and children from 5 to 12.

PADOVA

TREBASELEGHE
Pepper
Via Marco Polo 1, tel. 0499387226
Men's and women's classical and casual clothing. Also accessories and classical footwear for women.

ROVIGO

OCCHIOBELLO
Levi's Factory Store
Via Eridania 113, tel. 0425756992
End-of-season Levi's and Dockers gear.

TREVISO

CORNUDA
The North Face Outlet
Via Padova 21, tel. 0423839133
Sports clothing for men and women, The North Face brand (for high altitude sports and skiing).

MASÈR
Sport 1 Outlet Diadora Invicta
Via Enrico Fermi 1, tel. 0423950887
Sports shoes and clothing, ski gear, football, mountain climbing, tennis, running.

MOGLIANO VENETO
Coin Outlet
Zerman, Via Giotto 1, tel. 0415971241
End-of-season clothing for men, women and children. Household goods and textile furnishings.

VENEZIA

DOLO
Coin Outlet
Via Mazzini 102, tel. 041412110
www.coin.it
This outlet has clothing for men, women and children, household goods and textile furnishings.

VERONA

BUSSOLENGO
Swinger International
Via Festara 44, tel. 0456719806
Women's top designer clothes. The remaining stock from the previous year is sold 50% below the retail price.

VICENZA

TRISSINO
Factory Store
Via Stazione 93, tel. 0445424100
www.giorgioarmani.com
Clothes from the previous year's collections, firsts and seconds from the Giorgio Armani group labels. Men's, women's and children's clothing from age 0 upwards. Household goods, too.

PORDENONE

Sport Outlet
Via Fornace 2, tel. 0434542095
www.sportoutlet.it
Men's, women's and children's clothing. Bags, sunglasses and other accessories.

SHOPPING

183

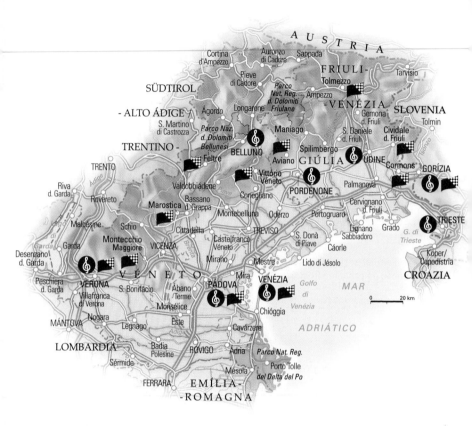

🎼 **MUSIC**

🏁 **FOLKLORE**

A melting pot of cultures from the hundreds of years of foreign dominance, the carnivals, theatrical and folklore events (including international folklore events) all help to make this northern area one of the most diverse and interesting in Italy. From the Verona amphitheatre to the "La Fenice" theatre in Venice, from the festivals that portray middle-European cultures and influence to the history of the Longobards, this area just overwhelms with interest. The Venice "Regata Storica" along the

Events

"Canal Grande" is now an internationally famous regata. The pomp and ceremony, the traditional highly coloured row boats and gondolas and the oarsmen in their traditional costumes give Venice that very special touch of class.

Highlights

■ Famous theatres: from the "La Fenice" in Venice to the opera house "Teatro Lirico Giuseppe Verdi" in Trieste

■ The solemn procession in memory of Saint Anthony in Padua; the chess game in 15th century costume on the main square in Maròsica

■ The "Festa dei Popoli della Mitteleuropa" in Cormòns and the world folklore festival in Gorizia

■ The main folklore festivals in Venice: the Carnival, the "Festa della Salute" and the "Rendentore"

Monteverdi, Vivaldi, Malipiero, Maderna and Nono: this region of Italy has always been at the forefront in the music world. The Lieder season at Palazzo Labia and the brief though striking episodes of chamber music with the music school "Scuola Grande di San Rocco" bear witness to a very real form of cultural revolt. Even traditional theatrical events, such as at the "Sociale di Rovigo" or "Comunale di Treviso" theatres, have managed to gain in popularity and compete with such places as the "Arena di Verona" amphitheatre and the famous "La Fenice" theatre in Venice. In some cases certain distinguished polyphonies brighten up the Sunday festivities as well as the main festivals and celebrations.

View from the gallery, the stalls and the stage in the famous "Teatro Sociale" theatre in Rovigo

BELLUNO

Cattedrale
The cathedral, with its majestic interior, is a suggestive setting for organ concerts.
Teatro Comunale
Piazza Vittorio Emanuele, tel. 0437940349
www.cultura.comune.belluno.it

PADOVA

Centro Artistico Musicale Padovano
This music arts centre organises concerts, lectures, lessons-cum-concerts, training periods and meetings. Piazza Capitaniato 7, tel. 0498274650, www.lettere.unipd.it/cmp/index.html
"Amici della Musica" concert season
October-May
Over 60 editions on, 20 concerts are planned for the concert season at the Auditorium "C. Pollini". Many internationally famous names stand along side those of the very best from the new generation. Information: tel. 0498756763, www.amicimusicapadova.org
Teatro delle Grazie
Via Configliachi 2/A, tel. 049650937
Teatro delle Maddalene
The artistic endeavours arranged by this theatre can be divided into two seasons: dance and contemporary theatre. Via XX Settembre 28,

tel. 049656692, www.tamteatromusica.it
Teatro Giuseppe Verdi
The main musical themes, mostly opera, are organised in collaboration with the Venice theatre "La Fenice". Via del Livello 32, tel. 04987770213, www.teatroverdipd.it

ROVIGO

Associazione Balletto Città di Rovigo
Via Martiri di Belfiore 60
tel. 042523113, www.fabulasaltica.com
Conservatorio Statale di Musica Francesco Venezze
In 1922 the local council set up the music school "Liceo Musicale" at the "Palazzo Venezze". This school was later to become the music conservatory "Conservatorio Statale di Musica", initially a branch of the Verona conservatory and then a fully fledged autonomous entity. Corso del Popolo 241, tel. 042522273, www.conservatorio-rovigo.it
Teatro Sociale
Piazza Garibaldi 33, tel. 042521734
www.comune.rovigo.it/teatrosociale

TREVISO

Teatro Comunale
Corso del Popolo 31, tel. 0422546355
Teatro Da Ponte
Piazza S. Leonardo 1, tel. 0422513300
www.teatrispa.it
Teatro Eden
Via Monterumici, tel. 0422513310
www.fondazionecassamarca.it

VENEZIA

Chiesa di San Stae
The "San Stae" church plays host to some of the most well known orchestras

from the Venice lagoon area.
Campo San Stae, tel. 0412750462

Istituto Culturale Italo-Tedesco
For many years now this institute has been organising eminent musical festivals as a "gathering place": "Venezia", "Incontri Musicali a Venezia" and "Venezia d'Inverno", as well as exhibitions and shows closely tied to the cinema festival "Biennale del Cinema" and the visual arts show "Arti Visive". Palazzo Albrizzi, Cannaregio 4118, tel. 0415232544

Festival Internazionale di Musica Contemporanea
September-October
At this international contemporary music festival dozens of composers from all over the world perform in a sort of universal exhibition of contemporary music; the festival is organised by the "Biennale di Venezia". Information: tel. 041786511, www.teatrolafenice.it

Fondazione Giorgio Cini
This foundation plays host to the "Istituto Antonio Vivaldi". The building is also the home of the arts academy "Istituto per le Lettere", the "Teatro e il Melodramma" and the "Istituto di Musica". Ancient music seminars by the Italian harpsichord association "Seminari di Musica Antica dell'Associazione Clavicembalistica Italiana" are also held here.
Island of San Giorgio Maggiore, tel. 0412710206

Fondazione Ugo e Olga Levi
Founded in 1962, this foundation organises meetings, study seminars, congresses, monographs and recordings in all the fields of musicology.
Palazzo Giustinan Lolin, S. Vidal 2893, tel. 041786764

Società Veneziana dei Concerti
Palazzo Giustinan Lolin, S. Vidal 2893
tel. 041786764

Teatro La Fenice
Founded in 1786, this famous theatre was officially opened in 1792. On 29th January 1996 the entire world gasped in astonishment as a terrible blaze destroyed the "La Fenice" theatre, one of the theatres that helped to write so many pages of history on Italian opera and symphonic music. Everyone is longing for the theatre to rise out of the ashes, thanks to the painstaking masterly work of the hundreds of workers, skilled stuccowork craftsmen, marble cutters, carpenters, metal workers and plasterers

who have taken up a difficult challenge: to restore the Venice "La Fenice" theatre to its former glory and exactly where it was. San Marco 2847, tel. 041786511, www.teatrolafenice.it

Teatro Malibran
S. Giovanni Crisostomo, tel. 041786601
www.teatrolafenice.it

VERONA

Arena
Piazza Bra' 28, tel. 0458051891/905
www.arena.it

Estravagario Teatro Tenda
Via S. Teresa 1, tel. 045502638
www.estravagario.it

International Music Meeting
April-September
With over 15 editions behind it, this meeting offers music lovers the opportunity to listen to various kinds of music from China, Germany, Italy, the UK, Mexico and the USA: gospel, jazz, classical, pop. The concerts are held in various towns in the Province of Verona and Padua. Information: tel. 049630786, www.orchestragiovaniledelveneto.it

J&W Rassegna di Jazz e World Music
January-April
Every year the Veneto Jazz association organises this music season at the best theatres in Veneto together with numerous other events to mark the influence one sort of music has on another. Information: tel. 0423452069, www.venetojazz.com

Teatro Filarmonico
Via Mutilati 4, tel. 0458051811
www.arena.it

VICENZA

Teatro Olimpico
Stradella del Teatro Olmpico
tel. 0444222101
www.comune.vicenza.it/olimpico/teatro.htm

BASSANO DEL GRAPPA
Opera Estate
June-August
The summer festivals are dedicated to music (classical, opera, jazz), international dances, theatre and classical cinema. Information: tel. 0424521850-217810, www.comune.bassano.it

EVENTS

As of the 16th century Friuli Venezia Giulia has fallen under the control of different rulers and undergone numerous political-administrative border changes. The turning of events over the centuries has had a great influence on the development of local theatre architecture. In the first half of the 19th century theatres even began to spring up in the outskirts of towns. Right in the middle of the Hapsberg domination theatre shows excelled just about everywhere. In the 20th century cinema began to enter the theatres, causing great structural change and perverting the original purpose of these historical buildings. To these events we have to add the damage caused by fire and the bombing raids during the First World War. Not until the 1920s and 1930s did we see these buildings return to their original purpose. Given the aforesaid, there was a strong desire to refurbish those theatres throughout the territory that could cope with the music supply: a rescue process that goes to show how careful the region is in trying to develop cultural potential through a hard look at what is happening in other Italian and central European cities.

GORIZIA

Teatro Kulturni Dom
Via Bross 20, tel. 048133288
www.kulturnidom.it
Teatro Verdi
Via Garibaldi 1, tel. 048133090
www.comune.gorizia.it/teatrogv

CORMÒNS
Jazz and Wine of Peace Festival
Internationally famous jazz, ethno-jazz and world music musicians perform in the city's theatres and clubs with live concerts and shows. Information: www.controtempo.org

PORDENONE

Teatro Comunale Giuseppe Verdi
Via Umberto 153, tel. 0427709343
www.assoprosapn.it
Teatro Politeama Zancanaro
Viale Zancanaro 26, tel. 0434780623

TRIESTE

Conservatorio Giuseppe Tartini
Via C. Ghega 12, tel. 040363508

The opera house "Teatro Lirico Giuseppe Verdi" in Trieste

Festival Internazionale dell'Operetta
June-August
This international light opera festival is aimed at portraying the past and the present of light music theatre: Information: tel. 0406722111, www.teatroverdi-trieste.com
Teatro Lirico Giuseppe Verdi
Riva Tre Novembre 1, tel. 0406722111
www.teatroverdi-trieste.com
Teatro Politeama Rossetti
Viale XX Settembre 45, tel. 0403593511
www.ilrossetti.it
Teatro Stabile La Contrada
Via Ghirlandaio 12, tel. 040948471
www.contrada.it

UDINE

Centro Ricerca Divulgazione Musicale
The international chamber music festival "Festival Internazionale di Musica da Camera" includes a number of concerts in various towns in the Province of Udine. Piazza I Maggio, tel. 043225002
Conservatorio Statale di Musica Jacopo Tomadini
Piazza I maggio 29, tel. 0432502755
Teatro Nuovo Giovanni da Udine
Via Trento 4, tel. 0432248411/419
www.comune.udine.it

CIVIDALE DEL FRIULI
MittelFest
July
Prose, music, dance, poetry, cinema and visual arts, a blending of western culture and the cultures of central European countries. Information: tel. 0432701553, www.regione.fvg.it/mittelfest

FOLKLORE IN THE VENETO

Every year this region arranges and puts on numerous events that go far back in time, many of which have a religious bearing. Many of these events are performed in traditional period costumes and even the visitors tend to get caught up in the spirit of the time. In the wake of the famous Venice Carnival almost all the Veneto cities have their own carnivals. The following is a list of only the most typical events.

BELLUNO

FELTRE
Palio di Feltre
Historical centre
First weekend in August
The pageant starts on the Friday with the dinner of the four city quarters. The athletic competitions start on the Saturday and the historical procession with the participants wearing 15th century costumes is on the Sunday. To cap the event, a horse race and prize giving ceremony, medieval entertainment with jesters. Information: tel. 04392540

SAPPADA
Carnevale
Historical centre
During carnival period
This is one of the most interesting carnivals in the Alps and features carved wooden masks. On the Saturday the carts parade by. The so-called "Rollate" mask is the traditionally worn mask; the name comes from the word "rollen", the large round iron bells worn around the waist. Monday is dedicated to the parade of the "Rollate". Information: tel. 0435469131, www.infodolomiti.it

PADOVA

Festa e Transito di Sant'Antonio
Historical centre
12 and 13 June
The solemn procession in honour of Saint Anthony's transit takes place in two stages. The "transito del santo" takes place on the evening of the 12th, a procession that retraces the dying saint's last journey. At the end of the procession the bells sound out to mark the saint's transit. On the afternoon of the 13th there is another procession during which relics of the saint are carried through the streets. The celebrations terminate with a firework display. Information: tel. 0498767918

TREVISO

Rogo della Vecchia
Thursday in mid Lent
A large effigy of an old woman is hung over the River Sile. A people's tribunal is formed and there is long dialogue in the local dialect blaming the old woman for all the bad things that happened to the town during the year. In the end the effigy is burnt; the purifying flames are accompanied by singing, dancing and libation. Information: tel. 0422547632, www.turismo.provincia.treviso.it

VITTORIO VENETO
Secolare Fiera di S. Augusta
Third week in August
This pageant goes far back in time. Concerts, dancing, fairground entertainment, stalls and the children's market all take place in the historical centre. On the evening of the 21st August a bingo session is held for charity and then a firework display. Information: tel. 043857088

VENEZIA

Carnevale
Piazza S. Marco and historical centre
Carnival week. The traditional Venice Carnival has witnessed surprising rebirth since the 1970s, so much so that it has become a really international affair. Apart from the theatrical events the real centre pieces of the carnival are the masks, all based on imaginative re-makes of bygone costumes. The carnival centres around Saint Mark's square with jugglers, acrobats and artists of all sorts. Information: tel. 0412747762, www.comune.venezia.it

EVENTS

189

Festa della Salute
Canal Grande
21 November
The Festa della Salute (Health Festival) is in memory of the awful Venice plague of 1630. When the plague had been eradicated the Republic had the wonderful church built. For the inauguration, a floating bridge on boats was built for the religious procession. The square throngs with stalls selling a sort of doughnut called *frittelle* and sweets. Information: tel. 0412747762, www.comune.venezia.it

Festa del Redentore
Third Sunday in July
This is a thanksgiving pilgrimage to the church, which was built in 1592 after the doge vowed he would build it if the plague ended. Tradition has it that a floating bridge was built across the Canal Grande on eighty boats and that the procession walked across the bridge. A floating bridge is still built to connect the Zattere side of the Canal Grande with the Giudecca side. Thousands of boats gather in front of the island ready for the firework display. Information: tel. 0412747762, www.comune.venezia.it

STRA
Riviera Fiorita, corteo acqueo e rievocazione storica
Along the Brenta river
Second Sunday in September
Every year a procession of the same boats used in the Venice Regata Storica sails along the River Brenta. The event starts with the arrival of a noble guest dressed in period costume at Villa Pisani di Stra and the Venice doge with his court who then board the boats and gondolas. Mid-morning and the procession reaches Dolo where the members parade through the town. Then on to Mira for lunch in front of Villa Contarini. In the afternoon the procession continues on to Gambarare, Oriago and finally to Malcontenta where the doge takes leave of the dignitaries and returns to Venice. Information: tel. 0415298711, www.riviera-brenta.it

VERONA

Bacanal del Gnoco
Carnival Friday
The Verona Carnival is a consequence of something that happened in 1531. A local doctor came to the aid of the starving population by handing out a great quantity of *gnocchi*. The central figure of the carnival is the "Papà del Gnoco" (*gnocchi* father), represented as an old man wearing a white costume with inlaid pieces of red cloth and gold embroidery, a cloak and a large top hat. He moves through the town on a donkey holding a large fork with an enormous *gnocco* on it and oversee the free distribution of *gnocchi*. Information: tel. 045592829, www.larenadomila.it/bacanal.htm

VICENZA

MARÒSTICA
Partita a scacchi
Piazza Castello
Second week in September, even years
Legend has it that this event dates back to something that happened in 1454. It is said that two noblemen fell in love with the podesta's daughter and decided to have a chess tournament to conquer her. The sumptuous ceremony reliving the legend takes place in the main city square, which looks like an enormous chess board made of white and red marble: on the board, pawns, knights, king and queen all dressed in 15th century costumes. The herald shouts out each move. The event ends with the *l'incendio*, a cascading firework display at the castle. Information: tel. 042472127, www.marosticaonline.it

MONTECCHIO MAGGIORE
La Faida
In the area of Rocche Scaligere
End April to beginning May
The locals relive the feud between the Montecchi and Capuleti families against a medieval background, and the suggestive setting of Romeo and Juliet's castles. There is much entertainment, a parade of the nobility and knights in costume followed by jugglers and jesters, and a market with local handmade products. The festivities end on 1st May with two teams, representing the Montecchi and Capuleti families, playing each other in a number of games and trials. Information: www.faida.it

FOLKLORE IN FRIULI VENEZIA GIULIA

Acornerstone of most of the celebrations and traditional popular pageants in Friuli Venezia Giulia is the involvement with surrounding populations. Indeed, we can mention the Festa dei Popoli della Mitteleuropa which takes place in Cormòns, or the participation of folklore groups from the five continents of the world, the Festival Mondiale del Folclore in Gorizia or the Festival Internazionale del Folclore in Aviano in the Province of Pordenone.

GORIZIA

Festival Mondiale del Folclore
Piazza Cesare Battisti
From Wednesday to Sunday last week in August
During this world folklore festival an international congress on popular traditions and an intercontinental folklore parade are held with some twenty folklore groups taking part. It is one big party with people from all five continents bringing to Italy customs, dances, colours and sounds from their distant homes. The festival ends on the Sunday: in the afternoon the parade and flag flyers, musical bands followed, at 6 p.m., by the prize giving ceremony.
Information: tel. 048138622

CORMÒNS
Festa dei Popoli della Mitteleuropa
Near Brazzano
Third Sunday in August
The Festa dei Popoli della Mitteleuropa takes place on the anniversary of the birth of Francesco Giuseppe (18 August 1830), the last Austrian and Hungarian emperor. Amid a lot of waving of flags with the double eagle (the emblem of Austria), bands dressed in costume parade through the streets playing Italian, German and Slovak songs. There is also a market for heirlooms and many traditional Austrian-cum-Hungarian traditional dishes can be tasted. Information: tel. 0481637110

PORDENONE

AVIANO
Festival Internazionale del Folclore
Piancavallo
From 6 to 15 August
Folklore groups from all over the world

mesmerise the public with their enthralling extremely different shows. Plus: cabaret in the Friuli dialect, theatrical shows, ethnic music and lyrics. To cap the festival, multiethnic food and an evening just for games.
Information: tel. 0434660750

UDINE

CIVIDALE DEL FRIULI
Fiera di San Martino
Borgo di Ponte
Sunday before or after 11 November
The San Martino festival is a return to the traditional agricultural fair and animal market. There are numerous events during the festivities including the actual market with over 70 stalls. Information: tel. 3287179561

Knights in traditional Friuli folklore costume

TOLMEZZO
Torneo delle Tredici Casade
Piazza Unità d'Italia
Third weekend in September
The tournament of the thirteen families is held in honour of the city's founding fathers, the hero Tergesteo and Lady Bora. The tournament is preceded by a parade in medieval costume with members from each of the thirteen *casade*, (the most powerful families). The tournament consists of a sort of jousting competition where two armed groups fight each other. The winner is then appointed "Cavaliere della Buriana" (knight of the Buriana) and receives the legendary sward that will give rise to gales to protect the town when it is in danger. There are markets, flag flyers, fire eaters, singers, musicians, jesters, medieval craftsmen and workshops. Information: tel. 3357431214, www.13casade.com

EVENTS

THERMAL SPA

HEALTH CENTER

Since Roman times man has exploited the therapeutic properties of hot springs. The Veneto has a wide range of elegant, long-established wellness centers built around its many hot springs, particularly around the Euganean Hills. Àbano Terme is one of Italy's best-known spas. Thermal treatments, mud therapy and many other cures are available to treat a wide range of ailments.
Friuli-Venezia Giulia has a good range of traditional wellness centers based on hot springs, but those on the coast also specialize

Wellness

in thalassotherapy (the beneficial effects of sunshine). Whether you seek thermal or esthetic treatments, hydro-massage, a particular diet or pure relaxation, the spas of this region can accommodate you in beautiful, restful, healthy surroundings.

Highlights

- Àbano Terme and the thermal springs of the Euganean Hills: when it surfaces at 87°C/188°F the water is slightly radio-active and rich in minerals including salt, bromine and iodine.
- Recoaro Terme and its numerous, thermal springs have been visited by many famous people, including Friedrich Nietzsche.
- In Friuli Venezia Giulia, the towns of Grado, Lignano Sabbiadoro specialize in thalassotherapy and beach health cures – swimming in salt water, heliotherapy and psammotherapy.

Inside

ÀBANO TERME ♨ 🏊

The water supply to the thermal spas around the Euganean Hills has its source 100 km further north. The water penetrates underground to a depth of 3,000 m, where the heat raises the temperature of the water to 87°C/188°F. It takes about 50 years to complete the journey, and as it does so it acquires certain minerals, including salt, bromine and iodine, and becomes slightly radioactive. The water is so plentiful and the area served by springs so vast that every hotel in the area has its own thermal water supply. At Àbano's 70 hotels people are treated for circulatory problems, skin complaints, motory problems, respiratory problems, problems of the urinary tract and metabolism disorders. Treatments

Pedestrian precinct in the center of Àbano Terme

include aerosols, therapeutic mud baths, steam-cave therapy and insufflations.

Àbano Grand Hotel ✦✦✦ 🏊
Via Valerio Flacco 1
tel. 0498248100
www.gbhotels.it
189 rooms, open all year
The building has two thermal swimming-pools, a sauna, a Turkish bath, vascular water trails, and a steam-cave. Treatments include lymph drainage, Ayurvedic massage, Shiatsu, kinesiology and acupuncture. Aromatherapy and chromotherapy are used

to promote psychological and physical wellness. The hotel also provides specific diets and thermal esthetic face and body treatments. Thermal treatments include mud therapy and inhalation therapy.

Àbano Ritz Hotel Terme ✦✦✦ 🏊
Via Monteortone 19
tel. 0498633100
www.abanoritz.it
141 rooms, open all year
The complex has two swimming-pools, a swimming-pool fed with thermal water, a sauna and a solarium. Here, standard thermal treatments are enhanced by programs of Bach Flower remedies and yoga to restore a correct psychological and physical balance. The manipulative and therapeutic treatments include acupuncture, Shiatsu massage, kinesiology. It also offers special diets, as well as

facial and body treatments. Thermal treatments include mud therapy and hydro-kinesitherapy.

G. H. Trieste & Victoria ✦✦✦t 🏊
Via Pietro d'Àbano 1
tel. 0498665100
www.gbhotels.it
174 rooms, closes January - March
Surrounded by a beautiful garden, it has thermal indoor and outdoor pools, a pool with hydro-massage and a steam-cave. Manipulative treatments include acupuncture, connective tissue massage, Shiatsu massage and chiropractice. For psychological and physical wellness: aromatherapy and Bach flower remedies. It provides special diets, and thermal esthetic treatments for the face and body. Thermal treatments include mud therapy and hydro-kinesitherapy.

BATTAGLIA TERME ♨

Hotel Terme Euganee
Viale S. Elena 34, tel. 049525055
www.asconet.com/termeeuganee
The treatments here are similar to those offered by other thermal spa establishments around the Euganean Hills. However, here the offering is enhanced by the combination of salt

bromine iodic water at 87°C/188°F, locally mined clay and algae which thrive in thermal water. Thermal treatments include aerosols, therapeutic baths, mud therapy and hydro-massage. The water is particularly effective in the treatment of circulatory, motory and respiratory disorders.

BIBIONE ♨

Bibione Thermae
Via delle Colonie 3, tel. 0431441111
www.bibioneterme.it
Open March - December
The water here is classified as hyper-thermal (52°C/125°F), is alkaline and contains bicarbonate, sodium and fluoride. It is used for mud therapy and balneotherapy at temperatures of 32-37°C/89-98°F. The complex also has a steam-cave where the water not only heats the environment but saturates it with steam at between 27°C and 45°C/80°F-113°F. Thermal treatments include aerosols, mud therapy, steam-caves, hydro-massage and lung ventilation. The water is beneficial in the treatment of circulatory, motory, respiratory and urinary ailments, and metabolism disorders.

Swimming-pool with hydro-massage and water fountains at Bibione

CALALZO DI CADORE ♨

Croda Bianca
Via Stazione 19, tel. 043532348
www.hotelcalalzo.it
Open all year
The thermal water of this lake has always been known to be beneficial to swimmers but was also used for washing, because of the whitening properties of the water. The water is alkaline and contains earth, sulfur and bicarbonate, surfacing at 10.7°C/51°F. It is beneficial whether taken by mouth, or used for inhalation and mud therapy. The treatments, which are recommended in the cure of circulatory disorders, liver and skin complaints, digestive problems, and motory and respiratory problems, involve aerosols, therapeutic baths and hydro-massage.

COMÈLICO SUPERIORE ♨

Terme delle Dolomiti - Valgrande Padola
Via Valgrande, tel. 0435470153
Open all year
The sulfurous water of Bagni di Valgrande is a remedy for intestinal ailments and skin complaints. This highly innovative hotel and spa complex specializes in the cure of skin and mucous membrane disorders. The water contains sulfur, calcium and magnesium, surfaces at 6.6 °C/43°F and is used in the treatment of circulatory problems, liver and skin complaints, and problems of the digestive and respiratory tracts. Treatments include aerosols, therapeutic baths, therapeutic showers, hydro-massage, insufflation, water therapy, fitness trails, breathing exercises, hydro-kinesitherapy, massage, anti-stress programs and rehabilitation.

WELLNESS

GALZIGNANO TERME ♨ ⚲

This spa uses salt bromine iodic water which surfaces at 87°C/188°F, and is used for making mud with local clay and algae. Four modern hotels are located in a spa park with an astonishing range of bathing facilities (8 swimming-pools, 6 of which are fed with hot spring water) and sports facilities (a golf course and practice range, tennis courts). The water here is recommended in the treatment of circulatory and skin problems, and motory and respiratory problems. Treatments include aerosols, therapeutic baths, therapeutic showers, mud therapy, steam-caves and hydro-massage, water therapy, fitness trails, breathing exercises, massage and rehabilitation.

Steam-cave at Galzignano Terme

Terme di Galzignano Resort ★★★ ⚲
Viale delle Terme 82
tel. 0499195555
www.galzignano.it
414 rooms
Closes from mid-December thru January
Set in a private park, this hotel complex has a golf course, 6 tennis courts and a gym. Each hotel has a spa building, and departments for mud therapy, massage and inhalations. There are 8 swimming-pools fed with hot spring water, hydro-massage facilities and a beauty farm. Manipulative and therapeutic therapies include therapeutic lymph drainage, Ayurvedic massage and craniosacral therapy. Psychological and physical wellness techniques include chromotherapy, relaxation and meditation techniques.

LAZISE ♨

Parco Termale del Garda Villa dei Cedri
Colà, Piazza di Sopra 4
tel. 0457590988, www.villadeicedri.it
Open all year
The Villa dei Cedri spa complex grew up when the hot spring was discovered. The water contains bicarbonate and calcium and has a high percentage of magnesium, potassium and silicon. It surfaces at 37°C/98°F and is so abundant that a lake has been converted into a pool for balneotherapy. An esthetic center offers facial and body treatments. The thermal treatments include hydro-massage and a pool fed with hot spring water.

Lazise overlooks the middle of Lake Garda from the side closest to Verona

MONTEGROTTO TERME ♨ 🏃

Here, archaeologists have uncovered the remains of the splendid Roman baths named after the Emperor Nero (Terme Neroniane), a huge spa complex surrounded by a theater, public buildings and temples. As at Àbano Terme, the marine salt bromine iodic water surfaces at 80-87°C/176-188°F and is used for mud therapy. In addition to mud and balneotherapy, the inhalation techniques available here are effective in the treatment of pathologies of the respiratory tract. Thermal treatments available include aerosols, therapeutic baths, mud therapy and hydro-massage. Other treatments include kinesitherapy, hydro-kinesitherapy and massage.

View of the swimming-pool of the Hotel Esplanade Tergesteo

Esplanade Tergesteo ★★★ 🏃
Via Roma 54, tel. 0498911777
www.esplanadetergesteo.it
139 rooms, closes from mid-January thru February
Facilities at this hotel include a gym, a tennis court and a kids' playground. The properties of the water and the constant temperature of approximately 35°C/95°F are beneficial to all the muscles in the body. Both swimming-pools are fed with hot spring water. The manipulative and therapeutic treatments available include acupuncture and Ayurvedic massage. Esthetic treatments include crystal massage and anti-cellulite treatment. Thermal treatments include mud therapy and hydro-kinesitherapy.

G. H. Terme ★★★ 🏃
Viale Stazione 21
tel. 0498911444
www.grandhotelterme.it
119 rooms, open all year
This spa complex, set in a large park, has two

swimming-pools fed with hot spring water with hydro-massage facilities and a steam-cave. Manipulative and therapeutic treatments include Ayurvedic massage, Shiatsu massage and acupressure. Esthetic thermal facial and body treatments are available, also balneotherapy and mud therapy.

RECOARO TERME ♨

Terme di Recoaro
Via Fonti Centrali 1
tel. 044575016
Open from May to October
This spa complex has five hot springs (Lelia, Lorgna, Amara, Nuova and Lora) and there are 4 more (Giuliana, Capitello, Franco and Aureliana) in the surrounding area. The water at the Aureliana, Capitello and Giuliana springs is alkaline and surfaces at 10°C/50°F. It has a medium mineral content and contains earth, bicarbonate, iron, carbon and lithium. The water at the Lelia, Amara, Nuova and Lorgna springs is alkaline and surfaces at 11-12°C/51-53°F and contains earth, bicarbonate, sulfur, iron and carbon. The water at the Lora spring surfaces at 6.4°C/43°F and has a low mineral content. The thermal treatments available include aerosols and mud therapy.

WELLNESS

197

Pavilions of the spa complex at Arta Terme

Terme di Arta-Fonte Pudia
Via Nazionale1, tel. 0433929320
www.termediarta.it
The Terme di Arta spa establishment is housed in two buildings linked to a spring called Fonte Pudia. The water surfaces at 9°C/48°F, contains calcium, magnesium and sulfur, and is effective in the treatment of circulatory diseases, complaints of the liver and bile ducts, skin complaints, problems of the digestive tract, and motory, respiratory, urinary and metabolism problems. The treatments include aerosols, therapeutic baths, nasal douches, mud therapy, hydro-massage, gum and nose irrigation, nebulizations and a swimming-pool fed with spring water. It also offers numerous esthetic treatments.

Gardel ★★★
Piano d'Arta, Via Marconi 6/8
tel. 043392588, www.gardel.it
55 rooms, closed in March
Also closes mid-November to mid-December
Here the water from Fonte Pudia surfaces at 9°C/48°F and contains calcium magnesium and sulfur. Relaxation therapies include a Finnish sauna, a Turkish bath, hydro-massage and a solarium.

Manipulative and therapeutic treatments include connective tissue massage, lymph drainage, craniosacral therapy, foot reflexology, posture correction and acupressure. Psychological and physical treatments include oligotherapy, aromatherapy and relaxation techniques. Esthetic treatments include customized diets, diet improvement and esthetic face and body treatments.

Strictly speaking, Grado is not a spa but it has a long tradition as a thalassotherapy center. The town's beginnings as a health resort date back to an Imperial Decree of 1892 which conferred official status on a town that was already the favorite holiday destination of the Habsburg nobility. The Terme Marine complex overlooks the main beach. The many facilities include an esthetic center and a dermo-esthetic medicine center, a fitness center, a sauna, a solarium and, in summer, special activities for kids, as

G. H. Astoria ★★★
Largo S. Grisogono 3
tel. 043183550
www.hotelastoria.it
120 rooms, closed from Epiphany to February and the second half of December
At the beginning of the 20th century, this spa establishment

was much frequented by the Habsburg nobility. Next to the panoramic swimming-pool is the thalassotherapy center. Manipulative and therapeutic treatments include foot reflexology and lymph drainage. Esthetic treatments include face and body treatments, peeling, pedicures and manicures. Thermal treatments include mud therapy, electrophoresis, kinesitherapy, ultrasound treatment, inhalation therapies and thalassotherapy.

Savoy ★★★
Via Carducci 33
tel. 0431897111
www.hotelsavoy-grado.it
83 rooms, closed from November until mid-March

The Savoy Beauty Spa and Wellness Center opened in 1992 and has a comprehensive range of facilities. They include indoor and outdoor salt-water pools, a swimming-pool with hydro-massage, a sauna, a Turkish bath and a solarium. Manipulative and therapeutic treatments include thalassotherapy, relaxation massage, lymph drainage, foot reflexology, aromatherapy massage, peeling massage, Shiatsu hydro-therapy, hydro-massage with essential oils and algae skin packs. Esthetic treatments include esthetic treatments for the face, body and hands. Thermal treatments include inhalation therapies and mud therapy.

Large salt-water swimming-pool at Grado

well as a cinema and a concert hall. Santa Croce mineral water has a low mineral content and surfaces at 6.5°C/43°F. Treatments include aerosols, therapeutic baths, steam-caves, hydro-massage, humid-hot inhalations and nebulizations. This water is particularly effective in the treatment of circulatory problems, skin complaints, and for motory and respiratory problems.

LIGNANO SABBIADORO 🎋 🏃

Terme di Lignano

Lignano Riviera, lungomare R. Riva 1/B
tel. 0431422217, www.sil-lignano.net
The Terme di Lignano, which opened in 1962, specializes in thalassotherapy, hardly surprising given the site's exceptional location. Facilities include a heated indoor salt-water pool, hydro-massage and a gym. In addition to traditional thalassotherapy treatments they also offer physical and rehabilitation

therapy. They also use the sulfurous water from the Terme di Tabiano for nebulizations for treating respiratory disorders. The esthetic center offers special treatments and massages. Thermal treatments include aerosols, therapeutic baths, hydropinic treatments (drinking the spring water), nasal douches, mud therapy, hydro-massage, humid-hot inhalations, insufflations, nasal irrigation and nebulization.

Golf Inn ★★★ 🏃
Via della Bonifica 3
tel. 0431427701
www.golfinn.it
24 rooms, open all year
This inn situated in the grounds of the prestigious Golf Club di Lignano provides accommodation for golfers. In addition to using the 18-hole golf course and the practice range, its guests can use the pool and the fitness center at the nearby Hotel Marina Uno. There is a highly respected beauty farm, a small pool with hydro-massage, a solarium, a gym, a sauna, vascular water trails, thermal armchairs, a lily pond and a relaxation area where guests can enjoy the benefits of the various treatments. Manipulative and therapeutic treatments include massotherapy, Thai massage, Shiatsu massage, sports massage and foot reflexology. Esthetic

treatments include facial and body treatments and peeling. Thermal treatments include kinesitherapy and vascular water trails.

Marina Uno ★★★ 🏃
Riviera, Viale Adriatico 7
tel. 0431427171
www.marinauno.it
78 rooms, closed November to March
The center, which has an Olympic-size swimming-pool, a kids' pool, a sauna and a Turkish bath, specializes in esthetic treatments. Manipulative and therapeutic treatments include massotherapy, hot stone massage, lymph drainage, relaxation massage and mud therapy. Esthetic treatments include face and body treatments, karité butter body treatment, body thalasso scrub, algae body treatments, leg bandaging and massage, manicures and pedicures.

GETTING TO

By plane to the Veneto

VENICE – Marco Polo International Airport
Information about flights and services
tel. 0412609240/2609250, www.veniceairport.it
Lost luggage tel. 0412609222.
To and from Venice Airport – Piazzale Roma (Venice's main car park and bus terminus): ATVO (information tel. 0421383672, www.atvo.it/airport); ACTV No. 5 bus service (information tel. 0412722111).
To and from airport/Mestre train station: ATVO FLY BUS shuttle and ACTV No. 5 bus service
Motor-launch services: Alilaguna (information tel. 0415235775, www.alilaguna.it), Consorzio Motoscafi Venezia (information tel. 0412406711, www.motoscafivenezia.it), Venice Water Taxi (information 041717273, www.venicewelcome.com for on line reservations).
VERONA – Valerio Catullo International Airport

Information tel. 0458095611, www.aeroportoverona.it
Lost luggage 0458095715
A shuttle service runs (both ways) between the airport and Verona's main train station. For taxis, call Cooperativa Taxi Villafranca (tel. 045914047).
TREVISO – San Giuseppe Airport
Information tel. 0422315111, www.trevisoairport.it.
Ticket office tel. 0422315331
ATVO runs a shuttle service between the airport and the main towns in Eastern Veneto and Friuli (information tel. 0421383671, www.atvo.it).
Services between the airport and Mestre (train station) and Venice (Piazzale Roma) are operated by Transavia.com (tel. 0422315327).
VICENZA – Tommaso Dal Molin Airport
General information (tel. 0444927711/12, www.airportvicenza.it)
AIM Vicenza Trasporti S.p.A. operates the No. 9 bus service between the airport and the city center (tel. 0444394909, www.aimvicenza.it). Taxis are available at the airport, tel. 0444920600.

By plane to Friuli Venezia Giulia

FRIULI VENEZIA GIULIA AIRPORT
Trieste International Airport – Ronchi dei Legionari (Gorizia)
General information tel. 0481773224, www.aeroporto.fvg.it, ticket office tel. 0481773232
Lost luggage, tel. 0481773227
APT (Azienda Provinciale Trasporti, tel. 800955957, www.aptgorizia.it) operates the bus services to and from the airport: to Gorizia (bus service No.1, then bus service No. 51), to Monfalcone (bus service No. 10), to Udine (bus service No. 51 – also non-stop on the highway bus), and Trieste (bus service No. 51).
The Trieste highway is also served by services to and from Slovenia and Croatia (www.autostradetrieste.it e www.saf.ud.it).

By train

For timetables and fares:
TRENITALIA, tel. 892021, every day, from 7 to 21, only from Italy, www.trenitalia.com; tel. ticket office 199166177, every day from 7 to 21.

TRANSPORT

Train

All the main towns in the Veneto and Friuli can be reached by train.
TRENITALIA operates services all over the region. For information, tel. 892021, telephone ticket office 199166177, www.trenitalia.com
Trenitalia operates the following special deals:
Carta Verde Railplus: only for young people up to 26 years of age, lasts one year, only valid for one person; entitles the holder to 10% discount on the price of 1st and 2nd class tickets and on journeys in sleeper or couchette, and a 25% discount on the prices of international tickets;
Carta Argento: only for people aged 60 and over, lasts one year, only valid for one person; entitles the holder to a 15% discount on 1st and 2nd class tickets and 10% off journeys in sleeper or couchette. Both cards are on sale at the ticket offices and travel agencies of Trenitalia.

Coach in the Veneto

BELLUNO – DolomitiBus operates services between Belluno, Àgordo, Calalzo Cortina and Feltre (tel. 043721711, www.dolomitibus.it)
PADOVA AND ROVIGO – SITA operates local long-distance coach services in the provinces of Padova and Rovigo (with connections into neighboring provinces, ordinary bus services to Venice, Vicenza, Treviso, and seasonal services to Jèsolo and Asiago) and local services in the municipality of Rovigo. Tel. 0498206811 (Padova), tel. 0425377711 (Rovigo), www.sitabus.it
TREVISO – ACTT operates bus services in the city and to nearby towns. Tel. 0422327253, www.actt.it
VENEZIA – ACTV is the company which operates the transport services in and around Venice, in the lagoon ("vaporetti" (water-buses), motorboats, ferries, motor-vessels) and on the mainland. Tel. 0412722111, www.actv.it

VERONA – AMT S.p.A. operates public trnsport services in and around the city of Verona. Vicenza. Tel. 0458871111, www.amt.it
VICENZA – Public transport services in and around Vicenza are operated by AIM Trasporti Vicenza. Tel. 0444394909, www.aimvicenza.it; VTF operates bus services in the Province of Vicenza. Tel. 0444223115, www.ftv.it

Coach in Friuli Venezia Giulia

GORIZIA – APT (Azienda Provinciale Trasporti) operates local bus services in the city, coach services to Monfalcone and Grado, and international coach services to Nova Gorica. Freephone 800955957, www.aptgorizia.it
PORDENONE – ATAP operates local services and long-distance links to Oderzo, Sacile, Spilimbergo, and other destinations). Tel. 0432224466, freephone 800101040, www.atap.pn.it

Practical info

By car

Motorway information center: tel. 0643632121, 24 hours a day, freephone 800269269, www.autostrade.it

AUTOVIE VENETE is a subsidiary of the following highways: the A4 Venice – Trieste, the A23 Palmanova – Udine Sud and the A28 Portogruaro – Pordenone – Conegliano. For information call freephone 800996099, www.autovie.it).

Radio information: Isoradio FM 103,3 and Viaradio FM 102,5

By boat

VENICE – Since 1997, Venezia Terminal Passeggeri has been responsible for managing passenger traffic (cruises, ferries, hydrofoils and yachts) in the port of Venice. Information: tel. 0412403001, www.port.venice.it

TRIESTE – The port of Trieste has been a free port since 1719, and, today, much of the port is still subject to this law and regarded as being outwith the customs area of the European Union. The port is organized into various terminals, all operated by private companies. Information: Attività Portuale Trieste, tel. 0406731, www.porto.trieste.it

TRIESTE – Trieste Trasporti operates the city's bus services. Freephone 800016675, www.triestetrasporti.it

UDINE – SAF operates local, long-distance, inter-regional and international coach services. Freephone 800915303, www.saf.ud.it

Car rental

You will find all the major car hire companies in the Veneto and in Friuli Venezia Giulia with an efficient network of agencies.

AVIS – Booking center 199100133, www.avisautonoleggio.it
"Marco Polo" Airport – Venice, tel. 0415415030
"Valerio Catullo" Airport – Verona, tel. 045987571
"San Giuseppe" Airport – Treviso, tel. 0422433351
Padua, tel. 049664198
"Friuli Venezia Giulia" Airport – Ronchi dei Legionari, tel. 0481777085
Pordenone, tel. 043421925
Udine, tel. 0432501149

TOURIST INFORMATION

Website of Regione Veneto: www.regione.veneto.it
Website of Regione Friuli Venezia Giulia: www.regione.fvg.it
Most of the websites of the various municipalities have similar addresses, for example: www.comune.belluno.it

HERTZ – Booking center 199122211, www.hertz.it
"Marco Polo" Airport – Venice, tel. 0415416075
"Valerio Catullo" Airport – Verona, tel. 0458619042
"San Giuseppe" Airport – Treviso, tel. 0422264216
Padova, 0498752202
"Friuli Venezia Giulia" Airport – Ronchi dei Legionari, tel. 0481777025
Udine, tel. 0432200210

EUROPCAR – Booking center 8000014410, www.europcar.it
"Marco Polo" Airport – Venice, tel. 0415415654
"Valerio Catullo" Airport – Verona, tel. 0458600477
"San Giuseppe" Airport – Treviso, tel. 042222807
"Friuli Venezia Giulia" Airport – Ronchi dei Legionari, tel. 0481778920
Udine, tel. 0432501389

Inside

Hotels and restaurants
Tourist information
Museums and monuments
At night

EMERGENCY NUMBERS
113 General public emergency number
112 Military Police
115 Fire Brigade
117 Financial Police
118 Medical emergencies
1515 Forest fires
1530 Coastguard
116 Road Assistance

ÀBANO TERME

ⓘ Ufficio Informazioni e Accoglienza Turistica
Via Pietro d'Àbano 18,
tel. 0498669055
www.termeeuganeeapt.net

Hotels

Ariston Molino Terme *ఓ* ⚂
Via Augure 5, tel. 0498669061
www.aristonmolino.it
Open mid-March to November
175 rooms. Restaurant, parking, air-conditioned, swimming pool, sauna, tennis, gym
Credit cards: American Express, Diners Club, Visa, Mastercard
A modern building in a quiet location, surrounded by a vast garden. Run by same family for many years, thermal and beauty treatments available, Internet point.

Bristol Buja *ఓ* ⚂ ★
Via Monteortone 2,
tel. 0498669390
www.bristolbuja.it
139 rooms. Restaurant, parking, air-conditioned, swimming pool, sauna, tennis, gym
Credit cards: American Express, Diners Club, Visa, Mastercard
Offers hospitality and thermal treatments in an elegant, efficient ambience. The rooms, suites and mini-suites have all modern comforts. Special agreements with three local golf courses.

Due Torri *ఓ* ⚂
Via Pietro d'Àbano 18,
tel. 0498632100
www.gbhotels.it
133 rooms. Restaurant, parking, air-conditioned, swimming pool, gym
Credit cards: American Express, Diners Club, Visa, Mastercard
Formerly an 18th-century stately home. Spacious rooms, junior suites and suites, some of which overlook the garden; facilities include: communicating thermal swimming pools, modern fitness and beauty centers, indoor thermal treatments. Restaurant with garden service in summer, breakfast room with veranda and terrace.

Harrys' *** ★
Via Marzia 50, tel. 049667011
www.harrys.it
Open March-November
66 rooms. Restaurant, parking, air-conditioned, swimming pool, tennis, gym
Credit cards: American Express, Diners Club, Visa, Mastercard

In a quiet location, surrounded by a large garden; in addition to thermal treatment zone, thermal swimming pool with hydro-massage for use of guests. Keep-fit classes, walks, bikes for use of guests, live music at dinner.

La Residence & Idrokinesis *ఓ* ⚂
Via Monte Ceva 8,
tel. 0498247777
www.gbhotels.it
146 rooms. Restaurant, parking, air-conditioned, swimming pool, sauna, gym
Credit cards: American Express, Visa
Plenty of ideal places to relax; large hall, large sitting rooms, spacious bedrooms with lift to swimming pools. Wide-ranging program of cures and beauty treatments, with a new physiotherapy department.

Terme Savoia *ఓ* ⚂
Via P. d'Àbano 49,
tel. 0498231111
www.savoiaterme.it
Open March-November and over Christmas
172 rooms. Restaurant, parking, air-conditioned, swimming pool, sauna, tennis, gym
Credit cards: American Express, Visa, Mastercard
The elegance, rational layout and comfort of the communal areas, the garden and the bedrooms have resulted in a high level of refined hospitality and a relaxing, healthy atmosphere.

Restaurants

Aubergine ⅋⅋ ★
Via Ghislandi 5, tel. 0498669910
Closed Wednesday
Cuisine: traditional
Credit cards: American Express, Diners Club, Visa
Elegant decor adds to the charming atmosphere of this venue; meat, game and fish, and they change the menus every month. Also pizza.

Gambrinus ⅋ ⚂ ★
Via Marzia 92, tel. 0498668829
Closed Tuesday
Cuisine: Veneto
Credit cards: Visa, Mastercard
In a quiet area, a well-lit venue with modern decor. Regional cuisine, with excellent "primi piatti" made with vegetables, horse-meat and stockfish.

Museums, Monuments and Churches

Pinacoteca Civica al Montirone
Via Pietro d'Àbano 20,
tel. 049667129-0498245268

www.abanoterme.net
Opening times: Summer: Tuesday-Sunday 10.00-12.00, 16.00-19.00. Winter: Tuesday-Sunday 10.00-12.00, 15.00-18.00.

ADRIA

Rural Lodgings

Scirocco ★
Voltascirocco 3,
tel. 042640963
Restaurant
Family hospitality in a 19th-century mansion. Large garden with poplars, ideal for children. From March to May and September to mid-November educational activities for schoolchildren.

Restaurants

Molteni ⅋⅋
Via Ruzzina 2, tel. 042621295
Closed Saturday
Cuisine: Polesine and traditional
Credit cards: Visa, Mastercard
A pleasant venue with exposed beams and natural brick walls. Fish and meat specialties, grilled meats, game during hunting season, selection of cheeses. A wide selection of first-class wines and spirits.

Museums, Monuments and Churches

Museo Archeologico Nazionale
Via Badini 59, tel. 042621612
Opening times: Monday-Sunday 9.00-20.00.

ÀGORDO

Restaurants

Erice ⅋⅋
Via IV Novembre 13/B,
tel. 043765011
Closed Monday except in summer
Cuisine: local
Credit cards: American Express, Diners Club, Visa
Wood dominates this building with large windows, a comfortable, well-lit venue.

Due Mori ⅋⅋
Borgo Bassano 149,
tel. 0499401422
www.hotelduemori.it
Closed Sunday evening and Monday
Cuisine: Veneto and traditional
Credit cards: American Express, Diners Club, Visa, Mastercard
Can seat large numbers (especially receptions) and serves traditional dishes. The chef recommends duck with balsamic vinegar and pistachios; sushi dishes (on request).

Museums, Monuments and Churches

Collezioni Ottiche e Occhiali - Raccolta Rathschüler-Luxottica
Corso Patrioti 3, tel. 043762641
Opening times: May be visited by arrangement.

Museo della Storia Mineraria
Istituto Geotecnico Minerario "Follador", via V Maggio 16, tel. 043762015
www.follador.bl.it/museo.html
Opening times: During the school year: Monday-Saturday 8.30-13.00. During the summer, may be visited by arrangement at the same times.

ÀLLEGHE

> ☑ **Ufficio Informazioni e Accoglienza Turistica**
> Piazza Kennedy 17, tel. 0437523333

Hotels

Alla Posta *★*
Caprile, piazza Dogliani 19, tel. 0437721171
www.hotelposta.com
Open Christmas-mid-April and mid-June-September
55 rooms. Restaurant, parking, swimming pool, sauna, tennis, gym
Credit cards: American Express, Diners Club, Visa, Mastercard
A sophisticated hotel with a long tradition of hospitality, bedrooms and reception rooms furnished in rustic style. Facilities include: indoor pool, fitness center, sauna and pool with hydro-massage.

Barance ★★★ &
Masarè, corso Venezia 45, tel. 0437723748
www.hotelbarance.com
Open December-April and June-September
27 rooms. Restaurant, parking, swimming pool, sauna, tennis
Credit cards: Diners Club, Visa, Mastercard
Elegant venue with rustic decor and wooden furnishings, with a warm, pleasant atmosphere; family run; facilities for keep-fit enthusiasts; restaurant serving traditional and imaginative dishes, extra accommodation in the "Liliana" annex.

Sport Hotel Europa *★*
Via Europa 10, tel. 0437523362
www.sporthoteleuropa.com
Open mid-December-mid-April and mid-June-mid-September
36 rooms. Restaurant, parking, sauna, gym
Credit cards: American Express, Diners Club, Visa, Mastercard

Quiet location on lake shore, elegant, spacious rooms and suites and large reception rooms; complete range of facilities for relaxation and esthetic treatments.

ASIAGO

> ☑ **Azienda di Promozione Turistica**
> Via Stazione 5, tel. 0424/462221
> *www.ascom.vi.it/asiago/*

Hotels

Da Barba ★★★ ★
Via Pöslen 40, tel. 0424463363
www.dabarba.it
22 rooms. Restaurant, parking, sauna, gym
In a panoramic position, attractive ambience with mountain-style decor. Excellent service and home cooking; some suites, keep-fit circuit, giant chess-board with hand-carved pieces.

Erica ★★★ ★
Via Garibaldi 55, tel. 0424462113
www.hotelerica.it
Open December-mid-April and June-September
33 rooms. Restaurant, parking, gym
Credit cards: Visa
A charming, comfortable small hotel close to the ski facilities. Three types of rooms, some in attic. Has been run by same family, attentive to their guests' needs, since 1952.

Golf Hotel Villa Bonomo *★* &
Via Pennar 322, tel. 0424460408
www.hotelvillabonomo.it
11 rooms. Restaurant, parking, sauna
Credit cards: American Express, Diners Club, Visa, Mastercard
Converted old farm and hunting-lodge. Rustic yet elegant with a "Stuben". Special terms at the local golf course which, in winter, becomes a cross-country ski track. Restaurant with Puglia cuisine.

Linta Park Hotel *★*
Via Linta 6, tel. 0424462753
www.altopiano-asiago.com/linta
Open Christmas-mid-March and mid-June-mid-September
101 rooms. Restaurant, parking, swimming pool, sauna, tennis, gym
Credit cards: Visa
Modern complex with large, well furnished reception rooms and comfortable bedrooms, including some suites; facilities for keeping fit and sport, and a kids' playground. Included in the

price: swimming pool, sauna, gym, sauna, Turkish bath, entertainment, kids' club, tennis courts, small football pitch.

Restaurants

Casa Rossa ⁑ &
Kaberlaba, via Kaberlaba 19, tel. 0424462017
Closed Thursday
Cuisine: Veneto
Credit cards: American Express, Diners Club, Visa, Mastercard
An old converted farmhouse, with typical local dishes such as home-made pasta, "soppressa", grilled meats and game. Wide selection of spirits and quality wines.

Da Riccardo al Maddarello ⁑
Via Val Maddarello 88, tel. 0424462601
Closed Monday and Tuesday except July and August
Cuisine: Veneto and creative
Credit cards: American Express, Diners Club, Visa, Mastercard
Riccardo and Dora add their own creative touch to traditional recipes. Wide range of cheeses, extensive list of wines and spirits, good choice of coffees and desserts.

Museums, Monuments and Churches

Museo del Sacrario Militare
Viale degli Eroi, tel. 0424463088
Opening times: May 16-September: Monday-Sunday 9.00-12.00, 14.00-18.00. October-15 May: Monday-Sunday 9.00-12.00, 14.00-17.00.

Museo Naturalistico Didattico
Via Bertacchi 14, tel. 0424460124-0424464081
www.comune.asiago.vi.it/da
Opening times: May be visited by prior arrangement.

ÀSOLO
Hotels

Al Sole *★* &
Via Collegio 33, tel. 0423951332
www.albergoalsole.com
23 rooms. Restaurant, parking, air-conditioned, gym
Credit cards: American Express, Visa, Mastercard
The atmosphere of this sophisticated 16th-century palazzo conjures up memories of how Asolo used to be. Charming bedrooms and suites with all mod cons, fax and internet access. Well-equipped massage parlor, romantic restaurant serves unique dishes of local cuisine with a creative touch.

Villa Cipriani *✮*
Via Canova 298, tel. 0423523411
www.sheraton.com/villacipriani
31 rooms. Restaurant, parking, air-conditioned, sauna, gym
Credit cards: American Express, Diners Club, Visa, Mastercard
Housed in a charming 17th-century villa, a prestigious hotel with garden. The ideal place for those seeking relaxation in a sophisticated ambience. Bedrooms tastefully furnished and reception rooms have a dream-like quality.

Restaurants

Ca Derton 🍴
Piazza G. D'Annunzio 11, tel. 0423529648
Closed Sunday evening and Monday
Cuisine: Veneto
Credit cards: American Express, Diners Club, Visa, Mastercard
An 18th-century palazzo, a venue with classic decor with Venetian style furniture; the chef favors traditional cuisine.

Ai Due Archi 🍴
Via Roma 55, tel. 0423952201
Closed Wednesday evening and Thursday
Cuisine: traditional
Credit cards: Diners Club, Visa, Mastercard
Upmarket venue, with antiques and wooden decor; traditional dishes, such as home-made pasta, "primi piatti" with asparagus, vegetables in season and aromatic herbs.

Museums, Monuments and Churches

Museo Civico
Via Regina Cornaro 74, tel. 0423952313
www.asolo.it/museo
Opening times: Saturday and Sunday 10.00-12.00, 15.00-19.00.

BASSANO DEL GRAPPA

> ℹ️ **Ufficio Informazioni e Accoglienza Turistica**
> *Largo Corona d'Italia 35, tel. 0424524351*
> *www.vicenzae.org*

Hotels

Al Camin *✮*
Cassola, via Valsugana 64, tel. 0424566134
www.bestwestern.it/alcamin_vi
45 rooms. Restaurant, parking, air-conditioned
Credit cards: American Express, Diners Club, Visa, Mastercard
Well equipped, with great attention to detail, rooms furnished in different styles but all with hydro-massage. Restaurant with Venetian decor and local cuisine.

Alla Corte *** 👍
Sant'Eusebio, via Corte 54, tel. 0424502114
www.hotelallacorte.com
32 rooms. Restaurant, parking, air-conditioned
Credit cards: American Express, Visa, Mastercard
In a quiet, concealed location, yet close to the town center, this 1920s building has been converted to provide all modern comforts; spacious bedrooms (some with balcony and mountain views) and conference facilities; buffet breakfast, with home-made bread and cakes; local cuisine with an imaginative touch.

Bonotto Hotel Belvedere *✮* 👍 ★
Piazzale Generale Giardino 14, tel. 0424529845
www.bonotto.it
87 rooms. Restaurant, parking, air-conditioned, gym
Credit cards: American Express, Diners Club, Visa, Mastercard
This 15th-century palazzo has beautifully furnished superior rooms and elegant suites, with hydro-massage bath. Excellent facilities for conferences and business meetings.

Victoria *** 👍
Viale A. Diaz 33, tel. 0424503620
www.hotelvictoria-bassano.com
23 rooms. Parking, air-conditioned
Credit cards: American Express, Diners Club, Visa, Mastercard
A palazzo in the old town center, with excellent amenities; comfortable bedrooms in period style and buffet breakfast.

Villa Ca' Sette *✮* 👍 ★
Via Cunizza da Romano 4, tel. 0424383350
www.ca-sette.it
19 rooms. Restaurant, parking, air-conditioned
Credit cards: American Express, Diners Club, Visa, Mastercard
Just behind the town, an 18th-century Venetian villa converted into a hotel with charming bedrooms and suites. Elegant garden with olive trees, lake and fountains.

Rural lodgings

Villa Brocchi Colonna
Contrà San Giorgio 98, tel. 0424501580
www.villabrocchicolonna.it
Bikes for use of guests
Credit cards: American Express, Diners Club, Visa, Mastercard
A country residence with a warm, welcoming ambience, thanks to the owners' hospitality. Good breakfasts with home-made cakes and biscuits. Perfect place to chill out. Riding stables and golf course nearby.

Restaurants

Al Ponte 🍴
Via Volpato 60, tel. 0424219274
www.alpontedibassano.com
Closed Monday and Tuesday lunch-time
Cuisine: Veneto
Credit cards: American Express, Diners Club, Visa, Mastercard
From the restaurant you can see Palladio's wooden bridge. Large, modern venue, with a veranda in the summer. Fun, imaginative cooking; particularly good home-made pastries, chocolates and cakes.

Belvedere 🍴🍴 👍 ★
Viale delle Fosse 1, tel. 0424524988
www.bonotto.it
Closed Sunday
Cuisine: Veneto and traditional with a new angle
Credit cards: American Express, Diners Club, Visa, Mastercard
Smart, traditional ambience. A true gastronomic benchmark for the area, serving traditional local dishes, prepared with a modern touch with absolutely fresh local ingredients. Wide selection of especially local wines and spirits.

Ca' 7 🍴🍴 👍 ★
Via Cunizza da Romano 4, tel. 0424383350
www.ca-sette.it
Closed Sunday evening and Monday
Cuisine: local with a modern touch
Credit cards: American Express, Diners Club, Visa, Mastercard
In this refined setting, the dishes are prepared using top-quality ingredients, with a menu ranging from meat and game to fish. Carefully selected wine-list.

Da Renzo-alla Trinità 🍴
Via SS. Trinità 9, tel. 0424503055
Closed Tuesday and Wednesday lunch-time
Cuisine: Venetian
Credit cards: American Express, Diners Club, Visa, Mastercard
18th-century palazzo with informal atmosphere, traditional decor with a seafaring motif, views of mountains and olive-groves; cuisine based mainly on fish, but the menu includes traditional "primi piatti" and dishes made with asparagus

and "radicchio di Treviso".
Outdoor terrace in summer.

At night

Decò
Via Gaggion 3/B, tel. 0424504335
Disco

Museums, Monuments and Churches

Museo Civico
Piazza Garibaldi, tel. 0424522235
www.museobassano.it
Opening times: Tuesday-Saturday 9.00-18.30; Sunday 15.30-18.30. The graphic display can only be visited by appointment.

Museo degli Alpini
Via Angarano 2, tel. 0424503650-0424503662
Opening times: Tuesday-Sunday 8.30-20.00.

Museo della Ceramica - Palazzo Sturm
Via Schiavonetti, tel. 0424524933
www.museobassano.it
Opening times: Tuesday-Saturday 9.00-12.30, 15.30-18.30; Sunday 10.00-12.30, 15.30-18.30.

Museo della Grappa "Jacopo Poli"
Via Gamba 6, tel. 0424524426
www.poligrappa.com
Opening times: Monday-Sunday 9.00-19.30.

BELLUNO

> ℹ️ *Azienda di Promozione Turistica*
> *Piazza V. Emanuele II 2, tel. 0437940300*
> *www.dolomiti.it*

Hotels

Delle Alpi ★★★
Via J. Tasso 13, tel. 0437940545
www.dellealpi.it
40 rooms. Parking, air-conditioned
Credit cards: American Express, Diners Club, Visa, Mastercard
Not far from the train station, a traditional, comfortable hotel with a refined ambience; taxis and minibuses available on request.

Olivier ★⅔★
Nevegal, via Col de Gou 341, tel. 0437908165
www.dolomiti.it/olivier
Open December-March and June-September
54 rooms. Restaurant, parking, gym.
Credit cards: Visa, Mastercard
A modern hotel with welcoming ambience, set in pine trees; the fields, football, volleyball and

basketball pitches opposite belong to the hotel. Excellent conference facilities and restaurant with traditional cuisine.

Villa Carpenada ★★★
Via Mier 158, tel. 0437948343
28 rooms. Restaurant, parking, air-conditioned
Credit cards: American Express, Visa, Mastercard
A 17th-century villa in a quiet location not far from town center, with fine wooden ceilings in the reception rooms; buffet breakfast and restaurant serving Italian cuisine and local specialties.

Rural Lodgings

Fulcio Miari Fulcis ♿
Modolo Castion, tel. 0437927198
Mountain bikes for use of guests
Refined farm-stay for horse-riding and winter-sports enthusiasts; dignified ambience. Unusual "white weeks" with skiing in the morning and riding in the afternoon. Horse-riding courses and trekking available.

Sant'Anna
Castion, via Pedecastello 27, tel. 043727491
www.aziendasantanna.it
Mountain bikes for hire
On the edge of the Parco delle Dolomiti Bellunesi, this farm-stay is ideally located between lovely Belluno and the mountains, which have much to offer in winter and summer.

Restaurants

Al Borgo ⅰ♿ ★
Via Anconetta 8, tel. 0437926755
www.alborgo.to
Closed Monday evening and Tuesday
Cuisine: local Belluno
Credit cards: American Express, Diners Club, Visa, Mastercard
An 18th-century villa in rural setting with charming atmosphere; local cuisine includes barley and bean soup, mushrooms, game and home-made salamis. Carefully selected wines and spirits.

Delle Alpi ⅰ♿ ★
Via J. Tasso 15, tel. 0437940302
Closed Sunday
Cuisine: traditional Veneto and fish
Credit cards: Diners Club, Visa, Mastercard
Attention to detail in terms of decor, service and menus (mainly fish, one evening a week is devoted to cheese or chocolate); smaller rooms available for working lunches.

At night

Cecchet
Via Montelungo 2, tel. 043983774
Pub

Museums, Monuments and Churches

Museo Civico
Piazza del Duomo 16, tel. 0437944836
www.comune.belluno.it
Opening times: May-September: Tuesday-Sunday 10.00-13.00, 16.00-19.00; Sundays and public holidays 10.30-12.30. October-April: Monday-Saturday 9.00-13.00; Thursday-Sunday 15.00-18.00. Closed 1 May, 15 August and 1 November.

BIBIONE

> ℹ️ *Ufficio Informazioni e Accoglienza Turistica*
> *Viale Aurora 111, tel. 0431442111,*
> *www.bibionecaorle.it*

Hotels

Ariston ★★★ ♿ ★
Corso Europa 98, tel. 043143138
www.hotelaristonbibione.it
Open mid-April-September
44 rooms. Restaurant, parking, air-conditioned, swimming pool
Credit cards: American Express, Diners Club, Visa, Mastercard
In quiet location near the beach, with garden, swimming pool with hydro-massage, attentive hospitality in a traditional, elegant ambience. Restaurant with an interesting new approach.

Corallo ★⅔★
Via Pegaso 38, tel. 0431430943
www.corallo.bibione.it
Open May-September
76 rooms. Restaurant, parking, air-conditioned, swimming pool, tennis, gym
Credit cards: American Express, Visa, Mastercard
Facing the sea, great for seaside holidays: rooms refurbished with modern decor, good amenities.

G.H. Esplanada ★⅔★
Bibione Pineda, via delle Dune 6, tel. 0431430831
www.clementihotels.it
Open mid-May-mid-September
74 rooms. Restaurant, parking, air-conditioned, swimming pool, tennis
Credit cards: Visa
Modern hotel set in pine trees, 50 m from the beach; rooms refurbished, cool terrace and pleasant garden with swimming pool, solarium, kids' playground and tennis court.

Villaggio Turistico Internazionale - Resort
Via delle Colonie 2, tel 0431442611
www.vti.it
185 bungalows, 40 apartments, parking, private beach, swimming pool, sport facilities, pets welcome.
Credit cards: Mastercard, Visa.
Closed: October-April.
Set in a pine grove, with access to the sea via the equipped beach, this site is notable for its large range of amenities, masonry villas, care and order.

At night

Top Ten
Via Perseo 40, tel. 043143606
Disco

BURANO

Restaurants

Da Romano ǁ ♿
Piazza B. Galuppi 221, tel. 041730030
www.daromano.it
Closed Tuesday
Cuisine: Venetian
Credit cards: American Express, Diners Club, Visa, Mastercard
A favorite haunt of celebrities in the 20th century. The same atmosphere prevails thanks to the collections of paintings, plates and copper pans on the walls. Menus mainly fish, risottos, seafood and shellfish starters, trolley of home-made sweets; some serious wines.

Gatto Nero-da Ruggero ǁ ♿ ★
Fondamenta della Giudecca 88, tel. 041730120
www.gattonero.com
Closed Monday
Cuisine: Venetian with an interesting new approach
Credit cards: American Express, Diners Club, Visa, Mastercard
Charming ambience, high-class service with porcelain and terrace overlooking the canal. Genuine hospitality and excellent cuisine, including traditional dishes; fresh pasta and the sweets are all home-made, impressive olive-oil list.

Museums, Monuments and Churches

Museo del Merletto
Piazza Galuppi 187, tel. 041730034
www.museiciviciveneziani.it
Opening times: April-October: 10.00-17.00; November-March: 10.00-16.00 (last tickets sold 30 mins before). Closed Tuesday, 25 December, 1 January, 1 May.

CÀORLE

Hotels

Airone **** ♿
Via Pola 1, tel. 042181570
www.hotelairone.it
Open May-September
70 rooms. Restaurant, parking, air-conditioned, swimming pool, tennis, gym
Credit cards: Visa
Good facilities at this hotel which has a garden, a fitness center and is near the sea. Also has junior suites with hydro-massage; traditional cuisine.

Garden *** ♿
Piazza Belvedere 2, tel. 0421210036
www.hotelgardencaorle.com
Open mid-April-October
62 rooms. Restaurant, parking, air-conditioned, swimming pool, sauna, tennis
Credit cards: Visa, Mastercard
This refurbished, well-run hotel on the beach is surrounded by pine trees. Comfortable rooms, one suite with a bath with hydro-massage; good facilities for sport and relaxation.

Metropol *** ★
Via Emilia 1, tel. 042182091
www.metropolhotel.it
Open mid-May-mid-September
44 rooms. Restaurant, parking, air-conditioned, swimming pool, tennis
Credit cards: American Express, Diners Club, Visa, Mastercard
Modern hotel in quiet location with good facilities and pleasant decor. Informal restaurant with Veneto cuisine.

Rural Lodgings

Lemene ♿ ★
Marango, strada Durisi 16, tel. 3358015776
www.agriturismolemene.it
Open Easter-mid-November
Bikes for use of guests
Credit cards: Visa
Country house, offers real hospitality, ideal for families with children. The beach is close by but so is the enchanting world of the lagoon with its wildlife.

Restaurants

Duilio ǁ
Via Strada Nuova 19, tel. 0421210361
www.promoservice.com/diplomatic
Closed Monday unless public holiday (except May to September)
Cuisine: Veneto
Credit cards: American Express, Diners Club, Visa, Mastercard
Vast, with pleasant atmosphere, a real benchmark of local gastronomy and extremely popular. Interesting selection of cheeses, impressive wine-cellar.

Sporting ǁ ★
Via Venier 1, tel. 0421210156
www.orologio.net
Closed Sunday evening and Monday (from October to April)
Cuisine: Veneto
Credit cards: American Express, Diners Club, Visa, Mastercard
Elegant dining-rooms and a pleasant patio. The cooking here brings out the best flavors of fish and seafood. Also tasty meat dishes and traditional Venetian soups.

Tituta ǀ
Viale Panamà 2, tel. 0421210022
Closed Tuesday (from September to May)
Cuisine: Veneto
Credit cards: American Express, Diners Club, Visa, Mastercard
In a small palazzo, this large restaurant has 2 dining-rooms with modern decor; traditional local cuisine in which fish has to be the main attraction.

Museums, Monuments and Churches

Museo Sacro del Duomo
Piazza Vescovado 6, tel. 042181028
Opening times: Saturday 20.30-22.30; Sunday 10.00-12.00, 20.00-22.00.

CASTELFRANCO VENETO

Ufficio Informazioni e Accoglienza Turistica
Via Preti 66, tel. 0423491416

Hotels

Alla Torre **** ♿ ★
piazzetta Trento e Trieste 7, tel. 0423498707
www.hotelallatorre.it
54 rooms. Air-conditioned
Credit cards: American Express, Diners Club, Visa, Mastercard
This restored palazzo with a good central position makes a charming hotel; buffet breakfast.

Al Moretto **** ★
Via S. Pio X 10, tel. 0423721313
www.albergoalmoretto.it
46 rooms. Parking, air-conditioned, swimming pool
Credit cards: American Express, Diners Club, Visa, Mastercard
Extremely comfortable 16th-century palazzo. Well appointed rooms, bathrooms with Veneto terracotta tiles; reading room,

evening piano bar; buffet breakfast.

Restaurants

Alle Mura ⚑ ♿
Via Preti 69, tel. 0423498098
Closed Thursday
Cuisine: traditional
Credit cards: American Express, Diners Club, Visa, Mastercard
Next to the old town walls, this refined ambience has exposed beams and an open fire; garden service in summer. Mainly fish.

Barbesin ⚑ ★
Salvarosa, circonvallazione Est, tel. 0423490446
www.barbesin.it
Closed Wednesday evening and Thursday
Cuisine: Veneto
Credit cards: American Express, Diners Club, Visa, Mastercard
A modern, rustic ambience; its vegetable dishes are particularly good; excellent list of wine and spirits, a wide selection of olive oil and cheeses.

Museums, Monuments and Churches

Museo Agricolo e Museo dell'Arte Conciaria "Chiminelli"
Sant'Andrea oltre Muson, via Lama 1, tel. 0423482072
Opening times: May be visited by prior arrangement.

Museo Civico Casa del Giorgione
Piazza S. Liberale, tel. 0423725022
www.bibliotecacastelfranco veneto.tv.it
Opening times: Tuesday-Sunday 10.00-12.30, 15.00-18.30. Closed: 1 January, Easter Sunday, 15 August, and 25, 26 and 31 December.

CASTELNUOVO DEL GARDA

Hotels

Dorè ★★★ ♿
Via Milano 23, tel. 0457571341
www.hoteldore.it
33 rooms. Restaurant, parking, air-conditioned, sauna, gym
Credit cards: American Express, Diners Club, Visa, Mastercard
Low building with pleasant decor suited to people travelling between the town and the lake and businessmen; buffet breakfast, choice of menu at dinner.

La Meridiana ★★ ♿
Sandrà, via Gen. Zamboni, tel. 0457596306
14 rooms. Restaurant, air-conditioned

Credit cards: American Express, Visa, Mastercard
Small hotel with adequate facilities in terms of rooms and services, situated in a small village, in good position for one-night stays. Buffet breakfast, restaurant with Venetian cuisine.

Rural Lodgings

Finilon
Finilon 7, tel. 0457575114
This farm was built in the 18th and 19th centuries around a large courtyard. Lake Garda is about 10 km away, but for people seeking peace and quiet, there is always the alternative of the morainic hills above the Mincio.

CAVALLINO-TREPORTI

Hotels

Fenix ★★★ ★
Via Tirreno 6, tel. 041968040
www.hotelfenix.it
Open mid-May-mid-September
64 rooms. Restaurant, parking, air-conditioned, swimming pool, tennis
Credit cards: American Express, Visa, Mastercard
Located between the country and the sea, ideal for a relaxing holiday. Well run by a family constantly working to improve the hotel by adding new facilities, such as the small garage, mini-bars and air-conditioning.

Park Hotel Union Lido ★★★ ♿
Via Fausta 270, tel. 041968884
www.unionlido.it
Open Easter-September
78 rooms. Restaurant, parking, air-conditioned, swimming pool, sauna, tennis, gym
Credit cards: Visa, Mastercard
Set in pine trees a few meters from the beach, you are guaranteed a comfortable stay here thanks to its modern facilities. Pleasant air-conditioned rooms, fitness center and entertainment programs for adults and kids alike; Veneto and traditional cuisine at the "Ai Pini" restaurant.

Restaurants

Antica Dogana ⚑ ♿
Via della Ricevitoria 1, tel. 0415302040
www.anticadogana.info
Closed Monday and Tuesday lunch-time (in summer closed only Monday lunch-time)
Cuisine: Venetian
Credit cards: American Express,

Diners Club, Visa, Mastercard
In splendid position, once a customs post of the Austrian Empire, now a serious, elegant venue serving excellent local dishes, mainly fish.

Da Achille ⚑
Piazza S. Maria Elisabetta 16, tel. 041968005
www.ristoranteachille.it
Closed Monday
Cuisine: Veneto
Credit cards: Visa, Mastercard
Guests are greeted by a modern wine-bar, while the decor in the three dining-rooms is rustic, with stone walls, exposed beams and high ceilings. Menu concentrates on fish. Good wine list.

Faro Piave ⚑
Via Vespucci 13, tel. 0415370568
Closed Monday
Cuisine: Veneto with a new angle
Credit cards: American Express, Visa, Mastercard
Venue has a seafaring motif; well-known and popular for its dish with a selection of raw fish, presented as a "carpaccio", with tartare sauce or marinated.

CITTADELLA

Hotels

Cittadella ★★★ ♿ ★
Via Monte Pertica 3, tel. 0499402434
www.hotelcittadella.it
49 rooms. Restaurant, parking, air-conditioned, swimming pool, sauna, gym
Credit cards: American Express, Diners Club, Visa, Mastercard
A former factory cunningly converted into a charming hotel; comfortable, well-appointed rooms with modern decor. The "Dom Mario" restaurant serves dishes prepared with local products in season; wine-bar nearby.

Due Mori ★★★
Borgo Bassano 149, tel. 0499401422
www.hotelduemori.it
26 rooms. Restaurant, parking, air-conditioned
Credit cards: American Express, Diners Club, Visa
Set in a former 15th-century monastery, a traditional atmosphere and very comfortable; elegant reception rooms, breakfast served in the garden, popular restaurant.

Filanda Palace ★★★ ♿
Via Palladio 34, tel. 0499400000
www.filandapalace.it
70 rooms. Restaurant, parking,

air-conditioned, swimming pool, sauna, gym
Credit cards: American Express, Diners Club, Visa, Mastercard
An elegant hotel complex created by cleverly converting a 19th-century spinning mill. Extremely comfortable bedrooms and good leisure and sport facilities.

Restaurants

Due Mori ⅋⅋
Borgo Bassano 149,
tel. 0499401422
www.hotelduemori.it
Closed Sunday evening and Monday
Cuisine: Veneto and traditional
Credit cards: American Express, Diners Club, Visa, Mastercard
Can seat large numbers and serves traditional cuisine; in summer, lunch and dinner are served in the romantic garden with a gazebo.

Museums, Monuments and Churches

Museo Archeologico Torre di Malta
Stradella del Cristo,
tel. 0499404485
www.comune.cittadella.pd.it/?p=Cultura/Musei/Index
Opening times: May be visited by prior arrangement on Saturday and Sunday 15.00-19.00.

CONEGLIANO

> ℹ️ **Ufficio Informazioni e Accoglienza Turistica**
> Via XX Settembre 61,
> tel. 043821230

Hotels

Canon d'Oro ★★★ & ★
Via XX Settembre 131,
tel. 043834246
www.hotelcanondoro.it
51 rooms. Restaurant, parking, air-conditioned
Credit cards: American Express, Diners Club, Visa, Mastercard
Stately residence with fine 16th-century facade; warm, hospitable atmosphere and tasteful decor. Size of rooms variable, comfortable reception rooms.

Cima ★★★
Via XXIV Maggio 61,
tel. 043822648
www.hotelcima.it
19 rooms. Restaurant, parking, air-conditioned
Credit cards: American Express, Diners Club, Visa, Mastercard
Comfortable villa in quiet location, traditional bedrooms in terms of decor and size; restaurant serves typical specialties of local cuisine.

Restaurants

Città di Venezia ⅋⅋
Via XX Settembre 77/79,
tel. 043823186
Closed Sunday evening and Monday
Cuisine: mainly fish
Credit cards: American Express, Diners Club, Visa, Mastercard
Historic venue with original 15th-century floors and ceiling. This "osteria" also serves typical local dishes, some meat dishes, at a reasonable price.

Tre Panoce ⅋⅋⅋ &
Via Vecchia Trevigiana 50,
tel. 043860071
Closed Sunday evening and Monday
Cuisine: Veneto with an interesting new approach
Credit cards: American Express, Diners Club, Visa, Mastercard
Elegant, romantic venue in late 17th-century building; the menu changes according to the ingredients available; carefully selected wines, also sold by the glass, home-made cakes and pastries.

Museums, Monuments and Churches

Casa-Museo Giambattista Cima
Via Cima 24, tel. 043822494
Opening times: Summer: Saturday and Sunday 16.00-19.30. Winter: Saturday and Sunday 15.00-18.30. May also be visited by prior arrangement.

Museo Civico del Castello
Piazzale Castelvecchio 8,
tel. 043822871
www.comune.conegliano.tv.it
Opening times: Summer: Tuesday-Sunday 10.00-12.30, 15.30-19.00. Winter: Tuesday-Sunday 10.00-12.30, 15.00-18.30. Closed Monday unless public holiday and for 3 weeks in November (except Saturday and Sunday).

CORTINA D'AMPEZZO

> ℹ️ **Azienda per la Promozione Turistica**
> P.tta S. Francesco 8,
> tel. 04363231
> www.apt-dolomiti-cortina.it

Hotels

Ancora ★★★ &
Corso Italia 62, tel. 04363261
www.hotelancoracortina.com
Open December-April and June-October
49 rooms. Restaurant, parking, gym

Credit cards: American Express, Diners Club, Visa, Mastercard
The oldest hotel in Cortina, it dates from 1826; charming, comfortable and well-equipped for winter and summer, with a lovely terrace; has some suites. Elegant dining-room for candle-lit dinners, with a "culture corner" for exhibitions and cultural evening events.

Bellevue ★★★ &
Corso Italia 197, tel. 0436883400
www.bellevuecortina.it
Open mid-December-mid-April and June-mid-September
65 rooms. Restaurant, gym
Credit cards: American Express, Diners Club, Visa, Mastercard
Efficient residence hotel with all-round comfort in rooms and elegant suites; busy restaurant "L'Incontro", terrace bar, cake-shop. Modern beauty parlor.

Concordia Parc Hotel ★★★
Corso Italia 28, tel. 04364251
www.concordiacortina.it
Open Christmas-March and July-August
58 rooms. Restaurant, parking, air-conditioned
Credit cards: American Express, Diners Club, Visa, Mastercard
A beautiful hotel built in 1907, surrounded by extensive garden; menu ranges from the flavors of the Veneto to international cuisine.

Cortina ★★★
Corso Italia 92, tel. 04364221
www.hotels.cortina.it/cortina
Open December-mid-April and mid-June-mid-September
48 rooms. Restaurant, parking, sauna
Credit cards: American Express, Diners Club, Visa, Mastercard
Restaurant serves traditional dishes with an interesting new approach. A complete overhaul has increased the number of rooms and suites, and added a wellness center and a conference room.

Cristallo Reconditioning and Beauty Hotel ★★★★ &
Via Menardi 42, tel. 0436881111
www.cristallo.it
Open December-April and July-September
73 rooms. Restaurant, parking, air-conditioned, swimming pool, sauna, gym
Credit cards: American Express, Diners Club, Visa, Mastercard
Prestigious hotel complex with extensive wellness center. Elegant rooms with all modern comforts; the "La Veranda" restaurant occupies a large veranda with splendid views of the Valle d'Ampezzo, and serves Veneto and international cuisine.

De la Poste ★☆★
Piazza Roma 14, tel. 04364271
www.delaposte.it
Open Christmas-mid-April and June-September
80 rooms. Restaurant, parking, air-conditioned
Credit cards: American Express, Diners Club, Visa, Mastercard
One of Cortina's historic hotels, completely refurbished in a warm, elegant mountain style.

Miramonti Majestic G.H. ☆☆
Peziè 103, tel. 04364201
www.geturhotels.com
Open Christmas-March and June-September
121 rooms. Restaurant, parking, swimming pool, sauna, tennis, gym
Credit cards: American Express, Diners Club, Visa, Mastercard
In an elevated position, the hotel occupies the rooms of a castle in the Art Nouveau style, in a Natural Park, a haven of peace and quiet; luxurious atmosphere with excellent sports facilities (the hotel has its own golf course).

Parc Hotel Victoria ★☆★ ★
Corso Italia 1, tel. 04363246
www.hotelvictoriacortina.com
Open December-March and June-September
41 rooms. Restaurant, parking, air-conditioned
Credit cards: American Express, Diners Club, Visa, Mastercard
Welcoming ambience, with antiques; the restaurant "Il Cirmolo" serves dishes from the Veneto and Alto Adige. Mountain bikes, table tennis and billiards available.

Restaurants

Baita Fraina ⫪
Via Fraina 1, tel. 04363634
www.baitafraina.it
Closed Monday in low season
Cuisine: of the Valle d'Ampezzo
Credit cards: American Express, Diners Club, Visa, Mastercard
Three dining-rooms with rustic decor and a pleasant terrace for lunches in summer, with very local cuisine. Some rooms.

El Toulà ⫪⫪
Via Ronco 123, tel. 04363339
www.toula.it
Open Christmas-Easter and mid-July-August
Closed Monday
Cuisine: of the Valle d'Ampezzo and traditional
Credit cards: American Express, Diners Club, Visa
A converted hay-barn, with elegant decor; menus range from very local cuisine to traditional dishes; it is a base for all the Toulà family living in various parts of the world.

La Tavernetta ⫪
Via del Castello 53, tel. 0436868102
Closed Wednesday
Cuisine: of the Valle d'Ampezzo
Credit cards: Visa
A typical rustic mountain restaurant with a warm, friendly atmosphere. Traditional local cuisine.

At night

Hippo
Lg. Poste 35, tel. 04362333
Disco

Metrò Discoteque
Gall. Nuovo Centro 8, tel. 04364366
Disco

Museums, Monuments and Churches

Ciasa de ra Regoles
Via del Parco 1, tel. 0436866222-04362206
www.musei.regole.it
Opening times: June-September: Tuesday-Sunday 10.00-12.30, 16.00-19.30. July-August-Christmas break: Monday-Sunday 10.00-12.30, 16.00-20.00. January-April: Monday-Sunday 16.00-19.30. Groups may also visit by prior arrangement.

Musei della Grande Guerra di Cortina d'Ampezzo ★
Passo di Valparola, passo Falzarego, tel. 0436861112
www.grandeguerra.dolomiti.org
Opening times: Summer: Forte Tre Sassi, Monday-Sunday 10.00-12.30, 13.30-17.00. the open-air museums of Lagazuoi and Cinque Torri are open every day.

FELTRE

> ℹ **Ufficio Informazioni e Accoglienza Turistica**
> P.tta Trento e Trieste 9, tel. 04392540

Hotels

Doriguzzi ★★★
Viale Piave 2, tel. 04392003
www.hoteldoriguzzi.it
23 rooms. Parking, air-conditioned
Credit cards: Diners Club, Visa
Palazzo in the Art Nouveau style, good central position, comfortable rooms, buffet breakfast, tables on outside terrace when fine.

Nuovo ★★★
Via Fornere Pazze 5, tel. 04392110
25 rooms. Parking, air-conditioned
Credit cards: American Express, Visa
This modern hotel (no restaurant) with recently refurbished rooms has been run by the same family for three generations.

Rural Lodgings

Meneguz Aurelia
Villabruna, via Arson 113, tel. 043942136
Restaurant
This farm is situated in the Parco Nazionale delle Dolomiti Bellunesi and makes an ideal base for walkers and climbers. The rooms are in stone buildings with wooden decor and magnificent views.

Museums, Monuments and Churches

Galleria d'Arte Moderna "Carlo Rizzarda"
Via Paradiso 8, tel. 0439885234
www.comune.feltre.bl.it
Opening times: April-October: Tuesday-Friday 10.30-12.30, 16.00-19.00; Saturday and Sunday 9.30-12.30, 16.00-19.00. November-March: Tuesday-Friday 10.30-12.30, 15.00-18.00; Saturday and Sunday 9.30-12.30, 15.00-18.00. Closed Monday unless public holiday, 25-26 December, 1 January.

Museo Civico
Via Luzzo 23, tel. 0439885241-0439885242
www.comune.feltre.bl.it
Opening times: April-October: Tuesday-Friday 10.30-12.30, 16.00-19.00; Saturday and Sunday 9.30-12.30, 16.00-19.00. November-March: Tuesday-Friday 10.30-12.30, 15.00-18.00; Saturday and Sunday 9.30-12.30, 15.00-18.00. Closed Monday unless public holiday, 25-26 December, 1 January.

GARDA

> ℹ **Azienda per la Promozione Turistica**
> Lungolago Regina Adelaide, tel. 0457255279
> www.aptgardaveneto.com

Hotels

Bisesti ★★★ ★
Corso Italia 34/36, tel. 0457255766
www.hotelbisesti.it
Open mid-April-mid-October
90 rooms. Restaurant, parking, air-conditioned, swimming pool
Credit cards: Visa, Mastercard
Informal, only a few meters from the lake, rooms furnished in 19th-century style; good management.

Conca d'Oro ★★ ★
Lungolago Europa 2, tel. 0457255275
www.hotelconcadorogarda.it

Open mid-March-mid-November
19 rooms. Restaurant, parking, air-conditioned
Credit cards: Diners Club
Austere hotel on the lakeside. Most of the rooms have views, well appointed with pleasant decor.

Locanda San Vigilio *⁑*
San Vigilio, tel. 0457256688
www.punta-sanvigilio.it
Open March-November
7 rooms. Restaurant, parking, air-conditioned
Credit cards: American Express, Visa, Mastercard
Converted 16th-century villa with comfortable, sophisticated rooms and suites; à la carte restaurant, with garden service in summer beside the lake.

MALCÉSINE

ℹ *Ufficio Informazioni e Accoglienza Turistica*
Via Capitanato 6/8, tel. 0457400044

Hotels

Alpi ***
Campogrande, tel. 0457400717
45 rooms. Restaurant, parking, air-conditioned, swimming pool, sauna
Credit cards: Visa, Mastercard
Set among olive trees, austere, elegant atmosphere. Restaurant serves traditional cuisine, buffet breakfast.

Maximilian *⁑*
Val di Sogno, tel. 0457400317
www.hotelmaximiliam.com
Open April-mid-October
33 rooms. Restaurant, parking, air-conditioned, swimming pool, sauna, tennis, gym
Credit cards: Visa, Mastercard
Set in a large garden/olive grove directly overlooking the lake, this hotel has good facilities including a popular beauty center; other rooms available in two annexes.

Park Hotel Querceto *⁑*
Campiano, tel. 0457400344
www.parkhotelquerceto.com
Open April-September
22 rooms. Restaurant, parking, swimming pool, sauna
Credit cards: Visa, Mastercard
Rural setting, pleasant hotel with warm, welcoming ambience, pleasant comfortable rooms furnished with style; relax on the viewing terrace, and recharge your batteries with a sauna or hydro-massage.

Restaurants

Vecchia Malcesine ⅌
Via Pisort, tel. 0457400469

www.vecchiamalcesine.com
Open evenings only (except Sunday and public holidays)
Closed Wednesday
Cuisine: creative
Credit cards: American Express, Diners Club, Visa, Mastercard
Romantic terrace with lake view and a small, inviting dining-room; the small number of tables means that booking is essential. The chef is very good, he uses very fresh fish and carefully selected ingredients. Wide selection of wines and spirits.

Museums, Monuments and Churches

Musei del Castello Scaligero
Via del Castello, tel. 0456570333
www.comunemalcesine.it
Opening times: Monday-Sunday 9.30-20.00.

MARÒSTICA

Hotels

Due Mori *** ⅙ ★
Corso Mazzini 73, tel. 0424471777
www.duemori.com
12 rooms. Restaurant, parking, air-conditioned
Credit cards: American Express, Diners Club, Visa, Mastercard
Inside the medieval walls, period residence converted to elegant design. The "Sotoportego" restaurant serves local cuisine with imaginative touches added by the chef. Week-end deals focusing on aspects of culture, wine or gastronomy.

La Rosina *** ★
Valle San Floriano, via Marchetti 4, tel. 0424470360
www.larosina.it
12 rooms. Restaurant, parking, air-conditioned
Credit cards: American Express, Diners Club, Visa, Mastercard
In beautiful location, on a charming hill in rural setting. Well-appointed rooms, comfortable ambience. Restaurant serves dishes made with local products in season and an extensive wine-cellar with Italian and international wines.

Restaurants

Al Castello Superiore ⅌ ⅙
Via Cansignorio della Scala 4, tel. 042473315
www.castellosuperiore.it
Closed Wednesday and Thursday lunch-time
Cuisine: Veneto
Credit cards: American Express, Diners Club, Visa, Mastercard
This venue harks back to the time of the fortress of the Scaligeri.

Cuisine prepared with carefully selected basic ingredients; locally produced cheeses, salamis and cured meats. Wide selection of wines and spirits, menu with medieval recipes.

Museums, Monuments and Churches

Museo "Cappelli di Paglia di Maròstica"
Castello Inferiore, tel. 0424479120-0424479121
www.retemusealealtovicentino.it
Opening times: Saturday 16.00-18.00; Sunday 10.30-12.00, 16.00-18.00. May also be visited by prior arrangement.

Museo dei Costumi della Partita a Scacchi
Piazza Castello 1, tel. 042472127
www.marosticascacchi.it
Opening times: Monday-Sunday 10.00-12.00, 14.30-18.00.

Museo Ornitologico "Angelo Fabris"
Via Cansignorio della Scala 2, tel. 0424471097
Opening times: Saturday and Sunday 10.00-12.30, 15.30-18.00. May be visited by prior arrangement from Monday to Friday.

MESTRE

Hotels

Alexander *⁑*
Via Forte Marghera 193/C, tel. 0415318288
ww.hotelalexander.com
61 rooms. Restaurant, parking, air-conditioned
Credit cards: American Express, Diners Club, Visa, Mastercard
Modern hotel in strategic position with all modern comforts.

Ambasciatori *⁑*
Corso del Popolo 221, tel. 0415310699
www.ambasciatori.it
94 rooms. Restaurant, parking, air-conditioned, gym
Credit cards: American Express, Diners Club, Visa, Mastercard
Not far from the station, refurbished palazzo with comfortable rooms and facilities geared to business and conference tourism. Warm welcome; new fitness center.

Bologna & Stazione *⁑*
Via Piave 214, tel. 041931000
www.hotelbologna.com
112 rooms. Restaurant, parking, air-conditioned
Credit cards: American Express, Diners Club, Visa, Mastercard
Opposite the train station,

comfortable rooms and facilities for conferences and business meetings. Buffet breakfast and well-run restaurant serving Veneto cuisine.

Garibaldi ★★★ ★
Viale Garibaldi 24,
tel. 0415350455
www.hotelgaribaldi.it
28 rooms. Parking, air-conditioned
Credit cards: American Express, Diners Club, Visa, Mastercard
The air-conditioned rooms and tasteful decor, internet point and comfortable reception rooms make this a perfect place for holiday and business clientele.

Plaza ★★★ ★
Viale Stazione 36, tel. 041929388
www.hotelplazavenice.com
226 rooms. Restaurant, air-conditioned
Credit cards: American Express, Diners Club, Visa, Mastercard
Imposing, luxurious complex, with large reception rooms and diverse facilities. Busy à la carte restaurant serving Veneto and traditional cuisine and new "Plaza Café" with modern decor.

Restaurants

Alla Pesa ⅋⅋
Favaro Veneto, Via Altinia 119,
tel. 041630555
Closed Wednesday
Cuisine: Venetian
Credit cards: American Express, Diners Club, Visa, Mastercard
Not far from the airport, typical Venetian trattoria where the dishes are only prepared with absolutely fresh fish. Good selection of wines from the Veneto.

Dall'Amelia ⅋⅋⅋ ★
Via Miranese 113, tel. 041913955
www.boscaratoristorazione.it
Closed Wednesday
Cuisine: Veneto with an interesting new approach
Credit cards: American Express, Diners Club, Visa
Elegant venue, a favorite with "aficionados" of regional cuisine, also popular for cultural get-togethers. Carefully selected olive oils from all over Italy; wide selection of wines and spirits.

Marco Polo ⅋⅋
Via Forte Marghera 67,
tel. 041989855
www.ristorantemarcopolo.it
Closed Sunday
Cuisine: Veneto and Sardinian
Credit cards: American Express, Diners Club, Visa, Mastercard
This old fisherman's house makes a delightful venue, with modern paintings on the walls;

also serves Veneto and Sardinian specialties, home-made cakes and pastries.

Trattoria al Passo ⅋⅋
Campalto, via Passo 118,
tel. 041900470
Closed Monday and Tuesday
Cuisine: local and creative
Credit cards: American Express, Diners Club, Visa, Mastercard
Typical fish restaurant. The decor has a seafaring motif, and the cuisine concentrates mainly on cooked and raw fish starters. Remarkable wine-list.

MOGLIANO VENETO

Hotels

Campiello ★★★ ⅋ ★
Via Montegrappa 2 ang.
Via Roma, tel. 0415904595
www.campiellohotel.it
40 rooms. Restaurant, parking, air-conditioned
Credit cards: American Express, Visa, Mastercard
Conveniently situated, a small palazzo with modern interior; professional management particularly attentive to needs of families with children. Buffet breakfast.

Duca d'Aosta ★★★ ⅋ ★
Piazza Duca d'Aosta 31,
tel. 0415904990
www.ducadaostahotel.it
43 rooms. Parking, air-conditioned
Credit cards: American Express, Diners Club, Visa, Mastercard
Refurbished early 20th-century palazzo, well-appointed bedrooms and inviting reception rooms with modern decor; great buffet breakfast.

Villa Condulmer ★★★ ★
Zerman, via Preganziol 1,
tel. 0415972700
www.hotelvillacondulmer.com
45 rooms. Restaurant, parking, air-conditioned, swimming pool
Credit cards: American Express, Diners Club, Visa, Mastercard
Surrounded by a garden and golf course, this charming villa dating from 1743 has an unusually refined interior; classy atmosphere and excellent hospitality.

Restaurants

Da Bimbari ⅋ ⅋
Campocroce, via Zero Branco 120, tel. 041454632
Closed Monday
Cuisine: local Treviso cuisine
Credit cards: American Express, Diners Club, Visa, Mastercard
A simple venue with rustic decor and an informal atmosphere.

The cuisine is based on genuine flavors and traditional recipes. The desserts are all home-made.

Beccofino ⅋ ⅋
Via Marconi 17/A, tel. 0415936236
Closed Sunday
Cuisine: Veneto
Credit cards: American Express, Diners Club, Visa, Mastercard
This small rustic building in the town center has a wooden coffered ceiling and an open fire; regional cuisine with dishes which vary according to the season.

Museums, Monuments and Churches

Villa La Marignana - Museo Toni Benetton
Marocco, via Marignana 112,
tel. 041942111
www.museotonibenetton.com
Opening times: May-October: Saturday and Sunday 15.00-19.00. May be visited by prior arrangement on other days.

MONSÉLICE

Hotels

Ceffri ★★★ ⅋
Via Orti 7/B, tel. 0429783111
www.ceffri.it
44 rooms. Restaurant, parking, air-conditioned, swimming pool
Credit cards: American Express, Diners Club, Visa, Mastercard
Dominated by the Rocca, this elegant restaurant is a fine blend of style and modern functionality; it serves traditional dishes alongside typical Veneto recipes.

Rural Lodgings

Castello di Lispida
Via IV Novembre 4,
tel. 0429780530
www.lispida.com
Swimming pool, bikes for use of guests
In this charming old monastery converted into a comfortable castle with a lake fed with hot spring water, the rooms are located in the former granaries. Receptions are held in the former refectory, with its 16th-century barrel-vault ceiling.

San Bartolomeo
San Bartolo, via Chiesetta 33,
tel. 0429783676
www.agriturismosanbartolomeo.it
Restaurant
Credit cards: Visa, Mastercard
This business began as a farm restaurant and then expanded into an old farm. Between meals guests can go to the riding stables, play golf on the local golf courses, or go for walks.

Restaurants

La Torre ⊺⊺
Piazza Mazzini 14, tel. 042973752
Closed Sunday evening and Monday
Cuisine: Veneto and traditional
Credit cards: American Express, Diners Club, Visa
Situated near a medieval castle, intimate and inviting ambience. Varied wine list, extensive selection of spirits.

Museums, Monuments and Churches

Castello e Antiquarium Longobardo ★
Via del Santuario 17, tel. 042972468
www.castellodimonselice.it
Opening times: Tuesday-Friday and Sunday 10.00-12.00, 15.00-17.30, Saturday if booked beforehand.

Museo delle Macchine Termiche "Orazio e Giulia Centanin"
Via Petrarca 44, tel. 042521530
www.turismocultura.it
Opening times: April-September: Saturday 15.00-19.00; Sunday 10.00-13.00, 14.00-19.00. October-March: Saturday 14.00-18.00; Sunday 9.00-13.00, 14.00-18.00. May also be visited by prior arrangement.

MURANO

Restaurants

Ai Frati ⊺
Fondamenta Venier 4, tel. 041736694
Open only at lunch-time
Closed Thursday
Cuisine: Venetian
Credit cards: Visa, Mastercard
Traditional atmosphere and cuisine and courteous hospitality, run by same family since 1950.

Busa alla Torre ⊺⊺
Campo S. Stefano 3, tel. 041739662
Open only at lunch-time
Cuisine: Venetian
Credit cards: American Express, Visa, Mastercard
Two rooms of an old house, and in fine weather it sets up tables in the little square outside. Traditional cuisine.

Museums, Monuments and Churches

Museo Barovier & Toso
Fondamenta dei Vetrai 28, tel. 041739049
www.barovier.com
Opening times: Guided tours only. September-July: Monday-Friday 10.00-12.00, 15.00-17.00. Closed August, 25 December.

Museo del Vetro
Fondamenta Giustinian 8, tel. 041739586
www.museicivicineveneziani.it
Opening times: April-October: 10.00-17.00. November-March: 10.00-16.00 (last admission 30 mins before). Closed Wednesday, 1 January, 1 May, 25 December.

Museo Parrocchiale San Pietro Martire
Campiello Michieli, tel. 041739704
Opening times: Summer: Monday-Friday 9.00-18.00; Saturday 15.30-18.00. Winter: Monday-Friday 9.00-18.00; Saturday 15.30-18.00. Sunday (summer and winter) 13.00-17.00.

ODERZO

> ℹ️ **Ufficio Informazioni e Accoglienza Turistica**
> Piazza Castello 1,
> tel. 0422815251

Hotels

Primhotel ★★★ ♿ ★
Via Martiri di Cefalonia 13, tel. 0422713699
www.primhotel.it
50 rooms. Parking, air-conditioned, sauna, gym
Credit cards: American Express, Diners Club, Visa, Mastercard
This hotel has tastefully furnished rooms and suites with all mod cons. Well-equipped room for small and medium-size conferences; buffet breakfast.

Restaurants

Gaia da Camino ⊺⊺ ♿
Via Comunale di Camino 80, tel. 0422717886
www.ristorantegaiadacamino.it
Closed Monday
Cuisine: Veneto
Credit cards: American Express, Diners Club, Visa, Mastercard
Steaks and chops are barbecued on a huge grill, excellent after a pumpkin risotto; great selection of cheeses.

Museums, Monuments and Churches

Museo Civico Archeologico "Eno Bellis"
Via Garibaldi 63, tel. 0422713333
www.oderzocultura.it
Opening times: Wednesday-Saturday 9.00-12.00, 15.30-18.30; Sunday 15.30-18.30.

Museo di Storia Naturale "Brandolini-Rota" e "Giol"
Via Brandolini 6, tel. 0422712041
www.murialdo.it/brandolini
Opening times: May be visited by prior arrangement.

PADOVA

> ℹ️ **Azienda per la Promozione Turistica**
> Riviera Mugnai 8,
> tel. 049 8767911
> www.apt.padova.it

Hotels

Accademia Palace ★★★ ♿
Via del Pescarotto 39, tel. 049998341
www.accademiahotelpadova.it
95 rooms. Restaurant, air-conditioned
Credit cards: American Express, Visa
Elegant hotel with comfortable rooms and restaurant serving traditional cuisine. Three conference rooms.

Best Western Hotel Biri ★★★ ★
Via Grassi 2, tel. 0498067700
www.bestwestern.it/biri_pd
92 rooms. Restaurant, parking, air-conditioned, gym
Credit cards: American Express, Diners Club, Visa, Mastercard
Modern hotel with refurbished rooms and room for business meetings; warm hospitality, residence formula also available. Restaurant with terrace and local cuisine.

Europa ★★★
Largo Europa 9, tel. 049661200
www.hoteleuropapadova.com
64 rooms. Restaurant, air-conditioned
Credit cards: American Express, Diners Club, Visa, Mastercard
In the old town center, comfortable rooms and buffet breakfast; for other meals, the "Zaramella" restaurant serves specialties of regional cuisine and has facilities for working lunches or receptions.

Garibaldi ★★★ ★
Ponte di Brenta, via S. Marco 63, tel. 0498932466
www.hotelgaribaldi.com
47 rooms. Parking, air-conditioned
Credit cards: American Express, Diners Club, Visa, Mastercard
Close to the motorway exit, comfortable hotel with new, well-appointed, tastefully furnished, elegant rooms.

Grand'Italia ★★★ ♿ ★
Corso del Popolo 81, tel. 0498761111
www.hotelgranditalia.it
61 rooms. Air-conditioned
Credit cards: American Express, Diners Club, Visa, Mastercard
Elegant palazzo in the Art Nouveau style, in the town

center; elegant reception rooms, sound-proofed bedrooms and suites and modern decor.

Le Padovanelle *⁑* ★
Ponte di Brenta, via Chilesotti 2, tel. 049625622
www.hotelpadovanelle.it
40 rooms. Restaurant, parking, air-conditioned, swimming pool, tennis
Credit cards: American Express, Diners Club, Visa
Easy to access from motorway, popular with business clientele. Pleasant ambience, relaxed atmosphere and leisure facilities.

Piroga Padova *⁑* & ★
Selvazzano Dentro, via Euganea 48, tel. 049637966
www.hotelpiroga.com
62 rooms. Restaurant, parking, air-conditioned, sauna, gym
Credit cards: American Express, Diners Club, Visa, Mastercard
Functional, comfortable hotel; spacious rooms, suites; conference room, good restaurant with specialties of the Veneto and traditional cuisine.

Sheraton Padova Hotel *⁑* &
Corso Argentina 5, tel. 0498998299
www.sheratonpadova.it
234 rooms. Restaurant, parking, air-conditioned, gym
Credit cards: American Express, Diners Club, Visa, Mastercard
Situated near the Padova-Est exit of the motorway to Venice; has everything that a tourist or business clientele require. Restaurant based on Veneto and international cuisine, piano bar in the evening.

Restaurants

Antico Brolo ⑪ ★
Corso Milano 22, tel. 049664555
www.anticobrolo.it
Closed Monday
Cuisine: Veneto and traditional
Credit cards: American Express, Visa, Mastercard
A 16th-century palazzo with an elegant dining-room and a lovely terrace for meals outside; the pizzeria has plain stone walls. Meat, game and fish dishes with an imaginative touch, based on products in season; wide selection of wines and spirits.

Antica Osteria dal Capo ⑪
Via degli Obizzi 2, tel. 049663105
Closed Sunday, Monday lunch-time
Cuisine: Veneto
Credit cards: American Express, Diners Club, Visa, Mastercard
The chef serves traditional dishes prepared with carefully selected ingredients; try his "bigoli in salsa", "zuppa in pagnotta" and "baccalà alla vicentina". Limited but interesting wine-list, wide range of spirits.

Bastioni del Moro ⑪ & ★
Via P. Bronzetti 18, tel. 0498710006
www.bastionidelmoro.it
Closed Sunday
Cuisine: Veneto and traditional
Credit cards: American Express, Diners Club, Visa, Mastercard
Elegant ambience in three small dining-rooms and a garden in the summer. Regional cuisine, with dishes based on seasonal ingredients and fresh fish, a good selection of wines, and wide range of spirits, olive oil and cheese.

Belle Parti ⑪ &
Via Belle Parti 11, tel. 0498751822
Closed Sunday
Cuisine: Veneto and traditional
Credit cards: American Express, Diners Club, Visa, Mastercard
In the 16th-century Palazzo Prosdocimi, fish and meat dishes are carefully prepared to a variety of regional recipes; good choice of olive oil, cheese, salamis and cured meats, wide selection of wines and spirits.

Dotto di Campagna ⑪ &
Ponte di Brenta, via Randaccio 4, tel. 049625469
www.hotelsagittario.com
Closed Sunday evening and Monday
Cuisine: Veneto
Credit cards: American Express, Diners Club, Visa, Mastercard
Next to the "Sagittario" hotel, this venue has a century of experience of using local products. Garden service in summer; the dining-room used for receptions is ionized and climatized.

Enoteca Angelo Rasi ⑪
Riviera Paleocapa 7, tel. 0498719797
Open evenings only
Closed Monday
Cuisine: Veneto with a new angle
Credit cards: Visa
This wine-bar is the ideal venue for a romantic evening but also for having a glass of wine with snacks in the company of friends. Traditional cuisine, beautifully presented and sometimes with a creative touch in its preparation, always accompanied by the "right" wine. Small, but intimate dining-room and in summer they serve meals outside.

Trattoria ai Porteghi ⑪ ★
Via Cesare Battisti 105, tel. 049660746
www.trattoriaaiporteghi.com
Closed Sunday, Monday lunch-time
(in July and August also Saturday)
Cuisine: traditional
Credit cards: American Express, Diners Club, Visa, Mastercard
Warm and inviting, meat and fish dishes, accompanied by olive oil and wines from the best areas of production. The chef works until late; wide range of olive oil and cheese, served with "mostarda" and jams made on the premises.

At night

Black and White
Viale Navigazione Interna 49/B, tel. 0497389791
Disco

Cuarto de Tula
Riviera Francia 3/A, tel. 3479664203
Music Club

Museums, Monuments and Churches

Galleria "Guglielmo Tabacchi" - Safilo
Via Settima Strada 15, tel. 0496985679
www.safilo.com
Opening times: May be visited by prior arrangement: Monday-Friday 9.00-17.00.

Musei Civici agli Eremitani ★
Piazza Eremitani 8, tel. 0498204551
www.cappelladegliscrovegni.it
Opening times: Tuesday-Sunday 9.00-19.00. Closed Monday unless public holiday, 25, 26 December, 1 January, 1 May. Booking is compulsory to visit the Scrovegni Chapel (also on Monday) (tel. 0492010020).

Museo Antoniano e Mostra Antoniana della Devozione Popolare
Piazza del Santo 11, tel. 0498225656
www.basilicadelsanto.org
Opening times: Summer: Monday-Sunday 9.00-13.00, 14.30-18.30. Winter: Tuesday-Sunday 9.00-13.00, 14.00-18.00.

Museo del Precinema - Collezione Minici Zotti
Prato della Valle 1a, tel. 0498763838
www.minicizotti.it
Opening times: June 16-September 15: Monday, Wednesday-Sunday 16.00-24.00. September 16-June15: 10.00-16.00. Closed Tuesday and 1 January, Easter Sunday, 25 April, 1 May, 1 –15 August, 24, 25, 26 and 31 December.

Museo di Geologia e Paleontologia
Via Giotto 1, tel. 0498272086-0498272135
www.geol.unipd.it
Opening times: May be visited by prior arrangement.

Museo di Mineralogia
Corso Garibaldi 37,
tel. 0498272033
www.musei.unipd.it
Opening times: May be visited
by prior arrangement.

Museo Diocesano ★
Piazza Duomo 12,
tel. 0498761924-049652855
www.museodiocesanopadova.it
Opening times: Thursday-Saturday
14.00-18.00; Sunday 10.00-18.00.

**Museo di Scienze Archeologiche
e d'Arte**
Piazza Capitaniato 7,
tel. 0498274576-0498274611
www.musei.unipd.it/archeologia
Opening times: May be visited
by prior arrangement.

Museo di Storia della Fisica
Dipartimento di Fisica "Galileo
Galilei", via Loredan 10,
tel. 0498277153
www.musei.unipd.it/fisica
Opening times: May be visited
by prior arrangement.

**Museo "La Specola" INAF
Osservatorio Astronomico di Padova**
Vicolo dell'Osservatorio 5,
tel. 0498293469
www.pd.astro.it/museo-laspecola
Opening times: May-September:
Saturday at 11.00 and 18.00;
Sunday at 18.00. October-April:
Saturday at 11.00 and 16.00;
Sunday at 16.00. Groups must
book beforehand: Tuesday-
Friday 9.00-17.00. Closed 24, 25,
26 and 31 December.

**Nuovi Musei di Palazzo
Zuckermann**
Corso Garibaldi 33,
tel. 049665567-0498204551
www.padovanet.it/museicivici
Opening times: Tuesday-Sunday
9.00-19.00. Closed 1 January, 1
May, 25, 26 December.

Orto Botanico
Via Orto Botanico 15,
tel. 0498272119
www.ortobotanico.unipd.it
Opening times: April-October:
Monday-Sunday, public holidays
9.00-13.00, 15.00-18.00.
November-March: Monday-
Saturday 9.00-13.00.

PESCHIERA
DEL GARDA
Hotels

Fortuna *⁑*
Via Venezia 26, tel. 0457550111
www.fortunahotel.com
42 rooms. Restaurant, parking,
air-conditioned
Credit cards: American Express,
Diners Club, Visa, Mastercard
Recently built, with panoramic

restaurant; well-equipped rooms
and junior suites.

Puccini ★★★
Via Puccini 2, tel. 0456401428
www.hotelpuccini.it
32 rooms. Parking, air-
conditioned, swimming pool
Credit cards: American Express,
Diners Club, Visa, Mastercard
In a quiet residential area, pleasant
rooms with balconies and views;
swimming pool in the garden.

Saraceno ★★★ ♿
San Benedetto di Lugana, Via
De Amicis 4, tel. 0457550546
www.hotelsaraceno.it
38 rooms. Restaurant, parking,
air-conditioned, swimming pool
Credit cards: American Express,
Diners Club, Visa, Mastercard
Out of the center, has a large
garden with a swimming pool with
hydro-massage and a play area for
kids. Rooms and suites have all
mod cons, cuisine with choice of
menu, taverna with piano.

Restaurants

Nuova Barcaccia ⍟⍟ ★
Madonna del Frassino, via
Frassino 11, tel. 0457550790
Closed Wednesday
Cuisine: fish and seafood, and
traditional
Credit cards: American Express,
Diners Club, Visa, Mastercard
Rural setting, real home-made
cooking done by the family.

Piccolo Mondo ⍟⍟
Riviera Carducci 6,
tel. 0457550025
Closed Monday and Tuesday
Cuisine: fish and seafood
Credit cards: Visa, Mastercard
On the lake, an elegant ambience,
run by the same family since 1954,
cuisine is fish-oriented, good range
of local and Italian wines.

PIEVE DI CADORE
Hotels

Al Sole *⁑*
Via Municipio 26, tel. 043532118
www.dolomiti.it/alsole
32 rooms. Restaurant, parking,
air-conditioned
Credit cards: American Express,
Diners Club, Visa, Mastercard
This late 19th-century palazzo
with modern facilities has rustic
decor; apartments also available
with residence formula. They
serve Cadore specialties in the
restaurant.

Giardino ★★ ♿ ★
Via Carducci 20, tel. 043533141
www.giardino.dolomiti.com
24 rooms. Restaurant, parking,
air-conditioned

Credit cards: American Express,
Diners Club, Visa, Mastercard
Close to the town center,
simple, well-run hotel, recently
refurbished; the food is good,
prepared by the owners.

Museums, Monuments
and Churches

Casa Natale di Tiziano
Via Arsenale 4, tel. 043532262
www.magnificacomunitadicadore.it
Opening times: June 20
–September 10: Monday-
Saturday 9.30-12.30, 15.30-
18.30. August: Monday-Sunday
9.30-12.30, 15.30-18.30. Winter:
Monday-Saturday 8.30-12.00 (by
prior arrangement). Groups
must book beforehand..

**Museo Archeologico della
Magnifica Comunità di Cadore**
Piazza Tiziano 2, tel. 043532262
www.magnificacomunitadicadore.it
Opening times: June 20-
September 10: Monday-Saturday
9.30-12.30, 15.30-18.30. August:
Monday-Sunday 9.30-12.30, 15.30-
18.30. Winter: Monday-Saturday
8.30-12.00 (by prior arrangement).
Groups must book beforehand.

Museo dell'Occhiale ★
Tai, via degli Alpini 39,
tel. 0435500213
www.museodellocchiale.it
Opening times: July-August and
public holidays: 8.30-12.30,
16.00-19.00. September-June:
Monday-Saturday 8.30-12.30.

PORTOGRUARO
Hotels

Antico Spessotto ★★★
Via Roma 2, tel. 042171040
www.hotelspessotto.it
46 rooms. Restaurant, parking,
air-conditioned
Credit cards: American Express,
Diners Club, Visa, Mastercard
In the old town center, tastefully
furnished, with all mod cons;
lunch and dinner at restaurant
under separate management,
buffet breakfast.

Restaurants

Tavernetta del Tocai ⍟ ♿ ★
Pradipozzo, via Fornace 93,
tel. 0421204280
Closed Sunday evening
and Monday
Cuisine: Veneto
Credit cards: American Express,
Diners Club, Visa, Mastercard
Venue with rustic decor and two
open fireplaces. For over 50
years, the Bellotto family has
been handing down recipes of
local cuisine; don't miss the
"baccalà" (stockfish) evening.

Alla Botte ⫪ &
Via Pordenone 46,
tel. 0421760122
www.alla-botte.it
Closed Sunday in low season
Cuisine: Veneto and Friuli
Credit cards: American Express,
Diners Club, Visa, Mastercard
Here the cooking is done the
traditional way and is inspired
by what is available in the
various seasons of the year;
interesting range of salamis,
cured meats and cheeses, wide
selection of spirits and good,
varied wine-list.

Museums, Monuments and Churches

Museo Nazionale Concordiese
Via del Seminario 26,
tel. 042172674
www.comune.portogruaro.ve.it
Opening times: Monday-Sunday
9.00-20.00. Closed 25
December, 1 January, 1 May.

Museo Paleontologico "Michele Gortani"
Via del Seminario 5,
tel. 0421277340
www.comune.portogruaro.ve.it
Opening times: Monday-Friday
10.00-12.00.
Closed Saturday, Sunday
and public holidays.

RECOARO TERME

> ℹ️ Ufficio Informazione
> e Accoglienza Turiatica
> Via Roma 15,
> tel. 044575070

Hotels

Al Pittore ★★★
Via Roma 50, tel. 044575039
www.albergopittore.it
21 rooms. Restaurant, parking,
air-conditioned
Credit cards: Visa, Mastercard
Central location, this hotel has
good facilities and has been
refurbished. Restaurant serves
Veneto cuisine.

Carla ★★★
Via Campogrosso 25,
tel. 0445780700
www.hotelcarla.it
30 rooms. Restaurant, air-
conditioned
Credit cards: American Express,
Diners Club, Visa, Mastercard
Quiet location not far from town
center, good, modern comfort;
adjacent restaurant serves good
Veneto dishes and has an
excellent wine-list.

Trettenero ★‡★ &
Via Vittorio Emanuele II 18/20,
tel. 0445780380

www.recoaroterme.com/trettenero
53 rooms. Restaurant, parking,
gym
Credit cards: American Express,
Diners Club, Visa, Mastercard
This beautiful building has had
many famous guests and
gradually adapted to modern
requirements. In the restaurant,
the period furnishings and
interesting lighting create a
charming ambience.

Restaurants

Piccole Dolomiti La Guardia ⫪
Guardia di Campogrosso,
tel. 044575257
Closed Monday evening and
Tuesday
Cuisine: local Vicenza cuisine
The food at this venue often
frequented by walkers will be a
pleasant surprise. Adone is a
highly talented chef who
prepares meat, sometimes on
the grill, and has a real vocation
for cooking local game; good
home-made cakes and and
adequate range of wines.

At night

Banana Garden
Via Roma 29, tel. 0445780789
Disco

ROVIGO

> ℹ️ Azienda per la
> Promozione Turistica
> Via J. H. Dunant 10,
> tel. 0425/361481
> www.apt.rovigo.it

Hotels

Best Western Hotel Cristallo ★★★ ★
Viale Porta Adige 1,
tel. 042530701
www.bestwestern.it/cristallo_ro
48 rooms. Restaurant, parking,
air-conditioned
Credit cards: American Express,
Diners Club, Visa, Mastercard
Modern hotel with large terrace,
well-equipped bedrooms,
facilities for business meetings
and receptions. Popular
restaurant with traditional,
Polesine and vegetarian cuisine
and an extensive wine-list.

Corona Ferrea ★‡★
Via Umberto I 21,
tel. 0425422433
www.hotelcoronaferrea.com
30 rooms. Parking, air-conditioned
Credit cards: American Express,
Diners Club, Visa, Mastercard
Modern, comfortable, elegant
hotel (no restaurant) in the old
town center, professional
welcome, buffet breakfast

Europa ★★★
Viale Porta Po 92,
tel. 0425474797
56 rooms. Restaurant, parking,
air-conditioned
Credit cards: American Express,
Diners Club, Visa, Mastercard
Ideally situated for frequent
travelers, a modern hotel
complex with refurbished rooms;
well-equipped conference rooms,
busy restaurant with Polesine
and international cuisine and an
excellent wine-list.

Villa Regina Margherita ★‡★ &
Viale Regina Margherita 6,
tel. 0425361540
www.hotelvillareginamargherita.it
22 rooms. Restaurant, parking,
air-conditioned
Credit cards: American Express,
Diners Club, Visa
Situated in an avenue of ancient
plane trees, with an Art Nouveau
facade, elegant interior, quiet
rooms; in the restaurant, the
cooking is excellent and
everything served is home-made.

Rural Lodgings

Il Bosco
Via Tre Martiri 134,
tel. 042530130
www.agriturismoilbosco.it
Credit cards: American Express,
Diners Club, Visa, Mastercard
A haven of tranquillity, ideal for
a relaxing holiday, and for horse-
riding and golf enthusiasts; the
decor of the rooms reflects the
rural setting, with attention to
detail. Good base for visiting the
Po Delta and the artistic heritage
of the vicinity.

Museums, Monuments and Churches

Pinacoteca dell'Accademia dei Concordi
Piazza Vittorio Emanuele II 14,
tel. 042527991
www.concordi.it
Opening times: July-August:
Monday-Saturday 10.00-13.00.
September-June: Monday-Friday
9.30-12.30, 15.30-18.30; Saturday
and Sunday 10.00-12.00. Closed
from 25 December to 1 January;
Easter Sunday and Easter Monday;
15 August and public holidays. May
be visited by prior arrangement.

SAN BONIFACIO
Hotels

Bologna ★★★ &
Viale Trieste 55, tel. 0457610233
www.hotel-bologna.com
67 rooms. Restaurant, parking, air-
conditioned, swimming pool, gym
Credit cards: American Express,
Diners Club, Visa, Mastercard
Easy to reach, basic facilities in

conference rooms, often used by business clientele, cyclists and touring visitors. Restaurant serves traditional and Argentine cuisine. Fitness room and American bar.

Relais Villabella ★★★ ★
Via Villabella 72, tel. 0456101777
www.relaisvillabella.it
11 rooms. Restaurant, parking, air-conditioned, swimming pool
Credit cards: American Express, Diners Club, Visa, Mastercard
Surrounded by trees, 18th-century villa with very sophisticated rooms and a romantic atmosphere. The same level of sophistication prevails in the reception rooms.

Restaurants

I Tigli 2
Via Camporosolo 11, tel. 0456102606
Open evenings only
Closed Wednesday
Lively pizzeria in the old town center, with tables outside in summer: very simple, with only a few well-spaced tables and a take-away counter. The limited range of wines includes some French labels.

Relais Villabella ℿ ♿ ★
Villabella, Via Villabella 72, tel. 0456101777
www.relaisvillabella.it
Closed Sunday
Cuisine: Veneto and traditional
Credit cards: American Express, Diners Club, Visa, Mastercard
The cuisine here is mainly fish-oriented; the venue can handle large and small numbers with the same style and quality; excellent service and a well-stocked wine-cellar.

SAN DONÀ DI PIAVE
Hotels

Forte del 48 ★★★ ♿
Via Vizzotto 1, tel. 042144018
www.hotelfortedel48.com
46 rooms. Restaurant, parking, air-conditioned
Credit cards: American Express, Diners Club, Visa, Mastercard
Located in what was once a Habsburg fortress, this hotel has comfortable rooms and conference facilities. Busy restaurant with exposed beams, serves Veneto cuisine.

Kristall ★★★
Corso S. Trentin 16, tel. 042152861
www.hotelkristall.biz
42 rooms. Parking, air-conditioned
Credit cards: American Express, Diners Club, Visa
Behind the unusual curved facade of this hotel with its beautiful windows is a pleasant

interior with comfortable bedrooms; buffet breakfast.

Park Hotel Heraclia ★★★ ♿
Via XIII Martiri 229, tel. 042143148
www.hotelheraclia.com
58 rooms. Restaurant, parking, air-conditioned
Credit cards: American Express, Diners Club, Visa, Mastercard
All windows, concrete and glass, unmistakable; modern design and decor, new conference rooms, summer terrace and private garden.

SAN VITO DI CADORE
Hotels

Dolomiti ★★★
Via Roma 33, tel. 0436890184
www.hoteldolomiti.com
Open June-September and December-April
30 rooms. Restaurant, parking, air-conditioned
Credit cards: American Express, Diners Club, Visa, Mastercard
1930s mountain hotel, with traditional wood furnishings; local cuisine and home-made cakes and biscuits at breakfast.

Ladinia ★★★
Via Ladinia 14, tel. 0436890450
www.italiaabc.it/ladinia/
Open Christmas-April and mid-June-mid-September
36 rooms. Restaurant, parking, swimming pool, sauna, tennis, gym
Credit cards: Visa, Mastercard
In a panoramic position, near the ski facilities, traditional mountain hotel with Tyrolean decor and furnishings in rooms and reception rooms; functional wellness center.

Restaurants

La Scaletta ℿ
Chiapuzza, via Calvi 1, tel. 0436890469
www.hotelcimabelpra.com
Closed Monday (except in July and August)
Cuisine: Belluno
Credit cards: American Express, Diners Club, Visa, Mastercard
Modern and sophisticated, located in a comfortable hotel. Excellent local Belluno cuisine. Interesting wine-list.

SELVA DI CADORE
Hotels

Giglio Rosso ★★★
Pescul, tel. 0437720310
www.valfiorentina.it
19 rooms. Restaurant, parking, sauna

Credit cards: Visa, Mastercard
Alpine decor, good facilities and high level of comfort: hydro-massage and Turkish bath.

Nigritella ★★★
Santa Fosca, via S.Fosca 17, tel. 0437720041
www.dolomiti.it/nigritella
Open mid-December-mid- April and mid-June-mid-September
59 rooms. Restaurant, parking, swimming pool, sauna, gym
Credit cards: Visa, Mastercard
Centrally located, comfortable ambience, good facilities and piano bar evenings; buffet breakfast, Cadore and traditional cuisine specialties served in the restaurant.

Museums, Monuments and Churches

Museo Civico della Val Fiorentina "Vittorino Cazzetta"
Via IV Novembre 51, tel. 0437521068
www.valfiorentina.it/selva/cu/museo.htm
Opening times: Being refurbished in 2006.

SOAVE
Hotels

Cangrande ★★★ ♿
Viale del Commercio 20, tel. 0456102424
www.hotelcangrande.it
56 rooms. Restaurant, parking, air-conditioned
Credit cards: American Express, Diners Club, Visa, Mastercard
This complex has good general facilities and comfortable rooms with wardrobe vestibule; high level of cuisine and service in restaurant.

Roxy Plaza ★★★ ♿ ★
Via S. Matteo 4, tel. 0456190660
www.hotelroxyplaza.it
43 rooms. Air-conditioned, gym
Credit cards: American Express, Diners Club, Visa, Mastercard
Situated by the walls of the castle built by the Scaligeri, this elegant palazzo has spacious rooms, beautiful lounges and a new conference room with multimedia facilities.

Restaurants

Lo Scudo ℿ
Via S. Matteo 46, tel. 0457680766
www.loscudo.vr.it
Closed Sunday evening and Monday
Cuisine: Veneto
Credit cards: American Express, Diners Club, Visa, Mastercard
Former 16th-century monastery,

romantic, elegant ambience, with Venetian windows and candelabra; lunch served in garden (formerly the orchard) in summer. Varied sophisticated cuisine. Good range of wines and spirits.

STRA

Restaurants

Osteria da Caronte ▮▮
Paluello, via Dolo 39,
tel. 041412091
www.osteriadacaronte.it
Closed Tuesday evening
and Wednesday
Cuisine: local
Credit cards: Visa
Rustic interior with open fireplace and garden service in summer; local specialties; home-made breads and sweets.

Museums, Monuments and Churches

Museo Nazionale di Villa Pisani
Via Alvise Pisani 7,
tel. 049502074-049502270
www.beniculturali.it
Opening times: April-October: Tuesday-Sunday 9.00-19.00. November-March: Tuesday-Sunday 9.00-16.00. Closed 1 January, 25 December.

Museo Rossimoda della Calzatura d'Autore
Villa Foscarini Rossi, Via Doge Pisani 1, tel. 0499801091
www.villafoscarini.it
Opening times: April-October: Tuesday-Thursday 9.00-12.30, 14.30-18.00; Friday 10.00-12.30, 14.30-18.00; Saturday and public holidays 11.00-18.00; Monday: groups only, booking essential. November-March: Monday-Friday 9.00-12.30, 14.30-18.00. Closed from 25 December to 6 January.

TREVISO

▣ **Azienda per la Promozione Turistica**
Palazzo Scotti, via Toniolo 41, tel. 0422/540600
www.sevenonline.it/tvapt/index.htm

Hotels

Best Western Al Foghèr ★★★ ⚹ ★
Viale della Repubblica 10,
tel. 0422432950
www.bestwestern.it/alfogher_tv
55 rooms. Restaurant, parking, air-conditioned
Credit cards: American Express, Diners Club, Visa, Mastercard
The fair distance from the town

center is compensated by the quality of the facilities and services. Rooms in pastel shades, restaurant known for its Veneto cuisine, menu varies according to the season.

Carlton ★▮★ ★
Largo Porta Altinia 15,
tel. 0422411661
www.hotelcarlton.it
93 rooms. Restaurant, parking, air-conditioned
Credit cards: American Express, Diners Club, Visa, Mastercard
Spacious, comfortable interior with a touch of austere elegance, in a 1960s building situated by the old town walls; restaurant serves traditional and Treviso cuisine.

Maggior Consiglio ★▮★ ⚹
Via Terraglio 140, tel. 04224093
www.boscolohotels.com
121 rooms. Restaurant, parking, air-conditioned, swimming pool, sauna, gym
Credit cards: Diners Club, Mastercard
On the main road to Venice, a modern building with all mod cons and a well-equipped conference center. Elegant, spacious rooms; light-filled reception rooms and wellness center with sauna, swimming pool and gym.

Scala ★★★ ★
Viale Felissent ang. cal di Breda 1, tel. 0422307600
www.hotelscala.com
20 rooms. Parking, air-conditioned
Credit cards: American Express, Diners Club, Visa, Mastercard
An old mansion next to the garden of Villa Manfrin, pleasant bedrooms with parquet floors, functional bathrooms, a pleasant, comfortable ambience.

Rural Lodgings

Il Cascinale ⚹
Via Torre d'Orlando 6/B,
tel. 0422402203
www.agriturismoilcascinale.it
Restaurant
This rustic building is a stone's throw away from the center. This is the land of red chicory of Treviso and the restaurant serves it as a specialty.

Restaurants

Alfredo ▮▮▮
Via Collalto 26, tel. 0422540275
Closed Sunday evening and Monday
Cuisine: Veneto
Credit cards: American Express, Diners Club, Visa
Elegant, refined ambience, with designer windows which create

a warm atmosphere. Excellent cuisine, with fish specialties; "red chicory of Treviso week" from December to February.

Antica Torre ▮▮ ★
Via Inferiore 55, tel. 0422583694
vwww.anticatorre.tv
Closed Sunday, Thursday evening
Cuisine: local Treviso cuisine
Credit cards: American Express, Diners Club, Visa, Mastercard
A 13th-century tower in the old town center is a pleasant setting for tasting excellent local cuisine; good range of wines and spirits and carefully chosen olive oils and local cheeses.

Due Mori ▮▮ ⚹
Via Bailo 9, tel. 0422540383
Closed Tuesday evening and Wednesday
Cuisine: local Treviso cuisine
Credit cards: American Express, Diners Club, Visa, Mastercard
Typical trattoria in the center of town, since 1400, plenty of atmosphere and good cooking, specialties made with fish and red Treviso chicory; interesting selection of local wines.

Trattoria all'Antico Portico ▮▮
Piazza S. Maria Maggiore 18,
tel. 0422545259
www.anticoportico.it
Closed Tuesday
Cuisine: local Treviso cuisine
Credit cards: American Express, Visa, Mastercard
In the town center, a rustic 14th-century venue with exposed beams which, in fine weather, spreads onto a cool terrace. Personalized versions of local cuisine, "primi piatti" with fresh home-made pasta.

At night

Il Capriccio
Via Brandolini d'Adda 18,
tel. 0422583949
Pleasant pub with well-stocked cellar.

Lime Aperitivo Notturno
Ponte della Priula, Via IV Novembre 119, tel. 335330391
www.limeaperitivonotturno.com
The unusual feature of this venue is that aperitifs have been moved to... after dinner. Interesting variety of cocktails. Also food.

Museums, Monuments and Churches

Museo Civico presso la Chiesa di Santa Caterina ★
Via S. Caterina,
tel. 0422544864
www.comune.treviso.it
Opening times: Tuesday-Sunday 9.00-12.30, 14.30-18.00.

Museo del Seminario Vescovile
Piazzetta Benedetto XI 2,
tel. 04223247
Opening times: Sunday 9.00-
12.00. Groups may also visit by
prior arrangement.

Museo Diocesano di Arte Sacra
Via Canoniche 9,
tel. 0422416700
www.diocesitv.it
Opening times: Tuesday-Friday
and Saturday 15.00-18.00;
Wednesday and Thursday 9.00-
12.00. Closed Monday and
public holidays.

**Museo Etnografico Provinciale
"Case Piavone"**
Via Cal di Breda 130,
tel. 0422308910
www.provincia.treviso.it
Opening times: Thursday-
Sunday 9.30-12.30, 15.00-18.30.
Groups may visit on other days
by prior arrangement
(0422656706/7).

VENEZIA

i **Azienda per la
Pormozione Turistica**
Castello, fondamenta S.
Lorenzo, tel. 0415298711
**Ufficio Informazione
e Accoglienza Turistica**
Stazione ferroviaria Santa
Lucia, tel. 0415298711
www.turismovenezia.it

Hotels

Bauer ☆☆☆ ໒
S. Marco 1459, campo S. Moisé,
tel. 0415207022
www.bauervenezia.com
191 rooms. Restaurant, air-
conditioned, sauna, gym
Credit cards: American Express,
Diners Club, Visa, Mastercard
A name of great prestige,
elegant interior, efficient
service and plenty of comfort.
The complex comprises the
Hotel Bauer and "Il Palazzo",
located in an 18th-century
palazzo. Rooms and suites,
wellness center; buffet
breakfast in the "Settimo Cielo"
restaurant.

Bellini ☆☆☆
Cannaregio 116, lista di Spagna,
tel. 0415242488
www.boscolohotels.com
97 rooms. Restaurant, air-
conditioned
Credit cards: American Express,
Diners Club, Visa, Mastercard
An old palazzo on the Grand
Canal, comfortable rooms and
elegant reception rooms; some
suites also available and a small
conference room. Excellent
buffet breakfast.

**Best Western Biasutti (Villa
Adria-Urania, Villa Nora) ☆☆☆ ★**
Lido di Venezia, via E. Dandolo
27/29, tel. 0415260120
www.bestwestern.it/biasutti_ve
69 rooms. Parking, air-conditioned
Credit cards: American Express,
Diners Club, Visa, Mastercard
Elegant complex comprising 3
villas, south-facing and quiet,
linked by gardens and wide
terraces; open-air bar, meeting
room and private beach (extra
charge).

Bonvecchiati ☆☆☆ ໒
Calle Goldoni 4488,
tel. 0415285017
www.hotelbonvecchiati.it
117 rooms. Restaurant, air-
conditioned
Credit cards: American Express,
Diners Club, Visa, Mastercard
In a 19th-century palazzo,
superb furnishings and comfort;
restaurant also serves meals on
a pleasant terrace, large
reception rooms.

Boscolo G.H. dei Dogi ☆☆☆ ໒ ★
Fondamenta Madonna dell'Orto
3500-Cannaregio, tel. 0412208111
www.boscolohotels.com
72 rooms. Restaurant, air-
conditioned
Credit cards: American Express,
Diners Club, Visa, Mastercard
Former noble palace, sumptuous
ambience, thanks partly to the
views of the lagoon and the
internal garden. 18th-century
Venetian furnishings and decor.
Remarkable restaurant "Il
Giardino" with local and
international cuisine.

Ca' Pisani ☆☆☆ ໒
Dorsoduro 979/A, rio Terà
Foscarini, tel. 0412401411
www.capisanihotel.it
29 rooms. Restaurant, air-
conditioned
Credit cards: American Express,
Diners Club, Visa, Mastercard
Late 16th-century palazzo with
rooms and suites furnished with
original 1930s and 1940s
furniture; solarium terrace,
Turkish bath. Restaurant and
"La Rivista" wine bar.

Carlton Gran Canal ☆☆☆
S. Croce 578, fondamenta
S. Simeon Piccolo,
tel. 0412752200
145 rooms. Air-conditioned
Credit cards: American Express,
Diners Club, Visa, Mastercard
Right on the Grand Canal, as its
name suggests, elegant,
comfortable with a pleasant
Venetian courtyard overlooked by
some of the rooms, all of which
are magnificently furnished in the
18th-century Venetian style.

Cipriani ☆☆☆
Giudecca 10, fondamenta
S. Giovanni, tel. 0415207744
www.hotelcipriani.com
Open April-November
104 rooms. Restaurant, air-
conditioned, swimming pool,
sauna, tennis, gym
Credit cards: American Express,
Diners Club, Visa, Mastercard
Offers elegant accommodation
with a high degree of comfort.
Beautifully furnished rooms and
prestigious suites, a fitness
center and sports facilities, a
new wellness center: just some
of the features which distinguish
this famous hotel, which also
has accommodation at the
"Palazzo Vendramin" and the
"Palazzetto Nani Barbaro".

Concordia ☆☆☆ ★
Calle larga S. Marco 367,
tel. 0415206866
www.hotelconcordia.it
55 rooms. Restaurant, air-
conditioned
Credit cards: American Express,
Diners Club, Visa, Mastercard
The only hotel in Venice with
views over St Mark's Basilica. A
welcoming, elegant ambience,
small conference room. Buffet
breakfast, the intimate "Maison
de Lauren" restaurant serves
Venetian and traditional cuisine.

Danieli ☆☆☆
Castello 4196, riva degli
Schiavoni, tel. 0415226480
www.luxurycollection.com/danieli
233 rooms. Restaurant, air-
conditioned
Credit cards: American Express,
Diners Club, Visa, Mastercard
Possibly the most sophisticated
hotel in Venice; antique
furniture, Corinthian stuccoes,
Murano lampshades, decorated
ceilings. Also has prestigious
suites and junior suites. Meals
at the "Terrazza Danieli"
restaurant, buffet breakfast.

Des Bains ☆☆☆
Lido di Venezia, lungomare
Marconi 17, tel. 0415265921
www.starwood.com/italy
Open mid-March-mid-November
191 rooms. Restaurant, parking,
air-conditioned, swimming pool,
sauna, tennis, gym
Credit cards: American Express,
Diners Club, Visa, Mastercard
Palazzo in Art Nouveau style
facing the sea; rooms have
balcony or terrace; elegant
restaurant with coffered ceiling,
serves traditional fish and
vegetable dishes.

Gabrielli Sandwirth ☆☆☆
Castello 4110, riva degli
Schiavoni, tel. 0415231580

☆☆☆ ☆☆☆ ☆☆☆ ★★★ ★★ ★ Hotels   🍴🍴🍴🍴🍴 🍴🍴🍴🍴 🍴🍴🍴 🍴🍴 🍴 Restaurants   ໒ Disabled   ★ Special TCI Rates

www.hotelgabrielli.it

100 rooms. Restaurant, air-conditioned

Credit cards: American Express, Diners Club, Visa, Mastercard

Decorated with polychrome marble and furnished in the 18th-century Venetian style, internal courtyard used for meals outside in summer and a pleasant garden.

Giorgione *‡* ⚓ ★
Cannaregio 4587, campo
Ss. Apostoli, tel. 0415225810
www.hotelgiorgione.com

76 rooms. Air-conditioned

Credit cards: American Express, Diners Club, Visa, Mastercard

A 15th-century palazzo, this hotel offers a standard of service worthy of a higher category hotel. Well-equipped rooms, suites and junior suites and a courtyard with a fountain; restaurant and wine-bar with traditional Venetian cuisine.

Gritti Palace *‡‡
S. Marco 2467, campo S. Maria del Giglio, tel. 041794611
www.starwoodhotels.com/gritti palace

91 rooms. Restaurant, air-conditioned

Credit cards: American Express, Diners Club, Visa, Mastercard

In the charming setting of this 16th-century mansion, the hotel has authentic Venetian furnishings and maximum comfort. Either continental or buffet breakfast.

Kette *‡*
S. Marco 2053, piscina S. Moisé, tel. 0415207766
www.hotelkette.com

63 rooms. Air-conditioned

Credit cards: American Express, Diners Club, Visa, Mastercard

Near Piazza S. Marco, quiet location and well-appointed rooms furnished in the Venetian style with marble bathrooms.

La Fenice et Des Artistes *** ★
S. Marco 1936, campiello della Fenice, tel. 0415232333
www.fenicehotels.it

69 rooms. Air-conditioned

Credit cards: American Express, Diners Club, Visa, Mastercard

Frequented by celebrities, this historic palazzo has a new wing, both furnished in the typical Venetian style. Pleasant reception rooms with plenty of atmosphere; guests eat at the "Taverna la Fenice" nearby.

Londra Palace *‡*
Castello 4171, riva degli Schiavoni, tel. 0415200533

www.hotelondra.it

53 rooms. Restaurant, air-conditioned

Credit cards: American Express, Diners Club, Visa, Mastercard

Elegant hotel with rooms and suites with period furniture and reception rooms with a pleasant atmosphere, splendid paintings and antiques. Warm welcome with attention to detail.

Luna Hotel Baglioni *‡‡
S. Marco 1243, calle larga de l'Ascension, tel. 0415289840
www.baglionihotels.com

104 rooms. Restaurant, air-conditioned

Credit cards: American Express, Diners Club, Visa, Mastercard

The oldest hotel in Venice. The medieval Knights Templar stayed here. It has an elegant interior, frescoed public rooms; bedrooms furnished with period pieces and modern comforts, suites; Veneto and international cuisine in the adjacent "Canova" restaurant.

Metropole *‡* ★
Castello 4149, riva degli Schiavoni, tel. 0415205044
www.hotelmetropole.com

70 rooms. Restaurant, air-conditioned

Credit cards: American Express, Diners Club, Visa, Mastercard

16th-century patrician residence converted into a hotel in the early 1900s, with period furnishings and interesting collections of antiques; rooms in the Art Nouveau and Art Déco style, oriental bar overlooking the lagoon, suites and junior suites.

Monaco & Grand Canal *‡*
S. Marco 1332, calle Vallaresso, tel. 0415200211
www.hotelmonaco.it

99 rooms. Restaurant, air-conditioned

Credit cards: American Express, Diners Club, Visa, Mastercard

Elegant rooms; some suites and junior suites with views of the Grand Canal; the restaurant serves traditional and international cuisine. Excellent conference facilities.

Palazzo Sant'Angelo sul Canal Grande *‡* ⚓ ★
S. Marco 3488-3478/B, tel. 0412411452
www.palazzosantangelo.com

14 rooms. Air-conditioned

Credit cards: American Express, Diners Club, Visa, Mastercard

Once a patrician palazzo, its rooms and suites are tastefully furnished in the Venetian style, with all modern comforts, including hydro-massage.

Sofitel Venezia *‡* ★
S. Croce 245, Giardini Papadopoli, tel. 041710400
www.accorhotels.com/italia

97 rooms. Restaurant, air-conditioned

Credit cards: American Express, Diners Club, Visa, Mastercard

Has beautifully furnished bedrooms and some suites. Guests may use the "Cafebar Salotto Veneziano", the library and private motor-boat. The "Papadopoli" restaurant serves typical Venetian cuisine.

The Westin Excelsior *‡‡
Lido di Venezia, lungomare Marconi 41, tel. 0415260201
www.westin.com

Open mid-March-mid-November

196 rooms. Restaurant, parking, air-conditioned, swimming pool, tennis, gym

Credit cards: American Express, Diners Club, Visa, Mastercard

A careful overhaul has restored the Moorish charm of this jewel of exclusive hospitality which is part of the legend of the Lido; well-equipped rooms for conferences and other events, wellness center and beauty treatments, four restaurants.

Wildner ** ★
Riva degli Schiavoni 4161, tel. 0415227463
www.veneziahotels.com

16 rooms. Restaurant, air-conditioned

Credit cards: American Express, Diners Club, Visa, Mastercard

Quiet atmosphere, good, comfortable rooms, restaurant serves Venetian cuisine.

Rural Lodgings

Le Garzette
Malamocco, lungomare Alberoni 32, tel. 041731078
www.legarzette.on.to

Restaurant, bikes for use of guests

On the island of the Lido, you can stay in rural lodgings right next to the shore, which can be reached by a short walk past vegetable gardens and natural vegetation. At weekends, restaurant also open to non-residents.

Orto Arcobaleno ⚓
Zelarino, via Parolari 88, tel. 041680341

Swimming pool

In the Venetian hinterland, this farm-stay is set in beautiful old farmland; the farm provides a warm welcome; it has its own vegetable gardens and organic bee-hives.

Valdor
Ca' Savio, via Medina 5,
tel. 041966108
www.valdor.it
Restaurant, swimming pool
Country residence by the sea.
The farm offers accommodation
in simple rooms and
independent apartments, each
with its own garden. Facilities
include entertainment for kids, a
private beach and special terms
at the local golf club. The
restaurant serves typical
Venetian cuisine made with
products made or grown on the
farm.

Restaurants

Ai Mercanti ⅋⅋
S. Marco 4346/A, calle
dei Fuseri, tel. 0415238269
www.aimercanti.com
Closed Sunday, Monday lunch-
time
Cuisine: Veneto with an
interesting new approach
Credit cards: Visa, Mastercard
Not far from La Fenice, this
venue prepares traditional
cuisine with plenty of
imagination; good home-made
pasta and sweets, wide choice
of wines.

Al Conte Pescaor ⅋⅋ ♿ ★
S. Marco 544, piscina S. Zulian,
tel. 0415221483
Closed Sunday
Cuisine: Venetian
Credit cards: American Express,
Diners Club, Visa, Mastercard
In an authentic Venetian setting,
warm hospitality is accompanied
by good cooking and the typical
recipes of local cuisine. Good
selection of cheeses, interesting
wine-list.

Al Covo ⅋⅋
Castello 3968, campiello della
Pescaria, tel. 0415223812
Closed Wednesday and
Thursday
Cuisine: Venetian with personal
interpretation
Pleasant ambience, where fresh
and farmed fish is at its best
and therefore cooked very
simply. Very interesting wine-
list; wide selection of olive oils,
cheeses, salamis and cured
meats.

Al Graspo de Ua ⅋⅋
S. Marco 5094, calle dei
Bombaseri, tel. 0415200150
www.algraspodeua.com
Closed Monday
Cuisine: Veneto and traditional
Credit cards: American Express,
Diners Club, Visa, Mastercard
The menu is changed every day
here, based on non-repetitive

Venetian cuisine; cheese trolley
of fresh Italian and French
cheeses, with some meat and
vegetarian dishes.

Al Leon d'Oro ⅋⅋
Cannaregio 2345, tel. 041720693
www.alleondoro.com
Closed Wednesday
Cuisine: Veneto
Credit cards: Visa, Mastercard
A friendly "cicchetteria" (wine
bar with food) serving
traditional local fare; don't miss
their coconut biscuits and other
home-made desserts.

Antico Martini ⅋⅋⅋⅋ ★
S. Marco 1983, campo S. Fantin,
tel. 0415224121
www.anticomartini.com
Closed Tuesday, Wednesday
lunch-time
Cuisine: Venetian and creative
Credit cards: American Express,
Diners Club, Visa, Mastercard
Popular, elegant venue, part of
Venetian history; tasting menu
available at lunch or dinner-time,
or cheaper fixed menu. The
restaurant is open for dinner
after theatre performances, good
selection of cheeses, olive oils,
wines and spirits.

Antico Pignolo ⅋⅋⅋⅋ ★
S. Marco 451, calle dei
Specchieri, tel. 0415228123
Cuisine: Venetian and traditional
Credit cards: American Express,
Diners Club, Visa, Mastercard
Traditional Venetian ambience
with garden in summer. The chef
uses the best local ingredients
to prepare traditional lagoon
recipes with fresh fish;
exceptional wine-list.

Caffè Quadri ⅋⅋⅋⅋
Piazza S. Marco 120,
tel. 0415222105
www.quadrivenice.com
Closed Monday in winter
Cuisine: Veneto and traditional
Credit cards: American Express,
Diners Club, Visa, Mastercard
Elegant, sophisticated early
16th-century venue where
Venetians first drank Turkish
coffee in 1725; excellent range
of cheeses and spirits. A small
orchestra entertains its clientele.

Corte Sconta ⅋⅋ ♿
Castello 3886, calle del Pestrin,
tel. 0415227024
Closed Sunday and Monday
Cuisine: Venetian
Credit cards: Visa, Mastercard
Unusual venue in a secluded
courtyard, with a lively
atmosphere, with cuisine based
on fresh fish. Don't miss their
excellent starters, or "primi
piatti" made with home-made

pasta; wide range of cheeses
and olive oils.

Da Fiore ⅋⅋⅋
S. Polo 2202/A, calle
del Scaleter, tel. 041721308
www.dafiore.com
Closed Sunday and Monday
Cuisine: Veneto with an
interesting new approach
Credit cards: American Express,
Diners Club, Visa, Mastercard
Classy, delightful atmosphere,
cuisine based on the day's
catch, dishes prepared simply
so as not to conceal the true
taste.

De Pisis ⅋⅋⅋ ♿
S. Marco 1459, campo S. Moisé,
tel. 0415207022
www.bauervenezia.com
Open evenings only
Cuisine: Veneto with a new
angle
Credit cards: American Express,
Diners Club, Visa, Mastercard
Prestigious ambience, with
refined service; in summer,
meals are served on the terrace
overlooking the Grand Canal.
Sophisticated, varied cuisine,
carefully prepared and elegantly
presented; fine selection of
cheeses, serious range of wines
and spirits.

Do Forni ⅋⅋ ★
S. Marco 457, calle dei
Specchieri, tel. 0415230663
www.doforni.it
Cuisine: Venetian and traditional
Credit cards: American Express,
Diners Club, Visa
Comfortable venue with rustic
yet elegant atmosphere, where
culinary tradition and hospitality
go hand in hand; wide choice of
French and Italian cheeses,
typical regional salamis and
cured meats. Fine wines and
spirits.

Do Leoni ⅋⅋⅋⅋ ★
Castello 4171, riva degli
Schiavoni, tel. 0415200533
www.hotelondra.it
Cuisine: Venetian with a new
angle
Credit cards: American Express,
Diners Club, Visa
This restaurant has the elegance
of the prestigious hotel of which
it is part, an austere
atmosphere where traditional
cuisine is served with a modern,
elaborate touch. Varied wine-
list, impressive selection of
spirits; meals served until late
in the evening and enchanting
summer terrace.

Harry's Bar ⅋⅋⅋⅋ ★
S. Marco 1323, calle Vallaresso,
tel. 0415285777

Cuisine: Venetian and traditional
Credit cards: American Express, Visa, Mastercard

Myth and benchmark of a family tradition of Venetian hospitality, this venue has retained the charm and atmosphere that made it famous; à la carte, or two fixed menus which are changed from one day to the next.

Harry's Dolci ¶¶
Giudecca 773, fondamenta S. Biagio, tel. 0415224844
www.cipriani.com
Open April-October
Closed Monday evening and Tuesday
Cuisine: Veneto and traditional
Credit cards: American Express, Diners Club, Visa, Mastercard

Quality in an elegant, sophisticated ambience; view over the Canale della Giudecca from the summer terrace. Cuisine of various types, but almost always based on local traditions, with fresh home-made pasta.

La Furatola ¶¶
Dorsoduro 2869/A, tel. 0415208594
Closed Monday lunch-time and Thursday
Cuisine: Venetian
Credit cards: American Express, Diners Club, Visa, Mastercard

Typical Venetian trattoria with friendly, competent management. Interesting selection of Veneto and Friuli wines.

Le Bistrot de Venise ¶¶ ★
S. Marco 4685, calle dei Fabbri, tel. 0415236651
www.bistrotdevenise.com
Cuisine: historic
Credit cards: Visa, Mastercard

A meeting point for Venice's artistic elite; the kitchen serves recipes dating from the 14th century to the present day. Extensive range of cheeses; impressive, prize-winning wine-list.

Poste Vecie ¶¶¶ &
S. Polo 1608, rialto Pescheria, tel. 041721822
www.postevecie.com
Closed Tuesday
Cuisine: Venetian
Credit cards: American Express, Diners Club, Visa, Mastercard

Three small, quiet dining-rooms and a cool terrace where you can sample really traditional Venetian cuisine.

Taverna la Fenice ¶¶ &
S. Marco 1938, campiello della Fenice, tel. 0415223856
www.ristorantelafenice.com
Open evenings only

Closed Monday
Cuisine: Venetian and traditional
Credit cards: American Express, Diners Club, Visa, Mastercard

Elegant dining-rooms with period furnishings, local cuisine, mainly fish and mushrooms.

Tre Spiedi ¶ & ★
Cannaregio 5906, salizzada S. Canciano, tel. 0415208035
Closed Sunday lunch-time and Monday
Cuisine: Venetian
Credit cards: American Express, Diners Club, Visa, Mastercard

Run by two brothers and two sisters of the same family for over 20 years; mainly fish dishes and the traditional "fegato alla veneziana".

Vecio Fritolin ¶¶ ★
S. Croce 2262, calle della Regina, tel. 0415222881
www.veciofritolin.it
Closed Monday
Cuisine: Venetian with an interesting new approach
Credit cards: American Express, Diners Club, Visa, Mastercard

In the historic heart of Venice, a 16th-century venue which has retained its original appearance. In the kitchen, the tastes of Venice prevail.

Vini da Gigio ¶¶
Cannaregio 3628/A, fondamenta S. Felice, tel. 0415285140
www.vinidagigio.com
Closed Monday and Tuesday
Cuisine: Venetian
Credit cards: Diners Club, Visa

In a 15th-century palazzo, with a rustic ambience, local cuisine prevails, wide selection of wines and spirits, good selection of olive oils and cheeses.

Zucca ¶ ★
S. Croce 1762, ramo del Megio, tel. 0415241570
www.lazucca.it
Closed Sunday
Cuisine: traditional
Credit cards: American Express, Diners Club, Visa, Mastercard

Typical, revitalized Venetian "osteria", with the pumpkin ("zucca") in glory on the walls; the owners have devised a really original menu.

At night

Casanova Music Café
Cannaregio 158/A, tel. 0412750199
Music Club

The Fiddler's Elbow Irish Pub
Cannaregio 3847, tel. 0415239930
Typical Irish venue, Guinness, Kilkenny, Harp galore and traditional Irish coffee. Good program of live concerts.

Museums, Monuments and Churches

Ca' Pesaro - Galleria Internazionale d'Arte Moderna
Santa Croce 2076, tel. 041721127
www.museicivicivenezini.it
Opening times: April-October: Tuesday-Sunday 10.00-18.00 (last admission 1 hour before). November-March: Tuesday-Sunday 10.00-17.00 (last admission 1 hour before). Closed 25 December, 1 January, 1 May.

Ca' Rezzonico - Museo del Settecento Veneziano
Dorsoduro 3136, tel. 0412410100
www.museicivicivenezini.it
Opening times: April-October: Wednesday-Monday 10.00-18.00 (last admission 17.00). November-March: Wednesday-Monday 10.00-17.00 (last admission 1 hour before). Closed 25 December, 1 January, 1 May.

Casa di Carlo Goldoni
San Polo 2794, calle dei Nomboli, tel. 0412759325
www.museicivicivenezini.it
Opening times: April-October: Monday-Saturday 10.00-17.00. November-March: Monday-Saturday 10.00-16.00 (last admission 30 mins before). Closed 25 December, 1 January, 1 May.

Collezione Peggy Guggenheim
Dorsoduro 701, tel. 0412405440
www.guggenheim-venice.it
Opening times: Wednesday-Monday 10.00-18.00. Closed Tuesday, 25 December.

Galleria "Giorgio Franchetti" alla Ca' d'Oro
Cannaregio 3932, tel. 0415238790
www.artive.arti.beniculturali.it
Opening times: Monday 8.15-13.30; Tuesday-Sunday 8.15-19.15. Closed 1 January, 1 May, 25 December.

Gallerie dell'Accademia
Dorsoduro 1050, campo della Carità, tel. 0415222247
www.gallerieaccademia.org
Opening times: Monday 8.15-14.00; Tuesday-Sunday 8.15-19.15.

Museo Archeologico Nazionale
Piazza S. Marco 17 – Entrance from Museo Correr, tel. 0415225978
sbmp.provincia.venezia.it/mir/musei/venezia/home_a.htm
Opening times: Entrance from Museo Correr: 9.00-19.00 (last admission 18.00). Entrance from Piazzetta San Marco No. 17: 8.15-9.00. Closed 25 December, 1 January.

Museo Civico di Storia Naturale
Santa Croce 1730, fondaco dei
Turchi, tel. 0412750206
www.museicivicivenezia ni.it
Opening times: Saturday and
Sunday 10-16. Tours for schools
must be booked beforehand:
Tuesday-Friday 9.00-13.00;
Saturday and Sunday 10.00-
16.00. Only part of the museum
is open (the Dinosaur Room and
the "tegnue" aquarium).

Museo Correr ★
Piazza S. Marco, Ala
Napoleonica, tel. 0412405211
www.museicivicivenezia ni.it
Opening times: April-October:
Monday-Sunday 9.00-19.00 (last
admission 1 hour before).
November-March: Monday-
Sunday 9.00-17.00. Closed 1
January, 25 December.

**Museo d'Arte Orientale
a Ca' Pesaro**
Santa Croce 2070, San Stae,
tel. 0415241173
www.arteorientale.org
Opening times: April-October:
Tuesday-Sunday 10.00-18.00.
November-March: Tuesday-
Sunday 10.00-17.00. Last
admission 1 hour before. Closed
1 January, 1 May, 25 December.

**Museo delle Icone Bizantine
e Postbizantine**
Castello 3412, ponte dei Greci,
tel. 0415226581
www.istitutoellenico.org
Opening times: Monday-Sunday
9.00-17.00.

**Museo Diocesano d'Arte Sacra
di Santa Apollonia**
Castello, fondamenta della
Canonica 4312, tel. 0415229166
Opening times: Monday-
Saturday 10.00-18.00. Closed
Sunday and public holidays.

Museo di San Marco
Basilica di S. Marco, piazza
S. Marco, tel. 0415225205
www.museosanmarco.it
Opening times: April-September:
9.45-17.00. October-March: 9.45-
16.45. No admission during
Sunday morning mass.

Museo Ebraico di Venezia
Cannaregio 2902/b, campo del
Ghetto Nuovo, tel. 041715359
www.museoebraico.it
Opening times: June-September:
Monday-Friday, Sunday 10.00-
19.00. October-May: Monday-
Friday, Sunday 10.00-17.30. Closed
Saturday and Jewish festivals.

Museo Fortuny ★
San Marco 3780, campo
S. Beneto, tel. 0415200995
www.museicivicivenezia ni.it
Opening times: Open for temporary
exhibitions or other events.

Museo Querini Stampalia ★
Castello 5252, S. Maria
Formosa, tel. 0412711411
www.querinistampalia.it
Opening times: Tuesday-
Wednesday-Thursday and
Sunday 10.00-18.00; Friday and
Saturday 10.00-22.00.

Museo Storico Navale
Castello, riva degli Schiavoni
2148, tel. 0415200276
www.museonavale.191.it
Opening times: Monday-Friday
8.45-13.30; Saturday and day
before public holidays 8.45-
13.00. Closed Sunday and public
holidays.

Palazzo Ducale
San Marco 1. Entrance from
Porta del Frumento, piazzetta
San Marco, tel. 0412715911
www.museicivicivenezia ni.it
Opening times: April-October:
Monday-Sunday 9.00-19.00 (last
admission 1 hour before).
November-March: Monday-
Sunday 9.00-17.00. Closed 1
January, 25 December.

**Palazzo Mocenigo - Museo
di Storia del Tessuto
e del Costume ★**
Santa Croce 1992, tel. 041721798
twww.museicivicivenezia ni.it
Opening times: April-October:
Tuesday-Sunday 10.00-17.00.
November-March: Tuesday-
Sunday 10.00-16.00 (last
admission 30 mins before).
Closed 25 December, 1 January, 1
May.

**Pinacoteca e Museo dei Padri
Armeni Mechitaristi**
Isola di San Lazzaro degli
Armeni, tel. 0415260104
Opening times: Guided tours
only: Monday-Sunday 15.25-
17.25.

Pinacoteca Manfrediniana
Dorsoduro 1, campo della
Salute, tel. 0412743911
www.patriarcato.venezia.it
Opening times: May be visited
by prior arrangement.

**Sale Monumentali Biblioteca
Nazionale Marciana (Libreria
Sansoviniana)**
piazzetta S. Marco 13/a –
Entrance from Museo Correr,
tel. 0412407211
www.marciana.venezia.sbn.it
Opening times: April-October:
Monday-Sunday 9.00-19.00.
November-March: Monday-
Sunday 9.00-17.00. Closed 1
January, 25 December.

Scuola Grande dei Carmini ★
Dorsoduro 2617, tel. 0415289420
www.provincia.venezia.it/lartis/ar
tisti/carmini.htm
Opening times: April-October:

Monday-Saturday 9.00-18.00;
Sunday 9.00-16.00. November-
March: Monday-Sunday 9.00-
16.00.

**Scuola Grande di San Giovanni
Evangelista**
San Polo 2454, tel. 041718234
www.sgiovanniev.it
Opening times: May be visited
by prior arrangement: Monday-
Friday 9.30-12.30.

Scuola Grande di San Rocco ★
San Polo 3052, campo S. Rocco,
tel. 0415234864
www.scuolagrandesanrocco.it
Opening times: 28 March-2
November: Monday-Sunday
9.00-17.30 (last admission
17.00). 3 November-27 March:
Monday-Sunday 10.00-16.00
(last admission 15.30). Closed
25 December, 1 January and
Easter Sunday.

Tesoro della Basilica di San Marco
Basilica di S. Marco, piazza
S. Marco, tel. 0415225205
www.basilicasanmarco.it
Opening times: April-September:
Monday-Saturday 9.45-17.00;
Sunday and public holidays 14.00-
17.00. October-March: Monday-
Saturday 9.45-16.45; Sunday and
public holidays 13.00-16.45.

VERONA

Hotels

Accademia ★★★ ♿
Via Scala 12, tel. 045596222
www.accademiavr.it
94 rooms. Restaurant, air-
conditioned
Credit cards: American Express,
Diners Club, Visa, Mastercard
This 16th-century palazzo is now
an elegant hotel with tapestries
on the walls, antique furniture,
junior suites and comfortable
rooms; busy restaurant, under
separate management, known
for its refined cuisine.

**Best Western Hotel
Firenze ★★★ ♿ ★**
Corso Porta Nuova 88,
tel. 0458011510
www.bestwestern.it/firenze_vr
49 rooms. Air-conditioned
Credit cards: American Express,
Diners Club, Visa, Mastercard
Very central near Piazza Brà,
completely refurbished;
comfortable, well-appointed rooms,
elegant decor. Buffet breakfast.

★★★ ★★★ ★★★ ★★★ ★★ ★ Hotels   🏨 🏨 🏨 🏨 🏨 Restaurants   ♿ Disabled   ★ Special TCI Rates

Bologna ★★★ ★
Piazzetta Scalette Rubiani 3,
tel. 0458006830
www.hotelbologna.vr.it
32 rooms. Restaurant, air-conditioned
Credit cards: American Express, Diners Club, Visa, Mastercard
Traditional hotel in a 13th-century building, comfortable and well-appointed. The "Rubiani" restaurant serves local Verona and traditonal cuisine.

Due Torri Baglioni ★★★
Piazza S. Anastasia 4,
tel. 045595044
www.baglionihotels.com
91 rooms. Restaurant, air-conditioned
Credit cards: American Express, Diners Club, Visa, Mastercard
This luxurious hotel complex in a 14th-century palazzo offers maximum comfort in apartments furnished in different styles; the grand entrance hall has columns and a frescoed ceiling. The "All'Aquila" restaurant serves local and international cuisine.

Gabbia d'Oro ★★★
Corso Porta Borsari 4/A,
tel. 0458003060
www.hotelgabbiadoro.it
27 rooms. Air-conditioned
Credit cards: American Express, Diners Club, Visa
Small, sophisticated hotel with a warm, friendly atmosphere; comfortable, tastefully furnished rooms, and some suites.

Giberti ★★★ ★
Via Giberti 7, tel. 0458006900
www.hotelgiberti.it
80 rooms. Parking, air-conditioned
Credit cards: American Express, Diners Club, Visa, Mastercard
This elegant, functional hotel has comfy rooms and reception rooms with a refined ambience. Particularly suited to business clientele.

Giulietta e Romeo ★★★ ★
Via Tre Marchetti 3,
tel. 0458003554
www.giuliettaeromeo.com
30 rooms. Air-conditioned
Credit cards: American Express, Diners Club, Visa, Mastercard
Hotel with a longstanding tradition, located in the heart of the city; refurbishment has improved both facilities and comfort. Buffet breakfast.

Holiday Inn Verona ★★★ ★
San Michele Extra, via Unità
d'Italia 346, tel. 0458952501
www.alliancealberghi.com
112 rooms. Restaurant, parking, air-conditioned
Credit cards: American Express, Diners Club, Visa
Modern hotel complex; comfortable rooms and rooms for business meetings and receptions.

Novo Hotel Rossi ★★★ ★
Via delle Coste 2, tel. 045569022
www.novohotelrossi.it
38 rooms. Parcheggio, air-conditioned
Credit cards: American Express, Diners Club, Visa, Mastercard
Hotel (no restaurant) with modern decor, handy for the train station; buffet breakfast.

Victoria ★★★ ♿ ★
Via Adua 8, tel. 045590566
www.hotelvictoria.it
71 rooms. Parking, air-conditioned, gym
Credit cards: American Express, Diners Club, Visa, Mastercard
This old palazzo offers very well-appointed bedrooms and suites with hi-fi system; also has a small museum with finds from the walls and fragments of Roman mosaic. Buffet breakfast.

Rural Lodgings

Ca' del Rocolo ★
Quinto di Valpantena, via Gaspari 3, tel. 0458700879
www.cadelrocolo.com
Credit cards: Visa, Mastercard
Refurbished 19th-century farmhouse in the hills near Verona. Wonderful breakfast with organic products; offers courses in woodworking.

San Mattia ♿
Via S. Giuliana 2/A,
tel. 045913797
www.sanmattia.it
On the road to the hills, simple hospitality, suitable for people who wish to visit Verona but avoid the bustle. Spacious, bright rooms with modern furnishings.

Restaurants

Ai Teatri ⅋ ♿ ★
Via S. Maria Rocca Maggiore 8, tel. 0458012181
www.ristoranteaiteatri.it
Closed Sunday, lunch-time Monday (only Monday in July and August)
Cuisine: local with a new interpretation
Credit cards: American Express, Diners Club, Visa, Mastercard
Elegant ambience in an 18th-century palazzo with the original stuccoes and coffered ceilings; lunch and dinner (until 23.00) also in the pretty courtyard of a deconsecrated church. Olive oil from Lake Garda and Valpantena, cheeses from the Monti Lessini, home-made bread and desserts, wide selection of wines and spirits.

Arche ⅋⅋⅋⅋ ★
Via Arche Scaligere 6,
tel. 0458007415
www.ristorantearche.com
Closed Sunday, lunch-time Monday
Cuisine: Veneto
Credit cards: American Express, Diners Club, Visa, Mastercard
Housed in the palazzo of the family of Shakespeare's tragic hero Romeo, the ambience is one of quality in a warm, historic setting. Dishes are prepared with an interesting new approach, and attention to the smallest detail. Wide selection of wines.

Baracca ⅋⅋⅋
Via Legnago 120,
tel. 045500013
www.ristorantelabaracca.it
Closed Sunday
Cuisine: traditional
Credit cards: American Express, Diners Club, Visa, Mastercard
Elegant rustic ambience, 40 years of experience guarantee continuity in terms of atmosphere and quality traditional cuisine, with fish and seafood specialties; varied list of wines and spirits.

Bottega del Vino ⅋⅋ ★
Via Scudo di Francia 3,
tel. 0458004535
www.bottegavini.it
Closed Tuesday (except during trade-fairs and opera season)
Cuisine: Veneto
Credit cards: American Express, Diners Club, Visa, Mastercard
This restaurant in the heart of Verona is 100 years old, a rare example of continuity, with a capacity to match cuisine and fine wines to new tastes. Great selection of cheeses.

Dodici Apostoli ⅋⅋⅋⅋ ♿ ★
Vicolo Corticella S. Marco 3,
tel. 045596999
Closed Sunday evening and Monday
Cuisine: Veneto and traditional
Credit cards: American Express, Diners Club, Visa, Mastercard
Venue with plenty of atmosphere, known for its excellent cuisine but also for the friendliness of the owner, Giorgio, and his son Antonio; guests can visit the wine-cellar, which has Roman and medieval features.

Maffei ⑪ ★
Piazza delle Erbe 38,
tel. 0458010015
www.ristorantemaffei.it
Closed Sunday (from October to
March)
Cuisine: Mediterranean with a
new approach
Credit cards: American Express,
Diners Club, Visa, Mastercard
Elegant restaurant and wine-bar,
with elaborated Mediterranean
cuisine; good selection of olive
oils and cheeses, good variety
of wines and spirits.

Oste Scuro ⑪
Vicolo S. Silvestro 10,
tel. 045592650
Closed Sunday, lunch-time
Monday
Cuisine: Fish and seafood
Credit cards: American Express,
Diners Club, Visa, Mastercard
Informal venue, here they know
how to cook fresh fish in a
variety of different ways.
Impressive selection of wines
and spirits.

Re Teodorico ⑪
Piazzale Castel S. Pietro 1,
tel. 0458349990
www.ristorantereteodorico.com
Closed Wednesday, Sunday
evening
Cuisine: traditional
Credit cards: American
Express, Diners Club, Visa,
Mastercard
A warm, inviting ambience, with
a lovely cool terrace and
beautiful views over the city.

Tre Marchetti ⑪
Vicolo 3 Marchetti 19/B,
tel. 0458030463
Closed Sunday (Monday in July
and August)
Cuisine: local Verona cuisine
Credit cards: Visa, Mastercard
Set in a 14th-century palazzo,
this friendly restaurant is family-
run; its traditional cuisine is
based on numerous local Verona
dishes. Extensive, carefully
selected list of wines and
spirits, excellent selection of
cheeses, salamis and cured
meats.

At night

Berfis
Via Lussemburgo 1,
tel. 045508024
www.berfis.com
One of the trendiest venues in
town, a disco with restaurant
and live music. Organizes
private parties, company dinners
and birthday celebrations.

El Mariachi
Cerea, Via Pascoli 16/B,
tel. 3355775872

Mexican venue, wide selection
of Mexican and Cuban beers.
Latin American music on
Thursday.

Malastrana
Via Sottoriva 23,
tel. 04580009904
Pub open till late with music.

Museums, Monuments and Churches

**Fondazione Museo
Miniscalchi-Erizzo**
Via S. Mammaso 2/a,
tel. 0458032484
www.museo-miniscalchi.it
Opening times: Monday-Sunday
11.00-13.00, 16.00-19.00.

**Galleria d'Arte Moderna
e Contemporanea Palazzo
Forti** ★
Corso S. Anastasia (vicolo Due
Mori), tel. 0458001903
www.palazzoforti.it
Opening times: Open only for
temporary exhibitions.

**Museo Archeologico al Teatro
Romano** ★
Regaste Redentore 2,
tel. 0458000360
www.comune.verona.it/
Castelvecchio/cvsito/mcivici2.htm
Opening times: Monday 13.30-
19.30; Tuesday-Sunday 8.30-
19.30 (last admission 18.45).

Museo Canonicale
Piazza Duomo 29,
tel. 045592813
Opening times: Saturday 10.00-
13.00, 14.30-18.00; Sunday
14.30-18.00. Groups may visit on
other days by prior
arrangement.

Museo Civico di Castelvecchio ★
Corso Castelvecchio 2,
tel. 0458062611
www.comune.verona.it/Castelvec
chio/cvsito
Opening times: Monday 13.30-
19.30; Tuesday-Sunday 8.30-
19.30.

Museo Civico di Storia Naturale
Lungadige Porta Vittoria 9,
tel. 0458079400
www.museostorianaturaleverona.it
Opening times: Summer:
Monday-Saturday 10.00-17.00;
Sunday and public holidays
14.00-19.00. Closed Friday.

**Museo degli Affreschi
«Giovan Battista Cavalcaselle»
alla tomba di Giulietta** ★
Via Shakespeare,
tel. 0458000361
www.comune.verona.it/castelvec
chio/cvsito/mcivici3.htm
Opening times: Monday 13.45-
19.30; Tuesday-Sunday 8.30-
19.30 (last admission 18.45).

Museo Lapidario Maffeiano ★
Piazza Bra' 28, tel. 045590087
www.comune.verona.it/castelvec
chio/cvsito/mcivici1.htm
Opening times: Monday 13.30-
19.30; Tuesday-Sunday 8.30-
19.30 (last admission 18.45).

VICENZA

ℹ️ **Ufficio Informazione
e Accoglienza Turistica**
Piazza dei Signori 3,
tel. 0444544122

Hotels

Alfa Fiera ★★★
Via dell'Oreficeria 50,
tel. 0444565455
www.alfafierahotel.it
90 rooms. Parking, air-
conditioned, sauna, gym
Credit cards: American Express,
Diners Club, Visa
Near the Vicenza-Ovest
motorway exit, good, modern
amenities, extremely good
conference facilities.

De la Ville ★★★ ♿
Viale Verona 12, tel. 0444549049
www.boscolohotels.com
118 rooms. Restaurant, air-
conditioned
Credit cards: American Express,
Diners Club, Visa, Mastercard
300 meters from the pedestrian
precinct, this hotel has very
comfortable rooms and suites,
with a well-equipped conference
center and excellent Veneto and
Mediterranean cuisine at the "La
Cantina" restaurant.

Europa ★★★ ♿ ★
S.S. Padana verso Verona 11,
tel. 0444564111
www.sogliahotels.com
127 rooms. Restaurant, parking,
air-conditioned
Credit cards: American Express,
Visa, Mastercard
Well placed, with a high
standard of service; well-
appointed rooms, large
conference center for meetings.
Restaurant serves Vicenza
specialties.

Jolly Hotel Tiepolo ★★★ ♿ ★
Viale S. Lazzaro 110,
tel. 0444954011
www.jollyhotels.it
113 rooms. Restaurant, parking,
air-conditioned
Credit cards: American Express,
Visa, Mastercard
Hotel of very modern design.
Spacious, comfortable rooms,
conference rooms of various
sizes; "Le Muse" restaurant with
an excellent wine-bar.

Quality Inn Viest ★★★ &
Strada Pelosa 241,
tel. 0444582677
www.viest.it
86 rooms. Restaurant, parking,
air-conditioned, gym
Credit cards: American Express,
Diners Club, Visa, Mastercard
Modern and functional, at the
Vicenza-Est motorway exit;
bright, comfortable rooms, with
hydro-massage, safe; restaurant
with Veneto and traditional
cuisine.

Victoria ★★★ &
S.S. Padana verso Padova 52,
tel. 0444912299
www.hotelvictoriavicenza.com
123 rooms. Restaurant, parking,
air-conditioned, gym
Credit cards: American Express,
Diners Club, Visa, Mastercard
Modern complex on the edge of
town: the hotel now has a new
wing with junior suites and
mini-apartments with all mod
cons. Restaurant with Veneto
cuisine and traditional
ambience.

Restaurants

Cinzia e Valerio ⅋
Piazzetta Porta Padova 65/67,
tel. 0444505213
Closed Sunday evening and
Monday
Cuisine: Veneto
Credit cards: American Express,
Diners Club, Visa, Mastercard
By the old town walls, an
elegant, inviting ambience
where they have created a
typical Venetian courtyard. The
kitchen specializes in fish and
shellfish.

Da Remo ⅋ &
Via Caimpenta 14,
tel. 0444911007
Closed Sunday evening and
Monday
Cuisine: local Vicenza cuisine
Credit cards: Diners Club, Visa,
Mastercard
A large venue which still has all
the charm of being family-run.
Traditional cuisine which excels
in "baccalà alla vicentina", and
the trolleys of roast and boiled
meats.

Giardinetto ⅋ &
Viale del Sole 142,
tel. 0444966133
www.ristorantegiardinetto.com
Closed Sunday evening and
Monday
Cuisine: local Vicenza cuisine
Credit cards: American Express,
Diners Club, Visa, Mastercard
Modern ambience but traditional
cuisine with an emphasis on
local Vicenza cuisine.

Storione ⅋ &
S.S. Pasubio 62, tel. 0444566244
Closed Sunday
Cuisine: traditional
Credit cards: American Express,
Diners Club, Visa, Mastercard
Pleasant, interesting ambience,
specializing in excellent fish,
home-made pasta, grilled meats
and steamed vegetables; the
biscuits and cakes are home-
made, good list of local and
Italian wines.

At night

Long Playing
Contra' Riale 4, tel. 0444543166
Disco

Mizuo
Via degli Ontani 52,
tel. 0444349766
Disco

Nabis
Strada Biron di Sopra 68/70,
tel. 0444568548
Disco

Totem Club
Via Vecchia Ferriera 135,
tel. 0444291176
www.totemclub.it
In the center, venue with live
music and high-quality disco.

Museums, Monuments and Churches

Gallerie di Palazzo Leoni Montanari ★
Contrà S. Corona 25,
tel. 800578875
www.palazzomontanari.com
Opening times: Tuesday-Sunday
10.00-18.00.

Museo del Risorgimento e della Resistenza ★
Viale X Giugno 115,
tel. 0444322998
www.comune.vicenza.it/musei/vi
cenza.htm
Opening times: Tuesday-Sunday
9.00-13.00, 14.15-17.00.

Museo del Santuario di Monte Berico ★
Viale X Giugno 87,
tel. 0444320999
www.monteberico.it
Opening times: May be visited
by prior arrangement

Museo Diocesano di Vicenza
Piazza Duomo 12,
tel. 0444226400
Opening times: Thursday and
Friday: 10.00-12.30; Saturday
and Sunday: 15.30-18.30.

Museo Naturalistico e Archeologico ★
Contrà S. Corona 4,
tel. 0444320440
www.comune.vicenza.it/musei/vi
cenza.htm

Opening times: Tuesday-Sunday
and public holidays 9.00-17.00.
Closed 1 January, 25 December.

Pinacoteca Civica di Palazzo Chiericati ★
Piazza Matteotti 37/39,
tel. 0444321348-0444325071-
0444222813
www.comune.vicenza.it/musei/vi
cenza.htm
Opening times: Tuesday-
Sunday and public holidays
9.00-17.00.

Teatro Olimpico ★
Piazza Matteotti,
tel. 0444222800
www.comune.vicenza.it/vicenza/t
eatro/olimpico.php
Opening times: Tuesday-Sunday
9.00-16.45.

VITTORIO VENETO

> ℹ **Azienda per la Promozione Turistica**
> Piazza del Popolo,
> tel. 043857243

Hotels

Sanson ★★
San Giacomo di Véglia, piazza
Fiume 38/39, tel. 0438500161
www.hotelsanson.com
28 rooms. Parking, air-
conditioned
Credit cards: American Express,
Diners Club, Visa, Mastercard
This family-run hotel (no
restaurant) has recently
refurbished its rooms and
reception rooms. Ideal for
business clientele, courteous,
professional service.

Terme ★★★ ★
Via delle Terme 4,
tel. 0438554345
www.hotelterme.tv
39 rooms. Restaurant, air-
conditioned
Credit cards: American Express,
Visa, Mastercard
Not far from the train station,
this hotel has good facilities,
particularly for business
meetings. Comfortable rooms
and pleasant, spacious
reception rooms; the restaurant
serves specialties of Veneto
cuisine.

Rural Lodgings

Alice-Relais nelle Vigne
Carpesica, via Giardino 94,
tel. 0438561173
www.alice-relais.com
Credit cards: American Express,
CartaSi, Diners Club, Visa,
Mastercard
Set in hills, accommodation in
an old country farm. Rooms of
various types and sizes, all well-

appointed and with all the advantages of modern comforts. Option of short wine-tasting courses; trekking, golf and horse-riding nearby.

Le Colline
Cozzuolo, via S. Mor 13, tel. 0438560282
Restaurant, mountain bikes for hire
Credit cards: American Express, Diners Club, Visa, Mastercard
This hill-top farm-house has beautiful views of the Prosecco vineyards. In the other direction, it is only 15 km away from the forests of Cansiglio, with infinite scope for walkers.

Restaurants
Postiglione ▮▮
Via Cavour 39, tel. 0438556924
Closed Tuesday
Cuisine: local
Credit cards: American Express, Visa, Mastercard
Old post-house, inviting venue with beautiful decor and genuine hospitality. The kitchen prepares gastronomic specialties based on local resources, with a good selection of wines, olive oils and cheeses.

Museums, Monuments and Churches
Museo del Cenedese
Serravalle, piazza M. Flaminio 1, tel. 043857103
www.museocenedese.it
Opening times: Summer: Tuesday-Sunday 9.30-12.30, 16.00-19.00. Winter: Tuesday-Sunday 9.30-12.30, 14.00-17.00.

Museo della Battaglia di Vittorio Veneto
Piazza Giovanni Paolo I, tel. 043857695
www.museobattaglia.it
Opening times: Summer: Tuesday-Sunday 9.30-12.30, 16.00-19.00. Winter: Tuesday-Sunday 9.30-12.30, 14.00-17.00.

Museo Diocesano di Arte Sacra «Albino Luciani»
Largo del Seminario 2, tel. 0438948411
Opening times: May be visited by prior arrangement.

Museo di Scienze Naturali "Antonio De Nardi"
Largo del Seminario 2, tel. 0438948411
Opening times: September-June: every second Sunday of the month 15.00-17.00. School groups may visit on other days by prior arrangement.

Palazzo Minucci-De Carlo
Serravalle, via Martiri della

Libertà 35, tel. 043857193
Opening times: Tuesday-Saturday 9.00-12.00; Sunday 15.00-19.00. May be visited at other times by prior arrangement.

AQUILEIA

ℹ️ **Ufficio Informazione e Accoglienza turistica**
Piazza del Capitolo 4, tel. 0431919491
www.aquileiaturismo.info

Hotels
Patriarchi ★★★
Via Giulia Augusta 12, tel. 0431919595
twww.hotelpatriarchi.it
23 rooms. Restaurant, parking, air-conditioned
Credit cards: American Express, Diners Club, Visa, Mastercard
A warm welcome and excellent hospitality make this hotel the ideal place for a quiet holiday. Pleasant, comfortable rooms; buffet breakfast.

Rural Lodgings
Ca' Ospitale
Beligna, tel. 0431917423
www.caospitale.com
Open April-October
Swimming pool
Credit cards: Diners Club, Visa, Mastercard
Near the archeological site of Aquileia, delightful farm camp-site with orchards and wheatfields: the rooms are very clean and the camper park is well-equipped. Guests may use the large swimming pool, tennis court and football pitch. Walks nearby or guided tours of the archeological site.

Restaurants
Colombara ▮▮ ♿ ★
La Colombara, via S. Zilli 42, tel. 043191513
www.lacolombara.it
Closed Monday
Cuisine: Friuli and traditional
Credit cards: American Express, Diners Club, Visa, Mastercard
Two pleasant dining-rooms with traditional decor, with open fire; the kitchen specializes in fish, and dishes based on ancient Roman recipes. Local and Italian wines.

Patriarchi ▮ ♿ ★
Via Giulia Augusta 12/A, tel. 0431919595
www.hotelpatriarchi.it
Cuisine: Friuli
Credit cards: American Express,

Diners Club, Visa, Mastercard
Family atmosphere, suitable for large numbers and also receptions. Highly diversified menu with reputation for fish and meat specialties; good range of Friuli DOC wines.

Museums, Monuments and Churches
Museo Archeologico Nazionale
Via Roma 1, tel. 043191016
www.museoarcheo-aquileia.it
Opening times: Monday 8.30-14.00; Tuesday-Sunday 8.30-19.30.

Museo Civico del Patriarcato
Via Patriarca Popone, tel. 0431919451
www.comune.aquileia.ud.it
Opening times: scheduled to re-open in 2006.

Museo Paleocristiano Nazionale
Monastero, piazza Pirano, tel. 043191131
www.museoarcheo-aquileia.it
Opening times: Monday-Sunday 8.30-13.45.

CERVIGNANO DEL FRIULI

Hotels
Internazionale ★★★ ♿
La Rotonda, via Ramazzotti 2, tel. 043130751
www.hotelinternazionale.it
69 rooms. Restaurant, parking, air-conditioned
Credit cards: American Express, Diners Club, Visa, Mastercard
This 1960s hotel has recently been refurbished and furnished with care; comfortable, spacious bright interior.

Restaurants
Al Campanile ▮
Scodovacca, via Fredda 3, tel. 043132018
Closed Monday and Tuesday
Cuisine: Friuli
In the center, an early 20th-century building with two dining-rooms and traditional decor; garden service in summer.

La Rotonda ▮▮ ♿
La Rotonda, via Ramazzotti 2, tel. 043130751
www.hotelinternazionale.it
Closed Sunday and Monday
Cuisine: traditional
Credit cards: American Express, Diners Club, Visa, Mastercard
This venue serves various specialties prepared with imagination; good assortment of olive oils and typical cheeses.

CIVIDALE DEL FRIULI

ℹ Azienda Regionale per la Promozione Turistica
Corso Paolino d'Aquileia 10, tel. 0432731461
www.regione.fvg.it/benvenuti/cividale/welcome.htm

Hotels

Locanda al Castello ★★★ ♿
Via del Castello 12,
tel. 0432733242
www.alcastello.net
17 rooms. Restaurant, parking, air-conditioned
Credit cards: American Express, Diners Club, Visa, Mastercard
This charming 19th-century castle is now a modern hotel with comfortable rooms, furnished in different styles; in the restaurant (with a panoramic terrace), an old fireplace is used for grilling meat and vegetables. Traditional and Friuli cuisine.

Locanda Pomo d'Oro ★★★ ♿
Piazza S. Giovanni 20,
tel. 0432731489
www.alpomodoro.com
17 rooms. Restaurant
Credit cards: American Express, Diners Club, Visa, Mastercard
Set among medieval walls and capitals, in the quiet old town center, this is one of the oldest venues in town. Romantic atmosphere, reception rooms furnished in period style, with a delightful and comfortable annex and rooms.

Roma ★★★ ★
Piazza Picco, tel. 0432731871
www.hotelroma-cividale.it
53 rooms. Parking, air-conditioned
Credit cards: American Express, Diners Club, Visa, Mastercard
Very central, a hotel (no restaurant) refurbished to modern criteria; friendly welcome from the family and buffet breakfast.

Rural Lodgings

Rosa Rubini ♿
Spessa, Via Case Rubini 3,
tel. 0432716141
www.villarubini.net
Swimming pool, mountain bikes for use of guests
Credit cards: American Express, Diners Club, Visa, Mastercard
The farm has belonged to the Rubini for almost 200 years, and is one of the few historic buildings in the area, set in a very old garden which can be visited. The apartments are in a farm-house and the rooms are all different and suitable for the disabled.

Restaurants

Il Fortino ♕♕
Via Carlo Alberto 40,
tel. 0432731217
www.ristorantealfortino.it
Closed Monday evening and Tuesday
Cuisine: Friuli
Credit cards: American Express, Diners Club, Visa, Mastercard
A 14th-century palazzo in the old town center, local cuisine, mainly meat; good selection of cheeses, salamis and cured meats and extensive wine-list.

Il Monastero-La Taverna di Bacco ♕♕
Via Ristori 11, tel. 0432700808
www.almonastero.com
Closed Sunday evening and Monday
Cuisine: Friuli and traditional
Credit cards: American Express, Diners Club, Visa, Mastercard
In a former 18th-century monastery in the heart of the town, this venue has 4 dining-rooms, one of which has an open fire, with cotto floors, coffered ceilings or exposed beams, and wooden paneling.

Museums, Monuments and Churches

Museo Archeologico Nazionale
Piazza Duomo 13,
tel. 0432700700
www.soprintendenza.fvg.it/musei/musei.htm
Opening times: Monday 9.00-14.00; Tuesday-Sunday 8.30-19.30.

Museo Cristiano and Tesoro del Duomo
Via Candotti 1, tel. 0432731144
www.cividale.com/citta/museocristiano.asp
Opening times: Summer: Monday-Saturday 9.30-12.00, 15.00-19.00; Sunday and public holidays 15.00-19.00. Winter: Monday-Saturday 9.30-12.00, 15.00-18.00; Sunday and public holidays 15.00-18.00.

CORMÒNS

ℹ Pro Loco Castrum Carmonis
Via Matteotti 69,
tel. 0481639334
www.cormons.org

Hotel

Felcaro ★★★ ♿ ★
Via S. Giovanni 45, tel. 048160214
www.hotelfelcaro.it
58 rooms. Restaurant, parking, air-conditioned, swimming pool, sauna, tennis, gym
Credit cards: American Express, Diners Club, Visa, Mastercard
19th-century villa which has refurbished its reception rooms and bedrooms. Main building has rooms on two storeys, plus mini-apartments in annexes.

Tana dei Ghiri
Monte 40, tel. 048161951
www.italyone.com
5 rooms. Parking
Credit cards: Visa
18th-century farmhouse surrounded by woods and vineyards, has five large rooms with rustic decor and views across the Isonzo plain to the sea; buffet breakfast.

Rural Lodgings

Al Giardinetto
Via Matteotti 54,
tel. 048160257
www.jre.it
Restaurant
Credit cards: American Express, Diners Club, Visa, Mastercard
Elegant 18th-century palazzo in the typical Cormòns style. Restaurant with a reputation for creativeness in its regional and Central European cuisine, an impeccable selection of Friuli and Italian wines, and the delicious cakes served with coffee.

Casa Riz
Giassico 18, tel. 048161362
www.casariz.com
Restaurant, bikes for use of guests
Credit cards: CartaSi, Diners Club, Visa, Mastercard
Accommodation on the farm, a pleasant ambience, good food, a distinctly country experience.

Restaurants

Al Cacciatore della Subida ♕♕♕
Monte 22, tel. 048160531
www.lasubida.it
Open Monday, Thursday, Friday (evenings)
Closed Tuesday and Wednesday
Cuisine: Friuli and Slovene
Credit cards: Visa, Mastercard
Cuisine which combines the genuine flavors of real home cooking with the cooking skills and presentation of the best restaurants; the dishes sound strange but taste wonderful.

Felcaro ♕♕ ♿ ★
Via S. Giovanni 45,
tel. 048160214
www.hotelfelcaro.it
Closed Monday
Cuisine: Friuli

Credit cards: American Express, Diners Club, Visa, Mastercard
Game or products in season are served with home-made wines. Also tourist menu at reasonable price and tasting sessions with game or seasonal produce.

Giardinetto ▦ ♿
Via Matteotti 54,
tel. 048160257
www.ir.europe.com/algiardinetto
Closed Monday and Tuesday
Cuisine: innovative Friuli cuisine
Credit cards: American Express, Diners Club, Visa, Mastercard
In the old town center, a small venue with two dining-rooms in an 18th-century palazzo; garden service in fine weather. Good Central European cuisine. Has three comfortable suites; home-made sweets and wines for sale.

Terra e Vini ▦ ♿
Brazzano, via XXIV Maggio,
tel. 048160028
www.terraevini.it
Closed Wednesday
Cuisine: Friuli
Credit cards: American Express, Diners Club, Visa, Mastercard
After a long period of restructuring and refurbishment the historic "All'Orologio" "osteria" has re-opened with a new name and a new look, with stone walls and an old underground wine-cellar. Leda della Rovere serves dishes of Friuli cuisine, using ingredients in season and carefully selecting other products. Don't miss the experience of their local cheeses, salamis and cured meats, washed down with one of their excellent wines.

DUINO-AURISINA

Hotels

Dama Bianca ★★
Via Duino Porto 61/C,
tel. 040208137
www.alladamabianca.com
7 rooms. Restaurant, parking, air-conditioned
Credit cards: American Express, Diners Club, Visa, Mastercard
On a small bay near the harbor, a comfortable hotel with a few well-appointed rooms, all with sea views. Breakfast on the terrace, private beach.

Duino Park Hotel ★★★
Via Duino 60/C, tel. 040208184
www.duinoparkhotel.it
18 rooms. Parking, swimming pool
Credit cards: American Express, Diners Club, Visa, Mastercard

Near the old castle, a modern hotel in a haven of tranquillity. The rooms have large terraces with sea views. Some suites also available.

Restaurants

Dama Bianca ▦ ♿
Via Duino Porto 61/C,
tel. 040208137
www.alladamabianca.com
Closed Wednesday
Cuisine: local Trieste cuisine
Credit cards: American Express, Diners Club, Visa, Mastercard
On the harbor, a refined venue with seafaring decor and a panoramic terrace. Traditional fish cuisine, selection of local cheeses and a good wine-list.

Il Pettirosso ▯
Santa Croce, tel. 040220619
Closed Monday lunch-time and Thursday
Cuisine: local
Credit cards: American Express, Diners Club, Visa, Mastercard
The restaurant has one dining-room with a majolica stove, another smaller, more intimate room, and a cool pergola. Meat and fish dishes according to what is available; local and Slovene wines, extensive range of spirits.

Osteria Sardoc ▯
Slivia 5, tel. 040200146
www.sardoc.com
Closed from Monday to Wednesday
Cuisine: local
Credit cards: American Express, Diners Club, Visa, Mastercard
Informal, rustic "osteria", not far from the Trieste-Sistiana motorway exit, but away from busy roads, it has a splendid view as far as the sea. The cuisine includes good cured meats, gnocchi and roast shin of pork; mostly regional wines.

Museums, Monuments and Churches

Castello di Duino ★
Via Castello di Duino 32,
tel. 040208120
www.castellodiduino.it
Opening times: Monday-Sunday 9.30-17.30. Closed Tuesday. December, January and February: Saturday and Sunday.

GORIZIA

ℹ **Azienda di Informazione e Accoglienza Turistica**
Via Roma 5,
tel. 0481386222

Hotels

Euro Diplomat Hotel ★★★ ★
Corso Italia 63, tel. 048182166
www.eurodiplomathotel.it
70 rooms. Restaurant, parking, air-conditioned
Credit cards: American Express, Diners Club, Visa, Mastercard
Central position, a functional 5-storey hotel, with comfortable, well-appointed rooms and rooms for business meetings. Buffet breakfast and elegant dining-room.

Internazionale ★★★ ♿
Viale Trieste 173,
tel. 0481524180
www.hotelinternazionalegorizia.it
49 rooms. Restaurant, parking, air-conditioned, swimming pool, sauna, gym
Credit cards: American Express, Diners Club, Visa, Mastercard
The well-furnished bedrooms are in different colors, well-equipped room for business meetings, wellness area with swimming pool, solarium, Turkish bath and Finnish sauna, sophisticated restaurant serving Central European and traditional cuisine.

Nanut ★★★
Via Trieste 118, tel. 048120595
www.nanut.it
21 rooms. Restaurant, parking, air-conditioned, swimming pool
Credit cards: American Express, Diners Club, Visa, Mastercard
Small, away from the center, with good facilities and a parking charge; the same family also owns an annex opposite the hotel.

Restaurants

Alla Luna ▯ ♿ ★
Via G. Oberdan 13,
tel. 0481530374
Closed Sunday evening and Monday
Cuisine: local Gorizia and Slovene
Credit cards: Visa, Mastercard
This venue was a locanda in the mid-19th century; here the owners wear traditional Gorizia costume. Traditional cuisine with Slovene influence.

Al Ponte del Calvario-da Mirko ▯ ♿
Piedimonte del Calvario, vallone delle Acque 2, tel. 0481534428
mwww.alpontedelcalvario.com
Closed Monday (except July-August) and Tuesday evening
Cuisine: local
Credit cards: American Express, Diners Club, Visa, Mastercard

The ideal place for a meal out; it has a large car park and the woods nearby are perfect for walking; rustic ambience, local cuisine with influences from nearby Slovenia.

Majda ¶¶
Via Duca d'Aosta 71, tel. 048130871
Closed Tuesday and lunch-time Saturday (in summer, Sunday)
Cuisine: Friuli and Slovene
Credit cards: American Express, Diners Club, Visa, Mastercard
This old locanda has been refurbished and is now a delightful venue with an interesting wine-bar and a jolly restaurant, with avant-garde gigantic photos on the walls and 200-year-old ivy. The place is competently run and friendly and serves traditional cuisine.

Rosenbar ¶¶
Via Duca d'Aosta 96, tel. 0481522700
Closed Sunday and Monday
Cuisine: Friuli with an interesting new approach
Credit cards: American Express, Diners Club, Visa, Mastercard
Two informal dining-rooms and a cool garden for lunches in summer; regional cuisine prepared with a modern touch, echoes of Central Europe, using products in season, especially fresh fish and vegetables; mainly local wines.

At night

Fly Entertainment
Piazza Municipio 6, tel. 04813220
Disco Pub with house and revival music.

Museums, Monuments and Churches

Castello di Gorizia
Borgo Castello 36, tel. 0481535146
www.comune.gorizia.it
Opening times: April-September: 9.30-13.00, 15.00-19.30. October-March: 9.30-18.00.

Fondazione Palazzo Coronini Cronberg
Viale XX Settembre 14, tel. 0481533485
Opening times: Temporarily closed for restoration. Scheduled to re-open at the end of 2005.

Musei Provinciali di Gorizia - Sedi di Borgo Castello

Borgo Castello 13, tel. 0481533926
www.provincia.gorizia.it
Opening times: Tuesday-Sunday 10.00-19.00.

GRADISCA D'ISONZO

> ℹ️ **Azienda Regionale per la Promozione Turistica**
> *Via Cesare Battisti 36, tel. 048199180*

Hotels

Franz ★★★ ♿
Viale Trieste 45, tel. 048199211
www.hotelfranz.it
50 rooms. Restaurant, parking, air-conditioned, gym
Credit cards: American Express, Diners Club, Visa, Mastercard
Centrally located hotel with well-appointed, comfortable rooms, pleasant reception rooms and conference rooms for business meetings with a maximum capacity of 110. Restaurant serves Friuli cuisine.

Restaurants

Al Commercio ¶
Via della Campagnola 6, tel. 048199358
Closed Sunday evening and Monday
Cuisine: Friuli
Credit cards: American Express, Diners Club, Visa, Mastercard
Simple trattoria with strong propensity for fish.

Alle Viole ¶¶ ♿
Via Gorizia 44, tel. 0481961326
Closed Tuesday (in July and August Friday lunch-time)
Cuisine: innovative Friuli cuisine
Credit cards: American Express, Diners Club, Visa, Mastercard
Historical venue on the edge of town, with tables under a pergola in summer; cuisine concentrates on very good traditional dishes and modern fish dishes.

Museums, Monuments and Churches

Galleria Regionale d'Arte Contemporanea "Luigi Spazzapan"
Via C. Battisti 1, tel. 0481960816
www.provincia.gorizia.it
Opening times: Tuesday-Sunday 10.30-12.30, 16.00-20.00.

Museo Documentario della Città
Via Bergamas 30, tel. 0481967915
www.comune.gradisca-d-isonzo.go.it
Opening times: May be visited by prior arrangement.

GRADO

> ℹ️ **Azienda Promozione Turistica**
> *Viale Dante Alighieri 72, tel. 04318991*
> *www.gradoturismo.info*

Hotels

Abbazia ★★★ ♿ ★
Via Colombo 12, tel. 043181721
www.hotel-abbazia.com
Open April-October
51 rooms. Restaurant, parking, air-conditioned, swimming pool, sauna
Credit cards: American Express, Diners Club, Visa, Mastercard
Beautiful 1930s villa near the beach, with a pleasant mixture of modern furnishings and well-appointed bedrooms; family-run; the restaurant serves traditional Friuli cuisine.

Alla Città di Trieste ★★★
Piazza XXVI Maggio 22, tel. 043183571
www.hotelcittaditrieste.it
24 rooms. Restaurant, air-conditioned
Credit cards: American Express, Diners Club, Visa, Mastercard
In the old town center, small palazzo with modern, functional furnishings, overlooking the yachting harbor, not far from the beach. The restaurant serves fish and other specialties of Italian cuisine.

Diana ★★★ ★
Via Verdi 1, tel. 043182247
www.hoteldiana.it
Open March-October
63 rooms. Restaurant, parking, air-conditioned
Credit cards: American Express, Diners Club, Visa, Mastercard
Modern, functional hotel in terms of location and facilities, very comfortable, recently refurbished; organizes meetings and congresses on request.

Hannover ★★★ ♿ ★
Piazza XXVI Maggio 10, tel. 043182264
www.hotelhannover.com
24 rooms. Restaurant, parking, air-conditioned, sauna, gym
Credit cards: American Express, Diners Club, Visa, Mastercard
Centrally placed, small, late 19th-century palazzo with junior suites and spacious, comfortable rooms. Restaurant serves Friuli and traditional cuisine; buffet breakfast.

Restaurants

Alla Fortuna da Nico ¶¶
Via Marina 10, tel. 043180470

Closed Thursday
Cuisine: local
One of the oldest restaurants in town, serving typical local dishes, mainly fish. The wines are from Friuli.

De Toni ¶ &
Piazza Duca d'Aosta 37,
tel. 043180104
www.trattoriadetoni.it
Closed Wednesday
Cuisine: local
Credit cards: American Express, Diners Club, Visa, Mastercard
Pleasant, family-run trattoria; Roman remains can be seen under the glass floor. Wide selection of wines, some very prestigious labels, to accompany fish.

Tavernetta all'Androna ¶
Calle Porta Piccola 6,
tel. 043180950
www.androna.it
Closed Tuesday in low season
Cuisine: local with an interesting new angle
Credit cards: American Express, Diners Club, Visa, Mastercard
In the historic center, not far from the Duomo, characteristic, well-run venue with inviting ambience, in the entrance-hall of an old house (hence its name). The cuisine is simple, of a high standard, based on very fresh fish. Not only are the bread, pasta and desserts home-made, but also the ice-cream, with some unusual flavors: fennel, cinnamon, vanilla and balsamic vinegar; wide selection of especially local wines.

At night

Isola d'Oro
Viale Dante Alighieri 66,
tel. 043181259
Disco with commercial and house music.

Museums, Monuments and Churches

Museo Lapidario del Duomo di Sant'Eufemia
Campo Patriarchi, tel. 043180146
Opening times: Summer: Monday-Sunday 7.00-20.00. Winter: Monday-Sunday 8.00-18.00.

LIGNANO SABBIADORO

> ℹ **Azienda di Promozione Turistica**
> *Via Latisana 42,*
> *tel. 043171821*
> *www.aptlignano.it*

Hotels

Al Cavallino Bianco ★★★ &
Via dei Platani 88,
tel. 043171509
www.lignano.it/hotel/cavallino bianco
38 rooms. Parking
Credit cards: American Express, Diners Club, Visa, Mastercard
Simple hotel with somber ambience (no restaurant) in quiet location next to a sports complex with tennis, mini-golf and bowls; buffet breakfast.

Atlantic ★★★ &
Lungomare Trieste 160,
tel. 043171101
www.hotelatlantic.it
Open mid-May-mid-September
61 rooms. Restaurant, parking, air-conditioned, swimming pool
Credit cards: Visa, Mastercard
Hotel facing the sea, set in a lovely garden. Swimming lessons for kids, large games room, a mini-club with entertainment for kids and a restaurant.

Bellavista ★★★ &
Lungomare Trieste 70,
tel. 043171313
www.bellavistalignano.it
Open April-October
53 rooms. Restaurant, air-conditioned, swimming pool
Credit cards: Visa, Mastercard
Situated on the sea-front, modern facilities and furnishings, rooms with balconies, suitable for families, young people and sports enthusiasts; good restaurant.

Florida ★★★ &
Via dell'Arenile 22,
tel. 043720101
www.hotelflorida.net
Open end April-September
73 rooms. Restaurant, parking, air-conditioned, sauna
Credit cards: American Express, Visa, Mastercard
Near the beach, two buildings with bright interiors and facilities for keeping fit; activities for kids and internet point. The restaurant serves traditional cuisine; buffet breakfast.

Greif ★★★
Lignano Pineta, arco del Grecale 25,
tel. 0431422261
www.greifgroup.net
92 rooms. Restaurant, parking, air-conditioned, swimming pool, sauna
Credit cards: American Express, Diners Club, Visa, Mastercard
Set in a garden very close to the sea, the quality of the facilities at this hotel ensure a comfortable, peaceful holiday; comfortable suites and a beauty center. Friuli cuisine with meat and fish dishes.

Meridianus ★★★ ★
Lignano Riviera, viale della Musica 1, tel. 0431428561
www.hotelmeridianus.it
Open mid-May-September
83 rooms. Restaurant, parking, air-conditioned, swimming pool, sauna
Credit cards: American Express, Visa, Mastercard
A pleasant, welcoming atmosphere, set among umbrella pines and only a few meters from the sea; leisure facilities, for example heated swimming pools and swimming lessons on request. Friuli and traditional cuisine, buffet breakfast.

Restaurants

Bidin ¶ &
Viale Europa 1, tel. 043171988
www.ristorantebidin.com
Closed Wednesday in low season
Cuisine: Friuli and traditional
Credit cards: American Express, Diners Club, Visa, Mastercard
This family-run wine-bar is well-organized, with garden terrace. Elegant venue which serves fish specialties; good range of wines and olive oils.

La Rustica ¶
Viale Europa 39, tel. 043170601
www.lignano.it/tavola/default.htm
Closed Wednesday
Cuisine: traditional
Credit cards: American Express, Visa, Mastercard
Rustic atmosphere, enlivened by an aquarium with live fish and a charcoal grill. The menu includes meat and fish dishes.

At night

Cà Margherita
Via Alzaia 1, tel. 0431422780
Disco with house music.

Drago Club
Viale Centrale 1, tel. 043171661
www.dragoclub.com
This disco, always packed, organizes special events and parties.

MANIAGO

Hotels

Eurohotel Palace Maniago ★★★
Viale della Vittoria 3,
tel. 042771432
www.eurohotelfriuli.it
39 rooms. Restaurant, parking,

air-conditioned

Credit cards: American Express, Diners Club, Visa, Mastercard

In the town center, modern hotel with comfortable, elegant rooms; the same sophisticated furnishings are to be found in the reception rooms and the "Parco Vittoria" restaurant, which serves typical Friuli cuisine.

Restaurants

Osteria Vecchia Maniago ❦ ♿
Via Castello 10, tel. 0427730583
alpro.com/of/ovm.htm
Closed Tuesday and Monday evening
Cuisine: Friuli and creative
Credit cards: American Express, Diners Club, Visa, Mastercard
The tables are arranged in small, 17th-century rooms and there are tables in the garden in summer; here Friuli cuisine is interpreted with a creative flair; highly respectable wine-cellar, good range of spirits, olive oils and cheeses.

Museums, Monuments and Churches

Museo dell'Arte Fabbrile e delle Coltellerie
Via Battiferri 1,
tel. 0427733296-0427707223
www.comune.maniago.pn.it
Opening times: Saturday 16.00-18.00; Sunday 10.00-12.00, 16.00-18.00. Groups may visit by prior arrangement.

Museo Provinciale della Vita Contadina "Diogene Penzi" - Sezione lavorazioni legno e ferro
Ex Filanda, Via Battiferri 1,
tel. 0427707223
www.provincia.pordenone.it/serv izi/cultura/musei/musei.htm
Opening times: May be visited by prior arrangement.

MONFALCONE

⌨ **Pro Loco Monfalcone**
Via Mazzini 3,
tel. 0481411525
www.monfalcone.info

Hotels

Excelsior ★★★ ♿
Via dell'Arena 4, tel. 0481412566
www.hotelexcelsiormonfalcone.it
65 rooms. Air-conditioned
Credit cards: American Express, Diners Club, Visa, Mastercard
This 10-storey hotel (no restaurant) serves a buffet breakfast. Bedsits with kitchenette also available.

Lombardia ★★★ ♿
Piazza Repubblica 21,

tel. 0481411275
tww.hotelombardia.it
21 rooms. Restaurant, parking, air-conditioned
Credit cards: American Express, Diners Club, Visa, Mastercard
In the town center, this palazzo has comfortable, elegant rooms, and a small conference room; the "Lombardia" restaurant serves traditional and local cuisine.

Restaurants

Ai Campi di Marcello ❦ ♿
Via Napoli 7, tel. 0481481937
www.paginegialle.it/aicampi
Closed Monday and Tuesday
Cuisine: Friuli fish recipes
Credit cards: American Express, Diners Club, Visa, Mastercard
This locanda dates from the late 19th century. Family atmosphere. Menu mainly fish; home-made desserts and wide selection of wines.

Ai Castellieri ❦
Via dei Castellieri 7,
tel. 0481475272
Closed Tuesday and Wednesday
Cuisine: an interesting new approach to cooking
Credit cards: American Express, Diners Club, Visa, Mastercard
Carefully selected ingredients form the basis of a light, delicate cuisine, with refined culinary combinations. This pleasant rustic venue, set in a farm-house, is well-run and the prices are reasonable.

Museums, Monuments and Churches

Galleria Comunale d'Arte Contemporanea di Monfalcone "La Comunale"
Piazza Cavour,
tel. 048146262-0481494369
Opening times: Times vary.

Museo Paleontologico Cittadino della Rocca
Via Valentinis 134,
tel. 048140014
www.museomonfalcone.it
Opening times: April-July: Sunday and public holidays 10.00-12.00, 16.00-19.00. September-March: Sunday and public holidays 10.00-12.00, 14.00-17.00. Groups may also visit by prior arrangement. Closed August.

MUGGIA

Hotels

Sole ★★★
Strada per Lazzaretto 93,
tel. 040271106
www.hotelsolemuggia.it
23 rooms. Restaurant, parking,

swimming pool
Credit cards: American Express, Diners Club, Visa, Mastercard
Pleasant hotel, with comfortable rooms with balconies overlooking the bay and a beautiful pool in the garden. Restaurant serves Trieste specialties, especially fish.

Restaurants

Lido ❦ ♿
Via C. Battisti 22,
tel. 040273338
www.hotellido.com
Closed Sunday evening and Monday
Cuisine: Istrian and traditional
Credit cards: American Express, Diners Club, Visa, Mastercard
The elegant simplicity of this venue gives no inkling of the gastronomic delights prepared by Vilma and Giorgio Suraci. Suitable for receptions and working dinners.

Trattoria Risorta ❦
Riva De Amicis 1/A,
tel. 040271219
www.trattoriarisorta.it
Closed Sunday evening and Monday (in July-August also Sunday lunch-time)
Cuisine: Veneto and creative
Credit cards: Visa, Mastercard
Old trattoria with a refurbished panoramic terrace, where the cuisine favors fish dishes prepared with a creative flair; good selection of wines and spirits.

Museums, Monuments and Churches

Mostra Permanente del Presepio
Chiesa di S. Francesco, salita delle Mura 2/b, tel. 040271104
Opening times: Monday and Friday 10.00-12.00. May be visited by prior arrangement.

Museo di Muggia e del Territorio
Calle Oberdan 14,
tel. 040271778-0403360340
www.comune.muggia.ts.it
Opening times: Monday and Wednesday 10.00-12.00; Saturday 10.00-12.00, 17.00-19.00. May be visited by prior arrangement.

PALMANOVA

Hotels

Roma ★★
Borgo Cividale 27,
tel. 0432920674
www.hotelromapalmanova.it
34 rooms. Restaurant, parking
Credit cards: American Express, Diners Club, Visa, Mastercard
Centrally located, with simple,

comfortable interior and a garden for lunches in summer.

Museums, Monuments and Churches

Civico Museo Storico
Borgo Udine 4, tel. 0432929106
www.comune.palmanova.ud.it/turismo/musei.htm

Opening times: March-May, October-December: Monday, Tuesday, Thursday-Sunday 9.30-12.30. June-September: Monday, Tuesday, Thursday-Saturday 9.30-12.30, 16.00-18.00; Sunday 9.30-12.30. Closed Wednesday, January, February. May also be visited by prior arrangement.

Museo Storico Militare
Dongione di Porta Cividale, tel. 0432923535-0432928175
www.comune.palmanova.ud.it/turismo/musei.htm

Opening times: Summer: Monday-Saturday 9.00-12.00, 16.00-18.00; Sunday 9.00-12.00. Winter: Monday-Saturday 9.00-12.00, 14.00-16.00; Sunday 9.00-12.00.

PORDENONE

> ### ℹ️ Agenzia di informazione e accoglienza turistica
> *Via Damiani 2/C, tel. 0434520381*
> *www.pordenone-turismo.com*

Hotels

Best Western Park Hotel ★★★ ♿ ★
Via Mazzini 43, tel. 043427901
www.bestwestern.it/park_pn
66 rooms. Parking, air-conditioned
Credit cards: American Express, Diners Club, Visa, Mastercard
Central, individually regulated heating and AC systems in the rooms and suites, pleasant reception rooms.

Palace Hotel Moderno ★★★ ♿ ★
Viale Martelli 1, tel. 043428215
www.palacehotelmoderno.it
94 rooms. Restaurant, parking, air-conditioned, sauna, gym
Credit cards: American Express, Diners Club, Visa, Mastercard
Modern, centrally lcated hotel; high standard of comfort in refurbished rooms, 3 suites and good facilities for conferences or business meetings, fitness center with sauna; à la carte menu.

Residence Italia ★★★ ★
Piazza Costantini 6, tel. 043427821
www.hotelresidenceitalia.com
44 rooms. Parking, air-conditioned
Credit cards: American Express,

Diners Club, Visa, Mastercard
In the town center, rooms with modern decor and kitchenette. Well-equipped conference room and internet point.

Villa Ottoboni ★★★ ♿
Piazzetta Ottoboni 2, tel. 0434208891
www.geturhotels.com
96 rooms. Restaurant, parking, air-conditioned, gym
Credit cards: American Express, Diners Club, Visa, Mastercard
Late 15th-century villa, with a café, restaurant (Friuli and traditional cuisine), reception, internet point and rooms for conferences and business meetings; the suites and rooms are located in an adjacent building with elegant furnishings.

At night

Uagamama
Via Fornace 2, tel. 0434540949
www.uagamama.it
A splendid place to spend an evening with friends listening to good music. Stylish ambience.

Museums, Monuments and Churches

Museo Civico d'Arte
Corso Vittorio Emanuele II 51, tel. 0434392311
www.comune.pordenone.it
Opening times: Tuesday-Saturday 15.30-19.30; Sunday 10.00-12.30, 15.30-19.30. In July and August also Thursday 20.30-22.30.

Museo delle Scienze
Via della Motta 16, tel. 0434392315
www.comune.pordenone.it
Opening times: Tuesday-Saturday 15.00-19.00; Sunday 10.00-13.00, 15.00-19.00.

Museo Diocesano d'Arte Sacra
Via Revedole 1, tel. 0434524340
www.ibisweb.it/pn11
Opening times: Tuesday 9.00-13.00; Wednesday-Friday 14.30-18.30; Saturday 9.00-12.30.

SAN DANIELE DEL FRIULI

> ### ℹ️ Ufficio Turistico Pro San Daniele
> *Via Roma 3, tel. 0432940765*
> *www.infosandaniele.com*

Hotels

Alla Torre ★★★ ♿
Via del Lago 1, tel. 0432954562
www.hotelallatorre.com
27 rooms. Air-conditioned

Credit cards: American Express, Diners Club, Visa
In the historic center, quiet, comfortable hotel (no restaurant), with elegant decor; buffet breakfast.

Al Picaron ★★★ ♿
Via S. Andrat 3, tel. 0432940688
www.alpicaron.it
36 rooms. Restaurant, parking, air-conditioned, tennis
Credit cards: American Express, Diners Club, Visa, Mastercard
A large country house on a hilltop, refurbished with modern decor; the restaurant serves local regional cuisine. Special menus and facilities for kids.

Restaurants

Alle Vecchie Carceri ⍙
Via Guarnerio d'Artegna 16, tel. 0432957403
www.allevecchiecarceri.it
Closed Sunday evening and Monday
Cuisine: local
Credit cards: American Express, Visa, Mastercard
Set in a former Austrian prison, family-run, serves traditional dishes, sometimes very old recipes. Wonderful cheese trolley and excellent choice of home-made cakes and biscuits.

Cantinon ⍙
Via C. Battisti 2, tel. 0432955186
Closed Thursday (also Friday lunch-time in winter)
Cuisine: Friuli
Credit cards: American Express, Diners Club, Visa, Mastercard
In a former wine depot, this charming venue serves traditional dishes, expertly made and served with style; excellent range of wines.

Osteria al Ponte ⍙
Via Tagliamento 13, tel. 0432954909
www.osteriaalponte.com
Cuisine: Friuli
Credit cards: American Express, Diners Club, Visa, Mastercard
Typical Friuli trattoria. In winter they cook kebabs on the open fire while in summer, lunch is served in the garden, under a gazebo. Only meat dishes cooked to local recipes, with home-made pasta and desserts.

Museums, Monuments and Churches

Museo del Territorio
Via Udine 4, tel. 0432954484-0432954934
www.comune.sandanieledel friuli.ud.it

Opening times: Tuesday-
Saturday 9.30-12.30. Sunday
guided tours by prior
arrangement.

SAN VITO
AL TAGLIAMENTO
Hotels

Patriarca ★★★ ♿ ★
Via Pascatti 6,
tel. 0434875555
www.hotelpatriarca.it
29 rooms. Restaurant, air-
conditioned
Credit cards: American Express,
Diners Club, Visa, Mastercard
Modern hotel with restaurant
close by at the trattoria "La
Piramide", which serves Friuli
cuisine. Special terms at nearby
golf course, swimming pool,
gym and tennis club.

Restaurants

Rosa ❦ ♿
Rosa, Via Rosa 49,
tel. 043480141
Closed Monday
Cuisine: Puglia
Credit cards: Diners Club, Visa,
Mastercard
Puglia cuisine, fish. Small
dining-room, meals served on
terrace in summer.

Museums, Monuments
and Churches

**Museo Civico "Federico
de Rocco"**
Via P. Amalteo 1,
tel. 043480405
Opening times: Winter: Monday-
Friday 8.00-12.30, 14.00-18.30.
Summer: Monday, Tuesday and
Thursday 8.00-12.30, 14.00-
18.30; Wednesday and Friday
8.00-12.30. First Sunday of the
month 8.00-20.00.

**Museo Provinciale della Vita
Contadina "Diogene Penzi"**
Via Altan 47, tel. 0434833275
www.provincia.pordenone.it/serv
izi/cultura/musei/musei.htm
Opening times: Monday-Saturday
9.00-12.30. Closed Sunday.

SAURIS

> ℹ️ **Azienda di Informazione
> e Accoglienza Turistica
> della Carnia**
> Sauris di Sotto, terminal
> 91, tel. 043386076
> www.sauris.com

Hotels

Schneider Meublé ★★
Sauris di Sotto, piazzale Kursaal
92/A, tel. 043386220
8 rooms

Credit cards: Visa, Mastercard
Recently built, it carries on the
tradition of an old locanda.
Tastefully-furnished rooms and
guests are greeted in the
morning with a breakfast of
delicious local products. No
restaurant but guests can eat at
the nearby "Alla Pace", also run
by the Schneider family.

Restaurants

Alla Pace ❦
Sauris di Sotto, via Roma 38,
tel. 043386010
Closed Wednesday (in low
season)
Cuisine: local Carnia cuisine
Credit cards: Visa, Mastercard
This 19th-century venue has two
lovely dining-rooms and a cozy
Stube; traditional ambience with
good local cuisine and game
and mushrooms when in
season.

Kursaal ❦❦ ★
Sauris di Sotto, piazzale Kursaal
91/B, tel. 043386202
Closed Sunday evening and
Monday
Cuisine: local Carnia cuisine
Credit cards: Visa, Mastercard
In a small town encircled by
mountains, this small restaurant
has a traditional atmosphere.
Unforgettable specialties which
constitute the best of the rich
gastronomy of the Carnia
region; good selection of local
cheeses, carefully chosen local
wines

SESTO AL REGHENA
Hotels

In Sylvis ★★★ ♿
Piazza Aquileia 15,
tel. 0434694911
www.hotelinsylvis.com
37 rooms. Restaurant, parking,
air-conditioned
Credit cards: American Express,
Diners Club, Visa, Mastercard
A neoclassical building,
comfortable rooms and
adequate facilities for all
requirements. Restaurant serves
various types of cuisine.

Restaurants

Abate Ermanno ❦ ♿
Piazza Aquileia 15,
tel. 0434694911
www.hotelinsylvis.com
Closed Monday lunch-time
Cuisine: Friuli and Veneto
Credit cards: American Express,
Diners Club, Visa, Mastercard
Part of a new hotel, under
separate management; the
interior of the restaurant is
spacious, with a restful

atmosphere. Traditional local
cuisine with risottos and game.

Museums, Monuments
and Churches

**Museo dell'Abbazia di Santa
Maria in Sylvis**
Piazza Castello 3,
tel. 0434699014
www.comune.sesto-al-
reghena.pn.it
Opening times: Monday-Sunday
8.00-12.00, 15.00-19.00.

SPILIMBERGO
Hotels

Afro ★★★ ♿
Via Umberto I 14, tel. 04272264
www.spilimbergo.it
8 rooms. Restaurant, parking,
air-conditioned
Credit cards: American Express,
Diners Club, Visa, Mastercard
Set in a medieval town, it has
retained the simplicity and
warmth of a late 18th-century
building; tastefully furnished
rooms, breakfast served inside
or outdoors.

G.H. President ★★★ ♿ ★
Via Cividale 10, tel. 042751002
33 rooms. Parking, air-
conditioned, sauna
Credit cards: American Express,
Visa, Mastercard
Hotel organized for conferences
and business meetings; has all
mod cons and also suitable for
holiday clientele. Music hall for
private parties and other events.

Restaurants

La Torre ❦❦
Piazza Castello 8,
tel. 042750555
www.ristorantelatorre.net
Closed Sunday evening and
Monday
Cuisine: Friuli with an
interesting new approach
Credit cards: American Express,
Diners Club, Visa, Mastercard
In the charming setting of
Palazzo Dipinto, inside
Spilimbergo castle; both the
unusual atmosphere and the
cuisine of chef Marco Talamini
will impress you. Wide selection
of quality wines. Good range of
cheeses.

Osteria da Afro ❦❦ ♿ ★
Via Umberto I 14, tel. 04272264
www.spilimbergo.it
Closed Sunday evening
Cuisine: Friuli
Credit cards: American Express,
Diners Club, Visa, Mastercard
Old "osteria", also a wine-bar.
Simple cuisine using excellent
local ingredients, also good

wines and spirits, which accompany risottos, home-made pasta dishes and mixed boiled meats; also vegetarian food.

TARCENTO

Hotels

Centrale ★★
Via Garibaldi 1,
tel. 0432785150
26 rooms. Parking, tennis
Credit cards: American Express,
Diners Club, Visa, Mastercard
Characteristic Friuli ambience,
dates from the 17th century, run
by the De Monte family for over
a century.

Restaurants

Costantini ⌘ &
Collalto, Via Pontebbana 12,
tel. 0432792004
www.albergocostantini.com
Closed Sunday evening and
Monday
Cuisine: Friuli
Credit cards: American Express,
Diners Club, Visa, Mastercard
Pleasant venue with stone and
wood decor; regional specialties
include "cialzons" and steamed
leg of roe-deer with pears and
Montasio cheese.

Da Gaspar ⌘
Zomeais, via Gaspar 1,
tel. 0432785950
Closed Monday and Tuesday
Cuisine: Friuli
In quiet countryside, this 18th-
century former mill has been
run by the Boezio family for 3
generations. The cuisine is
based on genuine ingredients
and follows the rhythm of the
seasons. Some of the salamis
and all the desserts are home-
made; mainly local wines.

Mulin Vieri ⌘ &
Via dei Mulini 10,
tel. 0432785076
Closed Monday and Tuesday
Cuisine: Friuli and traditional
Credit cards: American Express,
Diners Club, Visa, Mastercard
Overlooking the River Torre, 2
lovely dining-rooms: one
traditional and elegant, the
other rustic. Here they cook
fresh pasta, meat, fish,
mushrooms and ingredients in
season; great dessert menu,
carefully selected wines.

Osteria di Villafredda ⌘ &
Loneriacco, via Liruti 7,
tel. 0432792153
www.villafredda.com
Closed Sunday evening and
Monday
Cuisine: Friuli
Credit cards: American Express,

Diners Club, Visa, Mastercard
Country house with rustic
interior, garden service in
summer and areas for painting
exhibitions. Run by a family who
prepare traditional recipes with
local products.

TRIESTE

ℹ **Azienda di Promozione Turistica**
Via S. Nicolò 20,
tel. 04067961
www.trietetourism.it

Hotels

Abbazia ★★★
Via della Geppa 20,
tel. 040369464
www.albergoabbazia.com
21 rooms. Air-conditioned
Credit cards: American Express,
Diners Club, Visa, Mastercard
In the center of town, this hotel
(no restaurant) is comfortable
and functional. Simple rooms,
buffet breakfast.

Best Western San Giusto ★★★ ★
Via dell'Istria 7 ang. via C. Belli
3, tel. 040764824
www.bestwestern.it/sangiusto_ts
62 rooms. Parking, air-
conditioned
Credit cards: American Express,
Diners Club, Visa, Mastercard
Near the hill of San Giusto, this
functional hotel has modern,
comfortable, recently
refurbished rooms, well-
equipped room for business
meetings; buffet breakfast.

G.H. Duchi d'Aosta ★★★ &
Piazza Unità d'Italia 2,
tel. 0407600011
www.magesta.com
55 rooms. Restaurant, air-
conditioned, swimming pool
Credit cards: American Express,
Diners Club, Visa, Mastercard
This beautiful palazzo of 1873
has a Central European
atmosphere, elegant furnishings
and modern comforts. Rooms
have hydro-massage and Turkish
bath, refurbished stuccoes,
meeting room for small business
meetings and "Harry's Grill", a
refined restaurant serving Friuli
and traditional cuisine. New
wellness center with pool.

Jolly Hotel ★★★ & ★
Corso Cavour 7, tel.
0407600055
www.jollyhotels.it
174 rooms. Restaurant, air-
conditioned
Credit cards: American Express,
Diners Club, Visa, Mastercard
Modern and comfortable with

some suites. Buffet breakfast,
the "La Matta" restaurant serves
regional and traditional cuisine.

Starhotels Savoia Excelsior ★★★ ★
Riva del Mandracchio 4,
tel. 04077941
www.starhotels.com
155 rooms. Restaurant, air-
conditioned
Credit cards: American Express,
Diners Club, Visa, Mastercard
The old facade conceals a
modern interior, efficient
facilities and delightful rooms;
large conference center; the
"Savoy Inn" restaurant serves
Trieste and traditional cuisine.

Restaurants

Ai Fiori ⌘
Piazza Hortis 7, tel. 040300633
www.aifiori.com
Closed Sunday and Monday
Cuisine: local Trieste cuisine
Credit cards: American Express,
Diners Club, Visa, Mastercard
Everything here is home-made,
from the bread to the desserts.
Mainly fish, and an extensive
range of wines and spirits; good
choice of olive oils and cheeses.

Al Granzo ⌘ &
Piazza Venezia 7,
tel. 040306788
www.algranzo.it
Closed Wednesday, Sunday
evening
Cuisine: Istrian and traditional
Credit cards: American Express,
Diners Club, Visa, Mastercard
Old fishermen's venue converted
into a restaurant with a
seafaring theme, with old and
new photos and prints of Trieste
on the walls. Menus for
business lunches (also single
servings with home-made pasta
and shellfish), but also dishes
made to customers' requests,
with fish from the Adriatic; good
selection of quality olive oils,
mainly regional wines.

Antica Trattoria Suban ⌘ &
Via Comici 2, tel. 04054368
Closed Monday lunch-time and
Tuesday
Cuisine: local Trieste cuisine
Credit cards: American Express,
Diners Club, Visa, Mastercard
Historic venue, frequented by
celebrities and the cuisine has
Central European leanings.
Interesting range of wines and
spirits.

**Antipastoteca di Mare alla
Voliga** ⌘ ★
Via della Fornace 1,
tel. 040309606
www.cat-trieste.com
Closed Sunday evening and
Monday

Cuisine: local Trieste and Istrian cuisine
Very close to San Giusto, seafaring theme; wonderfully tasty selections of seafood, fish served with polenta.

Bandierette ⅱ
Riva N. Sauro 2, tel. 040300686
Closed Monday
Cuisine: Fish and seafood
Credit cards: American Express, Diners Club, Visa, Mastercard
Opposite the Stazione Marittima, traditional early 20th-century ambience where they serve fish, especially "spaghetti ai calamaretti"; good range of labels and the kitchen stays open till after 22.00.

Elefante Bianco ⅱ
Riva 3 Novembre 3, tel. 040362603
www.elefantebianco-trieste.com
Closed Sunday, lunch-time Monday
Cuisine: Mediterranean
Credit cards: American Express, Diners Club, Visa, Mastercard
Next to Teatro Comunale Giuseppe Verdi, comfortable ambience, with meals served on garden terrace in summer. Kitchen stays open till midnight, mainly fish.

Trattoria Tre Merli ⅰ ⅰ
Barcola, viale Miramare 42, tel. 040410884
www.tremerli.ws
Closed Monday
Cuisine: Mediterranean
Credit cards: American Express, Diners Club, Visa, Mastercard
Fish and seafood, served on a shady veranda and a terrace overlooking the sea in fine weather; fish grilled or baked, grilled meats. Also pizza.

At night

Dancing Paradiso
Via Flavia 3, tel. 040812391
Disco with South American ambience.

Vertigo
Via del Canale Piccolo 2, tel. 040368116
Disco with commercial and house music; theme evenings.

Museums, Monuments and Churches

Civico Acquario Marino
Molo Pescheria 2, tel. 040306201
www.triestecultura.it
Opening times: April-October: Tuesday-Sunday 9.00-19.00. November-March: Tuesday-Sunday 8.30-13.30. Closed on public holidays.

Civico Museo del Castello di San Giusto ★
Piazza Cattedrale 3, tel. 040309362
www.triestecultura.it
Opening times: Temporarily closed for restoration.

Civico Museo della Risiera di San Sabba - Monumento Nazionale
Via Palatucci 5, tel. 0408262024040310500
www.risierasansabba.it
Opening times: Monday-Sunday 9.00-19.00. Closed 1 January and 25 December.

Civico Museo del Mare
Via Campo Marzio 5, tel. 040304987-040304885
www.triestecultura.it
Opening times: Tuesday-Sunday 8.30-13.30. Closed on public holidays.

Civico Museo del Risorgimento and Sacrario Oberdan
Via XXIV Maggio 4, tel. 040361675-040310500
www.triestecultura.it
Opening times: Tuesday-Sunday 9.00-13.00. Closed on public holidays.

Civico Museo di Guerra per la Pace "Diego de Henriquez"
Via Revoltella 37, tel. 040948430
www.triestecultura.it
Opening times: Monday, Wednesday 9.00-16.00; Tuesday, Thursday, Friday 9.00-13.00. Closed Saturday, Sunday and public holidays. The part of the museum at Via Cumano 24 (heavy vehicles and artillery) may only be visited by prior arrangement.

Civico Museo di Storia e Arte and Orto Lapidario ★
Piazza Cattedrale 1, tel. 040310500
www.triestecultura.it
Opening times: Tuesday, Thursday-Sunday 9.00-13.00; Wednesday 9.00-19.00. Closed on public holidays.

Civico Museo di Storia Naturale
Piazza Hortis 4, tel. 0406758659-0406758661
www.triestecultura.it
Opening times: Tuesday-Sunday 8.30-13.30.

Civico Museo Mario Morpurgo de Nilma ★
Via Imbriani 5, II piano, tel. 040636969-040310500
www.triestecultura.it
Opening times: Tuesday, Thursday-Sunday 9.00-13.00; Wednesday 9.00-19.00. Closed public holidays.

Civico Museo "Pasquale Revoltella" - Galleria di Arte Moderna ★
Via Diaz 27, tel. 0406754350-0406754158
www.museorevoltella.it
Opening times: Monday, Wednesday-Sunday 9.00-13.30, 16.00-19.00. Open evenings in summer.

Civico Museo Teatrale Fondazione Carlo Schmidl ★
Via Rossini 4, tel. 0406754072-040310500
www.triestecultura.it
Opening times: Tuesday, Thursday-Sunday 9.00-13.00; Wednesday 9.00-19.00. Closed on public holidays.

Museo della Comunità Ebraica "Carlo e Vera Wagner"
Via del Monte 5/7, tel. 040633819-040371466
www.triestebraica.it
Opening times: Sunday 17.00-20.00; Tuesday 16.00-19.00; Thursday 10.00-13.00. Closed Saturday and Jewish festivals.

Museo della Farmacia Picciola
Via Caccia 3, tel. 040632558
www.retecivica.trieste.it
Opening times: May be visited by prior arrangement.

Museo Ferroviario di Trieste Campo Marzio
Via Giulio Cesare 1 - stazione di Campo Marzio, tel. 0403794185
www.triestecultura.it
Opening times: Saturday, Sunday and Wednesday 9.00-13.00. May also be visited by prior arrangement.

Museo Petrarchesco Piccolomineo
Piazza Hortis 4, tel. 0406758184
www.retecivica.trieste.it
Opening times: Monday-Saturday 9.00-13.00, 15.00-19.00.

Museo Postale e Telegrafico della Mitteleuropa ★
Piazza Vittorio Veneto 1, tel. 0406764294
www.triestecultura.it
Opening times: Monday-Sunday 9.00-13.00.

Museo Storico del Castello di Miramare
Grignano, Castello di Miramare, tel. 040224143
www.castello-miramare.it
Opening times: Monday-Sunday 9.00-19.00.

Museo Sveviano
Piazza Hortis 4, tel. 0406758182
www.retecivica.trieste.it

Opening times: Monday-Saturday 9.00-13.00, 15.00-19.00; study room: Monday-Saturday 9.00-13.00.

UDINE

ℹ️ **Azienda di Promozione Turistica**
Piazza I Maggio 7,
tel. 0342295972
www.regione.fvg.it

Hotels

Ambassador Palace ★★★ ♿ ★
Via Carducci 46, tel. 0432503777
www.ambassadorpalacehotel.it
80 rooms. Air-conditioned
Credit cards: American Express, Diners Club, Visa, Mastercard
Centrally located, this hotel offers the highest standards of comfort combining the old with the new.

Astoria Hotel Italia ★★★ ★
Piazza XX Settembre 24, tel. 0432505091
www.hotelastoria.udine.it
75 rooms. Restaurant, air-conditioned
Credit cards: American Express, Diners Club, Visa, Mastercard
Hotel situated in the historic center, elegant, traditional-style rooms and suites. Meeting room for small and medium-size conferences. Large private garage. The restaurant serves Friuli, Italian and international cuisine.

Best Western La' di Moret ★★★ ♿ ★
Viale Tricesimo 276, tel. 0432545096
www.ladimoret.it
82 rooms. Restaurant, parking, air-conditioned, swimming pool, sauna, tennis
Credit cards: American Express, Diners Club, Visa, Mastercard
Traditional Friuli hospitality since the early 20th century. Elegant, comfortable rooms and suites; 4 rooms for meetings and conferences; Turkish bath, sauna and indoor pool.

Executive ★★★ ♿
Cussignacco, via A. Masieri 4 ang. viale Palmanova, tel. 0432602880
www.hotelexecutive.net
87 rooms. Restaurant, parking, air-conditioned, sauna, gym
Credit cards: American Express, Diners Club, Visa, Mastercard
Hotel designed for business and holiday clienteles alike; elegantly furnished, sound-proofed rooms and suites, restaurant and conference center.

San Giorgio ★★★ ★
Piazzale G.B. Cella 2, tel. 0432505577
www.hotelsangiorgioudine.it
37 rooms. Restaurant, parking, air-conditioned
Credit cards: American Express, Diners Club, Visa, Mastercard
Ideally placed for the train station and the town center, a small 1950s palazzo furnished with care; the kitchen serves traditional Friuli cuisine.

Restaurants

Agli Amici 🍴🍴🍴 ♿
Gòdia, via Liguria 250, tel. 0432565411
www.agliamici.it
Closed Sunday evening (in summer also at lunch-time) and Monday
Cuisine: Friuli with an interesting new approach
Credit cards: American Express, Diners Club, Visa, Mastercard
Just outside town, warm, pleasant venue, where the 5th generation has given the cuisine a modern slant. Remarkable selection of cheeses; competent wine suggestions, broad choice of spirits.

Alla Vedova 🍴🍴
Via Tavagnacco 9, tel. 0432470291
Closed Sunday evening and Monday
Cuisine: Friuli
Credit cards: Visa, Mastercard
In the late 19th century it was called the "Kaiser"; today, this trattoria still serves real home-cooking accompanied by a selection of home-produced wines; typical rooms with open fire, decorated with collections of copper objects and paintings. Meals served in garden in summer.

La' di Moret 🍴🍴🍴 ♿ ★
Viale Tricesimo 276, tel. 0432545096
www.ladimoret.it
Closed Sunday evening and Monday lunch-time
Cuisine: Friuli and traditional
Credit cards: American Express, Diners Club, Visa, Mastercard
From being a "osteria" serving meals and a post-house in the early 20th century, it has become an elegant venue, where the 4th generation of the Marini family carries on the tradition: great variety of olive oils from the best areas of production, variety of salamis, cured meats, cheeses, and good selection of wines and spirits.

Vitello d'Oro 🍴🍴🍴 ♿ ★
Via Valvason 4, tel. 0432508982
www.vitellodoro.com
Closed Sunday (Wednesday in winter) and lunch-time Monday
Cuisine: Friuli and traditional
Credit cards: American Express, Diners Club, Visa, Mastercard
Historic late 19th-century venue, below the second set of city walls. The cuisine follows the rhythms of the seasons, with a propensity for fish; wisely selected cheeses, broad and diversified range of wines and spirits.

At night

ABC Gold
Via Feletto 35, tel. 0432482845
Disco and disco bar with various kinds of music: Latin-American, house, funky, hip hop.

Birrificio Udinese
Piazzale Osoppo
Home-made beer brewed by a Czech master brewer.
Pub and sandwich bar.

Gattomatto
Viale Venezia 464
Disco Pub with live music and evenings with rock, commercial and revival music.

Museums, Monuments and Churches

Civica Galleria d'Arte Moderna - GAMUD ★
Via Ampezzo 2, tel. 0432295891
www.comune.udine.it
Opening times: Tuesday-Saturday 9.30-12.30, 15.00-18.00; Sunday and public holidays 9.30-12.30.

Civici Musei e Gallerie di Storia e Arte Antica ★
Piazzale del Castello 1, tel. 0432271591
www.comune.udine.it
Opening times: Tuesday-Saturday 9.30-12.30, 15.00-18.00; Sunday 9.30-12.30.

Museo del Duomo
Piazza del Duomo, tel. 0432506830
www.spaziocultura.it/duomoud
Opening times: Tuesday-Saturday 9.00-12.00, 16.00-18.00; Sunday 16.00-18.00.

Museo Diocesano and Galleria del Tiepolo
Piazza Patriarcato 1, tel. 043225003
Opening times: Wednesday-Sunday 10.00-12.00, 15.30-18.30.

METRIC CONVERTIONS

DISTANCE

Kilometres/Miles		Meters/Feet	
km to mi	**mi to km**	**m to ft**	**ft to m**
1 = 0.62	1 = 1.6	1 = 3.3	1 = 0.30
2 = 1.2	2 = 3.2	2 = 6.6	2 = 0.61
3 = 1.9	3 = 4.8	3 = 9.8	3 = 0.91
4 = 2.5	4 = 6.4	4 = 13.1	4 = 1.2
5 = 3.1	5 = 8.1	5 = 16.4	5 = 1.5
6 = 3.7	6 = 9.7	6 = 19.7	6 = 1.8
7 = 4.3	7 = 11.3	7 = 23.0	7 = 2.1
8 = 5.0	8 = 12.9	8 = 26.2	8 = 2.4

WEIGHT

Kilograms/Pounds		Grams/Ounces	
kg to lb	**lb to kg**	**g to oz**	**oz to g**
1 = 2.2	1 = 0.45	1 = 0.04	1 = 28
2 = 4.4	2 = 0.91	2 = 0.07	2 = 57
3 = 6.6	3 = 1.4	3 = 0.11	3 = 85
4 = 8.8	4 = 1.8	4 = 0.14	4 = 114
5 = 11.0	5 = 2.3	5 = 0.18	5 = 142
6 = 13.2	6 = 2.7	6 = 0.21	6 = 170
7 = 15.4	7 = 3.2	7 = 0.25	7 = 199
8 = 17.6	8 = 3.6	8 = 0.28	8 = 227

TEMPERATURE

Fahrenheit/Celsius	
F	**C**
0	-17.8
5	-15.0
10	-12.2
15	-9.4
20	-6.7
25	-3.9
30	-1.1
32	0
35	1.7
40	4.4
45	7.2
50	10.0
55	12.8
60	15.5
65	18.3
70	21.1
75	23.9
80	26.7
85	29.4
90	32.2
95	35.0
100	37.8

LIQUID VOLUME

Liters/U.S. Gallons		Liters/U.S. Gallons	
L to gal	**gal to L**	**L to gal**	**gal to L**
1 = 0.26	1 = 3.8	5 = 1.3	5 = 18.9
2 = 0.53	2 = 7.6	6 = 1.6	6 = 22.7
3 = 0.79	3 = 11.4	7 = 1.8	7 = 26.5
4 = 1.1	4 = 15.1	8 = 2.1	8 = 30.3

PICTURE CREDITS

Agenzia Marka, p. 138, 140, 143

Archivi Alinari, p. 111

Archivio Buysschaert &Malerba, p. 137

Archivio TCI: p. 150, 151 top, 194 top, 195, 196, 197 bottom, 198 top, 199 top

Archivio teatro ed enti musicali, p. 185, 186, 188

P. Bumbaca, p. 92

A. Campanile, p. 34, 36, 39, 41, 47, 60 top, 61, 79, 189

Foto Campanile, p. 151 bottom, 152, 153, 154, 155, 173

G. Carfagna, p. 16, 20, 48, 52, 60 bottom, 73, 81, 106

E. Caracciolo, p. 132, 133, 134

G. Cervi, p. 115

Comune di Belluno, p. 6

Consorzio del Prosciutto di San Daniele, p. 147

Il Dagherrotipo: M. Fraschetti p. 178

F. Fiori, p. 97, 99

V. Giannella, p. 117, 122

P. Gislimberti, p. 118

Jolanda de Colò, p. 148

S. Lunardi, p 91, 96, 100, 101, 105, 108, 112, 114, 121, 129

Macelleria Gemmo Aldreghetti, p. 146

Mairani, p. 158, 163

Marka: D. Donadoni, p. 109, 179, 191

Panda Photo: G. Cappelli, p. 124 bottom; B. Midali, p. 123; L. Vinco, p. 124 top

Photos.com, p. 142

Realy Easy Star, p. 22

Realy Easy Star: R. Bianchi, p. 71; M. Bruzzo, p. 44, 63, 82, 90; C. Concina, p. 74; F. Iorio, 49; L. Pessina, p. 65, 75, 89; T. Spagone, p. 15, 57, 69, 84, 85, 176, p. 177 bottom, 201; F. Tanel, 17, 21, 29, 32, 88, 193

E. Rossaro, p. 53, 62, 59, 64, 66

Rossaro/Scarpa, p. 38

S. Scatà, p. 180

M. E. Smith, p. 58, 70, 83

Studio90, p. 166 bottom, p. 169 bottom

Drawings by Antonello and Chiara Vincenti

Illustration on pages 30-31, 94-95 by Giorgio Pomella pages 50-51 by Isabella Salmoirago

Some owners of photographic copyright have been impossible to trace; they are invited to contact the publisher

Altar-piece
Painting or sculpture, placed behind or above an altar

Ambo
A raised platform in an early Christian church from which parts of the service were conducted

Ambulatory
Open-air walkway flanked by columns

Amphitheater
An oval or round building with tiers or seats around a central arena, used in Ancient Roman times for gladiatorial contests and spectacles.

Arboretum
Collection of live trees

Atrium
The forecourt of an early Christian church, flanked or surrounded by porticoes. Also an open-air central court around which a house is built.

Capital
Part which links a column to the structure above.

Caryatid
A sculptured female figure used as a column

Cenotaph
A monument erected in memory of a deceased person, whose remains are buried elsewhere.

Chemin-de-ronde
A continuous gangway providing a means of communication behind the rampart of a fortified wall.

Chiaroscuro
Term used to describe paintings which rely on gradations between brightness and darkness

Codex (pl. Codices)
A manuscript book, esp. of Scriptural or Classical texts, usually on vellum.

Colonnade
A series of regularly spaced columns supporting an entablature and usually one side of a roof structure

Corinthian order
The most ornate of the five classical orders, developed by the Greeks in the 4th century BC but used more extensively in Roman architecture. The columns are characterized by a deep bell-shaped capital decorated with acanthus leaves.

Cryptoporticus
A series of underground corridors, often used for storage in classical times

Diptych see Polyptych

Doric order
The oldest and simplest of the five classical orders of decoration, characterized by fluted columns with plain, cushion-shaped capitals

Exedra
A large apsidal extension of the interior volume of a church; usually a semi-circular area.

Iconostasis
A screen or partition separating the presbytery from the nave

Incunabulum (pl. incunabula)
Book printed before 1501

Keep
The innermost and strongest structure or tower of a medieval castle

Loggia
A colonnaded or arcaded space within the body of a building but open to the air on one side, often at an upper storey overlooking an open court; also used as a decorative motif.

Machicolation
A projecting gallery at the top of a castle wall supported by corbeled arches with openings in the floor through which molten lead, stones, or boiling oil could be poured onto the enemy below.

Maenad
A woman participant in orgies in honor of Dionysus, the Greek god of wine

Martyrion
Burial-place of a martyr

Matroneum
Gallery reserved for women in early Christian churches

Merlon
One of the solid parts between the crenels of a battlement

Narthex
Vestibule in front of a Christian basilica

Necropolis
Pre-Christian tombs grouped in or over a particular area, or the area itself.

Nymphaeum
Originally a temple of the Nymphs, decorated with the statues of goddesses

Olivetan
An order of monks

Orchestra
The front of the stage in an ancient Greek theater; orchestra pit.

Parterre
An ornamental garden with paths between the beds

Pediment
A wide, low-pitched gable surmounting a colonnade or a major division of a facade.

Peristyle
A colonnade surrounding a building or courtyard.

Pilaster
A shallow, rectangular feature projecting from a wall, having a capital and a base and architecturally treated as a column.

Pluteus (Latin, pl. plutei)
Kind of balustrade, or division in an early Christian church, often with low reliefs.

Polyptych
Altar-piece consisting of a number of panels. A diptych has two panels; a triptych has three.

Portal
A doorway, gate or entrance, especially an imposing one emphasized by size and stately architectural treatment

Portico
A porch having a roof supported by columns, often leading to the entrance of a building

Presbytery
The part of the church reserved for the officiating clergy

Pronaos
An open vestibule before the cella of a classical temple or porch in front of a church.

Relief
The projection of a figure or form from the flat background from which it is formed

Sgraffitto
A decorative technique achieved by scratching through a layer of paint or other material to reveal a ground of different color

Sinopia
A red ochre used in fresco painting

Stele
Upright stone bearing a monumental inscription

Transenna
Stone slab, sometimes pierced or sculpted, placed vertically to close off reserved areas, for example the presbytery of a church

Transept
Area perpendicular to the nave, often extending out at the sides and giving the building a cross-shaped ground-plan.

Triptych see Polyptych

Notes

VILLAGGIO TURISTICO
INTERNAZIONALE
★ ★ ★ ★

Villette
Suites
Maxicaravan
Camping - Disco
Tennis - Animations
Swimming Pools
Acquascivolo - Private
Beach - Cinema
Bowling

BIBIONE
THERMAE

100 mt weit

EMAS
Polo Turistico
di Bibione

TÜV
ISO 14001

ADAC Super-Platz
2005

Veneto
Tra la terra e il cielo

www.vti.it
Villaggio Turistico Internazionale
30020 BIBIONE (VENEZIA)
Tel. 0431.442611 - Fax 0431.43620 e-mail info@vti.it

La Faula Home — Ravosa di Povoletto (Ud) Tel. +39 0432 666394 www.faula.com

---

Hotel Bisesti

**Corso Italia, 34/36
I-37016 Garda (Verona)
Tel.: +39-045-7255766
Fax: +39-045-7255927
www.hotelbisesti.it**

The Bisesti Hotel warmly welcomes you to spend a peaceful holiday on lake Garda. In a central but peaceful position 150 meters from the beach and from the old town.

90 rooms furnished in 19th century venetian style, all with shower, wc, hairdyer, telephone, sat television

Types of rooms: standard double rooms (some with the possibility do add the third bed on request); double rooms with air-conditioned; double rooms with balcony and air-conditioned

3 bars, 2 restaurant rooms, party and conference room, swimming pool, shady parking in the ground. The swimming pool with spring water is located in the hotel park with deckchairs and parasols availalbe free of charge.

Breakfast is provided as a vast range of buffet dishes. Lunches are arranged with a great variety of options provided à la carte. In the evening the waiter service is particulary pleasant, with various courses and different selections from one day to the next. Other services: internet point, safe rent

Credit cards: Visa, Eurocard, Mastercard, Carta si.

**** Hotel Due Leoni, Sacile (Pordenone)

On an island, surrounded by the arms of the river Livenza, medieval "Piazza Del Popolo" (people's square) retains intact, with its venetian palazzi, its bridges and the nearby 15th century cathedral, its role as the center of city life and its tranquil yet noble atmosphere.

During the recent renovation of one of the piazza's ancient and prestigious palazzi, two stone lions, symbols of the Venetian rule, were discovered and gave the "Hotel Due Leoni" its name. Since 1274 one of Italy's oldest festivals is held in the piazza every August.

Sixty spacious rooms offer a fine view of the historical piazza and the charming bights of the Livenza river. Thanks to their modern conception they ensure a comfortable stay for both business people and refined tourists.

The "Hotel Due Leoni" combines elegant surroundings and a sophisticated ambience with a relaxing atmosphere and offers its guests the comforts of modern technology and service.

t. 0039. 0434. 788111 - www.hoteldueleoni.com

★★★ **hotel Gardesana ristorante**

Torri del Benaco

Piazza Calderini, 20
37010 Torri del Benaco (Verona)
Tel. +39 045.7225411 - Fax +39 045.7225771
www.hotel-gardesana.com
info@hotel-gardesana.com

The peaceful bobbing up and down of the boats in the little medieval port, the romantic atmosphere of an evening's concert under the arches, the solemn presence of the turreted fourteenth century castle, the pleasure of a gastronomic evening on the terrace which overlooks the lake, the relaxed conversation between friends who meet at the bar to sip the specialities of the House in front of the unique scenery of the historic little square.

All this surrounds the guest with magic charm like a dream.